GLORIA STEINEM was a founding editor of *New York Magazine* and its political columnist until 1971. One of the leading spokespersons for the feminist movement in America, she currently writes regularly for *Ms.*, which she helped found in 1972. Gloria Steinem travels and speaks extensively. This is her first book.

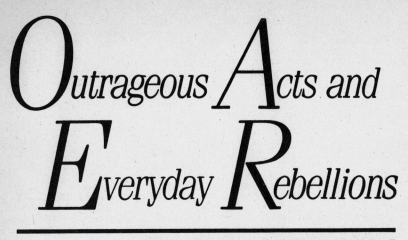

Outrageous Acts and Everyday Rebellions

GLORIA STEINEM

A PLUME BOOK

NEW AMERICAN LIBRARY

NEW YORK AND SCARBOROUGH, ONTARIO

ACKNOWLEDGMENTS AND COPYRIGHT NOTICES

"I Was a Playboy Bunny" originally appeared as a two-part article, "A Bunny's Tale,"
Show magazine, 1963 "Campaigning" includes excerpts from: "Coming of Age with Mc-
Govern: Notes from a Political Diary" *Ms.* magazine, October 1972, 39. "The City on the
Eve of Destruction" coauthored by Lloyd Weaver, *New York* magazine, 1968. "Trying to
Love Eugene," *New York* magazine, 1968. "In Your Heart You Know He's Nixon," *New
York* magazine, 1968. "Nelson Rockefeller: The Sound of One Hand Clapping," *New York*
magazine, 1969. "Sisterhood" was published in *Ms.* magazine, 1972. "College Reunion"
originally appeared as "Reunions: When College Never Ends," *Ms.* magazine, September
1981, 30. "Words and Change" is excerpted from "The Way We Were—and Will Be,"
Ms. magazine, 1979, and "The Stage Is Set," *Ms.* magazine, July/August 1982, 77. "In
Praise of Women's Bodies" was published in *Ms.* magazine, April 1981, 28. "The Importance of Work" was published as "Why Do Women Work?", *Ms.* magazine, March 1979,
45. "The Time Factor," *Ms.* magazine, March 1980, 45. "Men and Women Talking" was
published as "The Politics of Talking in Groups: How To Win the Game *and* Change
the Rules," *Ms.* magazine, May 1981, 43. "The Politics of Food," *Ms.* magazine, February
1980, 48. "Networking" was published as "How to Survive Burn-Out, Reagan, and Daily
Life: Create Psychic Turf," *Ms.* magazine, February 1982, 95. "Transsexualism" was published as "If the Shoe Doesn't Fit, Change the Foot," *Ms.* magazine, February 1977, 76.
"Why Young Women Are More Conservative" was published as "The Good News Is:
These Are Not the Best Years of Your Life," *Ms.* magazine, September 1979, 64. "Erotica
vs. Pornography" is adapted from "Erotica and Pornography: A Clear and Present Differ-
ence," *Ms.* magazine, November 1978, 53, and "Pornography—Not Sex But the Obscene
Use of Power," *Ms.* magazine, August 1977, 43. "Marilyn Monroe: The Woman Who
Died Too Soon," *Ms.* magazine, August 1972, 35. "Patricia Nixon Flying" is an excerpt
from "In Your Heart You Know He's Nixon," published in *New York* magazine, 1968.
"The Real Linda Lovelace" was published as "Linda Lovelace's 'Ordeal': 'Tell me, Linda,
what in your background led you to a concentration camp?'," *Ms.* magazine, May 1980,
72. "Jackie Reconsidered" was published as "Gloria Steinem on Jacqueline Kennedy Onas-
sis," *Ms.* magazine, March 1979, 46. "Do You Know This Woman? She Knows You: A
Profile of Alice Walker" was published in *Ms.* magazine, June 1982, 35. "Houston and
History" is adapted from "An Introductory Statement," *What Women Want: The National
Women's Conference*, Simon and Schuster, 1979. "The International Crime of Genital
Mutilation," *Ms.* magazine, March 1979, 65. "Rx Fantasies: For Temporary Relief of Pain
Due to Injustice . . . ," was published in *Ms.* magazine, July 1980, 99. "If Hitler Were
Alive, Whose Side Would He Be On;" was published in two parts: "The Nazi Connection:
If Hitler Were Alive, Whose Side Would He Be On?" and "The Nazi Connection: Authori-
tarianism Begins at Home," *Ms.* magazine, October 1980, 88 and November 1980, 14.
"Night Thoughts of a Media Watcher," *Ms.* magazine, November, 1981, 22. "Night Thoughts
of a Media Watcher" was published in *Ms.* magazine, 1981 and combined with parts of
"The Draft: Who Needs It?", *Ms.* magazine, April 1980, 20. "If Men Could Menstruate"
was first broadcast as a CBS *Spectrum*, 1977, then expanded in *Ms.* magazine, October
1978, 110, "Far From the Opposite Shore" was published as "Far From the Opposite
Shore: How To Survive Though a Feminist," *Ms.* magazine, July 1978, 65, and "The Stage
Is Set," *Ms.* magazine, July/August 1982, 77. "January 10, 1973" is from *Goodnight Willie
Lee, I'll See You in the Morning* by Alice Walker. Copyright © 1979 by Alice Walker. A
Dial Press Book. Reprinted by permission of Doubleday and Co., Inc. and the Julian Bach

(The following page constitutes an extension of this copyright page.)

Literary Agency, Inc. "New Face" and "Rage" are from *Revolutionary Petunias and Other Poems* © 1973 by Alice Walker. Reprinted by permission of Harcourt Brace Jovanovich, Inc. and the Julian Bach Literary Agency, Inc. "Playboy's Theme" is used by permission of copyright owner Edwin H. Morris & Company, Inc.

 PLUME TRADEMARK REG. U.S. PAT. OFF. AND FOREIGN COUNTRIES
REGISTERED TRADEMARK—MARCA REGISTRADA HECHO EN
WESTFORD, MASS., U.S.A.

SIGNET, SIGNET CLASSIC, MENTOR, PLUME, MERIDIAN,
and NAL BOOKS are published *in the United States* by
New American Library,
1633 Broadway, New York, New York 10019,
in Canada by The New American Library of Canada Limited,
81 Mack Avenue, Scarborough, Ontario MIL 1M8

Library of Congress Cataloging in Publication Data

Steinem, Gloria.
  Outrageous acts and everyday rebellions.

  1. Steinem, Gloria—Addresses, essays, lectures.
2. Feminists—United States—Biography—Addresses, essays,
lectures. 3. Feminism—United States—Addresses, essays,
lectures. I. Title.
HQ1413.S675A36   1983b   305.4   84-6875
ISBN 0-452-25579-1

First Plume Printing, August, 1984

1 2 3 4 5 6 7 8 9

PRINTED IN THE UNITED STATES OF AMERICA

*T*his book is gratefully dedicated to . .

. . . *Letty Cottin Pogrebin, who went through boxes of past writing, sold a sampling to Holt, and thus forced me to work on this book; to Suzanne Braun Levine, who gave loving and time-consuming advice on what to keep and where to put it; to my editor, Jennifer Josephy, whose good judgment is matched only by her great patience; to Joanne Edgar, who has spent a dozen years encouraging me to make space for writing, even when I didn't do it; to Robin Morgan, whose sisterly critiques I hope I never have to live without; to Robert Benton, whose long-ago listening to stories of a Toledo childhood helped show me that I needn't pretend to be someone else to be a writer; to Clay Felker, who never cared what gender of journalist a newsworthy idea came from; to the Woodrow Wilson International Center for Scholars at the Smithsonian Institution, whose fellowship provided time for much of the research herein; to Stan Pottinger for eight years of friendship, encouragement, and vitality; to Alice Walker for an honesty so strong that it lights an honest path for those around her; to Andrea Dworkin for an anger so righteous that it keeps others from confronting injustice without it; to Patricia Carbine, my friend and partner at* Ms. *magazine, who has given me and millions of others a forum for new ideas and dreams; to my father, Leo Steinem, who taught me to love and live with insecurity; to my mother, Ruth Nuneviller Steinem, who performed the miracle of loving others even when she could not love herself; and to all the courageous people I have met in twenty years of reporting and organizing—those women and men who dream of a justice that has yet to come and live on the edge of history.*

For rebellion is as the sin of witchcraft

—I Samuel 15·23

Contents

Within the text or at the end of each essay, you will find the year it was written. When related articles have been combined into one, the date of each is included. To allow each entry to stand on its own, some facts have been referred to more than once, but I also have cut overlaps within the context of this collection, updated with an occasional footnote or postscript, and restored or rewritten text that had been adapted for a particular magazine issue. In general, I've tried to make this book an entity in itself without changing the state of mind in which each of its various parts was written. Two essays, "Introduction: Life Between the Lines" and "Ruth's Song (Because She Could Not Sing It)," appear here for the first time.

*Outrageous Acts and
Everyday Rebellions*

Introduction: Life Between the Lines

*T*here have been days in the last ten or twelve years when I thought my collected works would consist entirely of fund-raising letters, scribbled outlines of speeches, statements hammered out at the birth of some new coalition, and introductions to other people's books.

I'm not regretful of the time I've devoted to those projects. Writing that leads to action, puts some common feeling into words, or introduces people to one another may be just as important in the long run as much of the fact and fiction published in conventional ways. If I were to name an emotional highpoint of my twenty or so years as a writer, it might be the two sleepless days I spent as an invited outside scribe for diverse caucuses at the 1977 National Women's Conference (an event also described here in "Houston and History"). Women representing every group of "minority" Americans, from Indian nations to new Vietnamese refugees, had decided to forge a shared resolution. As words were found to describe the common experiences of women of color while preserving the special issues of each group, and as that unprecedented shared resolution passed by acclamation of two thousand delegates representing every part of the country, I felt pride in being a writer that was at least as pleasurable as the pride that comes from seeing one's own more personal words in print.

In the same way, and supposing there is such a thing as posterity, I might be just as pleased if my part in it were much shorter than a book or an essay: perhaps the invention of something as brief and pithy as the phrase *reproductive freedom*, a democratic substitute for such old pater-

1

nalisms as *population control*, and a Fifth Freedom of special importance to the female half of the world. Finding language that will allow people to act together while cherishing each other's individuality is probably the most feminist and therefore truly revolutionary function of writers. Just as there can be no big social change without music (as Emma Goldman said, "If I can't dance, it's not my revolution"), there can be none without words and phrases that first create a dream of change in our heads

But it's one of the ironies of trying to be a writer and an activist at the same time that just when you feel you have the most to say, you have the least time to say it.

I regret very much, after more than a dozen years of traveling at least a couple of days a week as an itinerant speaker and feminist organizer, that I never kept a diary. Though most of the ideas and observations in this book were born during those travels (including its title, as you will see in the last essay, "Far from the Opposite Shore"), I could have written a book-length, blow-by-blow account of just one early year. For instance, one year that included being the first woman speaker for the powerful few at the National Press Club in Washington (they gave me a tie) and a Harvard Law Review banquet (where, being supplied with research from the few women students at this school that began admitting females only in the 1950s, I committed the sin of talking specifically about Harvard instead of generally about The World). Or finding three thousand people gathered for a speech in a basketball stadium in Wichita, Kansas, while the media was still reporting feminism as the invention of a few far-out women on either coast, and New York colleagues were predicting either indifference or the strong possibility of my being stoned to death. Or meeting women who were protesting everything from sex-segregated help-wanted ads in Pittsburgh to Nevada's practice of pressuring welfare mothers into prostitution in order to save money and increase tourist attractions.

Several more years like that one at the start of the 1970s taught me, despite deprecations the media were then reporting about "Women's Lib" or "bra burners," that daily rebellions and dreams of equality—inside families and in public life—were sprouting up everywhere. And these new ideas were not confined to any predictable demographics of age, race, education, or geography. If anything, rebellion was less rhetorical and more real in parts of the country where women's alternatives were more restricted than in the big cities of New York or California, and at economic levels where women's salaries were even more crucial than among the middle-class rebels who were the focus of the press.

Those regular travels also gave me good news to bring back to New York women writers and editors who were growing impatient with the old "feminine" and "masculine" stereotypes in the media, and who had just held historic sit-ins at *The Ladies' Home Journal* and *RAT*, a so-called radical paper that actually prospered on pornography. The good news was that there were more than enough readers for a new kind of women's magazine for, by, and about women. Though feminism was (and sometimes still is) a misunderstood word, many women readers wanted a magazine that supported its real definition: the equality and full humanity of women and men. After all, even those magazines directed to women were totally male-owned and controlled, and mostly edited by men. In order to right the balance, women needed a national forum—indeed, many such forums.

Meetings with other women in the publishing world uncovered war stories that either made you laugh or cry. *Look* magazine told Patricia Carbine, who had been essentially running that magazine for years as executive editor, that a woman could never have the editor's title. At *The Ladies' Home Journal* where I was an occasional consultant and writer, one of its two top editors (both men, of course) was so convinced that I was nothing like its readers (whom he described as "mental defectives with curlers in their hair") that he used to hand me a manuscript and say, "Pretend you're a woman and read this." Even at that, he was more flexible than the owner of *Seventeen*, who ordered an end to my editorial consulting there when he discovered I was raising money for the legal-defense fund of Angela Davis. An editor at *New York* magazine, where the women's movement was at least understood as an important news event, still insisted the whole thing was a minor upper-class discontent that could be solved by importing more maids from Jamaica. *The New York Times Magazine* seemed to be continuing its usual practice of allowing women, minorities, and homosexuals to write first-person confessional pieces, but, in the name of objectivity, assigning white male "authorities" to write definitive articles on these groups. A memo smuggled out by a woman office worker at *Playboy* magazine in Chicago was a three-page diatribe by Hugh Hefner against publishing an article on the women's movement that one of his editors had assigned to a professional male journalist, and thus had come out too "objective" and "well-balanced" for Hefner's purposes. As he wrote, "Doing a piece on the pros and cons of feminism strikes me as rather pointless for *Playboy*. What I'm interested in is the highly irrational, emotional, kookie trend. . . . These chicks are our natural enemies. . . . It is time to do battle with them. . . . What I want is a devastating piece . . . a really expert, personal demolition job on the subject." (I remember assuming that her release of that memo to the press would have a chilling effect on anyone who cared about journalism, if not women's equality, but it was treated with chuckles and smiles. Objectivity was for serious concerns, not for anything relating to women.)

There was an even bigger problem for women of color. Black women reported, for instance, that the senior editorial jobs of major national magazines included not one of their number. Even a brand-new magazine for black women was partly owned by *Playboy*, and, in the pattern of other women's magazines, was published by two men. As one woman put it, "At least you're getting hostility. We're still The Invisible Woman."

It was stories and meetings like those that rounded up the energy and professionalism for a national, inclusive, female-controlled magazine for women. With little capital and no intention of duplicating the traditional departments designed around "feminine" advertising categories—recipes to reinforce food ads, beauty features to mention beauty advertisers, and the like—we knew it would be economically tough. (Fortunately, we didn't know *how* tough. Attracting ads for cars, sound equipment, beer, and other things not traditionally directed to women still turns out to be easier than convincing advertisers that women look at ads for shampoo without accompanying articles on how to wash their hair, just as men look at ads for shaving products without articles on how to shave.) Given all these obstacles, we never would have continued if readers hadn't encouraged us. We produced one sample issue of this new editorial content—a magazine designed to stay on newsstands for three months—and it sold out in eight days.

There was a lot more hard work and uncertainty before we could begin publishing every month. Trying to start a magazine controlled by its female staff in a world accustomed to the authority of men and investment money should be the subject of a musical comedy.

Nonetheless, *Ms*. magazine was born, the place where the original versions of most of the writing in this book were eventually published.

At the same time, however, my life was less a magazine than a novel. For the four or five years surrounding the birth of *Ms.*, I was traveling and speaking as a team with a black feminist partner: first Dorothy Pitman Hughes, a child-care pioneer, then lawyer Florynce Kennedy, and finally activist Margaret Sloan. By speaking together at hundreds of public meetings, we hoped to widen a public image of the women's movement created largely by its first homegrown media event, *The Feminine Mystique*. (The English translation of Simone de Beauvoir's *The Second Sex* had caused a stir even earlier, but its message had been diminished by the idea that the rebellious women came from some other country, not our own.) Despite the many early reformist virtues of *The Feminine Mystique*, it had managed to appear at the height of the civil rights movement with almost no reference to black women or other women of color. It was most relevant to the problems of the white well-educated suburban homemakers who were standing by their kitchen sinks justifiably wondering if there weren't "more to life than this." As a result, *white-middle-class movement* had become the catch phrase of journalists describing feminism in the United States (unlike Europe, where early writings and actions were much more populist), and divisions among women were still deep.

There was little public understanding that feminism, by its very definition, has to include females as a caste across economic and racial boundaries, just as a movement against racial caste includes each individual marked by it, regardless of sex or class. There was even less understanding that sex and race discrimination are so pragmatically linked and anthropologically interdependent that one cannot be successfully uprooted without taking on the other.

So, to be feminist in both form and content, we went out in what Flo Kennedy used to describe cheerfully as "Little Eva teams—something for everyone." Or, as Margaret Sloan put it, "We travel in pairs—like nuns." After Dorothy Pitman Hughes and her husband Clarence had a baby who was nursing and so traveled with us, we were a trio for a while. Dorothy was convinced that some people might suspect us of renting this baby to demonstrate the integration of children into daily life; an important part of our message. In fact, one or two people behaved as if we had somehow given birth to a baby daughter by ourselves. It was a time when even one feminist speaker was a novelty, and interracial teams of feminists seemed to be unheard of since the days of Sojourner Truth.

That rarity brought us stares and opposition, but also great support. Our presence on the stage together made a point that women seemed hungry for, especially in the South. We attracted bigger and more diverse audiences than each of us would have had on our own, and we were complementary in other ways. As a journalist, my name was publicized, so I was more likely to attract the one paid speech around which we could build other meetings and benefits. On the other hand, Dorothy could talk personally about equality in marriage and parenthood, and both Flo and Margaret were far more experienced speakers. I always spoke first to lay a groundwork (as anyone in those audiences would tell you, speaking second also would have made me an anticlimax after the energy and style of Margaret or Flo), but the most important part of any lecture came after both of us—a long audience discussion and organizing meeting.

It was then that people began to answer one another's questions ("How can I stop feeling guilty about asking my husband to do housework?") with their own tried-and-true solutions ("Divide the housework as you would if you were living with another woman, and then don't lower your standards"). They informed one another of problems we never could have known about (a local factory that refused to hire women, a college hushing up a campus rape to protect its reputation, a high school counselor who advised girls to be nurses and minority boys to be veterinarians). They passed around literature from current feminist groups, sign-up sheets for new ones, and the addresses of politicians who deserved to be lobbied or demonstrated against. They picked up ideas or actions from the lengthening list we recited from our travels in other parts of the country, or they decided to do something entirely new.

Small all-women discussion groups that followed the lectures were even more honest, just as consciousness-raising or networking groups were (and still are, as reported here in an essay on "Networking") the basic cells of long-term change. But we discovered that the ideal proportion for a big public audience was about two-thirds women and one-third men. When matched by men in even numbers, women still restrained their response and looked to see how the men were reacting; but in clear majorities, they eventually forgot about any male presence at all and responded as women do when we are on our own. That gave many women a rare chance to speak honestly, and some men an even more rare chance to hear them.

Most of all, women in those audiences discovered they were not alone. And so did we.

Though we tried to focus on parts of the country that were most removed from the little feminist activity that then existed, there were so few feminist speakers that we ended by going to almost every kind of community and, I think, every state but Alaska. There were times when we felt like some combination of Susan B. Anthony and a lost company of *Blossom Time*.

In this book, the essay most directly related to such traveling is "Sisterhood," but other scenes come flooding back:

- Reporters at press conferences who routinely assumed I could answer questions about all women but Dorothy could answer only about black women, or perhaps only about the few black male leaders whose names they knew. Just as *male* was universal but *female* was limited, *white* was universal but *black* was limited. (We tried to turn this into a learning experience by letting the questions go on for a while—and then pointing the problems out.)

- White train conductors in the North who let me pass into the parlor car, then explained to Dorothy that the cheaper seats were in the rear.

- A black minister in Dorothy's tiny southern hometown who wouldn't let women in his church do anything but cook and sing—not even be deacons or pass the collection baskets that women's hard-earned coins did the most to fill.

- A white stewardess who pronounced Dorothy's nursing her baby onboard "obscene."

- An irate man in one audience who screamed at Dorothy to "go home to Russia where you belong," causing both her and the audience to break up with laughter at the idea of her Russian roots.

- A snobbish boys' prep school that gave us our toughest audience and a lifetime friend, the mother of one of the boys, who announced that she had an executive husband who liked to hunt, and two obnoxious sons who thought girls were inferior. She became a full-time volunteer for Dorothy's child-care center—where she worked for years thereafter.

- Margaret standing bravely with her arms crossed to block a man storming the stage against our "blasphemous" talk of equality.

- Late-night discussions in endless motel rooms where black women suggested we radicalize white women so they would stop offering themselves as doormats to black men, thus allowing some black men to accuse black women of being "too strong"; and where we listened to many women's stories of outrages to become known later as "sexual harassment," "battered women," or "displaced homemakers."

- A woman in Chicago who capsulized our long explanation of why welfare was a woman's issue (it was then considered an entirely racial one) by explaining that, with young children to care for, "most women in this country are only one man away from welfare."

- Gyms, auditoriums, church basements, and union halls filled to overflowing with women (and men) who applauded and laughed with relief at hearing the sexual politics of their lives described out loud.

- Stirring up rebellion at a women's university in Texas where campus guards were suspected of raping the women they were paid to protect, or among factory workers whose insurance covered men who had hair transplants but not women who had babies.

- Talking with Flo about her first book, *Abortion Rap*, in a Boston taxi and hearing its elderly Irish woman driver say the much-to-be-quoted words: "Honey, if men could get pregnant, abortion would be a sacrament."

- Trying to keep up with Flo's generosity and energy, from helping prostitutes organize against pimps and for decriminalization to encouraging rich wives to break the trusts that passed their family money from one generation of men to the next.

- Learning from Flo's experience as a lawyer how much more common were domestic violence and incest than I had ever dreamed. (She said, "Talk to any group of five or six women. One of them was probably sexually abused as a child by a man in her own family circle." I asked—and it was true.)

- Watching Flo transform lives by any available magic, from bullying an unconfident woman reporter into trying her own radio show, to convincing a shy clerk in a small-town dry-goods store that it was okay for Flo to buy her the purple pantsuit she'd been coveting for months.

- Most of all, learning from Flo's example that you didn't have to accept the opposition's terms. For instance, when a hostile man asked if we were lesbians (as frequently happened; why else would a white and black woman be colleagues?), Flo would just look him in the eye and ask, "Are you my alternative?"

It was Flo especially who taught me that a revolution without humor is as hopeless as one without music. Her own outrageousness allowed me to say things I might otherwise have confined to my former job as a writer of satire for the television show, "That Was the Week That Was," and feminism itself encouraged me to go beyond conventional subjects for humor (as you will see from a fantasy called "If Men Could Menstruate," an improvisation from later lectures). Flo also rescued me from a habit that might be okay in articles but is death in speeches: citing a lot of facts and statistics. After one such lapse before an audience that seemed especially skeptical about the existence of any discrimination at all, she took me aside. "Look," she said kindly. "If you're lying in the ditch with a truck on your ankle, you don't send somebody to the library to find out how much the truck weighs. You get it *off*."

The friendship and company of all three of my lecture partners helped me get over something else—an almost pathological fear of speaking in public. In the past, when magazines had booked me on a radio or television show, as writers routinely are asked to do, I had canceled out at the last minute so often that a few shows banned me as a guest. Though I wasn't shy about bearding lions on a den by den basis, as journalists must do, the very idea of speaking to a group, much less before a big audience, was enough to make my heart pound and my mouth go dry. The few times I tried it, I became obsessed with getting to the end of each sentence without swallowing, and then obsessed for days afterward with what I should have said.

It was self-conscious. It was wasteful. I berated myself for this idiotic inability to talk on my own. When I once did show up on television to talk about the organizing efforts of migrant workers, host Bill Cosby tried to still my chattering teeth by explaining during a break that I had no *right* to be so nervous when I was speaking for a man as important as Cesar Chavez. That didn't help at all. After experiencing police riots at the 1968 Chicago Democratic Convention, I got angry enough to try again, but only as a team with Jimmy Breslin, my colleague at *New York* magazine. That time, I got out about three sentences—and didn't even have the confidence to resist false eyelashes that television makeup men then glued on female guests, thus making the medium contradict the message.

On the theory that I knew no one in Canada and so failure wouldn't be as humiliating there, I did a Canadian television series in the late sixties that included long interviews with James Earl Jones, Congressman Adam Clayton Powell, and Prime Minister Pierre Trudeau. (I also didn't have the confidence to suggest women.) But that series offered the comfort of a very professional cohost and tapes that could be edited later. It was still a long way from standing in front of an audience with the sole responsibility for an hour of dead air.

I even consulted a speech teacher. She told me that writers and dancers had the most difficulty learning to talk in public, because each had chosen a profession in which they could communicate without speech. I had been both. Long before becoming a writer, I had been a semiprofessional dancer dreaming of tap dancing my way out of Toledo. I decided to give up on trying to say anything in public.

And I would have remained silent, like so many women who were giving up on various aspects of their human abilities, if I hadn't been lucky enough to live through a time when a few women were beginning to figure out that the gigantic lack of confidence in females wasn't all our individual faults. A profound system of sexual politics was at work here.

I say all this about speaking not only because it has been a major hurdle in my life, but also because it's a problem that seems to be common to many people who feel overly dependent on the approval of others. (Layers of political cause and effect peeled away more for me when I researched "Men and Women Talking," an essay included in this book.) One of the most helpful things ever said to me came from poet Sandra Hochman: "Don't think about it. Just pretend you're Eleanor Roosevelt and you have to do this idiotic television show before you can go on to do something *really* important." Perhaps this is the Art of Zen Speaking.

Years of actually getting up in front of audiences have taught me only three lessons: 1) you don't die; 2) there's no right way to speak, only *your* way; and 3) it's worth it. A mutual understanding can come from being in a room together, and a sense of character and intention can come through the television screen that could never happen on a printed page.

Now, I continue to travel and organize almost every week, sometimes alone, sometimes with other women, depending on the issue and audience at hand. If we were to do another road show like that earlier one (and perhaps we should), we would need a repertory company of a dozen or so women even to begin to symbolize who American feminists really are; from Chicana to Alaskan Native, from Puerto Rican to Pacific Islander. We would still need women who have made different choices, from a traditional homemaker who wants honor for her work to a lesbian who wants honor for her life-style. Indeed, we would now need some men, too. There are many more who can call themselves feminists with pride and justification. But the goal would still be the same: to give people a chance to hear feelings confirmed, know they are not alone, and thus discover they didn't need "outside agitators" after all. In any one audience, there is enough energy, skill, anger, and humor for a revolution.

As an itinerant organizer, my own two biggest rewards are still a sense of making a difference and the birth of ideas. The first would be enough in itself, for that is how we know we are alive, but the second is magic. On a good night, a roomful of people can set off a chain of thought that leads us all to a new place—a sudden explosion of understanding, a spontaneous invention. We hear ourselves saying things we had felt but never named. It will take a lifetime to write them all down.

*N*onetheless, I wouldn't be honest if I blamed only activism for the fact that, after more than twenty years of making a living as a writer, this is the first book I can call my own.*

Writers are notorious for using any reason to keep from working: over-researching, retyping, going to meetings, waxing the floors—anything. Organizing, fund raising, and working for *Ms.* magazine have given me much better excuses than those, and I've used them. As Jimmy

---

*There were two semibooks: *The Thousand Indias*, a guidebook I wrote for the Indian government while on a fellowship there in 1957 and 1958, but never published here; and *The Beach Book* (Viking, 1963) which was my anthology but mostly other people's writing.

Breslin said when he ran a symbolic campaign for a political office he didn't want, "Anything that isn't writing is easy." Looking back at an article I published in 1965, even when I was writing full-time and in love with my profession, I see, "I don't like to write. I like to have written."

That thought comes from "What's In It for Me," the subject on which *Harper's* had invited a group of writers to contribute. In fact, most of my reasons in that essay still hold.

- There is freedom, or the illusion of it. Working in spurts to meet deadlines may be just as restricting as having to show up at the same place every day, but I don't think so. . . . Writing about a disliked person or theory or institution usually turns out to be worthwhile, because pride of authorship finally takes over from prejudice. Words in print assume such power and importance that it is impossible not to feel acutely responsible for them.

- Writing, on the other hand, keeps me from believing everything I read.

- Women whose identity depends more on their outsides than their insides are dangerous when they begin to age. Because I have work I care about, it's possible that I may be less difficult to get along with when the double chins start to form.

- I don't have to specialize. If one year can include articles on suburban integration, electronic music, Saul Bellow, college morals, John Lennon, three Kennedys, the space program, hiring policies in television, hard-edge painting, pop culture, draftees for Vietnam, and James Baldwin, nonfiction writing may be the last bastion of the generalist.

- For me, writing is the only thing that passes the three tests of metier: (1) when I'm doing it, I don't feel that I should be doing something else instead; (2) it produces a sense of accomplishment and, once in a while, pride; and (3) it's frightening.*

Nevertheless, I'm surprised by the quantity of writing I was doing then; not just in that single year of 1965 but for most of the sixties. I hadn't reread these pieces until I dug them out for this collection and rejected

*"What's In It for Me," *Harper's*, November 1965, 169.

almost all of them as outdated or off-the-point. (Only two of the most personal ones survive, "I Was a Playboy Bunny" and the earlier parts of "Campaigning.") If I had realized at the time that trying to write like other reporters and essayists is precisely what makes the results more inter-changeable and perishable, I would have been less hesitant about writing in the first person. (You were supposed to say nothing more personal than "this reporter.") I was trying to be a professional writer-on-assignment; a worthy calling but not one that makes for much original thinking. Nonetheless, some themes of those articles emerge.

I was clearly trying to learn from other writers by choosing them as subjects for profiles. James Baldwin was high on the list because I identified with his sense of outrage and vulnerability (though at the time, I had no idea why I, a middle-class white person, should share these feelings). Saul Bellow's *The Adventures of Augie March* was the only novel that captured a certain crazy American class mobility I also had experienced while growing up in the Midwest with many books and show-business pretensions, but in either a housetrailer, or a house with rats and no heat. So I spent a memorable day following Bellow around as he revisited his childhood haunts in Chicago. I wrote about Truman Capote twice because I was so moved by his early fiction and its bitter-sweet evocation of an outsider's childhood, as well as by his ability to write seriously and empathetically about women (including the rape of a black woman trapped by white men in a roadside ditch—a scene I shall never forget). John Lennon was a subject I wrote about so long ago that I was more attracted by his pun-filled, Liverpudlian poetry than his music, but the only article I could sell was a pretty conventional account of following the Beatles during their first visit to New York. Interviewing Dorothy Parker, one of the few female writers about whom women's magazines cared enough to publish a profile, was like meeting an acerbic old friend. My mother had quoted her verses and I knew many by heart. In fact, we did become friends. Long after the article was published, I kept visiting her in the apartment where she was trapped by illness, and once got her out to a ballet. "My dear, that Round Table thing was *greatly* over-rated, you know," she said, with her delightful habit of debunking past glories. "It was full of people looking for a free lunch and asking, 'Did you hear the funny thing I said yesterday?' "

Most of my assignments reflected the media's interest in celebrities: Mary Lindsay, wife of the newly elected New York mayor, and actor

Michael Caine for *The New York Times Magazine*; Margot Fonteyn and Lee Radziwill for *McCall's*; Paul Newman and a newer star named Barbra Streisand for *The Ladies' Home Journal;* and many more. (The Newman assignment, typical of the hazards of working for certain women's magazines, was to find out "how that plain little girl hangs on to the world's handsomest movie star." When I reported back that Joanne Woodward was at least as interesting as her husband—and that, if anything, the balance seemed to be the other way around—my male editor said I couldn't write it that way. *Journal* readers would be threatened by interesting wives. When I finally did Newman on his own, it was a hard-won compromise.) I sneaked in a few less-well-known women whose work I admired: Marisol as an iconoclastic sculptor; Renata Adler as a very smart young writer and movie critic for *The New York Times*; Pauline Frederick as an older and excellent television reporter who might have been Walter Cronkite had she been a man and thus allowed to age on camera; Barbara Walters as the first woman on the "Today" show who wasn't a coffee-serving beauty-contest winner and who actually did her own reporting. But there weren't many of those. I didn't fight hard enough. I was grateful for celebrity profiles as a step up from the traditional "girl writer" assignments I was inevitably given and to which I sometimes succumbed.

They included things like: reporting on a hotel sale whose chief attraction was ZsaZsa Gabor's bed; going to London to interview a new hairdresser named Vidal Sassoon (who turned out to be a serious person, but *Glamour* wasn't interested in his life on a kibbutz); writing about designer Rudy Gernreich (who also turned out to be an innovator of comfortable clothes, but only a long fight with *The New York Times Magazine* got anything but his topless bathing suits included in the article); and, probably the low point in my writing life, a long, endlessly researched article on textured stockings. That last one was for *The New York Times Magazine*, the source of my most frivolous and seductive assignments. After turning down three or four on such subjects as a profile of Park Avenue (with instructions to stop where it entered Spanish Harlem and *Times* readers diminished), I would think, *Well, it is* The New York Times, and find myself writing on something I didn't care about. The good gray *Times* also had a high incidence of editors who asked you to go to a hotel with them in the afternoon, or, failing that, to mail their letters for them on the way out.

For *Life* magazine, I did write a long semisociological report on pop culture, but only after being sent home by the first editor I saw there. ("We don't want a pretty girl," he explained. "We want a writer.") There were also many protofeminist, philosophical essays for *Glamour*: a little saccharine but not without a germ of personal experience or real feeling. I still meet an occasional woman who tells me that she did or didn't have an affair, leave home, or otherwise do what she wanted to do anyway because one of those essays said it was okay. There were cultural columns for *Look* magazine; show business and college features for *Show* magazine and *Esquire*; such odd one-time projects as a concert booklet for Peter, Paul, and Mary; and book reviews for almost everybody.

In other words, I was making a living as a writer.

But most of this work was a long way from the writing I had hoped to do when I lived in India just after college, discovered that its standard of living, not ours, was the norm for most of the world, and kept a diary of walking through village caste riots with nothing but a cup, a sari, and a comb. After I first came home in 1958, I had naïvely tried to sell some of that writing, as well as a guidebook designed to lure Westerners into traveling beyond the Taj Mahal, but I was unknown and the time was much too early. Even the Beatles hadn't yet discovered India.

In fact, a lot of the work I published prefeminism was schizophrenic, even when compared to the life I was leading in New York.

I was volunteering for political campaigns, but writing *fumetti* and satirical photo captions for a successor to *Mad* magazine called *Help!*; sneaking endless pizzas and cigarettes to a group of Puerto Rican radicals, including some early feminists, while they occupied a church in Spanish Harlem, but writing about ancient Christmas traditional foods for *Glamour*; traveling in 110° heat with Cesar Chavez and his Poor People's March to the Mexican border in order to organize press coverage, but reporting on tropical vacations; raising bail and collecting clothes for migrant workers organizing on Long Island, but interviewing James Coburn about some James Bond–type movie.

As one of the few "girl reporters," I also was traveling among the Beautiful People I was writing about, and was sometimes photographed as one of their lesser members, yet at the same time, I was paying $62.50 a month for an apartment and having my American Express card—on which I had charged all the expenses of that march to the Mexican border that the farmworkers couldn't afford—repossessed.

Much of this disparity was my fault. I didn't take myself very seriously either. Besides, there had been the early mistake of accepting an
assignment from *Show* magazine to work as a Playboy Bunny in order to
write the exposé included in this book. Though I returned an advance
payment for its expansion into a book, thus avoiding drugstore racks full
of paperbacks emblazoned with my name, "I Was a Playboy Bunny," and
god-knows-what illustration, that article quickly became the only way I
was publicly identified. It swallowed up my first major signed article: an
Esquire report on the contraceptive revolution that had been published a
year earlier and was attracting assignments from other editors. (I see that
this twenty-one-year-old article ended with: "The only trouble with
sexually liberating women is that there aren't enough sexually liberated
men to go around." It's interesting that I could understand that much and
still be blind to all the rest.) I lost a hard-won assignment to do an
investigative article on the United States Information Agency, whose
accurate reflection of this country I had come to doubt after seeing its
operations in India. Instead, I got a leering suggestion that I pose as a call
girl and do an exposé of high-level prostitution.

Eventually, dawning feminism made me understand that reporting
about the phony glamour and exploitative employment policies of the
Playboy Club was a useful and symbolic thing to do. Posing as a call girl
(which I didn't do because I found the idea both insulting and frightening)
would have been an assignment worthy of Nellie Bly. But at the time, I
had no protection against the sex jokes and changed attitudes that the
Bunny article brought with it; and my heart sank whenever I was introduced as a former Playboy Bunny or found my employee photograph
published with little explanation in *Playboy*. (Even twenty years later,
both these events continue. The latter is *Playboy*'s long-running revenge.) Though I always identified emotionally with other women,
including the Bunnies I worked with, I had been educated to believe that
my only chance for seriousness lay in proving my difference from them.

It wasn't until *New York* magazine was founded in 1968 and I became
one of its contributing editors and political columnists that my work as a
writer and my own interests began to combine. For *New York*'s inaugural
issue, I wrote a short article called "Ho Chi Minh in New York"—a
probable American experience in the life of that mysterious anticolonial
leader whose affection for this country and respected status as "the

George Washington of South Asia" I knew from living in India after college. It was only now, a decade later, that I was able to use any experience from those two crucial years in my life. They also had taught me that a white woman was less threatening than a white man, and had an easier time traveling in other cultures. That helped when, after Martin Luther King was murdered and I sat staring mutely at my TV set, I got a call from *New York* editor Clay Felker to "get the hell up to Harlem, and just talk to people." I knew that, as in India, safety lay in staying close to other women for protection. I felt like a reporter for the first time. When a newly elected President Nixon sent Nelson Rockefeller on a tour of Latin America, I was assigned by *New York* to go along on the press plane. The result was an account of his very unpopular trip called "The Sound of One Hand Clapping." I reported on John Lindsay as mayor and Ed Koch as a congressman; on wounded Vietnam vets who returned to a hospital in Queens direct from the battlefield, only to find themselves victims of the peace movement as well as the war; on the discovery in the Bronx of kwashiorkor, a protein-deficiency disease once thought to be confined to the famines of Africa; neighborhood battles over child-care centers; anti-Vietnam demonstrations and peace mobilizations; and the attitudes of journalists on presidential campaign planes. (Samples of these travels are part of "Campaigning.") For the first time, I wasn't writing about one thing, while caring about something else.

Nonetheless, it wasn't until I went to cover a local abortion hearing for *New York* that the politics of my own life began to explain my interests.

In protest of an official hearing that had invited fourteen men and one nun to testify on the liberalization of New York State's anti-abortion laws, a local feminist group had asked women to testify about their real life experiences with illegal abortion. I sat in a church basement listening to women stand before an audience and talk about desperately trying to find someone who would help them, enduring pre-abortion rapes from doctors, being asked to accept sterilization as the price of an abortion, and endangering their lives in an illegal, unsafe medical underground. It was like the "testifying" I had heard in southern churches and civil rights meetings of the earlier sixties: emotional, rock-bottom, personal truths.

Suddenly, I was no longer learning intellectually what was wrong. I knew. I had had an abortion when I was newly out of college, and had told no one. If one in three or four adult women shares this experience, why should each of us be made to feel criminal and alone? How much power would we ever have if we had no power over the fate of our own bodies?

I researched as much as I could about reproductive issues and other wellsprings of a new feminism and wrote a respectable, objective article (not one *I* in the whole thing) called "After Black Power, Women's Liberation." It contained none of the emotions I had felt in that church basement, and certainly not the fact that I, too, once had an abortion. (Though hearing those women had made me free to say it for the first time, I still thought that writers were more credible when they concealed their personal experience. I had a lot to learn.) But I did predict that if these younger, more radical women from the peace and civil rights movements could affect what were then the middle-class reformists of the National Organization for Women, and join with poor women already organizing around welfare and child care, a long-lasting and important mass movement would result.

That article would now seem about as new as the air we breathe, but in 1970, a year after its publication, it won a Penney-Missouri Journalism Award as one of the first aboveground reports on this wave of feminism. From my male friends and colleagues, however, it won immediate alarm. Several took me aside kindly: Why was I writing about these crazy women instead of something serious, political, and important? How could I risk identifying myself with women's stuff when I'd worked so hard to get "real" assignments? Interestingly, the same men who had thought working as a Bunny and writing a well-publicized article was just fine for my career were now cautionary about one brief article on a political movement among women.

For the first time, I began to question the honor of being the only "girl reporter" among men, however talented and benevolent they might be. And all the suppressed anger of past experiences I had denied or tried to ignore came flooding back: the apartments I couldn't get because landlords assumed a single woman couldn't pay the rent (or if she could, she must be a hooker); the political assignments lost to younger and less-experienced male writers; the assumption that any work I did get was the result of being a "pretty girl" (even at a time, I suddenly realized, when all of my editors had been women); the lowered payments because women didn't really need the money; the innuendos that came along with any recognition ("easier than you think," was how *Newsweek* had captioned my photograph as a young writer—a quotation that turned out to be from my own statement that free-lance writing was "easier than you think"); the well-meaning friends who kept encouraging me to marry any man I was going out with who had talent or money; a lifetime of journalists' jokes about frigid wives, dumb blonds, and farmers' daughters that I had smiled at in order to be "one of the boys."

That was the worst of it, of course—my own capitulation to all the small humiliations, and my own refusal to trust an emotional understanding of what was going on, or even to trust my own experience. For instance, I had believed that women couldn't get along with one another, even while my own most trusted friends were women. I had agreed that women were more "conservative" even while I identified emotionally with every discriminated-against group. I had assumed that women were sexually "masochistic" even though I knew that trust and kindness were indispensable parts of my sexual attraction to any man. It is truly amazing how long we can go on accepting myths that oppose our own lives, assuming instead that we are the odd exceptions. But once the light began to dawn, I couldn't understand why I hadn't figured out any of this before.

I began to read every piece of feminist writing I could lay my hands on, and talk to every active feminist I could find. For the few magazines then interested, I wrote articles that reflected this growing movement: the possibility of a woman president in the White House for *Look*, more columns that commented on sexual politics for *New York*, an essay on "What It Would Be Like If Women Win" that ran with *Time* magazine's sensationalized cover story on Kate Millett, and others. (Though, as I discovered later, I was paid less than male journalists who had written similar *Time* essays—so much for women winning.)

But most magazines said, "Sorry, we published our feminist article last year." Or, "If we publish one article saying women are equal, then we'll have to be objective by publishing one right next to it saying they're not." Editors who had assumed I had some valuable biological insight into food, male movie stars, and textured stockings now questioned whether I or other women writers were biologically capable of writing objectively about feminism.

Responses like those drove me to try speaking instead of writing in order to report the deeper realities that I had first glimpsed the night of that abortion hearing. I began to learn from other women, to figure out the politics of my own life, and to experiment with telling the truth in public. That was the beginning.

But not the end. The first flash of consciousness reveals so much that it seems like the sun coming up. In fact, it's more like a first candle in the dark.

For instance, I could have collected those early profiles and articles long before they were out of date. I also could have attempted a single piece of work that would have been a book in itself. Why did I never do the former? And why, even now, do I continue to resist the latter?

Before feminism, I told myself that my work couldn't possibly be good enough. That excuse concealed the fact that I was still assuming my real identity would come from the man I married, not the work I did. It also kept me from admitting that I was too insecure to attempt a long and lonely piece of work. I needed the reinforcement that comes from short articles frequently published.

Immediately postconsciousness, I noticed that many of my male contemporaries who were felling forests and filling bookstores with their hard-cover works were not better writers than I. Some were much worse. Others had imitative ideas that hardly seemed worth the death of one tree. In the first light of early consciousness, I also noticed that most of them had wives, secretaries, and girl friends who researched, typed, edited, and said reverential things like, "Shhh, Norman is working." Meanwhile, I felt so "unfeminine" about admitting that I, too, loved and was obsessed with my work that, unlike those male colleagues, I never asked friends and lovers for help with research or other support, and rarely put writing ahead of their social schedules. I never even said firmly, "I want to work." Instead, I shuffled and apologized and said, "I'm terribly sorry, but I have this awful deadline."

Only later did I understand that a need for external emergencies to justify "unfeminine" work is common to many women (a phenomenon also explored in the essay on "The Importance of Work"). In fact, one measure of women's ingenuity may be the wide variety of ways we have found male authority, economic circumstance, or other good reasons to justify doing what we wanted to do anyway. This subterfuge allows us to maintain a passive, "feminine" stance while secretly rebelling. Like most deceptions, it is a gigantic waste of inventiveness and time.

Only much later did I realize that my resistance to undertaking a long piece of work—or to planning far into the future for any goal—was another common symptom of powerlessness. Even after I had stopped assuming that my life would be decided by whatever man I happened to marry (a pretty big "after"), I still had (and have) a hard time saying, "This is where I want to be in five years—or even next year." Class brings to poor men the same feeling of being out of control and subject to the whims of others, though rarely in the same degree as women who are trained to feel subject to the needs of a real or potential husband and children as well as to any lack of money. Writing "The Time Factor," an article included here, made me understand that planning ahead is a function of caste and class in general, and that I as an individual am just learning.

As old assumptions fall away, each layer of new observation has truth to it. Growing consciousness expands but doesn't negate the vision that went before. For instance, lately I've been wondering, *What is so sacred about a long and continuous piece of writing?* Life isn't always experienced in book-length themes. Shorter forms or a series of insights that surround a subject may be just as useful and give prose more of the economy and depth that poetry has always had. The idea of episodic techniques might release a lot of male writers who now struggle to create lineal and unrealistically neat connections, not to mention all the women writers who must work episodically at their kitchen tables with only a few hours to concentrate until the children come home. After all, spontaneity, flexibility, and a talent for living in the present are the other side of an inability to control our time and to plan. While women are discovering what we need to learn, we shouldn't jettison or undervalue what we already know.

For example, when I'm asked about the rewards and punishments of my life now, I always feel the need to come up with continuous themes and neat conclusions. In fact, I can only think of intense scenes and sense memories. Furthermore, the categories of reward or punishment aren't always clear. Some of the worst punishments turned out to be so instructive that they eventually were rewarding, and some of the supposed rewards are not only punishments but very difficult to complain about. (For instance, sympathies for the problems of becoming well-known are about as limited as sympathies for the rich.) Taking an intention to punish at face value, however, here are some scenes from the down side.

- Waking up to the "Today" show and an ad for an exploitation novel that features a scantily clad woman with my hair and glasses slinking toward a table on which there is a necklace with a large feminist symbol, while a male announcer's voice says something like: "The Symbol. She used men . . . but preferred women." In fact, this example of "any rebellious woman is a lesbian" turned out to be a useful lesson. Women who hadn't seen lesbianism as a feminist issue before wrote to say they now understood that all women could be stopped or divided by this accusation until we all succeeded in taking the sting out of it by making lesbianism an honorable choice.

- Opening a mass-mailed Christmas letter from a cousin and his wife with the misfortune of having the same last name as mine and, between the news of their fishing trip and other retirement activities, discovering an announcement that they had formally disowned me. As a feminist, I was "disloyal" to God, Man, and Country. Their announcement hurt my mother, but after I discovered they were still segregationists and had been at odds with my suffragist grandmother years before I was born, it began to seem like an honor and a family tradition.

- Watching Al Capp denounce me on television as both the "Shirley Temple of the New Left" and someone comparable to Richard Speck, the sadistic murderer of eight nurses—indeed, he went on to compare all "women's liberation leaders" with "mass murderers"—I guess on the theory that feminism kills women. Later, I discovered that Al Capp's public career was marred by allegations and a lawsuit about his own sexual approaches to young women while he was a frequent speaker on campus. But his words hurt nonetheless.

- Watching Richard Speck explain on television that not *all* the women he had murdered were "like Gloria Steinem." Though he was being interviewed in prison, his women hatred and gynocide are far from unique to him. His words were frightening.

- Being told by the elevator man that another tenant in my office building had said, "I hear Gertrude Stein works in this building. So how come I never see her in the elevator?" At first I thought this was only funny, until I realized that the image of one rebellious woman was being used to include all of us. We all look alike.

- Going to give a speech in Texas and seeing dozens of people outside the amphitheater with signs: GLORIA STEINEM IS A HUMANIST. I thought, *How nice, they must be friends.* But as I got closer and saw the hatred in their faces, I realized they were right-wing pickets to whom *humanist*—or any other word that means a belief in people instead of their authoritarian god—is the worst thing you can be.

- Being consistently opposed by the right (because feminism is "a leftwing plot to destroy the family") and occasionally by the left (because feminism is "a rightwing plot to divide the left"). From this I learned that Feminists Will Be Accused of Everything.

- Being accused both of communist agentry (because I went to two Soviet-sponsored Youth Festivals twenty-four and twenty-one years ago) and government agentry (because Americans who went to them were partly subsidized by foundations that wrongly took funds from the U.S. government). Or being accused of both things as a result of supporting lesbian rights (which have been called the inevitable "anti-family communist plot," and even "an FBI plot to discredit the Women's Movement"). I find such accusations unreasonably painful. They all imply that your mind and your acts are not your own.

- Being said to "use men" to get published, get ahead, even to succeed as a feminist—whatever. Since this accusation is generally leveled at women who succeed in anything, it may be the root cause of all of those above. As long as women who do well in the world are rare, even other women will wrongly assume that they must be following men's orders. The only question then is, *Which* men?

- Seeing displayed on newsstands all over New York a *Screw* magazine centerfold of a woman with my face and glasses, a nude body drawn in labial detail, a collection of carefully drawn penises bordering the page, and a headline instruction to PIN THE COCK ON THE FEMINIST. Feeling helpless and humiliated, I sent a lawyer's letter to *Screw*'s editor Al Goldstein—and got back a box of candy with a note that said "Eat It." Only Bella Abzug's humor rescued me from my depression.

When I explained to her about this nude centerfold in full labial detail with my face and head, she deadpanned, "and my labia."

There are, of course, the occasional bomb threats designed to clear the hall (generally phoned in by a self-described "Right-to-Lifer"), the hurtful articles you learn not to read because you can do nothing about them, the frustration at not being able to retain the legal rights to your own life, and the anger at seeing survival issues ridiculed or misunderstood. There is also the great reward of working full time at something I care about so much that I would do it for no money at all, plus the problems of making far less money than would be possible outside a social movement. The last would be okay if "rich and famous" weren't one phrase. Being resented for money that doesn't exist is not a great combination. Still, all of the punishments are somehow easier to describe than the rewards that mean much more. Perhaps women are more accustomed to singing the blues—even to using humor as a palliative for rage—than to victories and celebrations. In fact, there are many scenes and sense memories of emotional and factual rewards.

- Listening to five women say they have jobs they love that wouldn't have been open to them without feminism—a pregnant flight attendant, a fire fighter, the highest woman official in New York State, a union carpenter, and the first female astronaut—and hearing all of these in one day.

- Being stopped in the street by a truck driver who tells me that the woman he loves and has been living with for three years wouldn't marry him or have children because he didn't want her to go on working; then he heard some interview in which I asked men to consider how they would feel if they were exactly the same people but had been born female. He tried this exercise for a while, and changed so much that he and his friend were now happily married. He is thanking me—but the miracle is his own empathy.

- Seeing every day on my way to work a middle-aged black woman traffic cop who is the Toscanini of Manhattan's busiest intersection, who smiles at me and says "Give 'em hell," and leaves me with an unreasonable feeling of womanpride and well-being.

- Discovering that my excellent dentist has retired and left his practice to a calm, equally excellent young woman.

- Going on a speaking tour of Minnesota, from the Iron Range to farming villages, and finding that each church basement and school gym is full of women and men who matter-of-factly refer to themselves as feminists.

- Speaking at campuses that students warn me are "conservative" or "apathetic," and finding Women's Studies, clerical workers organizing, demonstrations against local porn theaters, a rape hot line, the beginning of child care for students and faculty, a partnership between women students and professors—all things that probably weren't there ten or even five years ago.

- Meeting a midwestern Catholic priest who prays to "God the Mother" as some reparation for five thousand years of patriarchy and who invites me to preach the homily from the pulpit; reading public statements by nuns who oppose their bishops' position against abortion; hearing a woman rabbi and a woman cantor who conduct a beautiful and inclusive memorial service for the death of a friend's mother in New York; meeting a woman Episcopalian priest in Washington who broke the barriers for herself and others with an ecclesiastical lawsuit; finding schools and Bible classes that honor as martyrs the millions of women burned as witches for resisting a cruel and patriarchal god.

- Getting on planes whose flight attendants tell me about their latest lawsuit, seat me in first class though I have a tourist ticket, come to lectures in strange cities, volunteer for lobbying, and send me home with slips of paper to remind me that they need news of this or that issue or the address of the nearest feminist group.

- Hearing over and over again "Feminism saved my life," or "Thank you for my mother," or "I understand my wife better now," or "My daughter will be what I never could have been"; and being constantly entrusted with the personal gratitude and triumphs of strangers.

- Sitting in an ethnic hall in Detroit, at a local celebration of *Ms.* magazine's tenth birthday, and being tapped on the shoulder by a small, gray-haired woman with gnarled, hardworking hands and a starched cotton housedress that is clearly her best. "I just want you to know," she says softly, "that you are the inside of me." All reward came together in one moment. Remembering now that woman's touch and words, I still feel the tears behind my eyes.

I used to have a recurring dream. I was fighting with one person or many people, struggling and kicking and hitting as hard as I could because they were trying to kill me or to hurt someone I loved. I fought with all my strength, as fiercely as I could, harder and harder; but no matter what I did, I couldn't hurt any of them. No matter how hard I fought, they just smiled.

In the 1970s, I told this dream to some other women and discovered that they shared similar emotions. My dream was a classic scenario of anger, humiliation, and powerlessness.

Sometime in the 1980s, I stopped having the dream. Thinking of that woman in Detroit, I realize now that I associate its disappearance with her words. They crystallized in one moment what women can do and are doing. We are offering each other a new and compassionate kind of power.

In fact, women and men have begun to rescue one another in many ways, large and small. I hope that you will find a rescuing moment or fact or idea within the pages of this book.

—New York City, 1983

LEARNING FROM EXPERIENCE

I *undertook a reporting assignment armed with a large diary and this ad:*

GIRLS:
Do Playboy Club Bunnies Really
Have Glamorous Jobs,
Meet Celebrities, And
Make Top Money?

Yes, it's true! Attractive young girls can now earn $200–$300 a week at the fabulous New York Playboy Club, enjoy the glamorous and exciting aura of show business, and have the opportunity to travel to other Playboy Clubs throughout the world. Whether serving drinks, snapping pictures, or greeting guests at the door, the Playboy Club is the stage—the Bunnies are the stars.

The charm and beauty of our Bunnies has been extolled in *Time, Newsweek,* and *Pageant,* and Ed Sullivan has called The Playboy Club " . . . the greatest new show biz gimmick." And the Playboy Club is now the busiest spot in New York.

If you are pretty and personable, between 21 and 24, married or single, you probably qualify. No experience necessary.

Apply in person at SPECIAL INTERVIEWS being held Saturday and Sunday, January 26–27, 10 A.M.–3 P.M. Please bring a swimsuit or leotards.

THE PLAYBOY CLUB
5 East 59th Street   PL 2-3100

THURSDAY, JANUARY 24th, 1963

I've decided to call myself Marie Catherine Ochs. It is, may my ancestors forgive me, a family name. I have some claim to it, and I'm well versed in its European origins. Besides, it sounds much too square to be phony.

FRIDAY 25TH

I've spent the entire afternoon making up a background for Marie. She shares my apartment, my phone, and my measurements. Though younger than I by four years (I was beyond the Bunny age limit), Marie celebrates the same birthday and went to the same high school and college. But she wasn't a slave to academics—not Marie. After one year she left me plodding along the path to a B.A. and boarded a tourist flight to Europe. She had no money, but short periods as a waitress in London, a hostess-dancer in Paris, and a secretary in Geneva were enough to sustain her between beachcombing and other escapades. Last year, she came back to New York and worked briefly as a secretary. Three mutual friends have agreed to give her strong personal recommendations. To know her is to love her.

Tomorrow is the day. Marie makes her first trip out of this notebook and into the world. I'm off to buy her a leotard.

SATURDAY 26TH

Today I put on the most theatrical clothes I could find, packed my leotard in a hatbox, and walked to the Playboy Club. It is impossible to miss. The discreet six-story office building and art gallery that once stood there has been completely gutted and transformed into a shiny rectangle of plate glass. The orange-carpeted interior is clearly visible, with a modern floating stairway spiraling upward at dead center. The total effect is cheerful and startling.

I crossed over to the club, where a middle-aged man in a private guard's uniform grinned and beckoned. "Here bunny, bunny, bunny!" He jerked his thumb toward the glass door on the left. "Interviews downstairs in the Playmate Bar."

The inside of the club was so dramatically lit that it took a few seconds to realize it was closed and empty. I walked down a short flight of stairs and was greeted by Miss Shay, a thin, thirtyish woman who sat at a desk in the darkened bar. "Bunny?" she asked briskly. "Sit over there, fill out this form, and take off your coat." I could see that two of the tables were already occupied by girls hunched over pencils, and I looked at them curiously. I had come in the middle of the interviews, hoping to see as many applicants as I could, but there were only three. "*Take off your coat*," said Miss Shay again, and she looked at me appraisingly while I did so. One of the girls got up and crossed to the desk, her high-heeled plastic sandals slapping smartly against her heels. "Look," she said, "you want these measurements with or without a bra?"

"With," said Miss Shay.

"But I'm bigger without," said the girl.

"All right," said Miss Shay wearily, "without." Two more girls came down the steps looking fresh and innocent of cosmetics. "Bunny?" said Miss Shay.

"Not really," said one, but the other took a card. Their long hair and loafers looked collegiate.

The application form was short: address, phone, measurements, age, and last three employers. I finished it and began to stall for time by looking at an accompanying brochure entitled *BE A PLAYBOY CLUB BUNNY!* Most of it was devoted to photographs: a group picture showed Bunnies "chosen from all over the United States" surrounding "Playboy Club President and *Playboy* Editor-Publisher Hugh M. Hefner"; there was a close-up of a Bunny serving Tony Curtis, "a Playboy Club devotee [who] will soon star in Hugh M. Hefner's film titled, appropriately enough, *Playboy*"; in another, two Bunnies smiled with Hugh M. Hefner on "Playboy's nationally syndicated television show"; Bunnies handed out copies of *Playboy* in a veterans' hospital as "just one of the many worthwhile community projects in which Bunnies participate"; a blond Bunny stood before a matronly woman, the "Bunny Mother," who offered "friendly personal counseling"; and, on the last page, a bikini-clad girl crouched on a yacht flying a Bunny flag. "When you become a Bunny," said the text, "your world will be fun-filled, pleasant, and always exciting. . . . " It cited an average salary of two hundred dollars a week.

Another girl came down the steps. She wore glasses with blue rims and a coat that looked as if she had outgrown it. I watched her as she nervously asked Miss Shay if the club hired eighteen-year-olds. "Sure," said Miss Shay, "but they can't work the midnight shift." She gave the girl an application card, glanced down at her plump legs, and did not ask her to take off her coat. Two more girls came in, one in bright pink stretch pants and the other in purple. "Man, this place is a gas," said Pink.

"You think this is wild, you should see Hefner's house in Chicago," said Purple. Miss Shay looked at them with approval.

"I don't have a phone," said Blue Glasses sadly. "Is it all right if I give you my uncle's phone? He lives in Brooklyn, too."

"You do that," said Miss Shay, and she called me over. She pointed to a spot three feet in front of her desk and told me to stand up straight. I stood.

"I want to be a Bunny so much," said Blue Glasses. "I read about it in a magazine at school."

Miss Shay asked me if I were really twenty-four. "That's awfully old," she warned. I said I thought I might just get in under the wire. She nodded.

"My uncle isn't home all day," the girl said, "but I'll go to his house and stay by the phone."

"You do that, dear," said Miss Shay and, turning to me, she added, "I've taken the liberty of making an appointment for you on Wednesday at six-thirty. You will come to the service entrance, go to the sixth floor, and ask for Miss Burgess, the Bunny Mother." I agreed, but then she added, "Are you sure you haven't applied before? Someone named Marie Ochs came in yesterday." I was startled: could Marie have escaped from my notebook? I had a thirty-second fantasy based on *Pygmalion.* Or was there another Marie Ochs? Possible, but not likely. I decided to brave it out. "How strange," I murmured, "there must be some mistake." Miss Shay shrugged and suggested I bring "bathing suit or leotard" on Wednesday.

"Could I call you?" said Blue Glasses.

"Don't do that, dear," said Miss Shay. *"We'll* call *you."*

I left the club worrying about the life expectancy of Marie Ochs. Would they find out? Or did they know already? When I got halfway up the block I saw the two college girls. They were leaning against a building, their arms wrapped around themselves in a spasm of giggles, and suddenly I felt better about everything.

Everything, perhaps, except the thought of Blue Glasses sitting by her uncle's phone in Brooklyn.

WEDNESDAY 30TH

I arrived at the club promptly at 6:30, and business appeared to be booming. Customers were lined up in the snow to get in, and several passersby were standing outside with their faces pressed to the glass. The elevator boy, a Valentino-handsome Puerto Rican, cheerfully jammed me in his car with two uniformed black porters, five middle-aged male customers, two costumed Bunnies, and a stout matron in a mink coat. We stopped at the sixth floor. "Is this where I get out?" said the matron.

"Sure, darling," drawled the elevator boy, "if you want to be a *Bunny.*" Laughter.

I looked around me. Dim lights and soft carpets had given way to unpainted cement block and hanging light bulbs. There was a door marked UNNIES; I could see the outlines where the B had been. A sign, handwritten on a piece of torn cardboard, was taped underneath: *KNOCK!! Come on, guys. Please cooperate?!!* I walked through the door and into a bright, crowded hallway.

Two girls brushed past me. One was wearing nothing but bikini-style panties; the other had on long black tights of fine mesh, and lavender satin heels. They both rushed to a small wardrobe room on my right, yelled out their names, collected costumes, and rushed back. I asked the wardrobe mistress for Miss Burgess. "Honey, we just gave her a going-away present." Four more girls bounced up to ask for costumes, collars, cuffs, and tails. They had on tights and high heels but nothing from the waist up. One stopped to study a bulletin-board list titled "Bunny of the Week."

I retreated to the other end of the tiny hall. It opened into a large dressing room filled with metal lockers and long rows of dressing tables. Personal notes were taped to the mirrors ("Anybody want to work B Level Saturday night?" and "I'm having a swingin' party Wednesday at Washington Square Village, all Bunnies welcome . . ."). Cosmetics were strewn along the counters, and three girls sat in a row applying false eyelashes with the concentration of yogis. It looked like a cartoon of a chorus girls' dressing room.

A girl with very red hair, very white skin, and a black satin Bunny costume turned her back to me and waited. I understood that I was supposed to zip her up, a task that took several minutes of pulling and tugging. She was a big girl and looked a little tough, but her voice when she thanked me was tiny and babylike. Judy Holliday could not have done better. I asked her about Miss Burgess. "Yeah, she's in that office," said Baby Voice, gesturing toward a wooden door with a glass peephole in it, "but Sheralee's the new Bunny Mother." Through the glass, I could see two girls, a blond and a brunette. Both appeared to be in their early twenties and nothing like the matronly woman pictured in the brochure. Baby Voice tugged and pulled some more. "This isn't my costume," she explained, "that's why it's hard to get the crotch up." She walked away, snapping her fingers and humming softly.

The brunette came out of the office and introduced herself to me as Bunny Mother Sheralee. I told her I had mistaken her for a Bunny. "I worked as a Bunny when the club opened last month," she said, "but now I've replaced Miss Burgess." She nodded toward the blond who was trying on a three-piece beige suit that I took to be her going-away present. "You'll have to wait a while, honey," said Sheralee. I sat down.

By 7:00 I had watched three girls tease their hair into cotton-candy shapes and four more stuff their bosoms with Kleenex. By 7:15 I had talked to two other prospective Bunnies, one a dancer, the other a part-time model from Texas. At 7:30, I witnessed the major crisis of a Bunny who had sent her costume to the cleaners with her engagement ring pinned inside. At 7:40, Miss Shay came up to the office and said, "There's no one left but Marie." By 8:00, I was sure that she was waiting for the manager of the club to come tell me that my real identity had been discovered. By 8:15, when I was finally called in, I was nervous beyond all proportion.

I waited while Sheralee looked over my application. "You don't look twenty-four," she said. *Well, that's that,* I thought. "You look much younger." I smiled in disbelief. She took several Polaroid pictures of me. "For the record," she explained. I offered her the personal history I had so painstakingly fabricated and typed, but she gave it back with hardly a glance. "We don't like our girls to have any background," she said firmly. "We just want you to fit the Bunny image." She directed me to the costume room.

I asked if I should put on my leotard.

"Don't bother with that," said Sheralee. "We just want to see that Bunny image."

The wardrobe mistress told me to take off my clothes and began to search for an old Bunny costume in my size. A girl rushed in with her costume in her hand, calling for the wardrobe mistress as a wounded soldier might yell, "Medic!" "I've broken my zipper," she wailed, "I sneezed!"

"That's the third time this week," said the wardrobe mistress sternly. "It's a regular epidemic." The girl apologized, found another costume, and left.

I asked if a sneeze could really break a costume.

"Sure," she said. "Girls with colds usually have to be replaced."

She gave me a bright blue satin. It was so tight that the zipper caught my skin as she fastened the back. She told me to inhale as she zipped again, this time without mishap, and stood back to look at me critically. The bottom was cut up so high that it left my hip bones exposed as well as a good five inches of untanned derrière. The boning in the waist would have made Scarlett O'Hara blanch, and the entire construction tended to push all available flesh up to the bosom. I was sure it would be perilous to bend over. "Not too bad," said the wardrobe mistress, and began to stuff an entire plastic dry-cleaning bag into the top of my costume. A blue satin band with matching Bunny ears attached was fitted around my head like an enlarged bicycle clip, and a grapefruit-sized hemisphere of white fluff was attached to hooks at the costume's rear-most point. "Okay, baby," she said, "put on your high heels and go show Sheralee." I looked in the mirror. The Bunny image looked back.

"Oh, you look *sweet*," said Sheralee. "Stand against the wall and smile pretty for the birdie." She took several more Polaroid shots.

The baby-voiced redhead came in to say she still hadn't found a costume to fit. A tiny blond in lavender satin took off her tail and perched on the desk. "Look," she said, "I don't mind the demerits—okay, I got five demerits—but don't I get points for working overtime?"

Sheralee looked harassed and turned to Miss Burgess. "The new kids think the girls from Chicago get special treatment, and the old kids won't train the new ones."

"I'll train the little buggers," said Baby Voice. "Just get me a costume."

I got dressed and waited. And listened:

" . . . he gave me thirty bucks, and I only got him cigarettes."

"Bend over, honey, and get yourself into it."

"I don't know, he makes Milk of Magnesia or something."

"You know people commit *suicide* with those plastic bags?"

"Then this schmuck orders a Lace Curtain. Who ever heard of a Lace Curtain?"

"I told him our tails were asbestos, so he tried to burn it to find out."

"Last week I netted thirty bucks in tips. Big deal."

Sheralee called me back into the office. "So you want to be a Bunny," she said.

"Oh yes, very much," I said.

"Well . . . "—she paused significantly— "we want you to be!" I was startled. No more interviews? No investigation? "Come in tomorrow at three. We'll fit your costume and have you sign everything." I smiled and felt foolishly elated.

Down the stairs and up Fifth Avenue. Hippety-hop, I'm a Bunny!

THURSDAY 31ST

I now have two bunny costumes—one orange satin and one electric blue. The color choice and the quality of satin are about the same as those in athletic-supply catalogs. Costume bodies, precut to body and bra-cup size, are fitted while you wait. I waited, standing on the cement floor in bare feet and bikini pants. The wardrobe mistress gave me a small bathroom rug to stand on. "Can't have brand new Bunnies catching cold," she said. I asked if she could follow the line of my bikini pants in fitting the bottom; the costume I had tried the day before was cut up higher than any I had seen in photographs. She chuckled. "Listen, baby, you think that was high, you should see *some*." The whole costume was darted and seamed until it was two inches smaller than any of my measurements everywhere except the bust. "You got to have room in there to stuff," she said. "Just about everybody stuffs. And you keep your tips in there. The 'vault' they call it."

A girl with jet black hair, chalky makeup, and a green costume stopped at the door. "My tail droops," she said, pushing it into position with one finger. "Those damn customers always yank it."

The wardrobe mistress handed her a safety pin. "You better get a cleaner tail too, baby. You get demerits running around with a scruffy old tail like that." More girls began calling for their costumes, checking them out in a notebook chained to the counter. I learned that costumes were not allowed out of the building and that each girl paid $2.50 a day to cover the cost of her costume's upkeep and cleaning. Bunnies also paid $5.00 a pair for their thin black nylon tights and could be given demerits if they wore tights with runs in them. The wardrobe mistress gave me swatches from my two costumes and told me to have shoes dyed to match. I asked if the club allowed us any money for shoes. "You crazy or something, baby?" she said. "This place don't allow you no money for nothing. Make sure you get three-inch heels. You get demerits, you wear 'em any lower."

I dressed and went to the Bunny Mother's room. Sheralee was at the desk. With her long hair pinned back she looked about eighteen. She gave me a large, shocking pink form marked "Bunny Application" and a brown plastic briefcase with a miniature nude girl and THE PLAYBOY CLUB printed on it in orange. "This is your Bunny bible," she said seriously, "and I want you to promise me you'll study it all weekend."

The application form was four pages long. I had already made up most of the answers for my biography, but some questions were new. Was I dating any Playboy Club keyholders, and what were their names? None. Did I plan to date a particular keyholder? No. Did I have a police record? No. The space for social security number I left blank.

Up one flight in the main office, I delivered the form to Miss Shay. The cement-floored room was checkered with desks, but, as personnel director, Miss Shay rated a corner position. She scanned the form and began taking more Polaroid pictures of me. "Be sure and bring your Social Security card tomorrow," she said, and I wondered what to do about the fact that Marie Ochs had none. A stout man in a blue suit, black shirt, and white tie approached and gestured toward a chubby girl standing behind him. "Mr. Roma told me to bring her over, and I'd sure appreciate anything you can do for her," he said, and winked.

"In cases of extreme personal recommendation," said Miss Shay coolly, "we do schedule a girl's interview right away." She signaled to Sheralee, who took the girl downstairs. The stout man looked relieved.

A red-haired woman and two men came over, but Miss Shay asked them to wait. The younger man tapped the redhead's chin with his fist and grinned. "You ain't got a thing to worry about, baby." She gave him a look of utter scorn and lit a cigarette.

I signed an income-tax form, a meal ticket, a receipt for the meal ticket, an application form, an insurance form, and a release of all photographs for any purpose—publicity, editorial, or otherwise—deemed fit by Playboy Clubs International. A harried-looking young man in shirt sleeves came to tell Miss Shay that two men working in the basement were going to quit. They had expected to work six days for seventy-five dollars and were working only five days for sixty dollars. They were upset about it because they had families to support. "I can't make changes," she said crisply. "I can only implement Mr. Roma's decisions."

Miss Shay stapled a set of Polaroid pictures to my employment form and gave me my schedule. "Tomorrow, you'll have makeup guidance at Larry Mathews's, this weekend is Bunny-bible study, and Monday I've made an appointment for you to see our doctor for a physical exam." She leaned forward confidentially. "A *complete* physical," she said. "Monday afternoon is the Bunny Mother lecture and Bunny Father lecture. Tuesday you'll have Bunny school, and Wednesday you'll train on the floor." I asked if I could go to my own doctor. "No," she said, "you must go to our doctor for a special physical. All Bunnies have to."

Miss Shay gave me one last form to sign, a request that Marie Ochs's birth record be sent to the Playboy Club. I signed it, hoping that the state of Michigan would take a while to discover that she did not exist. "In the meantime, I'll need your birth certificate," she said. "We can't let you work without it." I agreed to send a special-delivery letter home for it.

Of course I won't be allowed to serve liquor or work late hours without proof of age. Why didn't I think of that?

Well, Marie's future may be short, but she can still try to make it through Bunny school.

FRIDAY, FEBRUARY 1ST

I was fitted for false eyelashes today at Larry Mathews's, a twenty-four-hour-a-day beauty salon in a West Side hotel. As a makeup expert feathered the eyelashes with a manicure scissors, she pointed out a girl who had just been fired from the club "because she wouldn't go out with a Number One keyholder." I said I thought we were forbidden to go out with customers. "You can go out with them if they've got Number One keys," the makeup girl explained. "They're for club management and reporters and big shots like that." I explained that being fired for *not* going seemed like a very different thing. "Well," she said thoughtfully. "I guess it was the way she said it. She told him to go screw himself."

I paid the bill. $8.14 for the eyelashes and a cake of rouge, even after the 25-percent Bunny discount. I had refused to invest in darker lipstick even though "girls get fired for looking pale." I wondered how much the Bunny beauty concession was worth to Mr. Mathews. Had beauty salons sent in sealed bids for this lucrative business?

I am home now, and I have measured the lashes. Maybe I don't have to worry so much about being recognized in the club. They are three quarters of an inch long at their shortest point.

SUNDAY 3RD

I've spent an informative Sunday with the Bunny bible, or the *Playboy Club Bunny Manual,* as it is officially called. From introduction ("You are holding the top job in the country for a young girl") to appendix ("Sidecar: Rim glass with lime and frost with sugar"), it is a model of clarity.

Some dozen supplements accompany the bible. Altogether, they give a vivid picture of a Bunny's function. For instance·

. . . You . . . are the only direct contact most of the readers will ever have with *Playboy* personnel. . . . We depend on our Bunnies to express the personality of the magazine.

. . . Bunnies will be expected to contribute a fair share of personal appearances as part of their regular duties for the Club.

. . . Bunnies are reminded that there are many pleasing means they can employ to stimulate the club's liquor volume, thereby increasing their earnings significantly. . . . The key to selling more drinks is *Customer Contact* . . . they will respond particularly to your efforts to be friendly. . . . You should make it seem that [the customer's] opinions are very important. . . .

The Incentive System is a method devised to reward those table Bunnies who put forth an extra effort. . . . The Bunny whose [drink] average per person is highest will be the winner. . . . Prize money . . . will likewise be determined by over-all drink income.

There is a problem in being "friendly" and "pampering" the customer while refusing to go out with him or even give him your last name. The manual makes it abundantly clear that Bunnies must never go out with anyone met in the club—customer or employee—and adds that a detective agency called Willmark Service Systems, Inc., has been employed to make sure that they don't. ("Of course, you can never tell when you are being checked out by a Willmark Service representative.") The explanation written for the Bunnies is simple: "Men are very excited about being in the company of Elizabeth Taylor, but they know they can't paw or proposition her. The moment they felt they could become familiar with her, she would not have the aura of glamour that now surrounds her. The same must be true of our Bunnies." In an accompanying letter from Hugh Hefner to Willmark, the explanation is still simpler: "Our licenses are laid on the line any time any of our employees in any way engages, aids, or abets traffic in prostitution. . . . " Willmark is therefore instructed to "Use your most attractive and personable male representatives to proposition the Bunnies, and even offer . . . as high as $200 on this, 'right now,' for a promise of meeting you outside the Club later." Willmark representatives are told to ask a barman or other male employee "if any of the girls are available on a cash basis for a 'friendly evening.' . . . Tell him you will pay the girls well or will pay him for the girls." If the employee does act "as a procurer," Willmark is to notify the club immediately. "We naturally do not tolerate any merchandising of the Bunnies," writes Mr. Hefner, "and are most anxious to know if any such thing is occurring."

If the idea of being merchandised isn't enough to unnerve a prospective Bunny, there are other directives that may. Willmark representatives are to check girls for heels that are too low, runs in their hose, jewelry, underwear that shows, crooked or unmatched ears, dirty costumes, absence of name tags, and "tails in good order." Further: "When a show is on, check to see if the Bunnies are reacting to the performers. When a comic is on, they are supposed to laugh." Big Brother Willmark is watching you.

In fact, Bunnies must *always* appear gay and cheerful. (" . . . Think about something happy or funny . . . your most important commodity is personality") in spite of all worries, including the demerit system. Messy hair, bad nails, and bad makeup cost five demerits each. So does calling the room director by his first name, failing to keep a makeup appointment, or eating food in the Bunny Room. Chewing gum or eating while on duty is ten demerits for the first offense, twenty for the second, and dismissal for the third. A three-time loser for "failure to report for work without replacement" is not only dismissed but blacklisted from all other Playboy Clubs. Showing up late for work or after a break costs a demerit a minute, failure to follow a room director's instructions costs fifteen. "The dollar value of demerits," notes the Bunny bible, "shall be determined by the general manager of each club."

Once the system is mastered, there are still instructions for specific jobs. Door Bunnies greet customers and check their keys. Camera Bunnies must operate Polaroids. Cigarette Bunnies explain why a pack of cigarettes can't be bought without a Playboy lighter; hat-check Bunnies learn the checking system; gift-shop Bunnies sell Playboy products; mobile-gift-shop Bunnies carry Playboy products around in baskets, and table Bunnies memorize thirteen pages of drinks.

There's more to Bunnyhood than stuffing bosoms.

Note: Section 523 says: "Employees may enter and enjoy the facilities of the club as bona fide guests of 1 [Number One] keyholders." Are these the big shots my makeup expert had in mind?

MORNING, MONDAY 4TH

At 11:00 A.M. I went to see the Playboy doctor ("Failure to keep doctor's appointment, twenty demerits") at his office in a nearby hotel. The nurse gave me a medical-history form to fill out. "Do you know this includes an internal physical? I've been trying to get Miss Shay to warn the girls." I said I knew, but that I didn't understand why it was required. "It's for your own good," she said, and led me into a narrow examining room containing a medicine chest, a scale, and a gynecological table. I put on a hospital robe and waited. It seemed I had spent a good deal of time lately either taking off clothes, waiting, or both.

The nurse came back with the doctor, a stout, sixtyish man with the pink and white skin of a baby. "So you're going to be a Bunny," he said heartily. "Just came back from Miami myself. Beautiful club down there. Beautiful Bunnies." I started to ask him if he had the coast-to-coast franchise, but he interrupted to ask how I liked Bunnyhood.

"Well, it's livelier than being a secretary," I said, and he told me to sit on the edge of the table. As he pounded my back and listened to me breathe, the thought crossed my mind that every Bunny in the New York club had rested on the same spot. "This is the part all the girls hate," said the doctor, and took blood from my arm for a Wassermann test. I told him that testing for venereal disease seemed a little ominous. "Don't be silly," he said, "all the employees have to do it. You'll know everyone in the club is clean." I said that their being clean didn't really affect me and that I objected to being put through these tests. Silence. He asked me to stand to "see if your legs are straight." "Okay," I said, "I have to have a Wassermann. But what about an internal examination? Is that required of waitresses in New York State?"

"What do you care?" he said. "It's free, and it's for everybody's good."

"How?" I asked.

"Look," he said impatiently, "we usually find that girls who object to it strenuously have some reason . . ." He paused significantly. I paused, too. I could either go through with it or I could march out in protest. But in protest of what?

Back in the reception room, the nurse gave me a note to show Miss Shay that I had, according to preliminary tests at least, passed. As I put on my coat, she phoned a laboratory to pick up "a blood sample and a smear." I asked why those tests and no urine sample? Wasn't that the most common laboratory test of all? "It's for your own protection," she said firmly, "and anyway, the club pays."

Down in the lobby, I stopped in a telephone booth to call the board of health. I asked if a Wassermann test was required of waitresses in New York City? "No." Then what kind of physical examination *was* required? "None at all," they said

AFTERNOON, MONDAY 4TH

The Bunny Mother lecture turned out to be a casual and much-interrupted talk with Sheralee in her small windowless office. There were seven other trainees, two of them already in costume. There was also a delicate blond, the part-time model from Texas whom I had already met, a very big girl with very long hair who said she was a magician's assistant, a square-looking girl in a plaid suit, and a pretty brunette who never took off her coat.

For the most part, Sheralee's talk repeated the Bunny bible, but some points were new.

1. Because of the minimum wage in New York City, we must get a salary of fifty dollars a week for a forty-hour week. We get tips, but the club takes 50 percent of the first thirty dollars worth of those that are charged, 25 percent of amounts up to sixty dollars and 5 percent after that. "That means half of everything," whispered a girl in costume. "Who gets more than thirty dollars a day?"

2. We may keep all tips that are given to us in cash, but if we indicate any preference for cash tips, we will be fired

3. "We don't even want you kids to know what 'drink average' means," said Sheralee, and explained that it meant the number of drinks per customer. "But if you give good service, you're bound to get more reorders, and you get merits for good service. A hundred merits equals twenty-five dollars "

4. If we meet boyfriends or husbands after work, we must do it at least two blocks from the club. Customers must never see us meeting other men.

5. We should never leave money in our lockers. Two girls have just been fired for stealing.

6. Because of "special problems in New York," we can't be charged money for demerits, so we may buy them back with merits. "If a hundred merits are worth twenty-five dollars," I asked, "isn't it the same thing?" Sheralee said it wasn't.

7. Number One keyholders are given special treatment, i.e., we bring them telephone, pad, and pen immediately. Playboy International then "absorbs" the amount of their bill. Number One keys go to the executives of all the clubs, important members of the press, and a few other VIPs. We may also give them our names, accompany them in the club, and go out with them. The magician's assistant asked if we *had* to go out with them.

   Sheralee said, "Of course not."

   "But," the girl said, "one of the room directors got mad at me for not telling my last name to a Number One keyholder. I explained that I was married, but he said I should give my last name anyway." Sheralee said she was sure the room director didn't mean it. "You never have to do anything you don't want," she said comfortingly.

8. The apartment of Vic Lownes is used for Playboy's promotional parties in New York, just as Hugh Hefner's house is used in Chicago. ("Mr. Lownes used to run the clubs," Sheralee explained, "but now he's associated mostly with the magazine.") When we go to such parties, we are not allowed to bring men. "Not even husbands?" the magician's assistant asked. "Absolutely *no men*," said Sheralee. "But of course you don't have to go if you don't want to."

We all went down to the VIP Room for the Bunny Father lecture, but not before a Bunny stopped at the door of Sheralee's office and called "Gloria!" I froze. After what seemed an eternity, the Bunny sitting next to me answered. I have learned to answer to Marie. Now I must stop answering to Gloria.

There was no Bunny Father, but two slide shows with taped narration and jazz background were presented as his lecture. One was on Bunnies in general and offered nothing new except that when customers tried to "get familiar," we were to say, "Sir, you are not allowed to touch the Bunnies." The second half of the Bunny Father lecture was called "Cocktail Bunny" and showed how to set up trays, fill out checks, and place drinks on tables. The narration didn't synchronize with the slides, the room was cold, and I emerged with a splitting headache.

Sheralee said that Miss Shay wanted to see me. My heart sank.

The main office was the same fluorescent-lit chaos as before, but Miss Shay was an island of calm. I would need an identification card, she said, to get in and out of the building. I gave her the note from the doctor, and my real Social Security number. I explained that I had lost the card. She looked doubtful but took the number.

I wanted to ask about this morning's medical puzzle, but decided against it for the moment. By calling attention to myself, I might only jog her memory about the missing birth certificate. I told her that my file was complete except for a chest X ray, and I left. It's hard to believe that the efficient Miss Shay won't catch up with me soon, but I'll stay until discovered.

AFTERNOON, TUESDAY 5TH

At noon today I waited in line for a free chest X ray at the department of health, muttering "Flamingo gets cherry, orange, and lime circle. Mist gets lemon twist, cordials go in London docks" under my breath. These bits of wisdom from my drink script and all the other documents in that brown plastic briefcase were to be the subject of a written Bunny quiz at three o'clock.

I reported to Sheralee and she greeted me with a rush. "Oh, sweetie, I'm absolutely *desperate!*" She needed an "over-twenty-one girl," she said, to work the hat-check concession from seven-thirty that evening to four in the morning. Would I help her out? Of course I would, I said, if she thought I could handle it. "Oh, sure, sweetie," said Sheralee; "it's terrifically simple." My matching shoes weren't ready yet, but never mind, I could wear black, she said. All I had to do was to be there in makeup by seven. I was surprised and elated. I would have at least one night "on the floor." I would, that is, if I could successfully avoid Miss Shay.

The quiz turned out to be a list of sixty-one short-answer questions. Our class of eight scribbled seriously while Sheralee read the questions aloud. I could see the Texas model looking perplexed, her mouth slightly open, and the Bunny named Gloria was chewing on her knuckle. I decided it wouldn't pay to be too smart, and wrote down six wrong answers. We scored one another's papers and read out the results. I was top of the class with nine wrong, the magician's assistant had ten, and everyone else missed fourteen or more. Texas missed nearly thirty. When the club says a Bunny is chosen for "l) *Beauty*, 2) *Personality*, and 3) *Ability*," the order must be significant.

We went to the penthouse, a large fourth-floor room with a back-lit plastic panel depicting rooftops. Sheralee seated us at a row of deserted tables and began to quiz us on drinks. "What is Fleischmann's?"

"Gin."

"What is Vat Sixty-Nine?"

"I haven't studied these," said Texas.

"Scotch," said the pretty brunette.

"What's Courvoisier?"

"I know, I memorized that. It's . . . cognac!" said Gloria.

"What's Piper Heidsieck?" The delicate blond didn't know. "Haven't you ever had champagne?" asked Sheralee. The blond said no, she'd never seen it. "It looks just like ginger ale," said Sheralee, "only it costs lots and lots of money." After several rounds of quizzing, everyone except Texas had been able to answer a few. She hung her hennaed head, and Sheralee lectured her severely.

A very tall, very pale black girl came over and introduced herself as our training Bunny. She was as thin and fragile as a high-fashion model, and very pretty. "She's one of the oldest Bunnies here. Everybody just loves her," said Gloria. "The men call colored girls chocolate bunnies," said another girl, and giggled.

We spent a hurried hour learning the Bunny stance (a model's pose with one hip jutted out) and the Bunny dip (a back-leaning way of placing drinks on low tables without falling out of our costumes). We learned the ritual serving sentences: "Good evening, sir, I am your Bunny, Marie.

May I see the member's key, please? Are you the keyholder or is this a borrowed key? Thank you. Now I'll be happy to take your order." No deviation allowed. I wondered if the uniformity ever bored the customers. "Is there anything else I can get you, Mr. Jones?" "Thank you, Mr. Jones, come back and see us again." I was being programmed.

At home, I retreat behind greasepaint and false eyelashes. The club's office will be closed when I get there: no Miss Shay to forbid me to work. At least my career will include one night of "Customer Contact."

EVENING, TUESDAY 5TH

The Bunny Room was chaotic. I was pushed and tugged and zipped into my electric-blue costume by the wardrobe mistress, but this time she allowed me to stuff my own bosom, and I was able to get away with only half a dry cleaner's bag. I added the tiny collar with clip-on bow tie and the starched cuffs with Playboy cuff links. My nameplate was centered in a ribbon rosette like those won in horse shows, and pinned just above my bare right hipbone. A major policy change, I was told, had just shifted name tags from left hip to right. The wardrobe mistress also gave me a Bunny jacket: it was a below-zero night, and I was to stand by the front door. The jacket turned out to be a brief shrug of imitation white fur that covered the shoulders but left the bosom carefully bare.

I went in to be inspected by Bunny Mother Sheralee. "You look *sweet*," she said, and advised that I keep any money I had with me in my costume. "Two more girls have had things stolen from their lockers," she said, and added that I should be sure and tell the lobby director the exact amount of money I had with me. "Otherwise they may think you stole tips." Table Bunnies, she explained, were allowed to keep any tips they might receive in cash (though the club did take up to 50 percent of all their charge tips), but hat-check Bunnies could keep no tips at all. Instead, they were paid a flat twelve dollars for eight hours. I told her that twelve dollars a day seemed a good deal less than the salary of two to three hundred dollars mentioned in the advertisement. "Well, you won't work hat check all the time, sweetie," she said. "When you start working as a table Bunny, you'll see how it all averages out."

I took a last look at myself in the mirror. A creature with three-quarter-inch eyelashes, blue satin ears, and an overflowing bosom looked back. I asked Sheralee if we had to stuff ourselves so much. "Of course you do," she said. "Practically all the girls just stuff and stuff. That's the way Bunnies are supposed to look."

The elevator opened on the mezzanine, and I made my professional debut in the Playboy Club. It was crowded, noisy, and very dark. A group of men with organizational name tags on their lapels stood nearby. "Here's my Bunny honey now," said one, and flung his arm around my shoulders as if we were fellow halfbacks leaving the field.

"Please, sir," I said, and uttered the ritual sentence we had learned from the Bunny Father lecture: "You are not allowed to touch the Bunnies." His companions laughed and laughed. "Boy oh boy, guess she told *you!*" said one, and tweaked my tail as I walked away.

The programmed phrases of the Bunny bible echoing in my mind, I climbed down the carpeted spiral stairs between the mezzanine ("Living Room, Piano Bar, buffet dinner now being served") and the lobby ("Check your coats; immediate seating in the Playmate Bar"), separated from the street by only a two-story sheet of glass. The alternative was a broad staircase in the back of the lobby, but that, too, could be seen from the street. All of us, customers and Bunnies alike, were a living window display. I reported to the lobby director. "Hello, Bunny Marie," he said. "How's things?" I told him that I had fifteen dollars in my costume. "I'll remember," he said. I had a quick and humiliating vision of all the hat-check Bunnies lined up for bosom inspection.

There was a four-deep crowd of impatient men surrounding the Hat Check Room. The head hat-check Bunny, a little blond who had been imported from Chicago to straighten out the system, told me to take their tickets and call the numbers out to two "hang boys" behind the counter. "I'll give you my number if you give me yours," said a balding man, and turned to the crowd for appreciation.

After an hour of helping men on with coats, scarves, and hats, the cocktail rush had subsided enough for the Chicago Bunny to show me how to pin numbers on coat lapels with straight pins or tuck them in hatbands. She gave me more ritual sentences. "Thank you, sir, here is your ticket." "The information Bunny is downstairs to your right." "Sorry, we're unable to take ladies' coats." (Only if the club was uncrowded, and the coats were not fur, was the Hat Check Room available to women.) She emphasized that I was to put all tips in a slotted box attached to the wall, smile gratefully, and not tell the customers that the tips went to the club. She moved to the other half of the check room ("The blue tickets are next door, sir") and sent a tall, heavy-set Swiss Bunny to take her place.

The two of us took care of a small stream of customers and talked a little. I settled down to my ever-present worry that someone I knew was going to come in, recognize me, and say "Gloria!" If the rumor were true that one newspaper reporter and one news-magazine reporter had tried to become Bunnies and failed, the management must be alert to the possibility, and I had seen more than enough Sydney Greenstreet movies to worry about the club's reaction. If someone I knew did come in, I would just keep repeating "There must be some mistake" and hope for the best.

Dinner traffic began, and soon there was a crowd of twenty men waiting. We worked quickly, but coats going in and out at the same time made for confusion. One customer was blundering about behind the counter in search of a lost hat, and two more were complaining loudly that they had been waiting ten minutes. "The reason there's a line outside the Playboy Club," said one, "is because they're waiting for their coats." A man in a blue silk suit reached out to pull my tail. I dodged and held a coat for a balding man with a row of ballpoint pens in his suit pocket. He put it on, but backward, so that his arms were around me. The hang boy yelled at him in a thick Spanish accent to "Leave her alone," and he told the hang boy to shut up. Three women in mink stoles stood waiting for their husbands. I could see them staring, not with envy, but coldly, as if measuring themselves against the Swiss Bunny and me. High up on the opposite wall, a camera stared down at all of us and transmitted the scene to screens imbedded in walls all over the club, including one screen over the sidewalk: " . . . the closed-circuit television camera that flashes your arrival throughout the Club . . . " explained publicity folders. I was overcome by a nightmare sensation of walking naked through crowds but the only way back to my own clothes was the glass-encased stairway. As men pressed forward with coats outstretched, I turned to the hang boy for more tickets. "Don't worry," he said kindly, "you get used to it."

Business let up again. I asked the Swiss Bunny if she liked the work. "Not really," she shrugged. "I was an airline hostess for a while, but once you've seen Hong Kong, you've seen it." A man asked for his coat. I turned around and found myself face-to-face with two people whom I knew well, a television executive and his wife. I looked down as I took his ticket and kept my back turned while the boy found the coat, but I had to face him again to deliver it. My television friend looked directly at me, gave me fifty cents, and walked away. Neither he nor his wife had recognized me. It was depressing to be a nonperson in a Bunny suit, but it was also a victory. To celebrate, I helped a slight, shy-looking man put on his long blue-and-white scarf, asked him if he and the scarf were from Yale. He looked startled, as if he had been recognized at a masquerade.

There were no clocks anywhere in the club. I asked the hang boy what time it was. "One o'clock," he said. I had been working for more than five hours with no break. My fingers were perforated and sore from pushing pins through cardboard, my arms ached from holding heavy coats, I was thoroughly chilled from the icy wind that blew each time a customer opened the door, and, atop my three-inch black satin heels, my feet were killing me. I walked over to ask the Chicago Bunny if I could take a break.

"Yes," she said, "a half-hour to eat, but no more."

Down the hall from the Bunny Room was the employees' lounge, where our meal tickets entitled us to one free meal a day. I pulled a metal folding chair up to a long bare table, took my shoes off gingerly, and sat down next to two black men in gray work uniforms. They looked sympathetic as I massaged my swollen feet. One was young and quite handsome, the other middle-aged and graying at the temples: like all employees at the club, they seemed chosen, at least partly, for their appearance. The older one advised me about rolling bottles under my feet to relax them and getting arch supports for my shoes. I asked what they did. "We're garbage men," said the younger. "It don't sound so good, but it's easier than your job."

They told me I should eat something and gestured to the beef stew on their paper plates. "Friday we get fish," one said, "but every other day is the same stew."

"The same, except it gets worse," said the other, and laughed. The older one told me he felt sorry for the Bunnies even though some of them enjoyed "showing off their looks." He advised me to be careful of my feet and not to try to work double shifts.

Back downstairs, I tried to categorize the customers as I checked their coats. With the exception of a few teenage couples, the majority seemed to be middle-aged businessmen. Less than half had women with them, and the rest came in large all-male bunches that seemed entirely subsidized by expense accounts. I saw only four of the type pictured in club advertisements—the young, lean, nattily dressed Urban Man—and they were with slender, fashionable girls who looked rather appalled by our stuffed costumes and bright makeup. The least-confident wives of the businessmen didn't measure themselves against us, but seemed to assume that their husbands would be attracted to us and stood aside, looking timid and embarrassed. There were a few customers, a very few, either men or women (I counted ten), who looked at us not as objects but smiled and nodded as if we might be human beings.

The Swiss Bunny took a break, and a hang boy began to give me a gentle lecture. I was foolish, he said, to put all that money in the box. The tips were cash. If we didn't take some, the man who counted it might. I told him I was afraid they would look in my costume and I didn't want to get fired. "They only check you girls once in a while," he said. "Anyway, I'll make you a deal. You give me money. I meet you outside. We split it." My feet ached, my fingers were sticky from dozens of sweaty hatbands, and my skin was gouged and sore from the bones of the costume. Even the half-hour dinner break had been on my own time, so the club was getting a full eight hours of work. I felt resentful enough to take him up on it. Still, it would hardly do to get fired for stealing. I told him that I was a new Bunny and too nervous to try it. "You'll get over that," he said. "One Saturday night last week, this check room took in a thousand dollars in tips. And you know how much we get paid. You think about that."

It was almost 4:00 A.M. Quitting time.

The lobby director came over to tell us that the customer count for the night was about two thousand. I said that sounded good. "No," he said. "Good is four thousand."

I went back to the Bunny Room, turned in my costume, and sat motionless, too tired to move. The stays had made vertical indentations around my rib cage and the zipper had left a welt over my spine. I complained about the costume's tightness to the Bunny who was sitting next to me, also motionless. "Yeah," she said, "a lot of girls say their legs get numb from the knee up. I think it presses on a nerve or something."

The street was deserted, but a taxi waited outside by the employees' exit. The driver held a dollar bill out the window. "I got four more of these," he said. "Is that enough?" I kept on walking. "What'sa matter?" he said, irritated. "You work in there, don't you?"

The streets were brightly lit and sparkling with frost. As I walked the last block to my apartment, I passed a gray English car with the motor running. A woman was sitting in the driver's seat, smoking a cigarette and watching the street. Her hair was bright blond and her coat bright red. She looked at me and smiled. I smiled back. She looked available—and she was. Of the two of us, she seemed the more honest.

WEDNESDAY 6TH

I got up just in time to rush back to the club for my table-Bunny training at two o'clock, and arrived feeling that I had never left. As I changed into my costume, one of the Bunnies was reading aloud from a weekly tabloid called *Leo Shull's Show Guide*. "Listen to this," she said. "It says, 'Although a thousand girls were interviewed for the club and a hundred and twenty-five are working there now, the Playboy Club's fantastic business, the lines and crowds of customers thronging there daily, have made it necessary to add another fifty Bunnies.' " I had heard Sheralee say that only 103 Bunnies were on schedule. I asked the girl who was reading if we really needed fifty more. Probably, she said, because the club had opened with 140 Bunnies—and nearly 50 of them had quit.

Another girl disagreed. "I heard that twenty were fired and forty more quit—but I think it's more, because we've only got about a hundred now, and a lot of them are new Bunnies." I said I was going to ask Miss Shay, just out of curiosity, how many Bunnies quit. "Don't bother, sweetie. Nobody around here ever tells us anything."

I picked up the paper and read on: "The girls, in this reporter's opinion, are the most beautiful ladies ever seen together under one roof. Most of them have superior education as well, and fine breeding. They are trained to give the optimum in restaurant service. . . . Their earnings are three to ten times as much as they could earn in any similar position. Average earnings are two hundred to three hundred dollars, and 'Bunnies' meet the most attractive people. . . . " The article ended with the club's address and how to apply. "Two hundred dollars to three hundred a *what*?" said the dissident Bunny. "I got a hundred and eight dollars this week, and the girl with the biggest check got a hundred and forty-five." I asked if she was waiting on tables. She said she was.

"The next time Leo Shull comes in here," said the dissident, "I'm going to ask him where he gets his figures."

"Watch out," said the newspaper Bunny. "He's a Number One keyholder."

Sheralee called me into her office. She was still desperate for "over-twenty-one girls" who could work until four in the morning. Would I take the hat-check concession again? I deliberated. It was another chance to work before Miss Shay remembered that I had never turned in the requested birth certificate. On the other hand, I would be training as a table Bunny until six o'clock and going right back to a full day's work at seven-thirty. My feet were still so swollen that I could barely get my regulation three-inch heels on, and I had gauze wrapped around my middle where the costume had dug in and rubbed my skin raw. I decided to take a chance on not being found out for a little longer and explained my tiredness to Sheralee. Couldn't she find someone else? "I'll try," she said, and looked annoyed. "But if I can't, I'm still counting on you."

I took the elevator to the mezzanine again and crossed to the spiral stairs. To be in costume walking down that staircase seemed even more surrealistic in broad daylight with dozens of lunchtime shoppers staring in. One of the room directors was waiting for me at the bottom. "Go back up and come down again," he said, gesturing toward the crowds in the street. "Give the boys a treat."

Disobeying a room director was an automatic fifteen demerits, according to the Bunny bible. I searched for an excuse. "Look," I said, "I'm late to meet a Number One keyholder."

"Go ahead, kid," he said, and smiled approvingly. "Get a move on."

I walked down the stairs at the back of the lobby to the Playmate Bar, where I was to report for training. It had been dark and deserted when I came there for my first interview. Now it was alive with a lunchtime crowd, and the wall behind the bar glowed with blown-up color transparencies of seminude Playmates from the centerfold of *Playboy*.

I went to the service area at the end of the bar to set up a tray with a bar cloth, Playboy lighter, and all the other items that had been prescribed in

Bunny school. My training Bunny gave me checks from her pad and told me to follow her as she made the rounds of her station. At each table she said, "This is Bunny Marie, and she is a Bunny in training." Two men told me I would be okay if I did everything they said, and the first thing to do was get rid of my sourpuss training Bunny. "Don't pay any attention to those jerks," she said. "They've been guzzling all afternoon and just think they're smart." I asked if they could be from Willmark and just being difficult to test her. "Don't be silly," she said. "You can always spot a Willmark man. He never has more than two drinks."

Two of her tables were empty, and she told me to wait on anyone who sat there. My first two customers carried plastic briefcases and wore veterans' buttons in their lapels. Approaching them as confidently as I could, I embarked on the serving ritual. "Good afternoon, sir, I am your Bunny, Marie," I said and put a napkin in front of each man (" . . . this procedure informs the room director which guests have been served . . . "), taking care to look directly at him as I did so (" . . . eye-contact each of your guests immediately"). "May I see the member's key please?" One of the customers gave me his Playboy key together with a room key from the Hotel Astor. I gave it back and started to fill out the check.

"Well," he said, slapping the table with delight, "you can't blame a man for trying."

"Nope," said his friend, "you can't tell us your address, but nothing's to stop you from remembering ours."

I filled glasses with ice, called in their order at the bar for two Old Fashioneds, and asked how I was supposed to put in the proper "garbage"—Bunny-ese for drink garnishes. "With your hands, how else?" said the bartender. I picked up two orange slices and dredged around in a large trough full of juice until I found two cherries.

With the drinks balanced on my tray, I approached the two veterans. "Are you married?" asked the table slapper. I said no. "Well, it wouldn't matter anyway, because I'm married, too!" Pointing my right hip into the table, I bent my knees, inclined myself backward in the required Bunny dip, and placed the glasses squarely on the napkins. I felt like an idiot.

"You're doing just fine," my training Bunny whispered sweetly, and yelled, "One J & B, one CC, and two martinis straight up," at the bartender.

I waited on three more parties, all men. Two said, "If you're my

Bunny, can I take you home?" One asked if my picture was above the bar.

My veterans left me a dollar tip. I thanked them and told them they were my first customers. The table slapper punched his friend in the arm and doubled over with laughter. "This girl," he said, still laughing, "this girl's a *virgin Bunny*!" He wiped tears from his eyes.

At six o'clock, I turned my checks back in to the training Bunny. All tips charged on them went to her, presumably her reward for training. I told her the veterans had left a dollar. "You can keep it," she said magnanimously. I tucked it into the "vault," as I had seen the other Bunnies do, and went upstairs to change.

I was unfurling the plastic dry cleaner's bag from my bosom when Miss Shay entered the Bunny Room. I had never seen her there before. Had my lack of credentials caught up with me? She might not have been aware of my emergency hat-check duty, but she probably did know about tomorrow's assignment of serving drinks from eight o'clock to midnight. Miss Shay stopped next to me. "Keep up the good work," she said, confidentially. "I hear you're a very good Bunny."

I decided to risk asking about "the other Marie Ochs" she mentioned at my first interview. "What other Marie Ochs?" she said, and disappeared into the Bunny Mother's office.

I am at home and Sheralee has just phoned to say that she found another hat-check Bunny for tonight. My luck is holding.

THURSDAY 7TH

I went to the Bunny Room an hour early tonight to see what I could learn about my sister Bunnies. Newspapers described them as college girls, actresses, artists, and even linguists. I asked the Bunny dressing next to me about the linguists. She said yes, that there were quite a few foreign girls working the VIP Room. (As I had read in the Bunny bible, "That stands for Very Important Playboy, of course.") In fact, they had to speak English with a foreign accent in order to work that room specializing in dinner and midnight supper. Did Bunnies make a lot of money there? "Not really," she said. "It only seats fifty, and it's for dinner, so the turnover is slow. You're better off serving drinks and getting the jerks in and out fast." I asked about the college girls. "Oh, sure," she said, "I think there are three or four who go to classes during the week and work on weekends." How could they always get the weekends, which were the big tip nights? "Listen, friend," she said, "there are some people around here who get to pick whatever shift they want, and the rest of us get stuck with a week of lunches or that lousy hat-check bit. Mostly, it's the old girls from Chicago or somebody who's got an 'in' with the management." I asked if that couldn't just be seniority. "Sure," she said, searching for a place to put the Bunny ears on her upswept hairdo, "only there isn't supposed to be a seniority system. 'You're all treated alike'—that's what they tell us." I asked what she had done before becoming a Bunny. "Nothing much, a little modeling once in a while." And what did she hope working as a Bunny would lead to? "I thought maybe I could save enough money to get some test shots and a composite and I could be a real model," she said. "But after three months of this, I want to get married. Guys I wouldn't look at before, now I think they aren't so bad."

I moved to the other side of the dressing table where four girls were eating doughnuts and drinking chocolate milk (" . . . eating in the Bunny Room, five demerits . . . ") and introduced myself as a new Bunny. First-name introductions were made all around. They seemed glad for the diversion and offered me a doughnut. I asked about the college girls again. "Yeah, there are some," said one. "I met a girl the other day, she was taking a course in photography." I asked what they had done before and what they wanted to do. Three said they wanted very much to be models, not high-fashion, but in advertising or the garment industry. The fourth said she was married, had a baby, and was just picking up money as a Bunny because she wasn't trained to do anything. They asked about me, and I repeated what I had put on my application blank as a likely, but not startling, background for a Bunny: that I had worked as a waitress (true, though it was at college), that I had danced in nightclubs and once hoped to be a professional dancer (also true, though I had to do some switching of dates to make myself younger), and that I had most recently worked as a secretary (untrue, but it was the only thing I could make up references for).

"Say, you've done a lot," said the girl who was hoping to crash the garment industry. "If you can type, what the hell do you want to be a Bunny for?"

I told them that everything I'd heard about the club sounded great, and

I read to them the latest *Playboy Club News*: "Bunnies don't give up wages for glamour. A Bunny can easily earn twice the amount in a week that a good secretary averages. . . . An exciting extra is the anticipation of being discovered. Many Bunnies have moved on into the entertainment field and now can be seen in movies, nightclub acts, or as models. . . ." There was a small silence.

"Well, sure," said one, "if they say that, it must have happened to *some* girls." Another said that one of the Chicago Bunnies had been on the cover of *Playboy* about a year ago and that there was supposed to be a Bunny on a cover again soon.

"Yeah," said a third, "but I hear that's just because they're short of Bunnies and they're trying to get more."

It was nearly eight o'clock, time to put on my bright orange costume (more comfortable, I hoped, than the electric blue) and serve drinks in the Living Room.

Again I had a training Bunny whose checks I used, but this time I also had a whole station, because one table Bunny was missing. "Wouldn't you know it," said my training Bunny. "A girl gets in a car accident and it has to be from my shift."

My tables were in the "Cartoon Corner," that is, a corner of the Living Room whose walls were hung with mounted cartoons from *Playboy*. Because it was the depth of the building from the bar, with four steps to climb in between, it was considered a difficult station. The Bunny tray technique involved carrying our small round trays balanced high on the palm of the left hand as we looked straight ahead and did the stylish, faintly wiggly Bunny walk. It seemed simple enough, but after an hour of carrying trays loaded with ice cubes, full bottles of mixes, and a half-dozen drinks, my left arm began to shake and the blood seemed permanently drained from my fingers.

Furthermore, I still hadn't been paid. I complained to my training Bunny, but she said I had no grounds for it. The girls hired before the December opening of the club had trained for three weeks with no pay at all.

I did learn a lot. I served twenty-two customers, spilled two drinks (one on me and one on a customer), and got propositioned twice. I also learned from the musicians at the Piano Bar that there is a song called "Playboy's Theme." These are some of its lyrics:

If your boy's a Playboy,
Loosen your control.
If his eye meanders,
Sweet goose your gander's,
Just one more ornery critter,
Who goes for the glitter.
So if you've been over-heatin' your oven
Just remember that the boy is a Playboy,
And the gal that makes a fireside lovin' man of the boy,
Gets him to stay.
Never talks to him but sweetly,
When he plays it indiscreetly,
Never takes the play completely
Away.

One of the diverse duties of the Willmark men is to make sure that this theme is played at the beginning and end of every musical show every evening—like "God Save the Queen."

FRIDAY 8TH

I have finished my first night as a full-fledged professional table Bunny, and I am almost totally absorbed with my feet. They ache like bad teeth. They are so swollen that I can't even get sneakers on. My foremost fear is that my arches may be falling. Nonetheless, random impressions of this endless evening do come back.

Item. I had all the tables in Cartoon Corner, twice as many as last night, from seven-thirty to four o'clock in the morning with no break. With loaded trays balanced on one hand, I made sixteen round trips to the bar each hour until I lost count. I also had three iced drinks spilled down my back by customers who bumped into me or my tray, and two green olives to eat all evening. Why didn't I just give up, lie down, kick, refuse, quit? I wish I knew.

Item. The bartender in the Living Room is an artist. Fast, graceful, exact, and calm, he kept the room going almost single-handedly. "Last week, including overtime and bonus," he said, "I made a hundred and eighty dollars—and I'm the highest-paid bartender in the house." I asked him why he didn't quit. "I'm going to," he said.

Item. Employees eat on the run from communal plates of food swiped from the customers' buffet. We're one big family.

Item. $29.85 in cash tips—all in one-dollar bills and silver—makes for prosperity but a very uncomfortable costume. And I lost five pounds last night.

SATURDAY 9TH

My arches did not fall. I put on my rain boots and went to a chiropodist ("I do all the Copa girls"), who said there was nothing wrong with my feet except long hours, high heels, and muscle strain. "In a job like that," he said cheerfully, "your feet are bound to get a few sizes bigger."

I worked the Living Room again tonight, but at a station right next to the bar. By wearing borrowed shoes three sizes too large, wrapping my ribs in gauze inside the costume, and coaxing busboys to help me carry heavy trays, I managed to get through the night and was rewarded with the following information:

1. A Bunny who has been a Playmate—that is, who has posed for the fold-out picture in *Playboy*—gets five dollars a day more salary than other Bunnies. She is also obliged to approach customers with "I'm your Playmate Sue" instead of "I'm your Bunny Sue," and autograph her centerfold if requested.

2. In a letter written to mollify New Yorkers who had bought keys to a supposedly private club, which is now open to the public, Hugh Hefner said that nonmembers "must secure a temporary pass good for one visit only and they must pay cash in advance before they are served." Perhaps contrary to Mr. Hefner's instructions, Bunnies are told to collect *after* each round on cash sales, but there are few who do even that. Most allow cash customers to run up bar bills just as if they were keyholders. If anything, Bunnies prefer serving a nonmember, because they are assured of a cash tip instead of splitting a charge tip with the house

3. Bunnies and busboys have a love-hate relationship. A good busboy can make a Bunny wealthier by keeping her tables cleared for new customers. A bad busboy can whisk away cash tips before she sees them and insist that the customer "stiffed" her. As a result, a Bunny may spend all her working hours cajoling and vamping a boy whom she wouldn't dream of spending time with outside the club. It's a hothouse relationship, but a close one. Like some women and their hairdressers, they tell each other everything.

4. Many Bunnies regard plastic dry cleaner's bags as dangerous stuffing because they make you perspire, thereby causing a weight loss where you least want it. Kleenex and absorbent cotton are preferred.

5. The-Way-to-Get-Something-to-Eat, though a table Bunny, is to snitch it from the customers' buffet (on pain of instant dismissal, according to a recent memo) and hide it in the supply room. You can then grab a bite whenever you pass by. Almost no one goes to the employees' room to eat stew.

SUNDAY 10TH

I got home at four in the morning and had to be back at the club and in costume by eleven for publicity photos. I was furious at first (twenty-five demerits if I didn't show up), but once awake and outside, I was glad. It was the first time in nearly three days that I'd seen full daylight.

The *Playboy* photographer was posing girls on the broad curving staircase at the back of the lobby. Each of us was put through a cheesecake series: sitting on the steps with legs outstretched, standing with our hands posed on the railing ("bend over from the waist, dear; over a little more . . . "), and walking down the stairs with tray held high.

I asked what the photographs would be used for. "I don't know," he said, "I just got rush orders from Chicago." As a matter of routine, new Bunnies were asked to sign a release of all photographs. I asked if our pictures would turn up in some Playboy Club promotion, or in *Playboy* itself. No one knew.

A voice called to me from the darkness of the Playmate Bar. It was Miss Shay, sitting at the desk where I had first seen her, waiting for prospective Bunnies to come in for interviews. The photographer had asked if we could turn on taped music. "Marie will play," she said. "Marie plays the piano very well, don't you dear?" No, I said, I didn't play at all. "I'm sure you told me so when I interviewed you," she said firmly.

The oversight of my credentials, the other Marie Ochs, and now my piano playing. I thought of the several times I had heard the seemingly efficient Miss Shay call busboys by a first name that was the wrong one. For the first time, I was sure that, unless someone actually recognized me, I could work at the Playboy Club as long as I liked.

Out in the bright sunlight again, I wondered just how long I *did* want to stay. If Marie wasn't going to be discovered, Marie would have to end her own career.

Still, I had lived through those weekend nights, which were the worst of it. According to this week's Bunny schedule, I would be serving lunch for four hours each day and no more. It wasn't an envied assignment because the tips were bad, but it would give me more time to talk to Bunnies.

I decided Marie could live till Friday.

MONDAY 11TH

A story in today's *Metropolitan Daily* was the talk of the Bunny Room. Two ex-Bunnies are suing the club for back tips and "misrepresentation" of the amount of money a Bunny could earn. One has told reporters she received anonymous death threats immediately after filing the suit.

"I knew Phyllis Sands," said one girl, "but not this Betsy McMillan who got the threats." She studied their pictures. "They made sure to give out good publicity shots." Did she think the alleged threats were made up just for publicity? "Who knows?" she shrugged. "Maybe she wasn't told the club would take half her tips, and maybe her salary was a lot lower than she had expected. On the other hand, maybe she just had her boyfriend call up and threaten her so she'd get her name in the paper. Who knows?"

I went downstairs to the Playroom and began setting up tables for lunch. Of the six other Bunnies working there, I had met three: A Chinese Bunny, a Bunny who announced that *she* didn't *have* to stuff her bosom, and the big, baby-voiced redhead whom I'd met the first day in the Bunny Room. The room director assigned us our stations, and we sat down on the apron of the stage to wait for customers. The unstuffed Bunny talked about how much better tips were in Chicago. "They're dumber there," she said. "I mean it's easier to make them think you'll go out with them, and then they tip you more."

"It's lousy at the Miami Club, too," said Baby Voice. "One time we all got together and said we'd quit if they didn't pay us more, but they said to go right ahead, they'd just hire more girls."

I said, "Maybe the girls had been outbluffed."

A little dark-haired Bunny said, "Sure, it would cost the club a hell of a lot if we all quit together. What would they do?"

"Bring in girls from the other clubs," said Baby Voice. "You can't win." There was a piano at center stage. She went over to it and pretended to play a jazz arrangement that was being piped into the room. "Laaaa-tee-ta-tee-tum," sang Baby Voice.

A Bunny with long brown hair got up and went through the motions of a very professional striptease. "They asked me to be a Playmate once," she said, "but I couldn't do it now. I'm too thin." The little dark-haired Bunny told her it didn't matter because they always used a fake composite body anyway, and that she personally knew a girl who did the breasts. I said I doubted it because there's only so much you can do with an airbrush. "Anyway, they must use different girls," said the stripping Bunny, "because the breasts are in different shapes."

"They co-omme in different shapes," sang Baby Voice, and got up to do her own striptease. She took off her bow tie, collar, and cuffs and tossed them off the stage, accompanying each with an expert bump.

"Okay, girls," said the room director in a voice like ice. "Cut it." Three middle-aged customers, the first of the lunchtime onslaught, were squinting into the spotlit gloom from the doorway.

"Wouldn't you know it," said Baby Voice, disgusted. "Here come the suckers."

Serving lunch for four hours wasn't quite enough to open up all my old foot wounds, but the piled-up plates of roast beef (which is all we serve: our room director is called "The Roast Beef King") make a tray even heavier than a full load of drinks. The customers are all men: the heavy sprinkling of dates and wives in the evening crowd disappears. One told me over and over again that he was vice president of an insurance company and that he would pay me to serve at a private party in his hotel. Another got up from his fourth martini to breathe heavily down my neck. When I pulled away, he was sincerely angry. "What do you think I come here for," he said, "roast beef?"

At three o'clock, when the final table had been cleared, I went back to the Bunny Room. The wardrobe mistress stopped me. "Baby," she said, "that costume is way too big on you." It was true that I had lost ten pounds in the few days since the costume had been fitted, and it was also true that, for the first time, it was no more uncomfortable than a tight girdle. She marked the waist with pins where the tucks should be taken and told me to take it off. "I'll have it fitting you right when you come tomorrow," she said. "Needs two inches off on each side."

I took the *Playboy Club News* out of my locker and read aloud: "The Playboy Club world is filled with good entertainment, beautiful girls, fun-loving playboys . . . like a continuous house party. Cheerful Bunnies feel as though they are among the invited guests. . . . "

My co-workers from the Playroom giggled. "Some party," said Baby Voice. "You're not even supposed to go out with the customers." I asked if any of the Willmark representatives had tried to trap her into going out. "Nooooo," she said thoughtfully, "but one did offer another Bunny two hundred dollars just for promising she'd meet him after work—and she took it," said Baby Voice contemptuously. "She should have known. Nobody but a schmuck or a Willmark man would offer you the money *before*."

TUESDAY 12TH

Two of my classmates from Bunny school, Gloria and the magician's assistant, joined us in the Playroom today. I found myself explaining how to serve roast beef and convince customers that it was rare, medium, or well-done, though it was, in fact, all the same.

It was Lincoln's birthday and business was slow. I listened to the unstuffed Bunny explain that she liked older men because they gave you money. "I went out with this old guy I met in the club and fixed up two other Bunnies with his friends. You know, he gave me a hundred-dollar check just because he liked me?"

The unstuffed Bunny also explained that one of the Playboy executives had given her seven hundred dollars for a dress. "I had five hundred dollars," she said, "and I bought a dress for twelve hundred, and he took me to a party in it." A dark-haired Bunny said yes, she knew the same guy in Chicago. "Doesn't everybody?" said the unstuffed Bunny. "If you counted all the Bunnies who went out with that guy, you . . ."

The dark-haired Bunny looked pensive. "We had this crazy thing going for three weeks," she said. "It was wild. I guess I should have known that nothing would come of it . . ."

"*All* the girls think something will come of it," said the unstuffed Bunny comfortingly, "but it never does." They talked about this executive's huge apartment, great wealth, and romantic impulses. He sounded like an artist of overkill.

Unstuffed got up to serve a customer, and the dark-haired Bunny looked after her with disdain. "I don't believe he ever gave her seven hundred dollars for a dress," she said firmly. "*No*body ever gets money out of *him*."

WEDNESDAY 13TH

I've completed my unofficial list of Bunny bosom stuffers:

1. Kleenex
2. plastic dry cleaner's bags
3. absorbent cotton
4. cut-up Bunny tails
5. foam rubber
6. lamb's wool
7. Kotex halves
8. silk scarves
9. gym socks

I've also learned that we can not only go out with Number One keyholders but anyone they introduce us to. Also, anyone we meet at Vic

Lownes's parties. There is, however, only so far I'm willing to go with research.

FRIDAY 15TH

The Playroom was crowded with men drinking heavily at lunch because it was Friday. I carried plates of roast beef and the Friday-only alternate, trout. Bunny Gloria was standing with a tray loaded with cups, waiting for the coffee urn to be filled. "You know what we are?" she said indignantly. "We're *waitresses*!" I said maybe we ought to join a union.

"Unions just take your money," said Baby Voice, "and won't let you work double shifts."

The magician's assistant was serving a table next to mine and agreeing earnestly that our costumes were "so intelligently made, so flattering to a girl's body." She tried so hard to do things "like a gracious hostess," as the Bunny bible instructed, that she wasn't an efficient waitress. In programming us with, as one Bunny put it, "all that glamour shit," the club sometimes defeated itself.

It was my last day of lunches and I was glad. Somehow, the usual tail pullings and propositions and pinching and ogling seemed all the more depressing when, outside this windowless room of perpetual night, the sun was shining.

I found Sheralee in her office and told her the story I had chosen because it left the door open, should I need more information: that my mother was ill and I had to go home for a while. She was dismayed. "But we're so short of Bunnies *now*!" she said, and asked when I could come back. I told her I didn't know but I would call. She gave me my first week's paycheck: $35.90 net for two nights in the Living Room. I asked about my first night at the hat-check stand. "You don't get paid for training," said Sheralee. I protested that it wasn't training. "I'll talk to the bookkeeper," she said doubtfully.

THURSDAY 21ST

Nearly a week has passed. I called Sheralee to say I had just come back to pick up my clothes and that I would have to quit permanently. She pleaded with me to work the Playmate Bar just one more night, and somehow (might I learn something new?) I found myself saying yes.

FRIDAY 22ND

But it was just the same:

ROOM DIRECTOR: "That's your station, four fours and three deuces."

CUSTOMER: "If you're my Bunny, can I take you home with me?"

BARTENDER: "They keep changing the size of the shots—up and down, up and down. It's enough to drive you crazy."

BUNNY: "I worked that LoLo Cola private party, and they gave me a six-pack. Big deal."

CUSTOMER: "I'm in the New Yorker Hotel, Room six-twenty-five. Can you remember that?"

MAN: "If little girls were blades of grass, what would little boys be?"

BUNNY: "Ummm . . . lawn mowers?"

MAN: "No. Grasshoppers!"

Sign in supply room:
THIS IS YOUR HOME.
PLEASE DON'T THROW COFFEE GRINDS IN SINK.

BUSBOY: "The money's coming out of your costume, sweetie."

BUNNY: "He's a real gentleman. He treats you just the same whether you've slept with him or not."

*I*t was four in the morning. I went to the Bunny Room and took off my costume. A pretty blond was putting chairs together to sleep on. She had promised to take another girl's lunch shift after her regular eight hours in the Playmate Bar, and there wasn't time to go home in between. I asked why she did it.

"Well," she said, "the money's not too bad. Last week I made two hundred dollars."

At last I had found a girl who made at least the low end of the promised salary—but only by working round the clock.

In Sheralee's office, pinned to the bulletin board, was a list of cities next in line for Playboy Clubs (Pittsburgh, Boston, Dallas, and Washington D.C.) and a yellow printed sheet titled WHAT IS A BUNNY?

"A Bunny," began the text, "like the Playboy Playmate, is . . . beautiful, desirable. . . . We'll do everything in our power to make you—the Bunny—the most envied girl in America, working in the most exciting and glamorous setting in the world."

I turned in my costume for the last time. "So long, honey," said the blond. "See you in the funnies."

—1963

POSTSCRIPT

Among the short-term results of this article were:

A long letter from Hugh Hefner saying that "your beef about the physical given the girls before they start work at the club prompted my eliminating it." (He defended it as "a good idea" but noted that my article was not the first time it had been "misunderstood and turned into something questionable.") He also included the first seven installments of his own Playboy Philosophy. For most of the three-page letter, however, he insisted he didn't mind the article at all.

A one-million-dollar libel suit against me and a small, now defunct New York newspaper that had printed a report on my article, as well as allegations that the manager of the New York Playboy Club had clear Mafia connections. Though those allegations were not in any quote from me, I seem to have been included in the libel suit as a harassment gesture. I spent many unpleasant hours in depositions being threatened with punitive damages. Eventually, the newspaper settled out of court without reference to me. I was told by other reporters that such harassing actions, with or without actionable grounds, were a frequent way of discouraging or punishing journalists.

• Serving as a witness for the New York State Liquor Authority to identify printed instructions given to me as a Bunny so they could be entered in evidence in a case against the Playboy Club for maintaining a public liquor license while advertising as a private club. This was related to the fact that the Playboy Club had paid to get its liquor license, then turned state's evidence against the same officials. The State Liquor Authority fought back with the public/private suit in which they asked me to testify. Lawyers told me that other Bunnies they had approached had been afraid to testify, even on the simple question of identifying instruction sheets in which we were told to emphasize the private, exclusive nature of the club. Having seen many movies about courtroom proceedings in which justice prevailed, I agreed. After a Playboy Club lawyer had spent cross-examination time trying to demonstrate that I was a liar and a female of low moral character, I began to understand why the other Bunnies had refused. In the end, the Playboy Club kept their public liquor license.

• Several weeks of obscene and threatening phone calls from a man with great internal knowledge of the Playboy Club.

• Loss of serious journalistic assignments because I had now become a Bunny—and it didn't matter why.

Among the long-term results of this article are:

1. Feet permanently enlarged by a half size by the very high heels and long hours of walking with heavy trays.

2. Satisfaction two decades later when the Playboy Club's payments for a New York State liquor license were cited as one of the reasons for New Jersey's decision that Playboy Enterprises was unfit to operate a gambling casino in Atlantic City until its relationship with Hugh Hefner, its founder and principal owner, was severed.

3. Continuing publishing by *Playboy* magazine of my employee photo-graph as a Bunny amid ever more pornographic photos of other Bunnies. The 1983 version insists in a caption that my article "boosted Bunny recruiting."

4. Twenty years of occasional phone calls from past and present Bunnies with revelations about their working conditions and the sexual de-mands on them. In the first few years, my callers were amazed that I had used my own name on the article. One said she had been threatened with "acid thrown in my face" when she complained about the sexual use of the Bunnies. Another quoted the same alleged threat as a response to trying to help Bunnies unionize. All said they were amazed to find my name listed in the phone book. In recent years, for this and other reasons, I've had to switch to an unlisted phone.

5. Realizing that all women are Bunnies. Since feminism, I've finally stopped regretting that I wrote this article.

—1983

*T*he following excerpts, edited for chronological order, are taken from articles on George McGovern, Eugene McCarthy, Martin Luther King, Jr. (with co-author Lloyd Weaver), John Lindsay, Nelson Rockefeller, Robert Kennedy, and Richard Nixon.

JULY 1965

I am standing in the Boston airport, waiting for a ride to Vermont and happily contemplating a few days of listening to good political talk. Professor John Kenneth Galbraith and his family have kindly included me, a new and little-known journalist, in their invitation to an annual weekend gathering on their Vermont farm, and I have been looking forward to it for weeks.

I survey the passengers as they get off the Washington shuttle, but see no one who looks as if he might be the stranger appointed by the Galbraiths to rent a car and get us both to Vermont: the Democratic senator from South Dakota. There is only a tall, spare, rather round-shouldered man who has been surveying the crowd, too. At least he has looked up occasionally from studying the files he produces from an old and bulging briefcase.

The man walks over to me, turning out to be younger than he seemed at a distance. His wrinkled, too-big suit looks as if it were from a mail-order catalog and clearly betrays him as a man who doesn't give a damn about clothes. "Hello, I'm very sorry I didn't see you before," he says, the syllables sounding slow and plodding. "My name is George McGovern."

No "Senator," no nothing. I am a little disappointed. I haven't met many United States senators in my life, but this definitely doesn't look like one. Furthermore, he has a terrible time locating the rent-a-car booth and finally succeeds in making me feel worldly and efficient by comparison.

Once in the car, I gradually forget about the style and start to listen. The drive is long, but the time races by: three hours of unpretentious political talk, which assumes I am an equal and therefore allows me to both join in and learn something.

Mostly, McGovern talks about the current strategies of "doves" in the Senate, Ho Chi Minh as a historical force, President Kennedy's foreign-policy intentions before he died, and other influences on the war in Vietnam. But he also gives me careful advice on which doctor to see for my recurring back ailment; regrets that I won't meet his wife and daughters, who are on vacation in South Dakota; and repeats various Galbraithian witticisms of summers past with obvious delight. Furthermore, he is very trusting about my job as a journalist. Whether it's which senators are afflicted with alcoholism ("the political disease," as McGovern calls it) or his own opinion of various national leaders, he doesn't show the lack of candor I have grown to expect from politicians.

He also drives very fast and absentmindedly while talking, and relinquishes to me the difficult job of deciphering maps of Vermont's back roads. To my surprise, I read the damn things for the first time: a feat that seems to me partly a result of his confidence. I also offer a few political theories of my own, and begin to be more impressed with this unpretentious man: by not being overwhelming in the style of a "leader," he allows me, and probably others, to be more than a deferential listener.

I'm back in my listener's role, however, once the weekend's seminar of political luminaries is under way. Besides Galbraith and Arthur Schlesinger, Jr., there are other scholars from Harvard and the Kennedy administration, plus a variety of academic neighbors who drop in for meals. McGovern himself is the only other person who is as content to listen as he is to expound his own theories. He seems to be a respected outsider who enjoys the rhetorical battles of this urban group, but doesn't feel compelled to join them.

Only when we get on the subject of the draft do I, the youngest member of this group by far, get the courage to speak up. I say that I think a major draft-resistance movement is beginning. For the first time, it is respectable, even admirable, for many young men to get married, fake poor health, fake homosexuality—anything to avoid killing and getting killed in this immoral war.

Feeling out on a limb, I try to explain and document. In return, I get a kindly, tolerant listening and a few smiles. Certainly, the group agrees, this draft resistance is an interesting development, but it is bound to be limited to sophisticated antiwar groups like those in New York. It isn't likely to become a mass movement.

This is the reaction from everyone except McGovern. "Yes, it's going to happen," he says sadly. "I sense it around the country. Boys are willing to pay the price of resistance—they just won't accept this war the way they did the others, or even Korea."

On Sunday he adds this draft-resistance issue to a speech he's been writing, and passes it around the group for criticism. I read it and am surprised by the flat-out anger of his attack on Johnson's Vietnam policy. Alarmed on his behalf, I suggest he protect himself by explaining the fallacy of the Domino Theory: the argument that a Communist Vietnam will start an inevitable chain of other governments falling. It is sure to be used against him.

He listens carefully, then says he must disregard my caution. The speech will be given with all its anger intact. Though I have been cast in the role of New York radical and flagburner by some of the guests, McGovern has turned out to be less cautious than I. Later, when I research his record in the Senate, I realize that he is accustomed to being on the cutting edge. In 1963, with his friend and political ally Jack Kennedy still in the White House, he devoted his first speech on the Senate floor to warning that Vietnam was a tragic blunder that would "haunt us in every corner of this revolutionary globe." In 1964, while other politicians were still lamenting "the Negro problem," McGovern, then a freshman senator, was condemning "white racism."

The ride back to the Boston airport is delayed. McGovern forgot to turn the key off in the rented car that has been sitting all weekend, and the battery is stone dead. Galbraith has to use his car to push the rented one down miles of dirt roads to the nearest garage. The senator seems embarrassed.

I begin to understand that he shares my problem: he's great in emergencies but can't handle everyday life.

Once on the road back to Boston, he talks a little about growth as a result of pushing himself into areas he fears. He believes he would still be in a small South Dakota town, for instance, had it not been for the shyness that drove him into high school debating contests as a painful remedy. Eventually, his skill at presenting a cogent argument gave confidence to a quiet, unathletic boy. (One of the few debating contests he lost was to Eleanor Stegeberg, whom he later married. She had grown up with a very politically minded farmer for a father, and so had learned debating at the dinner table.) He discovered a second fear after signing up for flying lessons. (Not a luxury in South Dakota, where many farmers have small planes to cover hundreds of empty miles between the few towns.) He was "scared to death" to fly, and so pushed himself until he got a license. Very relieved, he thought he would never have to fly again, but having a license during World War II made him a likely candidate for training as a bomber pilot.

"I got over the fear of flying itself, but I was still afraid on every bombing mission. A man's a damn fool if he doesn't admit it. I wouldn't do it again, but I learned a lesson about war. Now I understand that the men who love war are mostly the ones who've never been in it."

Stubborn, tenacious, dogged—the way he went about trying to start a car or pursue a political point was probably as characteristic as was his reaction to flying or debating. However slow or doubtful he may seem, he just doesn't give up.

I say good-bye, thanking him for the lift. As he walks away at the airport, he looks ordinary, like any other tired, workaday commuter. But I am aware now that in his head there is anger and a sense of history. I wonder how this unpretentious, honest man became a politician.

SEPTEMBER 1967

Al Lowenstein and others in the Dump Johnson campaign had McGovern's name on the list of those who might enter the presidential primaries and challenge LBJ's policies in Vietnam. Al asked him, but apparently McGovern's conservative South Dakota staff was dead set against it. (One of them incredulously announced to McGovern, "George, there's some Jewish guy from New York here who wants you to run for president.")

In the end, McGovern decided his staff's concern about his own tough reelection campaign for the Senate next year was right. Besides, he is assuming that the real challenge to Lyndon Johnson still belongs to Bobby Kennedy. I gather he sent Al on to Senator Eugene McCarthy of Minnesota, who was also on the list. He doesn't have a reelection coming up, and is just mad enough at the president (who led him on about being vice-president and then chose Humphrey instead) to enjoy the idea of embarrassing Johnson in New Hampshire.

Also, McCarthy is not crazy about the Kennedys, considering them "bad Catholics," and he doesn't care if Robert Kennedy is the more logical challenger. Too bad McGovern said no. It would have been a brief flurry, but the country might have been made a little more aware of this man Robert Kennedy describes as "the only decent man in the Senate." Right now, he definitely is Mr. Obscure.

APRIL 1968

It was a seven-fifteen curtain for opening night, so Mayor John Lindsay missed the first bulletin on the shooting of Martin Luther King. At eight-thirty in the Alvin Theater, during a musical number called "Spring in the City," a black detective got the second bulletin and started moving down the aisle.

It wasn't the first time that Ernest Latty, a plainclothesman who serves as both aide and bodyguard, had summoned the mayor to an emergency in the midst of a theater or a public speech or the soundness of sleep, but there was a special urgency in his face as he leaned past Walter and Jean Kerr, who were seated on the aisle, to hand the mayor a note and beckon him outside. Lindsay turned to his wife, who signaled to go ahead, she would stay. *A good idea*, he thought; *this was an important opening night for actor Tom Bosley, an old friend, and it wouldn't do to have both of them leave*.

But all thoughts of musicals and opening nights left him as he read the fact of King's assassination, understood the enormity of it, and began to sense the loss. He thought: *It's stunning; it can't be true—like Kennedy.* He thought: *A wild reaction, all over the country.* He thought: *And here.*

He wanted to go to Harlem, that much was sure. Some kind of riots—over rats, garbage collection, welfare complaints, for instance—usually start in younger, more volatile ghettos like Brownsville or Bedford-Stuyvesant, spreading to Harlem only by contagion. But this one, the mayor knew, would be born in central Harlem, the country's oldest, most politically sensitive concentration of black leadership, if it were to happen at all. "Besides," he said grimly to his aides, "somebody just has to go up there. Somebody white just has to face that emotion and say that we're sorry."

It was a quiet ride, with the sweet spring air making the silence of the streets more ominous. At the Twenty-fifth Police Precinct in central Harlem, Lindsay got an intelligence report that the area was "heating up," then left the car with a very worried Dave Garth behind the wheel at Eighth Avenue and 125th Street, where people were gathering. He began talking to them in twos and threes, steadily moving toward Seventh Avenue so that a big crowd wouldn't form, expressing his sympathy to individuals.

Women stood with tears streaming down their faces. Groups gathered silently outside record shops, where loudspeakers blared the news of violence in other cities, or the recorded speeches of Martin Luther King himself. Both were frequently drowned out by sirens—a fire had started a few blocks away—or by the staccato of police calls from a nearby squad car.

At a city college campus uptown, several hundred students were watching a concert of African-American dance and music when somebody ran into the auditorium and announced that Dr. King was dead.

Leaving the auditorium in the middle of the concert, almost two hundred students, black and white joining hands, began marching down Convent Avenue to 125th Street, until they ran into Lindsay, who asked them to disband.

"We stopped," said one woman student in the march, "but other people had followed us, you know, and then they started this." The "this" was sporadic looting, rock throwing, and starting some of the fifty fires that were reported that night. The young student was shocked and confused as the march had moved into a world lit by the revolving red lights of the police vehicles, rising smoke, and screaming fire engines. "He didn't approve of violence," she mumbled, "and it isn't right to do this."

Like many, the marchers were children of the Black Power revolution. Their heroes were Stokely Carmichael, Malcolm X, and LeRoi Jones. In a student world of Camus, Fanon, and Malraux, Martin Luther King seemed antithetical to militancy. Nonetheless, his dream was more than the dream of their fathers.

"That's it for me," a neatly dressed young man said. "They do something like that to a man like King . . . a man like King."

For the leaders, the activist heroes, the dilemma was worse. Privately, most of them—even Rap Brown—had admitted that they hoped in their hearts King was right.

"Now," explained black militant author Addison Gayle, "we're all a little scared. Because we have to believe our own rhetoric."

*B*y one in the morning on Friday, refuse and broken glass littered the main streets, but many of the crowds of two hours ago had dispersed. There was no real riot. Yet.

At Gracie Mansion, Lindsay ordered an extra force of sanitation men to be out with hand brooms by six that morning, removing all traces of last night's violence. He had learned from two hot summers that slum dwellers who wake up to neatness and order are much more likely to keep it that way. (The usual consequence of riots is the refusal of sanitation men and other city employees to enter the area. In Newark, rioters were goaded on by garbage in the streets, as well as by tanks.) The psychology of despair is a delicate thing.

*A*t eight-thirty Friday night Jesse Gray, Harlem tenant leader, stood at the corner of 125th Street and Lenox, urging people to wait for the sound truck and the rally he had called. Jesse began: "The white man got off the *Mayflower* shooting and killing Indians . . . and now it is his objective to kill off the black people. Four years ago on July nineteenth, nineteen sixty-four, we served notice . . . it's been four years now, and there are more white cops now than in nineteen sixty-four."

The next speaker was Charles Kenyatta, the sword-carrying comman-der of a paramilitary group called the Harlem Mau Maus. He used the rhetoric of revolution—a militant leader has to stay ahead of his follow-ers—but he was telling the crowd to cool it. "Let me tell you something," he began. "If this city must be flattened, let's do it downtown. And I'm telling all of these leaders to put up or shut up, because a revolution don't have no leaders."

Livingston Wingate, a former director of Har-You-Act, was the next speaker. "Brothers and sisters of the colony of Harlem," he began, "they have us in another crisis, but we are the children of crisis. Before the white man killed King, they killed his movement. . . . King was simply waving the Constitution right back at them. . . . And they snatched it, put it in their hip pockets, and shot him down. . . ."

His voice trailed off as the crowd took up the chant "We want Whitey! We want Whitey!"

*B*usiness was brisk in Harlem and Brooklyn all Saturday. The burnt-out stores were being cleaned out and guarded by calm-looking police-men. Police had resisted pressures to make mass arrests for the looting last night. Harlem was returning to its normal condition of simple struggle for day-to-day survival.

*A*t a Community Youth in Action storefront in Bedford-Stuyvesant, at a looted store called Winston's TV, and anywhere people stopped to talk, Lindsay conducted instant seminars along Fulton Street. "Why don't you go back to Gracie Mansion!" shouted a man in one of the day's few sour notes. At the corner of Bedford Avenue, Chuck Willis, a Task Force worker, was standing with the mayor's groups, and so was Lindsay's aide Barry Gottehrer, but neither saw an elderly man get struck by a car until Lindsay dashed out to help. Apparently, all those walking tours have given him the eye of an Atlantic City lifeguard. An ambulance was sent for, and Lindsay stayed with the old man until it came.

In Washington there had been tear gas and crossfire and troops ringing the White House; there were even tanks on New Hampshire Avenue. In more than forty American cities, there had been disturbances serious enough for some form of martial law or weapons usually reserved for a battlefield. In New York, the biggest city, the place where everyone expected it to happen, there had been no riot.

The real reason was in the ghetto dwellers themselves. Restraint in the face of despair came from unexpected people, unexpected groups. Other reasons were smaller, more tenuous, but just as important: sweeping the streets, arranging a reconciliation, setting up an all-night phone system, having the mayor's Task Force ready to go, and electing a mayor who can and will go to the neighborhoods of the poor.

New York will need a lot of luck if all these variables are to hold together again.

"The patience of an oppressed people cannot endure forever."
                                          —Martin Luther King, Jr.

JUNE 1968

When Robert Kennedy was shot, I was watching that California victory scene on television. And I just kept on watching. Suddenly there was nothing else to do, nothing *worth* doing, so I stayed by the glass screen through that morning and the next day and the next, watching as each tragic step unfolded into the larger tragedy, then reliving the current sum of those steps as their taped and edited essence was played again.

It was a vigil almost as long as the one after President Kennedy was killed; our version of ancient ceremonies that brought comfort through repetition of ritual and a kind of self-hypnosis. Sometimes this electronic closeness keeps the country sane. If we only heard of the madhouse events in Dallas—without the civilized dignity of President Kennedy's funeral to turn to—we might have started a chain of vengeance more terrifying than the one that followed Lincoln's death.

*B*efore the 1968 New Hampshire primary, we used to meet after work in the barren expanses of the third-floor McCarthy for President headquarters on Columbus Circle: a few writers and editors with very different views on politics in general and the value of this anti-Vietnam campaign in particular, but with one thing in common—desperation.

I suppose the fact of our presence there excluded Establishment types on one hand and antivoting ones on the other, but we represented almost everything in the wide range between. Bobby-haters or those praying for Bobby to declare, old liberals for whom fighting their own kind was quixotic and brave, New Left radicals for whom working within the system at all was the same, even a Republican woman who hoped to strengthen the antiwar cause and therefore get Nelson Rockefeller nominated: we all pulled our rickety folding chairs into a circle, kept discussion of our differences to a minimum, and concentrated on our mutual hope of making an anti-Vietnam showcase out of the presidential primary

The odd thing was that none of us at those early brainstorming, McCarthy for President meetings was really for McCarthy. We knew that he made cautious but accurate statements about the war; that his voting record revealed a decent man, if not a social revolutionary; and, most of all, that he was willing to run in New Hampshire. The alternative was having a president whose word could not be trusted and whose considerable ego seemed bound up with "search and destroy." McCarthy might or might not be best, but he was clearly better

So we set out to like him, and we did.

Doing research for a piece of campaign literature then, I found it easy to concentrate on his many admirable features.

- He had begun speaking courageously against our Vietnam commitment in January 1966. (Of course, Galbraith was warning President Kennedy in 1962, and McGovern started criticizing our presence in Vietnam from the floor of the Senate in 1963—but neither of them was making the challenge in New Hampshire.)

- He was an early and lucid critic of the military-industrial complex. (But he voted appropriations for Vietnam, as did nearly everyone; and for civil defense, the Subversive Activities Control Board, and the National Board for the Promotion of Rifle Practice, as everyone did not.)

- He was an intellectual, a teacher who wrote books without ghostwriters and all his own speeches, a poet who enjoyed the company of poets and philosophers. (Never mind that his prose was very oversimplified, and his poetry seemed arch. How many politicians had on their office wall, not the usual party leaders, but a likeness of Sir Thomas More?)

• He had made the famous 1960 nominating speech for Adlai Stevenson—"Do not reject this man who made us all proud to be Democrats"—at great political risk. (On the other hand, McCarthy had gone to that convention as the probable vice-presidential choice of Lyndon Johnson, who was hoping to get the nomination as the result of a Stevenson-Kennedy standoff. But that possible motive didn't negate the force of a great speech.)

In February, the senator came to New York. There was to be a fund-raising dinner, some press conferences, a walk in the garment district (a Harlem walk proved impossible because black groups weren't interested in sponsoring it), and a meeting of potentially influential supporters.

Anybody at that last gathering will remember McCarthy's gift for diffusing enthusiasm. Wyatt Cooper had written a graceful and laudatory introduction. Virtually all of the several hundred guests were predisposed to like and applaud McCarthy for his record and for what he was doing in New Hampshire. But after the first few minutes of his speech, hopes and enthusiasm began to sink. He was cautious, uninspired, dry.

For me the next morning was worse. With three other volunteer writers, all of us working on a newspaper supplement for the primary states, I met with McCarthy at the St. Regis. Each of us asked questions about the senator's areas of strength in order to get quotes for the supplement. And after each question, McCarthy would turn to campaign manager Blair Clark or to a young press aide and say, "I think we talked about that in a Senate speech," or "Remember the piece *Look* didn't publish? Get them that." We asked and asked. We turned ourselves inside out with asking. (Somewhere, there is a tape of this fiasco that could be sold as a comedy record.) But we got not one spontaneous reply. Finally, I hit on a question that he couldn't have written about yet. How did this New Hampshire primary differ from his past congressional campaigns? "It doesn't," he said flatly. "They're exactly the same."

Spiritually speaking, McCarthy reminds me of the distinguished-looking clerk at Household Finance who used to lean back, put the tips of his fingers together in a steeple, and say to my father, "No, you can't have a loan."

It was the kids, of course, who transformed McCarthy into a symbol of hope. The Kennedy administration, so enshrined in nostalgic affection only months before, now seemed old and shopworn. When Bobby Kennedy belatedly announced on March 16 that he would run for the presidency after all, it was depressing for everyone. I could understand why he, with so much more at stake than McCarthy, had been seduced by bad advice and refused to run in New Hampshire. But he had lost his constituency.

At the McCarthy headquarters, however, it wasn't enough to be for him as a candidate. One also had to be against Robert Kennedy as a man. The air was thick with moral superiority. McCarthy, who had been something between a decent man and the Only Game in Town, was now the unassailable Man for All Seasons. His presence in New Hampshire had nullified all faults, just as Kennedy's absence had nullified all virtue.

Because of preference for one or another of two men whose platforms were not very different, friends no longer spoke to friends, and common goals were forgotten. Gossip about who had switched to whom politically was suddenly as juicy as who was having an affair with whom. But less tolerant.

Finally, I retired altogether—on the grounds that both campaigns were overpopulated anyway—to work for Cesar Chavez. And it was this Gandhian leader of the migrant workers in California who convinced me that Kennedy's compassion, his peculiar ability to identify with the excluded and deprived, was much more important than whether or not he had run in New Hampshire. The candidates' positions on Vietnam might be more or less the same, and even their voting records on civil rights, but only Kennedy had ambassador's credentials acceptable to the black colonial nation-within-a-nation. Only Kennedy had gone to help the Mexican migrant workers' strike in California in spite of the fact that the growers were crucial supporters of the Democratic party. Those Kennedy-ites who chanted "He can win" were doing him a disservice. The larger point was that perhaps he *should* win.

By the Oregon primary, however, McCarthy was attacking Kennedy not just politically, but personally. ("Bobby can't be Jack, and doesn't want to be himself" was a favorite jibe.) Stevenson's wit had been turned against himself, but McCarthy's was used to ridicule others. Fine. But why so personally vicious about Kennedy while Hubert Humphrey, McCarthy's real opponent on our policies in Vietnam, goes free?

Still, had McCarthy stood up at his first press conference after Kennedy's death and said he understood something had gone out of the world and would try to fill the gap, I and many others would have been for him all over again. Black people and poor people understood Bobby, though a lot of others were just beginning to. But McCarthy didn't. "Gene was shocked for the country," explained a friend, "and depressed that his campaign had to start all over again. But he considered Bobby a demagogue while he was alive, and he still does."

Having suffered Lyndon Johnson, a president with a heart and no moral structure, we might be in for the reverse. To find out, I accepted an assignment to cover the McCarthy campaign as a journalist in the old-fashioned sense: the keeper of a journal.

JULY 1968

First Day. The senator's campaign plane goes from Washington to Pittsburgh and back today; then begins what his campaign staff refers to as "McCarthy's southern swing"—no farther south than Virginia, Georgia, and Kentucky. Sitting across from the senator, I looked at McCarthy slouched in his seat like a countryfied Ray Milland, and a lot of resentment fell away. I understand now why critics are crueler to directors and playwrights than to actors: it's impossible to be too tough on someone whose vulnerable human form is right before your eyes. Peering through heavy-framed reading glasses at two *New York Times* ads for Rockefeller and Humphrey, his old-fashioned suspenders stretched over starched shirt and bony shoulders, he looked like someone's loved and overworked father poring over the family bills. A little out of place, a little removed—the sort of man who reads newspapers at the beach and wears street shoes with his bathing suit.

Second Day. Whether in New York, Pittsburgh yesterday, or on the plane right now, staff divisions are interesting. Traveling staff, local talent, or advance men, they all seem to fall into two groups: the True Believers for whom this campaign is a one-time crusade and the Pragmatists who see McCarthy only as the best alternative. The former are uncritical and continually shocked by the opinions of the latter (who dubbed them True Believers in the first place). Each group tends to restrict its talk when the other is around. Each group worries about the other's influence on the candidate.

Overlaid on that division is one among the staff in constant contact with McCarthy (mostly on the plane) and local or headquarters' workers. The first group is much cooler than the second, not because their enthusiasm for McCarthy is any less, but because they are devoted to imitating his style. They look down on any display of emotion. This cool, understated, slightly cynical demeanor is natural to McCarthy but sits strangely on the shoulders of young aides. It also makes them less likely to stir up enthusiasm for their candidate. "The kids are effective," observed one of our entourage, "in direct proportion to their distance from McCarthy."

"Look at this plane," said one aide, not a True Believer. "We could have any good man in the country on it—Mike Harrington, Galbraith, Pat Moynihan—but we've hardly got anyone. McCarthy doesn't think he needs them."

Third Day. Charlie Callahan, a quiet, Rock of Gibraltar young man who is McCarthy's personal aide, says I can sit next to the senator on the flight to Atlanta this afternoon. As usual on campaign planes, both staff and press are constantly focused on who has the candidate's ear.

I notice that compared to pre–New Hampshire days, McCarthy has begun that process peculiar to the theater and politics: he is metamorphosing into a star. Gray-white skin has been replaced by a light but even tan, silvery hair is worn longer and not slicked down, socks are now long enough to meet trouser cuffs; knit socks instead of short silk ones with clocks embroidered in them. But the metamorphosis has more to do with interior things, with changes wrought by constant scrutiny by the public and the obsessive attentions of a staff. Perhaps the change is power.

I ask, "Are there false impressions in other articles that this one could be used to correct?" It's my prepared attempt at a surefire question: nothing but the weather is as universally complained about as the press. He answers in his own deceptively mild way.

"All they're interested in is numbers of delegates, you know. And that's wrong. It's too early. Demonstrations and talking to delegates are fine, of course, but the most important thing to watch is the polls. The opinion polls are what count.

"But the papers, *The New York Times* for instance, they get caught up with reporting the way they think things *ought* to be: each time I did one of the things they said I couldn't do because I wasn't a serious candidate, they'd set up another. I might be in the White House and still not be considered 'serious.' " He smiled his sardonic half smile.

We talk for a while about today's news stories on the firing of his youthful aides. "It's no image change or conspiracy, the way reporters like to think it is. We've done well ever since the cold of New Hampshire by bringing young people into the political process. Why should we change? It's a combination of things—partly an economy move, partly a normal cutback after primaries. And then some of them are like ski bums in the summer. They ought to go home and get jobs. They just like to hang around."

The ski-bum image surprises me. Does he really think of the peace kids, the "Clean for Eugene" workers, as hangers-on? "Well no, not all of them, but they really should go home. And sometimes you have to get rid of a few good ones, too, because you can't just separate out the ones you'd like to go."

Wasn't he now pleased, I ventured ambiguously, that he hadn't become Lyndon Johnson's vice-president in '64? "Yes," he said, equally ambiguous, "vice-presidents don't have much influence on policy." But wouldn't it have eliminated all of his current anti-Establishment appeal? "Hmmm," he said. I waited for a moment. The key, I had figured out after that earlier interview when we showered him with questions, was to out-wait him. "I would have had to stay silent," he said finally, gesturing for another ginger ale.

I wanted him to say he would have resigned. Or spoken out against the war. Or called for Johnson's impeachment. But at least he wouldn't have lent his enthusiasm to "Communist containment," as Humphrey has done. The Johnson administration and Vietnam have made us grateful for small favors.

I also learned, by questions and silences, that most of the people he admired were "in history," but that he regretted not meeting C. S. Lewis, wanted to meet Isaiah Berlin and Pablo Casals ("I'm partial to cellists"), and "like everybody else" (a reference to Bobby Kennedy's choice of quotations?) he was an admirer of Camus. His desire to be a baseball player hadn't been very lasting, but he had always intended to be a teacher, either inside or outside the Catholic church. He wasn't personally interested in Africa or Asia. "The only underdeveloped country I would like to visit," he said whimsically, "is Ireland."

Was there another time in which he would rather have lived? "No," he said, "I like the present." Silence. Bobby, I volunteered, had answered that question with Periclean Greece—an interesting response—because men in that Golden Age could be leaders and artists and all things at once. "Of course," he said coolly, "an age of heroes. I wouldn't like that. Perhaps England when there were *no* heroes. And no nationalism. Sometime between the eleventh and sixteenth centuries. That's when the English language was being developed by men like Chaucer and Langland and Shakespeare. And Erasmus, don't forget Erasmus. That would have been an interesting time to live. A good time for intellectuals."

We are at the airport now with the inevitable band and banners and cameras. "I don't like these airport demonstrations," McCarthy said resentfully. "There's no time to say anything, and you have to shake hands."

At Pascal Brother's Restaurant in Atlanta, a snappy new building in a black neighborhood where Martin Luther King used to have *his* press conferences, McCarthy got his first hostile question. Q: "Why should black people vote for *you*?" A: "I never said they should. But I would hope that a cut in our inflated Vietnam budget, and the spending of that money on urban and poverty problems, would mean something to them."

Outside our hotel, a sweet-faced little boy was patted on the head by McCarthy—the first time I've seen him touch anyone voluntarily. He wiped his palm on the side of his trousers as he got in the car.

We sat in McCarthy's hotel suite that night, several aides and I. The candidate was in high spirits, a state marked by acerbic wit and a rare willingness to initiate conversation. With his long legs stretched out and a weak gin and tonic in hand, he answered a few questions, and frequently got laughs.

"The Moose—now there's a ridiculous story. Somebody told me there were a lot of Moose in Minnesota and it would help me to get elected senator if I joined a lodge. So I did, years ago. I don't even think I'm paid up on my dues. Now Eric Sevareid says there are no Negro Moose. If he makes an issue out of that, it's time CBS let him go."

Down in the lobby with the speech writers, I discovered why McCarthy was in such good spirits. For the first time in the campaign, he was the frontrunner in an opinion poll. Harris showed him at least four points ahead of Humphrey.

Perhaps that was why he had aimed his scornful wit at Humphrey for the first time. "I nominated Hubert in nineteen fifty-two," he told Fulton County Democrats, "and he was ripe just about then."

When peace candidate McCarthy uttered his famous epigram that "the only legitimate political motive is vengeance," we shouldn't have assumed he was kidding.

*T*his week, I happened to be on one of those late-night radio shows—so late that you're convinced no one is listening, and you begin to tell the truth. I was supposed to be talking about an article I had just written on the McCarthy campaign. "Probably," I heard myself saying, "George McGovern is the real Eugene McCarthy."

In the few days since then, I have received two dozen calls and telegrams. Apparently, there is a small underground movement to get McGovern to declare for the presidency. Its strategy goes like this: since McCarthy hasn't attracted a single additional delegate in weeks, Humphrey is pretty much assured of a first ballot. The remaining hope is the several hundred Kennedy and uncommitted delegates who don't want to go for either McCarthy or Humphrey. A third force who could win the allegiance of these delegates could break the first ballot.

The most practical of the phone calls came from the Kennedy Action Corps, a hundred or so activists and Peace Corps returnees who have been looking for someone to pick up an effective peace candidacy where Bobby left off. They had researched various candidates' records, decided on McGovern, and were meeting in marathon sessions to figure out how to draft him. Would I help by transmitting their message?

It's a crazy idea, but we're all desperate. Why not?

We are in a bad, flossy restaurant on Capitol Hill. McGovern and his secretary-assistant, Pat Donovan, are listening to my recitation of arguments from his would-be volunteers. Obviously, she thinks he should run, too, and her presence makes me feel less uncomfortable about urging him to attempt this odd three-week campaign.

McGovern listens: the ex-Kennedy kids have more than two thousand volunteers in New York State alone, they are pooling their money to open a Draft McGovern storefront, and there are similar groups in California. They have had one press conference to announce their Draft McGovern effort, and they are now conducting a telephone poll of New York delegates to see how many of them he might gain. Some ex-Humphrey and ex-McCarthy people have joined them.

He nods seriously, but it's impossible to tell whether he is pleased or not. Yes, this is a move he has been considering for some time. He has received a five-thousand-dollar check from a supporter in South Dakota, cashable only if he uses it for the presidency. Furthermore, McCarthy already has told McGovern that he knows he doesn't have a chance of beating Humphrey; that he's just going through the motions so he won't let his supporters down. (This admission has surprised and worried McGovern. The peace kids and antiwar groups still have a lot of faith in McCarthy's ability to win, and McGovern wonders what will happen when they realize the truth.)

Another crisis: one of the McGovern children, nineteen-year-old Terry, was arrested in South Dakota for possession of a small amount of marijuana. Because her arrest seems to have been politically motivated (the state attorney general's office admitted she had been watched "for months"), McGovern is more than ever conscious of the price his family pays for his choice of job. It especially troubles him in the case of Terry, a sensitive girl who takes everything very much to heart and who is now in despair over what she may have done to her father's career.

The family is going off to some isolated spot in the Black Hills, as they often do in times of decision. McGovern says he will return with a verdict about his candidacy.

AUGUST 1968

In the Senate caucus room today, surrounded by his family and banks of TV cameras, McGovern announced that he is running for the presidency. Contributions and phone calls have begun coming in to his Washington office and to the Draft McGovern storefront in New York. Hardly anyone has heard of this man before, but apparently his honest face and straightforward delivery are a welcome contrast to Nixon's circumlocution and Humphrey's bombast. So is the message: "Vietnam—the most disastrous political and military blunder in our national experience. That war must be ended now—not next year or the year following, but right now. Beyond this, we need to harness the full spiritual and political resources of this nation to put an end to the shameful remnants of racism and poverty that still afflict our land."

Terry stood beside him. Somewhere in the Black Hills, with each feeling guilty for putting an added strain on the other, they seem to have arrived at a peaceful agreement.

Politics is very personal. Ted Kennedy, whom McGovern barely knows, had called him with support at the time of his daughter's arrest. There is still some doubt there: McGovern has wondered aloud if Ted Kennedy isn't more a creation of his staff than a reality. But the call altered his feeling about Ted Kennedy's character.

Announcement or no, it's quite clear that few people in the country—or in the press—know who the hell George McGovern is. His habit of operating as a loner doesn't help.

McGovern just assumes his volunteers can do whatever needs to be done. Because there are so few people in this campaign, we all end up doing everything. So far, I have been pamphlet writer, advance "man," fund raiser, lobbyist of delegates, errand runner, and press secretary—consecutively or simultaneously. I'm telling myself it's educational.

One assignment, for instance, was to set up a series of luncheons in New York's great journalistic boardrooms: *The New York Times*, *Time*—the works. These meetings are part of the ritual for presidential candidates.

Apparently, however, the appearance of women at these events is not a part of the ritual. And I doubled the error by bringing along another woman: a public-relations expert who is also a McGovern volunteer. The result was some embarrassment, especially at *Time*, and endless "lady" jokes. (Much hesitancy over whether to serve us ale and cigars, for instance, and editors who excused themselves if they said "damn.") The other woman didn't mind, being toughened to such situations by her experience in business. But I was surprised by the editors' condescension, especially combined with the low intellectual quality of their questions. Are these the journalistic heights to which we've all been climbing?

Even Pierre Salinger, who had come along on McGovern's behalf, interrupted what serious discussion there was with political jokes, prefacing each one by excusing himself to "the ladies." One of the editors pointed out that *Time* had done away with waitresses "to avoid such problems of propriety." (Our food was served by obsequious men in uniform.)

Oddly, McGovern didn't seem to notice at all. He just plowed right on, very serious and very effective.

I smoked half the cigar, drank the ale, and got McGovern out of there in time for a picket-line appearance that we'd promised to the United Farm Workers. But I don't think I'm cut out for this job.

AUGUST/OCTOBER 1968

Chicago. Will the word always bring back memories of gas masks and pools of blood on Michigan Avenue? I have a feeling that many of us will be dividing our lives into "before" and "after" this so-called Democratic convention. And in addition to his enthusiastic support for the war in Vietnam, Hubert Humphrey now has to live down his refusal even to suggest to Chicago's Mayor Daley that he control rampaging police and stop the bloodshed in the streets.

Most incredible of all, many authorities now are trying to deny the reality of what happened there, to say television exaggerated it. I'm afraid television minimized it. The truth was much worse.

- McGovern, hanging out the window of his headquarters at the Blackstone Hotel, shouting obscenities at the teams of policemen ganging up on individuals. The cops used gloves weighted with pieces of metal, billy clubs, everything. A man and a woman were left lying in their own blood on the sidewalk. It was, and had been for two days, a police riot. Afterward, staff members in the room were surprised by two things: McGovern's language and his admission that he'd never seen police brutality before.

- Each day of the convention, Galbraith would call up and say, "Get George to say something nice about Gene." And each day, McGovern would dutifully pay tribute to McCarthy's lonely bravery in the snows of the New Hampshire primary. But it never did any good. McCarthy likes McGovern little more than he liked Robert Kennedy. I wonder if

he will ever forgive either one for sharing the support of an antiwar
constituency

• The California delegation meeting was the most spirited and constructive event in Chicago. It was also the only time that all three candidates appeared together in debate. Humphrey defended Johnson's
Vietnam policy and the "broad-based democracy" of the regime in
Saigon: not exactly a popular stance in front of the convention's most
antiwar delegation. Furthermore, his cheerful, all-American style
didn't fit well with the seriousness of his subject. McCarthy sniped
more at McGovern than at Humphrey or Johnson. He clearly felt that
he no longer should be asked to explain his policy positions. When
questioned by delegates, he often answered coldly, "My stand is clear
on that."

  The two candidates' speeches were a perfect prelude to McGovern,
who was free to be his best: angry about the waste of lives in Vietnam;
forceful on such convention issues as the resistance to seating the
Georgia delegation headed by Julian Bond; charitable toward individuals of goodwill who had made mistakes, including Hubert Humphrey. The contrast couldn't have been more clear, and the delegation
loved it, cheering and applauding every answer. In the end, delegates
already pledged to McCarthy had to be dissuaded from switching to
McGovern. After all, the two senators were in league, technically at
least, to break the first ballot, and that kind of loss would only have
angered McCarthy further.

  The room was jammed, and the debate was being televised nationwide. It was one of those electric moments when you know a person or
an idea is being born. Magically, McGovern had become a presidential candidate.

• Senator Ribicoff took on Mayor Daley and the whole convention
Establishment in his nominating speech. "With George McGovern,"
he said simply, "we wouldn't have Gestapo tactics in the streets of
Chicago." No one was more stunned than those of us who had been
standing backstage, taking a breather after working on that very
speech. Up to the last minute, Ribicoff had seemed primarily worried
about whether to wear his glasses or not, and there was no such
dynamite in the text as typed and approved. Frank Mankiewicz had

encouraged him to talk about the violence while they were waiting at the platform.

- When, in spite of this intense effort to break the first ballot, Humphrey won the nomination, McGovern finished on an equivocal note by consenting to stand on the platform arm-in-arm with Humphrey—a gesture of unity that McCarthy refused to make.

*B*ack in New York, anti-Vietnam groups even began to consider the possibility that Nixon, not being personally committed to the war, might end it faster than Humphrey who had publicly defended it for so long as vice-president. After all, lackadaisical Senator Eugene McCarthy, who once wanted to be Johnson's vice-president, had ended up as the symbol of opposition to Johnson's policies in Vietnam. And Robert Kennedy, who started out as a devoted anti-Communist and made Joe McCarthy godfather of his first child, ended up as the only American politician who seemed concerned about the fate of Vietnamese citizens as well as that of American soldiers. (The turning point, I've always thought, came when he was a twenty-nine-year-old traveler in the Soviet Union and a Communist doctor saved his life; but these human explanations aren't favored by political scientists.) Even Strom Thurmond, archsegregationist and defender of states' rights, was once a reformer and disciple of Franklin Roosevelt.

If these men had ranged back and forth across the political spectrum, wasn't it possible that Richard Nixon might do the same?

Though many disappointed Kennedy-McCarthy-McGovern supporters still regarded Nixon with a mixture of fear (would he still believe the Adlai Stevensons of the world were "spreading pro-Communist propaganda"?) and boredom (could we stand four years of having all human experience reduced to clichés?), he was suddenly a real alternative. Mightn't it be better to have a pragmatist with minimal philosophy who listened to opinion polls, than an ideologue like Humphrey who seemed still to believe the United States should be the world's policeman?

Besides, Nixon appeared destined to be president no matter what we did. The more we speculated, the less personal knowledge or hard information we could come up with about this man. As the only campaign worker in the press, I was designated to become a kind of Manchurian candidate on Nixon's campaign plane for some of these crucial fall days; a personal correspondent who would report not the respectful, circumspect news one reads in *The New York Times*, but Nixon's behavior, the atmosphere of the men around him, and anecdotes revelatory of character.

Thursday. A thousand-dollar-a-plate dinner here in New York and a simultaneous Agnew banquet in Los Angeles were being seen on closed-circuit television at banquets in other cities. The net take was said to be nearly five million dollars, but the impact on me was instant nostalgia; nostalgia for a midwestern childhood in which these banquet goers had been the respectable burghers and my high-school mates (football-playing, Negro-hating Hungarians and Poles) had gone to work in their factories and filling stations. Nothing had changed, not one florid face or cummerbund, or John Dewey heart. Could they have been flash-frozen since 1952?

The high point of the evening was a tanned and hearty Richard Nixon standing on stage with arms above his head, fingers moving up and down in his odd, benedictory V sign, to acknowledge a standing ovation. He was clearly at ease. He was, as Art Linkletter said in his introduction, "a man whose time has come."

Then came what the newsmen around me said was The Speech: that collection of good political generalities so inexorably the same that reporters could recite it with him and could interpret any minute change with the skill of Kremlinologists. Thus, a seemingly innocuous sentence like Nixon's paraphrase of Teddy Roosevelt, "This isn't going to be a good country for any of us to live in until it's a good country for all of us to live in," acquires more significance when it is left out in the South. Other stock phrases, like "The most important civil right is every American's right to safety," become more important simply because they are left in.

I am assured that more of tonight's gems are staples:

"I say to you that when the capital of the nation has become the crime capital of the world, when bus drivers in Washington, D.C., have to use scrip and carry guns from fear of robbery, when there have been riots in three hundred cities, and the president of the United States can't go to any city without fear of a demonstration, when a second-rate little country like North Korea can kidnap one of our ships on the high seas . . . then it's time for the quiet people, the Forgotten People, to stand up and demand a change!"

"I pledge to restore America as a first-rate military power . . . We must not lose at the conference table what our boys have died to win in Vietnam."

"People accuse me of not talking about issues. Well, I had my staff count up all the issues I've made statements on, and it came to one hundred and sixty-seven issues. Of course, Hubert's been on both sides of every question, so he has twice as many."

"I know these seem like bad times, but now I'm going to say something that may surprise you. As a student of history who has traveled all over this world, I would pick the United States in 1968 as the best time and place to live in."

There were some extra reassurances for this thousand-dollar-a-plate audience. ("You have succeeded beyond the wildest dreams of most Americans. You who are participating in this dinner are the luckiest people in the world. You are participating in the great events of your time.") But the rest was an Old Macdonald's Farm recitation of all the places he's been campaigning so far.

I had the feeling that, had I not been taking notes, I would have been left with no clear memory of what he said; only an impression of confidence. I turned to a waiter, the only other person in the room who hadn't heard this before. What did he think of Nixon's speech? "That guy," he said contemptuously, heaving a full tray to his shoulder. "He's such a schmuck he doesn't know what *schmuck* means." Clearly not one of the quiet men Nixon had in mind.

Friday. Today we go to Philadelphia on big chartered campaign jets, *The Tricia* and *The Julie*, with staff, Secret Service, and press corps aboard. (*The David*—named, of course, for Julie's fiancé David Eisenhower—will join us for a midwestern swing next week. Having that painted on a plane seems a big strain on a twenty-year-old's engagement.) After a ticker-tape parade and a statewide television show, the entire entourage will stay overnight at a Marriott Motor Hotel before starting a bus tour of nine shopping centers, zeroing in on down-the-middle white Americans.

On the plane I learn that chances of a personal interview are almost nil. Even press conferences only come about when a dozen or so important reporters band together and threaten headlines: NIXON HIDING FROM PRESS. Herb Klein, Nixon's polite and very intelligent press secretary with whom I registered my interview request, is so confident of no controversy and no crises that he frequently stays in New York, leaving most day-to-day press dealings to two personable young men: Pat Buchanan, a former newspaperman and Young Americans for Freedom adviser, who is brought in when the press gets obstreperous; and Ron Zeigler, formerly J. Walter Thompson's account executive for Disneyland, who takes care of the press when it's calm.

"Don't worry about it," said a kindly midwestern newspaperman. "You don't learn much anyway. His technique is to take the first question and run with it. Maybe he doesn't use the Western Behavioral Institute the way Reagan did: they fed issues cards into a computer, you know, and came out with all the positions that would fit a basically conservative frame of mind; Reagan just took out the card file when we asked him questions. But this campaign is being run by two psychologists in a back room somewhere. I'm sure of it."

At various campaign stops that day, Nixon himself favored leaving gun control up to the states and instituting a mandatory prison sentence for any crime committed with a gun; said of Johnson and Humphrey that "Neither Governor Agnew nor myself are raising questions of their loyalty" ("I'm glad there are no traitors running this year," muttered the *Time* correspondent to my left); said that air and water pollution could best be handled by "tax incentives to industry," not federal legislation; upheld his previous statement that the Rutgers professor who spoke well of the Vietcong should be fired (he was), and reiterated the Nixonian stand that he couldn't say what his Vietnamese policy would be while Paris negotiations were going on.

I went back to the hotel dragged down by an unreasoning depression. We were going back to the fifties again. "It's a phenomenon we all suffer from when we first join up," said a British journalist. "A sort of reentry phase. With this campaign, and with most Western countries right now, we're in for a time of reaction."

Saturday. An unprecedented event on the Nixon tour: a visit to a black neighborhood. The press and staff piled out of our three busses at Progress Shopping Plaza, a Philadelphia shopping center and office development being built by black capital and black management. Reverend Leon Sullivan—confident, good-looking, clearly accustomed to dealing with The Man—showed a very nervous oohing and ahing Nixon what the future layout would be. It was impressive. Supermarkets, shops, small factories for the making of clothes and electronic supplies, a management training school: Reverend Sullivan explained it all in loving detail while Nixon said, "Hmmm, I see," "Isn't that interesting," or "Right, right," and rubbed his sweating palms together. The candidate was clearly eager to say something.

"Now, what you fellas need," Nixon said seriously, "is economic power." Some of the younger men around Sullivan looked disbelieving, but the reverend just smiled and let The Man stand in the middle of a multimillion-dollar black-owned shopping center and deliver his high-school civics lecture. "I've said it before and I'll say it again," Nixon went on. "There's one door you people haven't gone through yet. Oh, you've accomplished some very important things, of course, but there's one door you must open, and that's the door to black capitalism. The boy in the slums must have hope he can one day own the grocery store on his corner; he must have something to work for. That's what my program of black capitalism is all about. You fellas have got to get *a piece of the action*."

Nixon stepped back looking pleased with his hip phrase, and Sullivan laughed heartily. "That's right," he said, giving Nixon a slap on the back that moved him over a couple of inches. "That's what Afro-Americans got to work for now, *black* power and *green* power. That's why I'm a political independent." Either Nixon was dismayed by that "political independent" or he had never heard "Afro-American" before, but his "Right, right, I see," was getting noticeably more nervous. The small talk drifted onto the fact that both he and Sullivan had once been designated Outstanding Young Men of the Year by the Junior Chamber of Commerce.

"Say," said Nixon, "you must know that fella who was a Young Man of the Year, too. You know, the one with a hook for an arm?" Sullivan looked bewildered, and said no, he didn't. Nixon insisted he must know him, though they hadn't been elected the same year, and there was no reason for them to be friends, and he insisted on describing him, gesturing to show where the hook came. Sullivan said no, he really didn't, and, after some more backslapping, the meeting came to an end. But not before an explanation of Nixon's mental connection had become painfully clear. Black skin and a man with a hook for an arm: two handicapped men must know each other.

Monday. In this easy, well-oiled campaign, Nixon stayed in his gold-and-white French-provincial apartment this morning surrounded by gifts from famous people, gifts that Mrs. Nixon rotates for display:

autographed photos from chiefs of state acquired while he was vice-president, four engraved views of Buckingham Palace from Queen Elizabeth, a permanent collection of two hundred curio elephants, and his most prized possessions—two paintings signed *D. D. Eisenhower* and one floral scroll by Madame Chiang Kai-shek. The change from thirty-thousand-dollar-a-year vice-president to two-hundred-thousand-dollar-a-year lawyer has meant a lot to the candidate. Dinner guests say that he sometimes looks around the spotless, gold-carpeted ten rooms at 810 Fifth Avenue and says, "Isn't this beautiful? Aren't I lucky to be here?"

A reporter told me that Nixon often asked guests in his California home to guess the cost of some particularly expensive piece of furniture, like a living version of "The Price Is Right." To the reporter, this was an example of smallness and lack of sophistication, but I found it suddenly endearing. At least Nixon wasn't pretending that he didn't care.

Wednesday. This campaign is run like IBM. There is an ideas department in charge of "packaging and merchandising the candidate." There is a production department to raise money, make campaign schedules, handle press, and take care of all the other elements involved in producing a "quota" of votes in each state.

Top aides do not speak of policy briefings but of "programming the candidate." The chain of command is definitely corporate, with John Mitchell, a fiftyish Wall Street lawyer who is a Nixon partner, as "chairman of the board" over both ideas and production.

Treatment of the press is impeccable. Do you wish to ask questions about Mr. Nixon's concept of the presidency? Here is the staffman in charge of that. About trade barriers and the gold flow? Here is the department head in charge of *that*. (The fact that there are no blacks on staff and not even a labor specialist goes almost unnoticed.) Baggage never gets lost, wire-service facilities are everywhere, and I was phoned twice, once at one in the morning, to make sure that I knew about a half-hour schedule change.

It's all very pleasant, even seductive, but there is a suspicion that the reporters are inmates and that the staff are their keepers; that if we said, "I don't like Richard Nixon," it would be like saying, "I am Napoleon." The keepers would smile their "We're the winners" smile, give us our room keys, and go right on.

In fact, what's most striking about the press is their air of disinterest in what the candidate does. On any Kennedy campaign plane, or even McCarthy's or Rockefeller's, there was a feeling of being at the second-best party: that no matter how interesting the reporters' discussions and dinners might be, the candidate and his chosen few were having a better time somewhere else. But not on Nixon's plane. Here reporters clearly feel themselves to be the first best, and going off to a rally or even a private interview is just part of the unexciting job.

Occasionally, one of the several reporters who has covered the White House will call other veterans around for a "one-minute reminder": he plays a tape of Johnson talking, and everybody jokes about how glad they are to be away. Occasionally, as if against their better judgment, other reporters are reminded of stories from the primaries: Bobby, the day before Oregon's primary, sitting on a suitcase in the aisle and singing "Where Have All the Flowers Gone" to somebody's guitar accompaniment; Bobby spending three days visiting South Dakota's Indians and responding to staff objections that there were no votes there, with "You sons of bitches, you don't really care about suffering." They tell their stories and then are silent for a moment, as each one tries to think of something cheerful to say.

In a way, both Kennedy and Nixon have been written about inaccurately because of reporters' discomfort with personal feeling. Many of them loved Bobby and so took care to conceal that fact with criticism. Many of them dislike or disdain Nixon and so give his viewpoints maximum weight. This desire to balance may be inevitable, but it's misleading. We who learned who Kennedy was only after he died may find out who Nixon is only after he is president.

Thursday. After Seattle and Denver, with half a dozen campaign stops and Nixon renditions of The Speech in each, I think I'm getting the hang of his new and improved speaking style.

It is a definite improvement over 1960. The New Nixon has given up the keep-your-elbows-in stance recommended by his high-school debating coach—but what doesn't show up on the short takes shown on television is the difference between form and content. For the phrase, "we must reach up . . ." he may stretch both arms downward; for "the whole world," he may gesture close to his chest, or tick off the first of two points on the third finger; for the one-arm thrust that marks important statements, he may find himself with his arm raised too soon, and pause visibly to get coordinated. This is a man who has, to an extraordinary degree, created himself; who has worked hard, who never stops working, to fulfill his idea of what a public man should be.

Colleagues say he has one of the highest IQs in Washington. The State Department officials who briefed him for his many trips as vice-president were invariably impressed that he had "done his homework." In recent years of law practice, fellow attorneys have commented on his ability to grasp all the essentials of a problem quickly, and to analyze afterward what did or did not go wrong. If it can be learned, Nixon will learn it.

But if it has to be understood, Nixon—and possibly the country—may be in deep trouble. He has worked so long and so consciously to better himself that instinct and spontaneity have somehow got buried. ("He has a better grasp of Africa's over-all economic problems than any other American politician," said a visiting official, "but he doesn't understand Africans.")

Over the years, aides have tried to humanize his image with everything from hobbies (in 1960, one of them said he was too neat and should take up something messy like chicken-raising) to posed photographs in sport clothes. Yesterday on the suburban tour, an announcement was made to all three busses that Nixon had lost a cuff link to the crowd. ("Next thing you know, someone will snatch the paperclips from Wallace's cuffs," said one reporter.) The emphasis now is on being statesmanlike instead of, as Nixon puts it, "a buddy-buddy boy," so the candidate seems much more at ease.

But there is a philosophical tree-in-the-forest question that will never be answered, one that he raises in our minds by being so relentlessly conscious, politically and personally, of the way he appears to others. When Nixon is alone in a room, is there anyone there?

Friday. We got a plane-side press conference today because there was a row about the lack of one last night. Reporters had wanted a reply to George Ball's accusation, just then on the wires, that Nixon didn't have the character or principles to handle world crises as president, and that Agnew was a "fourth-rate political hack." When he finally stood on the plane steps to take questions, the reporters were angry enough to bring out the Old Nixon. He accused them of putting words in his mouth, and his face actually shook with tension. Then he suddenly pulled himself together and added, "Of course, you boys have a right to put words in my mouth, that's your job."

In a Tampa auditorium for that night's rally, bleachers climbed up three sides from a floor full of folding chairs, making a solid valley of people. Max Frankel of *The New York Times* tossed us a note, "$1 reward still available for the first black face."

A choir began to sing "The Battle Hymn of the Republic." For a moment, it didn't quite sink in. "They shouldn't sing that," said a midwestern reporter softly. "It doesn't belong to them." June 8th, Bobby Kennedy's funeral, a long, slow funeral train. Old hopes that I had managed to forget since that first reentry phase a week ago washed over me again. Only worse.

Governor Kirk and Nixon stood with their arms around each other's shoulders. A banner read REGISTER COMMIES, NOT GUNS. It suddenly seemed that we were surrounded by antilife, conserving, neighbor-fearing people—or rather by good people whose neighbor-fearing instincts were being played upon—and that the enemy was going to win. And win not just this election, but the power to impose themselves, here and in many other countries where waves of reaction were beginning, for a long time to come. The hymn went on and on, and the Nixon cheers went on and on. It wasn't the victory of one man or the death of another. It was the death of the future, and of our youth, because we might be rather old before the conservers left and compassionate men came back.

Saturday. I woke up this morning in a Key Biscayne motel where the press corps is being pampered for the weekend, incorporating into a dream the chant, "Nixon afraid to debate Humphrey. *Why?*" I had the feeling it had been repeated over and over in the dream, and it continued awake: a small plane was circling overhead with a loudspeaker. And a wired-for-sound boat was cruising back and forth off the beach.

As usual, the Humphrey camp had miscalculated. Nixon was not staying at the motel, but with Bebe Rebozo, a longtime friend and local millionaire, who kept a posh vacation home nearby.

But reactions are truthful that early in the morning, and I discovered I was cheering that little misscheduled plane along. The chant was ridiculous, but I was glad to hear it. There was no rational choice between the Plastic Man and the Cowardly Lion, but there was an emotional one. What good is intelligence or pragmatism at the service of poor instincts?

JULY 1969

Politics is the unforeseen. Chappaquiddick happened last week.

Among the waves spreading out from it is a new look at McGovern and other presidential possibilities. Ironically, he had told Ted Kennedy recently that there should be several candidates next time, "in case one of us runs into a telephone pole on the way home."

Now there is a meeting under way to discuss McGovern's own potential campaign. He phoned to invite me to join the group being put together by Ribicoff, and asked that each of us give a little advance thought to our advice.

The truth is that I haven't thought about politics, at least not in the conventional sense that I would have five or six months ago, since I woke up to the fact that my own position, and the position of women in general, was political in the deepest sense. I'm told that it's called the Feminist Realization.

I thought about it as I hung up the phone. Six months ago, I would have been honored by McGovern's invitation to a "serious" (i.e., male and therefore grown-up) political meeting, but full of doubt about whether I could contribute in a "serious" (male) way. I had raised as much money and done as much political work as anyone in McGovern's last brief presidential effort and *still* had been treated like a frivolous pariah by much of McGovern's Senate staff, but I had refused to admit even to myself that this was so. In fact, one of his chief aides only stopped saying "get her out of here" when he discovered that I had brought in the single biggest contributor: a seventy-year-old first-generation Jewish meat-packer who pledged ten thousand dollars on the phone, without asking for any favors in return, because he cares about preserving the libertarian traditions that had brought him here. Nonetheless, the aide didn't like women in politics, and said he feared someone would think I was having an affair with the candidate.

Even in South Dakota, where many of us had gone to help McGovern get reelected to the Senate in spite of his conservative constituents' belief that "George became a hippie" in Chicago, I was made to feel that I had to dress dowdily (I actually went out and bought covered-up, mud-colored clothes) and lurk around corners.

Those events were echoes of every political campaign I had ever worked in as a volunteer, from Students for Stevenson in 1952 to McGovern. Like other women, I had either stayed at the edges doing menial jobs or been hidden away in some backroom because (a) it might be counterproductive to admit that a female was working on speeches or policy decisions, and (b) if she was under sixty and didn't have terminal acne, someone might think she was having an affair with the candidate.

Not only had I suppressed all those years of anger, just assuming that I was lucky to be allowed to volunteer for a campaign at all, but I also had defined politics very narrowly: the faraway events in Washington or Saigon or city hall. I couldn't admit that any power relationship in life is political: therefore politics also may be who's doing the dishes, or who's getting paid half the wages that a man would get for the same job, or who's expected to take the roles of service and support everywhere, including in political campaigns.

It's a realization I owe to those brave women whose meetings I started covering last winter. A lot of them were younger than I. Most had come out of the peace or civil rights movements, where they had figured out that if even those admirable and idealistic groups relegated women to doing mimeographing and making coffee, a woman-run movement against sexism was a necessity. They changed my life. It will never be the same.

That's why I'm looking forward to going to that meeting. For one thing, I can finally stop couching my suggestions in hesitancy and humor. That alone should save me a lot of time.

Nonetheless, I go happily off on one more standard political trip and journalistic assignment, joining dozens of reporters who are following Nelson Rockefeller around Latin America on a diplomatic mission he has accepted from President Richard Nixon, the very man he has politically opposed for so many years.

But then, who is more dependable than Nelson Rockefeller? Well-meaning, full of energy, a little Olympian, he seems to stride through the world with elephant's-paw pants legs flapping, palms the size of Easter hams outstretched in a perpetual handshake—the indefatigable politician and exemplary rich man of our time.

The question is: Dependable for whom? From interviewing him between countries, I discover that this peace candidate of a year ago is now helping Nixon strong-arm votes for the ABM. Furthermore, Rockefeller seems so delighted to have an international assignment that he is willing to ignore how unpopular this mission is. Even Venezuela, where he has owned a huge ranch for thirty years and is on a nickname basis with leaders, cancels his trip. Condemning such popular resistance as "Communist inspired," he seems not to care that the few countries who do welcome us have to provide armies to guard us, and ask that our Pan Am plane land at protected military bases. In Haiti he poses in "grinning embrace of the decrepit tyrant Duvalier," as *Life* magazine later explains in a caption. Unfortunate Haitians are brought in cattle cars to line the streets in a "spontaneous" welcome.

This last long trip makes me realize how tired I am of feeling estranged from the political leaders I am covering. As on the Nixon plane, one of the chief aides is convinced that I have been phoning ahead to notify demonstrators. The only difference is that the Rockefeller plane actually has one black reporter on it who is, of course, suspected of doing the same. Neither of us has. Maybe we should.

I am also tired of being the only woman among the press. ("Can you do twenty-five push-ups?" Rockefeller's press secretary asked me seriously when I applied for credentials. "No," I said, "not one." "That's a question I ask all women reporters," he explained cheerfully, "and hope they don't say yes.") I come home and write what I hope will be my last traditional political assignment: "Nelson Rockefeller in Latin America— The Sound of One Hand Clapping."

AUGUST 1969

At this year's Vermont weekend (which is fast becoming the only tradition in my life), McGovern explains apologetically that Ribicoff had deleted my name from the invitation list for the planning meeting for McGovern's candidacy. Ribicoff simply said: "No broads." According to McGovern, he then explained to Ribicoff that I had been his advance "man," helped to write speeches, raised money, and so on. Ribicoff listened patiently to all of it and then repeated, "No broads."

Moreover, McGovern now has a lot of political talent around him. Looking at Galbraith, Dick Goodwin, and two aides, I wonder what purpose I am serving here. Clearly, I haven't deepened their understanding of the political system as it affects women. (Mostly my fault: I haven't had the confidence or the consciousness to put up a fight.) I have served interchangeably with men, working longer and raising more money than most of them, but even those supposedly worthwhile acts haven't opened the doors for other women. McGovern, for instance, would never have let Ribicoff get away with saying, "No blacks" or "No Jews." "No broads" was somehow acceptable.

It isn't that the incident was very important, or even that McGovern's attitudes are bad. I've accepted dozens of similar situations, and McGovern, as the head of the Reform Commission that's changing the representation rules for the next convention, is one of the few politicians working to increase women's political participation. I think it's precisely *because* the meeting was such a common incident, *because* McGovern is probably the best of the political lot, that I feel so estranged.

I realize that, unless women organize, support each other, and force change, nothing basic is going to happen. Not even with the best of men. And I wonder: *Are women—including me—willing to face that?*

AUGUST 1971

The weekend in Vermont again. Nothing has changed—but everything is different.

McGovern is here, but, having formally declared for the presidency in January 1970, he is now a serious candidate for the Democratic nomination. Knowing he would have to buck the party and get grass-roots support, he has embarked on the longest campaign in presidential history. Gone are the baggy suits of 1965. Longer hair and sideburns make up for his incipient baldness. Henry Kimmelman, McGovern's dapper new finance chairman, is helping him metamorphose into a candidate.

The high point of these two days is to be a benefit for McGovern's candidacy—people are coming from miles around to drink punch in the Galbraiths' pasture. I've been recruited as one of the many speakers—a big change. Two years ago, I would have pled insanity or sickness rather than stand up in front of a group larger than four, but recently I've been teaming up with another woman to talk about the women's movement. (It's McGovern's theory of growth through conquering fear.)

What caused my inclusion, I'm sure, was women's recent political activity. After a year of work and planning, we held the founding conference of the National Women's Political Caucus in Washington last month. Though Secretary of State William Rogers and President Nixon were quoted by the press as saying that a photograph of Congresswomen Shirley Chisholm, Bella Abzug, and others of us who were founders of the caucus looked "like a burlesque," some media have reported this effort seriously.

Clearly no one knows what leadership has gone undiscovered in women of all races, and in black and other minority men. In deference to that, as well as to the symbolic but important candidacy of Shirley Chisholm, I end by praising McGovern as "the best white male candidate."

He smiles at that, neither flattered nor put off. He may be one of the few leaders who will let fundamental change happen.

FEBRUARY 1972

Now it's McGovern, not McCarthy, in the snows of New Hampshire. I've been working for Chisholm in the states where she is running in the primaries, and McGovern wherever she's not. Therefore, I'm here for McGovern. Five campaign meetings in one day: more than ever, I wonder how candidates can enjoy or even survive this as a steady diet.

The "advance man" for my trip is a woman. So is the candidate for delegate with whom I spoke at a rally. There are women involved in most areas of the campaign here, and they believe McGovern favors the economic and legislative changes they need. But, as in other states, the women are still more the workers than the decision makers, especially in the eyes of the young and sometimes-arrogant men who are managing the campaign.

"McGovern is fine," the delegate explained to me, "but he should discipline his staff. If the campaign managers here had the attitudes about black men that they do about all women, they would be fired."

It sounds painful and familiar. I promise to ask the staff in Washington to help, but I'm afraid only the women there will really listen. Question: Do *they* have any power?

MARCH 1972

The phone rings. It is McGovern, standing in some lonely airport, making political calls. He thanks me for a fund-raising speech in Florida and for New Hampshire, saying with some surprise that the women's issues had really turned out to be very effective against Congressman McCloskey, who had otherwise threatened to take away a crucial percentage of McGovern's antiwar support in New Hampshire.

I hope McCloskey now sees his folly in waffling on various equality issues. In fact, McCloskey, who followed the same campaign path days later, has admitted that most of the resistance he met was from women.

While the iron is hot, I mention the campaign problems. McGovern sounds a little resigned. After all, the New Hampshire campaign is over. There are other worries now.

There has been a lot of pressure to become a McGovern delegate. It's fish-or-cut-bait, because both Chisholm and McGovern will be on the ballot in New York State. As a Chisholm delegate, there is little chance of winning, but perhaps any woman who is in the least recognizable should offer to run on her slate.

Personally, I'd still feel much more at home going to the convention as a member of the press.

APRIL 1972

Went to my district meeting and became a Chisholm delegate after all. I think it was the surprise in McGovern's voice that did it: surprise at the strength of women's issues in New Hampshire, or that one benefit speech in Florida could bring ten thousand dollars in ticket sales into campaign coffers. He still doesn't understand the women's movement.

There are so many pressure groups pushing McGovern to the right. The Chisholm candidacy is one of the few forces on the left, and almost the only one focusing on the issues of women and other powerless groups.

It might help to educate McGovern and others a little more.

JUNE 1972

A dozen or so members of the National Women's Political Caucus met with McGovern in Washington. The object was to quiz him on many issues of concern to the women's vote, from welfare to military spending. Representatives of the caucus had done the same with each presidential candidate.

After some discussion of appointing women to high posts in government, with which McGovern fully agreed, we got into the most sensitive area—abortion. The problem was that McGovern had first inspired hope, and then waffled. Months after quietly taking the position that this was a decision for the individual conscience, not a subject for legislation at all, he found himself brutally attacked by anti-abortion groups during the primaries. Not having the gut instinct on this issue that he does on the war or the economy, he did something out of character—he backed down. First he said it was a question for the states to decide, then he implied the opposite by personally criticizing the New York law as too liberal. As a result, his position was neither consistent nor pleasing to either side.

As a way out of the dilemma, I suggested the wording of the "reproductive freedom" item in the caucus's own statement of purpose, since it might be adaptable for a political plank. For instance: "The Democratic party is opposed to government interference in the reproductive and sexual freedom of the individual American citizen." That covered the problem in its true proportions by including the repeal of laws on birth control, the remaining eugenics laws that allowed involuntary sterilization, and laws on sexual orientation—all concerns of men as well as women. On abortion, it incorporated the results of a Gallup poll showing that 57 percent of the American public and 54 percent of Catholic Americans felt abortion to be a decision for the individual and her doctor. It also took a stance against government interference with which both the right and the left could agree.

McGovern listened carefully, as he always does, and said he liked the wording, that he would think about it and get back to us that night.

The meeting's only point of disagreement was on the representation of women in the campaign staff. Betty Friedan, overstating in her own frenetic style, told him he had to have "more women visible in the campaign, because right now they just aren't there." McGovern responded quickly that her statement was "sheer nonsense—you just don't know what you're talking about." And indeed, Jean Westwood was in the room, as were several other top women from the McGovern staff.

One of them came to Betty's rescue by noting that, even though they were in the campaign, women weren't always listened to. McGovern himself was open, she explained, in what had become a truism of the campaign, but taking women's issues and women campaign aides seriously hadn't been impressed on the staff.

The meeting was disorganized but helpful. McGovern seemed distant and a little impatient, but still willing to listen and change. Only Shirley MacLaine, a volunteer for McGovern, seemed very disturbed at its end. Though she herself agreed with the right to reproductive and sexual freedom, she was afraid that Nixon, who had favored restrictive legislation in all these areas, could use the issue profitably against McGovern. And protecting McGovern, she felt, was an end to which any principle or issue should be sacrificed.

Had I been that obsessed with campaign-itis in my prefeminist days? Perhaps. It had taken me a long time to learn that no one would speak for these issues if their natural constituency did not, and it had taken even longer to understand that they could win.

One disturbing sentence came floating back in my mind as I left. When we had questioned McGovern on his welfare policy, he seemed bewildered: "Why is *this* group interested in welfare?" If he doesn't see welfare as a women's issue, how much communication has there been?

*S*hirley MacLaine has cut the reproductive-freedom plank out of the McGovern draft of the Democratic platform, without, she says, the knowledge of or instruction from her candidate. Women fear endangering men's approval so much, we don't even wait for them to say no. Or else we protect them, even if it means saying no to ourselves.

But Jennifer Wilke, a young delegate from Alaska, worked hard and got enough signatures to reintroduce it as a minority plank—minus the words "and sexual" because, in the meantime, representatives of the gay community had launched a plank of their own.

So the right to reproductive freedom will be raised at the convention anyway. It's the strength of the women's movement: some of us won't be told what to do anymore, not even by each other

JULY 1972

In this week before the convention in Miami, the NWPC has been meeting to make plans.

In fact, we have already been much more successful than expected, because women all over the country have had that Feminist Realization and have been willing to work.

1. There will be 40 percent women delegates, as opposed to 14 percent in 1968. The NWPC boosted that number by pressuring the Democratic National Committee to put enforcement teeth into the McGovern Reform Commission rules and by holding delegate training sessions around the country. But it was individual women who took the risks and who now have a toehold in their local political structures, no matter what happens in Miami.

2. There will be a woman cochairing the convention: Yvonne Brathwaite, a young black California legislator, who is also running for Congress.

3. There is a women's plank, including all the crucial issues except reproductive freedom, already in the majority report as it emerged from the Platform Committee. Congresswoman Bella Abzug organized other Platform Committee members to get that through.

4. Most of the challenges to delegations without a fair representation of women have already been won or negotiated to some compromise before the Credentials Committee.

The convention is bound to be a far cry from 1968, when most of the women were going to luncheons and fashion shows arranged for "the wives."

But we are still scared. I especially am scared because I am one of the two NWPC spokeswomen elected to coordinate our forces at the Democratic and Republican conventions respectively. Without the experience or money or computerized information available to most other forces on that convention floor, we will have to make a unified fight on at least four issues: any remaining challenges to delegations without enough women, the reproductive plank, a poor people's plank that has better welfare provisions than the majority report, and, if we get our nerve up, the vice-presidency.

*I*f you let Barnum & Bailey interpret a plot by Stendhal, it might come out to be something like the 1972 Democratic convention. I have memories of five days with no sleep, never getting anyone on the telephone, endless machinations to get floor passes, bloody internal problems with three or four women in the NWPC, frustration, anger, and oddly, when it was all over, a sense of accomplishment and community. For instance:

- We chose the South Carolina challenge as our floor fight on the representation of women; partly because a victory would have established a definition of "affirmative action" that would have helped all traditionally excluded groups.

  The first experience of political realism came when a South Carolina delegate, speaking against our challenge, implied heavily that white women would be replacing black men; a classic tactic of divide-and-conquer. The implication was false (the remedy explicitly stated that the racial balance not be changed), and especially angering when the women, black and white, had chosen this test precisely because it was a coalition issue.

  Did the tactic defeat us? We'll never know. Because the McGovern strategists got nervous about the possibility of a change in the total number of votes necessary to constitute a majority in the key California challenge, they started withdrawing votes halfway through the South Carolina roll call.

  We learned how it felt to be a football between the McGovern forces and the Stop McGovern forces. The issue itself—and McGovern's pledge of support—didn't matter a damn.

- The women's plank passed beautifully, as expected. In 1968 there was not one word about women in the Democratic platform. We would have celebrated, had we not been too busy.

- The challenge to the Chicago delegation of Mayor Daley—a group with far too few women, minorities, and young people—was supported. The non-Daley group took their seats. The spirit of '68 was officially dead.

The consensus of the meetings of women delegates held by the caucus had been to fight for the minority plank on reproductive freedom; indeed, our vote had supported the plank by nine to one. So fight we did, with three women delegates speaking eloquently in its favor as a constitutional right. One male Right-to-Life zealot spoke against, and Shirley MacLaine also was an opposition speaker, on the grounds that this *was* a fundamental right but didn't belong in the platform.

Far from the humiliating defeat we had feared and the danger of setting back efforts to repeal anti-abortion laws through the courts, we made a very good showing. Clearly, we would have won if McGovern's forces had left their delegates uninstructed and thus able to vote their conscience. The issue of reproductive freedom had been raised in a national political platform for the first time.

There remained only one afternoon to put together the vice-presidential candidacy of Frances "Sissy" Farenthold, the recent candidate for governor of Texas who had made such an unprecedented coalition of women, young people, blacks, Chicanos, and other workers. She had at least as good qualifications as Tom Eagleton, McGovern's announced choice. Like him, she was a Catholic from a southern state, and she was certainly no more obscure.

There was no time to lobby, so speakers on her behalf were picked to signal the important caucuses.

In one final, glorious push, our jerry-built system of floor contacts actually worked. Most of the women had never heard of Sissy Farenthold before Miami, yet they trusted their floor leaders' information enough to vote for another woman. Though Farenthold came in second, since McGovern obviously controlled enough votes to give the nomination to Eagleton, she beat out several men who had campaigned for months.

As a result, many fewer interviewers were asking superciliously, "But *is* there a qualified woman?"

Fannie Lou Hamer, a well-known black leader in Mississippi and an NWPC founder, had spoken on Farenthold's behalf. "I know how hard it is," she said, "for a white southern woman to fight like she does." After the vote, she added, "Next time, we'll win."

It is the morning after all these momentous events, and we are hoarse and shaky with fatigue. John Conyers, the gifted young black congressman from Michigan, has got an appointment with McGovern for our Clearinghouse Committee—a group of civil rights, women's, and other reform groups that have been coordinating all efforts before and during this convention.

Finally, we are ushered into a small room. McGovern is there in his shirt sleeves—suddenly not a distant candidate, but a calm and familiar face from the past.

We discuss future coordination, and he asks a leading staff member, one of the arrogant young men who have made life miserable for women working in the campaign, to apologize for a "misquote" in which he had said that there weren't enough women with political experience or who knew how to organize.

Women old enough to be his mother or grandmother, and who have been organizing all their lives, accept his apologies with good grace.

McGovern pauses on his way out, then falls silent. It is an odd and moving moment, as if I might be some reminder of the seven long years since 1965; as if time has suddenly washed over him in a remembering tide. The others in the room are silent, too. "It's . . . incredible, isn't it?" I say, not knowing what to do. "After Chicago, it's so hard to believe."

"Yes," he says finally, "it's hard to believe. But there's a long way to go."

If there is agitation, even anger around McGovern, it is because he inspires hope, as Richard Nixon does not. And hope is a very unruly emotion.

But women are never again going to be mindless coffee-makers or mindless policy-makers in politics. There can be no such thing as a perfect leader. We have to learn to lead ourselves.

A very, very long time ago (about three or four years), I took a certain secure and righteous pleasure in saying the things that women are supposed to say. I remember with pain—

"My work won't interfere with marriage. After all, I can always keep my typewriter at home." Or:

"I don't want to write about women's stuff. I want to write about foreign policy." Or:

"Black families were forced into matriarchy, so I see why black women have to step back and let their men get ahead." Or:

"I know we're helping Chicano groups that are tough on women, but *that's their culture*." Or:

"Who would want to join a women's group? I've never been a joiner, have you?" Or (when bragging):

"He says I write like a man."

I suppose it's obvious from the kinds of statements I chose that I was secretly nonconforming. I wasn't married. I was earning a living at a profession I cared about. I had basically—if quietly—opted out of the "feminine" role. But that made it all the more necessary to repeat the conventional wisdom, even to look as conventional as I could manage, if I was to avoid some of the punishments reserved by society for women who don't do as society says. I therefore learned to Uncle Tom with subtlety, logic, and humor. Sometimes, I even believed it myself.

If it weren't for the women's movement, I might still be dissembling away. But the ideas of this great sea-change in women's view of ourselves are contagious and irresistible. They hit women like a revelation, as if we had left a dark room and walked into the sun.

At first my discoveries seemed personal. In fact, they were the same ones so many millions of women have made and are continuing to make. Greatly simplified, they go like this: Women are human beings first, with minor differences from men that apply largely to the single act of reproduction. We share the dreams, capabilities, and weaknesses of all human beings, but our occasional pregnancies and other visible differences have been used—even more pervasively, if less brutally, than racial differences have been used—to create an "inferior" group and an elaborate division of labor. The division is continued for a clear if often unconscious reason: the economic and social profit of males as a group.

Once this feminist realization dawned, I reacted in what turned out to be predictable ways. First, I was amazed at the simplicity and obviousness of a realization that made sense, at last, of my life experience. I couldn't figure out why I hadn't seen it before. Second, I realized how far that new vision of life was from the system around us, and how tough it would be to explain this feminist realization at all, much less to get people (especially, though not only, men) to accept so drastic a change.

But I tried to explain. God knows (*she* knows) that women try. We make analogies with other groups that have been marked for subservient roles in order to assist blocked imaginations. We supply endless facts and statistics of injustice, reeling them off until we feel like human information-retrieval machines. We lean heavily on the device of reversal. (If there is a male reader to whom all my *pre*realization statements seem perfectly logical, for instance, let him read each sentence with "men" substituted for "women"—or himself for me—and see how he feels: "My work won't interfere with marriage. . . . "; " . . . Chicana groups that are tough on men. . . . " You get the idea.)

We even use logic. If a woman spends a year bearing and nursing a child, for instance, she is supposed to have the primary responsibility for raising that child to adulthood. That's logic by the male definition, but it often makes women feel children are their only function, keeps them from doing any other kind of work, or discourages them from being mothers at all. Wouldn't it be just as logical to say that the child has two parents, therefore both are equally responsible for child rearing, and the father should compensate for that extra year by spending *more* than half the time caring for the child? Logic is in the eye of the logician.

Occasionally, these efforts at explaining actually succeed. More often, I get the feeling that most women are speaking Urdu and most men are speaking Pali.

Whether joyful or painful, both kinds of reaction to our discovery have a great reward. They give birth to sisterhood.

First, we share the exhilaration of growth and self-discovery, the sensation of having the scales fall from our eyes. Whether we are giving other women this new knowledge or receiving it from them, the pleasure for all concerned is enormous. And very moving.

In the second stage, when we're exhausted from dredging up facts and arguments for the men whom we had previously thought advanced and intelligent, we make another simple discovery: women understand. We may share experiences, make jokes, paint pictures, and describe humiliations that mean little to men, but *women understand*.

The odd thing about these deep and personal connections among women is that they often leap barriers of age, economics, worldly experience, race, culture—all the barriers that, in male or mixed society, seem so impossible to cross.

I remember meeting with a group of women in Missouri who, because they had come in equal numbers from the small town and from its nearby campus, seemed to be split between wives with white gloves welded to their wrists and students with boots who used words like "imperialism" and "oppression." Planning for a child-care center had brought them together, but the meeting seemed hopeless until three of the booted young women began to argue among themselves about a young male professor. The leader of the radicals on campus, he accused all women unwilling to run mimeograph machines of not being sufficiently devoted to the cause. As for child-care centers, he felt their effect of allowing women to compete with men for jobs was part of a dreaded "feminization" of the American male and American culture.

"He sounds just like my husband," said one of the white-gloved women. "He wants me to have bake sales and collect door-to-door for his Republican party."

The young women had sense enough to take it from there. What difference did boots or white gloves make if they were all getting treated like servants and children? Before they broke up, they were discussing some subjects that affected them all (like the myth of the vaginal orgasm) and planning to meet every week. "Men think we're whatever it is we do for men," explained one of the housewives. "It's only by getting together with other women that we'll ever find out who we are."

Even racial barriers become a little less formidable once we discover this mutuality of our life experiences as women. At a meeting run by black women domestics who had formed a job cooperative in Alabama, a white housewife asked me about the consciousness-raising sessions or "rap groups" that are often an organic path to feminism. I explained that while men, even minority men, usually had someplace—a neighborhood, a bar, a street corner, something—where they could get together and be themselves, women were isolated in their houses and families; isolated from other females. We had no street corners, no bars, no offices, no territory that was recognized as ours. Rap groups were an effort to create something of our own, a free place—an occasional chance for total honesty and support from our sisters.

As I talked about isolation, about the feeling that there must be something wrong with us if we aren't content to be housekeepers and mothers, tears began to stream down the cheeks of this dignified woman—clearly as much of a surprise to her as to us. For the black women, some distance was bridged by seeing this white woman cry.

"He does it to us both, honey," said the black woman next to her, putting an arm around her shoulders. "If it's your own kitchen or somebody else's, you still don't get treated like people. Women's work just doesn't count."

The meeting ended with the housewife organizing a support group of white women who would extract from their husbands a living wage for domestic workers and help them fight the local authorities who opposed any pay raises; a support group without which the domestic workers felt their small and brave cooperative could not survive.

As for the "matriarchal" argument that I swallowed in prefeminist days, I now understand why many black women resent it and feel that it's the white sociologists' way of encouraging the black community to imitate a white suburban life-style. "If I end up cooking grits for revolutionaries," explained a black woman poet from Chicago, "it isn't my revolution. Black men and women need to work together: you can't have liberation for half a race." In fact, some black women wonder if criticism of the strength they were forced to develop isn't a way to keep half the black community working at lowered capacity and lowered pay, as well as to attribute some of black men's sufferings to black women, instead of to their real source—white racism. I wonder with them.

Looking back at all those male-approved things I used to say, the basic hang-up seems clear—a lack of esteem for women, whatever our race, and for myself.

This is the most tragic punishment that society inflicts on any second-class group. Ultimately the brainwashing works, and we ourselves come to believe our group is inferior. Even if we achieve a little success in the world and think of ourselves as "different," we don't want to associate with our group. We want to identify up, not down (clearly my problem in not wanting to join women's groups). We want to be the only woman in the office, or the only black family on the block, or the only Jew in the club.

The pain of looking back at wasted, imitative years is enormous. Trying to write like men. Valuing myself and other women according to the degree of our acceptance by men—socially, in politics, and in our professions. It's as painful as it is now to hear two grown-up female human beings competing with each other on the basis of their husband's status, like servants whose identity rests on the wealth or accomplishments of their employers.

And this lack of esteem that makes us put each other down is still the major enemy of sisterhood. Women who are conforming to society's expectations view the nonconformists with justifiable alarm. *Those noisy, unfeminine women*, they say to themselves. *They will only make trouble for us all.* Women who are quietly nonconforming, hoping nobody will notice, are even more alarmed because they have more to lose. And that makes sense, too.

The status quo protects itself by punishing all challengers, especially women whose rebellion strikes at the most fundamental social organization: the sex roles that convince half the population that its identity depends on being first in work or in war, and the other half that it must serve as docile, unpaid, or underpaid labor.

In fact, there seems to be no punishment inside the white male club that quite equals the ridicule and personal viciousness reserved for women who rebel. Attractive or young women who act forcefully are assumed to be either unnatural or male-controlled. If they succeed, it could only have been sexually, through men. Old women or women considered unattractive by male standards are accused of acting out of bitterness, because they could not get a man. Any woman who chooses to behave like a full human being should be warned that the armies of the status quo will treat her as something of a dirty joke. That's their natural and first weapon. She will *need* sisterhood.

All of that is meant to be a warning but not a discouragement. There are more rewards than punishments.

For myself, I can now admit anger and use it constructively, where once I would have submerged it and let it fester into guilt or collect for some destructive explosion.

I have met brave women who are exploring the outer edge of human possibility, with no history to guide them, and with a courage to make themselves vulnerable that I find moving beyond the words to express it.

I no longer think that I do not exist, which was my version of that lack of self-esteem afflicting many women. (If male standards weren't natural to me, and they were the only standards, how could I exist?) This means that I am less likely to need male values and approval and am less vulnerable to classic arguments. ("If you don't like me, you're not a real woman"—said by a man who is coming on. "If you don't like me, you can't relate to other people, you're not a real person"—said by anyone who understands blackmail as an art.)

I can sometimes deal with men as equals and therefore can afford to like them for the first time.

I have discovered politics that are not intellectual or superimposed. They are organic. I finally understand why for years I inexplicably identified with "out" groups: I belong to one, too. And I know it will take a coalition of such groups to achieve a society in which, at a minimum, no one is born into a second-class role because of visible difference, because of race or of sex.

I no longer feel strange by myself or with a group of women in public. I feel just fine.

I am continually moved to discover I have sisters.

I am beginning, just beginning, to find out who I am.

—1972

A few weeks before my twenty-fifth reunion last spring, a Washington reporter called to say she was writing an article on why so many women of accomplishment had gone to Smith College.

"Like who?" I asked cautiously, sensing a news peg. "Like Nancy Reagan and Barbara Bush," she said. "Don't you think it's remarkable that the two top women in the country went to the same college?"

There was a pause while both of us waited for me to find a diplomatic way to challenge the question. "Look," I said finally, "do you think a reporter is interviewing Mr. Thatcher's schoolmates to find out how they were trained to marry a chief of state? Is Mr. Thatcher one of the top men in England?"

The reporter laughed. She agreed this story was a dumb idea, especially since she herself had gone to Smith, but her editor had assigned it. "Did you know Jean Harris also went to Smith?" she added dryly.

I hadn't. I wondered if the connection among Jean Harris, Nancy Reagan, and other famous companions was the same in the reporter's mind as in mine: they were Olympic champions at the traditional feminine game of transferring their egos into the body of a male human being. It was the awful familiarity of this game that had made so many women, especially older women, feel both uncomfortable and sympathetic when Jean Harris's years of willing humiliation were laid bare in the press. She said she had intended to commit suicide when she accidentally shot Dr. Tarnower, her longtime lover whose money and affection were being distracted by a younger woman—and perhaps she had. Perhaps he *was* herself.

We skittered off this disturbing idea and onto something more positive. Even in the 1940s when Nancy Reagan and Jean Harris were students, Smith and other women's colleges were producing a disproportionate number of women scholars and professionals; especially those in such "unfeminine" fields as science and math. Though Smith was proud of the fact that men greatly outnumbered women on its faculty—a proof of seriousness highlighted in the college catalogue even when I was there in the 1950s—and though not one woman was president of Smith until the current one arrived in 1975, we still had many more women professors and role models than did coeducational schools. Equally important, there was never a danger of being made to feel like a female misfit in a mostly male classroom, the fate of so many women in co-ed schools, especially in fields like science or math.

But even as the reporter and I discussed those interesting reasons why Smith had produced more than its share of independent achievers, we knew that all of them put together were less newsworthy than one Nancy Reagan. Any First Lady, no matter what she does or doesn't do, is still more likely to top the lists of Most Admired Women than any woman who has succeeded on her own.

It's a social message that's especially painful for women who are encouraged toward personal accomplishment and excellence, and then expected to subordinate themselves to children and a husband's career. "If we're ever to have educated children," we were told at Smith in the 1950s, "we must have educated mothers." That impossible way of resolving the tension resulted in the prototypical class note of the *Alumnae Quarterly* each year: "Sophia Smith Jones, '56, has completed her Ph.D., done volunteer work, and begun several teaching jobs while having four children and following her husband John in his corporate career."

It was the question the reporter didn't ask that sent me back to my reunion: *How had we survived that double message of our educations?*

*T*he first important fact about women's college reunions is who *doesn't* come. "My God, who would want to?" went a frequent response. "It'll be so depressing." The reason often turned out to be some microcosm of contempt for women—ourselves and others. A few said they didn't want to go because they were "just housewives"; others because they were divorced and weren't "just housewives"; some others because they had gained too much weight; others because they were successful in their professions and assumed everyone else would be conforming to the suburban "Smith girl" image we still believed, whether or not we knew anyone who fit it. A few of the active feminists in the class had tried to enlarge what was, they thought, one inadequate panel on the double-role problem—"Can It All Be Done?"—with almost no time for discussion. At least one felt that legislation, sexuality, and other controversial topics were resisted. In frustration, she just didn't come.

In the end, 220 of the 657 living members of the Class of 1956 did show up, including some of those who had been disdainful at first. That was still a lower percentage than most twenty-fifth reunions at men's colleges. A total of 323 women responded to the "Where are we now?" questionnaire that three classmates had worked hard to prepare. As at the reunion, however, the most poorly represented group was the 5 percent who had never married at all. They were only half as likely to respond to the questionnaires as were those who had been married at least once (including the 10 percent who had been married twice or more). Eighty percent of those responding were currently married, with only 42 percent doing paid work full-time, plus another 31 percent part-time. Clearly, the image of "successful Smith graduate" attracted more of those who felt they fit it.

When we arrived in those eerily familiar dorm rooms on our green New England campus, however, the few women who had brought husbands along were the subjects of mild complaint. Having a husband was one thing, but bringing him along was another. Spouses, children, and lovers might be okay at men's reunions, but definitely not at women's. "That's because women take men's reunions seriously but not vice versa," said one classmate whose Peck & Peck exterior concealed a rebellious heart. "Besides, families mean support and an audience to men. To women, they just mean more work."

We gathered in a local motel for our class supper; a noisy, tentative crowd of women who eyed one another with furtive curiosity while insisting stoutly that all of us looked "just the same."

In fact, the age span among us, based on visual evidence alone, could have been twenty years. A waitress thought some were in our late twenties, while others seemed far over our real average age of forty-six.

Without the dark lipstick, round collars, and hairdos of the 1950s, however, most of us seemed substantially younger than the few husbands present. They looked alarmingly paternal. Clearly, a lot of us had listened to our cultural instructions to marry older, wiser, taller men who both weighed and earned more than we did. According to the class question-naire, most of our husbands were somewhere between forty-eight and sixty-two.

The centerpiece of the evening was another small age shock. We were now as old as our college president. Since Jill Kerr Conway was both the first woman to occupy that position and a 1956 graduate of her own university in Australia, we inducted her as an honorary member of our class.

In return, she spoke to us personally about her dreams of adventure as a child living on an isolated Australian farm, her hopes for accomplish-ment as a student and young scholar, and the sex barriers that had impeded her along the way. As a professor, she had pressed for change on behalf of women faculty and workers on campus, and that activism eventually resulted in her first administrative job. As a scholar and historian, she had reconciled herself to the idea of remaining single, and was still surprised to have found a husband and colleague who valued her work as much as his own. As someone who couldn't have children, she was aware that her successful career would have been difficult or impossi-ble for most women with children.

When she made a plea for less obsessive, masculine-style work patterns in society, she got a long applause. When she reported that she had surveyed professional women who spent an average of thirty thousand dollars a year on household help, the audience groaned. When she admitted that, when first married, she assumed she had to clean bathrooms—until her husband stopped her by saying he hadn't married her to clean bathrooms—there was the silence of envy.

Of course she said nothing about a man's responsibility for raising children, cleaning bathrooms, or otherwise limiting his career, as women have traditionally done, when there isn't enough money for household help. In describing her dawn-to-midnight day as president, she made no mention of her ongoing fights with conservative members of the Smith faculty who oppose women's studies, or with alumnae who complain about lesbian students who no longer feel the need to lie about their identity.

"That's because she's a great manipulator," a new graduate explained later. "She doesn't want to alienate husbands or turn off any contributors. She may be the best fund raiser Smith has ever had."

But President Conway had spoken to us personally, understanding, feminist-style, that the personal is political, and she had touched us. "I'm so glad I brought my husband," said one woman with tears in her eyes. "I've been trying to tell him what it's like for twenty years."

I had been worried that having no husband or children, plus a public identity, would isolate me from women who had been my friends. I had forgotten the phenomenon of reunions: you go right back to where you left off twenty-five years before. Proust's tea cake has nothing on one hour in a college dorm.

I also discovered that being famous is not the worst crime a woman can commit—perhaps because fame as anything other than a wife is still controversial and thus a mixed blessing at best. No, the worst crime is to be thin. Since I understand this discomfort with thin people very well (I have always struggled with being overweight and there are only a few minutes each day when I'm not thinking about food), I tried hard to explain that my being thin at the moment didn't mean I wasn't a food junkie, any more than being sober doesn't mean one isn't an alcoholic.

Even so, I couldn't always connect across the weight barrier. The only classmate who later published a hostile comment (that I had come "not to see but to be seen") didn't mention events or conversations at all, just that I was "an anachronism from the 1970s in size-six designer jeans talking sisterhood." (Actually, they were neither size six nor designer, but I knew what she meant.)

Nonetheless, it was from a real event—the issue of the placards for the Alumnae Day Parade—that I learned the most.

*B*eginning with the oldest living graduates, this traditional procession across campus includes all the reunioning classes. Each group wears its class color in a sash over white clothes, plus some special symbol of its era. At the end of the parade come the young women who will graduate the next day. Their white dresses may vary from designer elegance to bed sheets stolen defiantly from the dorms, but each of them carries a long-stemmed rose.

It's a tradition that depends partly on sentiment, partly on the imagination of costumes and signs. (I remember with gratitude the banner carried by some very old and bawdy women who led the parade while I was a student: HARDLY A MAN IS NOW ALIVE, WHO REMEMBERS THE GIRLS OF '95.) It's also a place where social change is visual. Only with the 1960s do the groups begin to show much racial diversity. My class, for instance, included not one black student, no Hispanic women, and only a handful of Asian Americans. (As a freshman, I had asked a professor why none of the black applicants from my town had been admitted. His answer was a classic of racism and sexism: one had to be very careful about educating Negro girls because there weren't enough educated Negro men to go around.) In dramatic contrast, the current graduating class was 29 percent women of color.

Together with Phyllis Rosser, a classmate and a colleague at *Ms.* magazine, I had helped make placards that we hoped would bridge the years between us and marchers both older and younger:

THE SECOND WAVE OF FEMINISM SALUTES THE FIRST.

WE SURVIVED JOE MCCARTHY-WE CAN SURVIVE
REAGAN AND THE MORAL MAJORITY

'56 REMEMBERS OUR SISTERS WHO DIED OF ILLEGAL
ABORTIONS. DON'T LET IT HAPPEN AGAIN!

WOMEN GET MORE RADICAL WITH AGE.

We knew that these slogans had more political content than "Focus '56," the theme set by our reunion committee as a pun on middle-age and bifocals. That was why we brought our signs—with two copies of each, which was all we had time to make—in the first place. But given the results of the questionnaire, we didn't think they would be too controversial. The Class of '56 had voted against Reagan by almost three to one, and 98 percent thought abortion should be a safe and legal choice.

When we laid our extra placards on the grass where the Class of 1956 was forming in the parade, women picked them up with enthusiasm.

The only other substantive slogan in sight was GROWING UP FREE ALL OVER AGAIN, a possible reference to second careers. There was much groaning over a neighboring placard, NOW OUR AGE IS THE SAME AS OUR BUSTLINE.

Nonetheless, I noticed several women pointing to our signs, and a queasiness in my stomach told me something was amiss. I ignored it as a remnant of my passive 1950s self who never carried placards, and who thought women had been "given" the vote.

A member of our reunion committee came over looking severe. Who had authorized these signs? My heart sank. She went on to explain that all slogans had been approved months in advance.

"By whom?" said one of my unknown sign-carrying sisters. "The whole class didn't vote on those slogans, either."

Our official went away to confer with other committee members. She came back with the news that if even one classmate disapproved of our slogans, we couldn't carry them at all. (Not that one *did* disapprove, but someone *might*.) With all my 1950s fear of conflict returning fast, I explained that we weren't censoring anybody else's signs, nor were we asking them to carry ours. Didn't freedom of speech allow each classmate to carry what she pleased?

As a compromise, another committee member suggested that our group march at the end of our class so we wouldn't interfere with the order of the signs in the "Focus" theme. We agreed.

But more conferencing was afoot, and the compromise was withdrawn. We would have to march at the end of the whole parade in order to have no association with our class at all. I said this would make us very conspicuous indeed, but the first official was adamant. No sign could be carried if it hadn't been okayed by the reunion committee or if even one person might disapprove. With alarmingly little spine left, I agreed.

"She can't keep us from marching with our class," insisted one of our unknown sign-carriers, braver than I. "We can march wherever we damn well please." The others chimed in. Feeling guilty by now both for bringing the signs and for giving in, I fell in with our rebellious group as our class entered the parade.

The committee sent over a young student marshal to move us back on the sidelines. "I think this is stupid," she said kindly, "but they say you've got to wait here for the end of the parade."

And that's where we were, waiting on the sidelines, when the Class of 1966 came by. News of our plight had filtered back through the ranks. These women ten years younger had decided to invite us to march with them, and they made space for us in their lines. "We were so glad to see you," said one as we filed in, our blue sashes conspicuous among their red ones. "A student in our class died from a coat-hanger abortion. It was all hushed up—but we knew."

As we moved slowly across the campus, shouts and applause began to ripple through the bystanders as they spotted our signs. "Good for all of you!" "It's about time!" "Give 'em hell!" An older woman darted out of the crowd to tell us we were "the only worthwhile group in this whole goddamn parade." When we finally passed in front of the president's house, where the new graduates were waiting, there were special cheers and fists raised in salute from a cluster of young black graduates; then more applause from other seniors and their families. By the time we arrived at our destination in the beautiful, sun-dappled quad, all feelings of conflict had gone. Most of our sign-carrying group had tears in our eyes.

"I'm going to take my sign to my son's graduation at Yale," said one woman.

"It was interesting to see how different groups responded," said another. "Maybe the quiet ones disapproved of us, but most people just seemed so pleased."

"I'm proud of my class," said one of the 1966 marchers. "Everybody is outraged that yours threw you out."

As with one voice, we defended our 1956 classmates. "The majority would have agreed," we explained. "It's just that nobody asked them." Not one of us, no matter how angry or embarrassed we had felt at being turned away, wanted to see this moment of celebration become a division.

A signal had been sent out. The results came rippling back for the rest of the weekend.

Members of the new graduating class sought us out to explain that they had met late the previous night, trying to decide whether to unfurl a banner, U.S. OUT OF EL SALVADOR, from a dormitory behind the platform for their outdoor graduation. They were divided. A few members felt that unanimity, not majority rule, should prevail, and no substantive banner could get unanimous support

"Do you ever get unanimity on anything?" one of them asked. "I don't think so," I said. "For me, that's a way of avoiding controversy and any action at all."

They decided to let down their bed-sheet El Salvador banner, as well as one that read STOP THE HLA. Including this so-called human life amendment that would outlaw abortion had been an afterthought inspired by our signs. Smith had changed, but not quite enough to make students take women's issues as seriously as those that men assumed to be more so.

Still later that night, a campus feminist group found us. "You should have let us know in advance. We could have had a thousand people out there," one young activist said with pride. "We never dreamed alumnae would do *anything*."

At our farewell breakfast Sunday, the committee member who had been most opposed to our signs said, "It isn't that most of us don't agree with those sentiments. It's just that these things had been decided in advance." We said we understood, and parted friends. Had we polled the class six months before, what would have happened? I don't know. The fear of conflict was still strong in me twenty-five years later, and I'd had much more opportunity to conquer it than most. Perhaps even one dissenting voice would have been too much.

*D*oes a "feminine" education break the link between thought and action? Perhaps even between thought and speech? Black colleges have been the think tanks of the civil rights movement. They taught black history and black pride even when those subjects were least popular. Yet women's colleges have rarely taught us to fight for ourselves, much less for other women. Women's history courses, plus feminist faculty and administrators, are beginning to change all that, but many of us are still overcoming the "advantages" of our traditional educations.

*J*ust before that college reunion, I had gone back to Toledo where nearly all of my teenage years were spent. I met women whom I had not seen since junior high school, women from the factory-working neighborhoods that I had tried so hard to escape. Most had not gone to college at all or had gone part-time and with great difficulty. Most had to work to support themselves and their families.

As a group those women were alive, outrageous, full of energy and self-confidence. Some had brought discrimination suits against local factories years before feminism brought more middle-class women together in consciousness-raising groups. Others had organized successfully against a recent anti-abortion ordinance in Toledo. Still others were going back to get degrees now, radicalizing the younger or more privileged women they met in class. All of them seemed to assume that education was supposed to lead to action.

Perhaps well-to-do women and unemployed ghetto teenagers have something in common. Neither group has been allowed to develop the self-confidence that comes from knowing you can support yourself.

Yet those same women are made to feel special, privileged by their educations. Separated from much of the world by class (or rather, by the class of their husbands), they are the most likely to marry men with demanding careers and the ability to support a wife. At the same time, society doesn't admit that raising children and homemaking are economically valuable jobs. Which, of course, they are.

I think we deserve to be proud that so many "Smith girls" of the 1950s survived educations that trained us to fit the world, or at least to fear the conflict that comes from trying to make the world fit us.

And how odd to find, after all these years, that I might owe my own survival to the very East Toledo neighborhood I worked so hard to escape.

—1981

*H*appy or unhappy, families are all mysterious. We have only to imagine how differently we would be described—and will be, after our deaths—by each of the family members who believe they know us. The only question is, Why are some mysteries more important than others?

The fate of my Uncle Ed was a mystery of importance in our family. We lavished years of speculation on his transformation from a brilliant young electrical engineer to the town handyman. What could have changed this elegant, Lincolnesque student voted "Best Dressed" by his classmates to the gaunt, unshaven man I remember? Why did he leave a young son and a first wife of the "proper" class and religion, marry a much less educated woman of the "wrong" religion, and raise a second family in a house near an abandoned airstrip; a house whose walls were patched with metal signs to stop the wind? Why did he never talk about his transformation?

For years, I assumed that some secret and dramatic events of a year he spent in Alaska had made the difference. Then I discovered that the trip had come after his change and probably been made because of it. Strangers he worked for as a much-loved handyman talked about him as one more tragedy of the Depression, and it was true that Uncle Ed's father, my paternal grandfather, had lost his money in the stockmarket Crash and died of (depending on who was telling the story) pneumonia or a broken heart. But the Crash of 1929 also had come long after Uncle Ed's transformation. Another theory was that he was afflicted with a mental problem that lasted most of his life, yet he was supremely competent at his work, led an independent life, and asked for help from no one.

Perhaps he had fallen under the spell of a radical professor in the early days of the century, the height of this country's romance with socialism and anarchism. That was the theory of another uncle on my mother's side. I do remember that no matter how much Uncle Ed needed money, he would charge no more for his work than materials plus 10 percent, and I never saw him in anything other than ancient boots and overalls held up with strategic safety pins. Was he really trying to replace socialism-in-one-country with socialism-in-one-man? If so, why did my grandmother, a woman who herself had run for the school board in coalition with anarchists and socialists, mistrust his judgment so much that she left his share of her estate in trust, even though he was over fifty when she died? And why did Uncle Ed seem uninterested in all other political words and acts? Was it true instead that, as another relative insisted, Uncle Ed had chosen poverty to disprove the myths of Jews and money?

Years after my uncle's death, I asked a son in his second family if he had the key to this family mystery. No, he said. He had never known his father any other way. For that cousin, there had been no question. For the rest of us, there was to be no answer.

*F*or many years I also never imagined my mother any way other than the person she had become before I was born. She was just a fact of life when I was growing up; someone to be worried about and cared for; an invalid who lay in bed with eyes closed and lips moving in occasional response to voices only she could hear; a woman to whom I brought an endless stream of toast and coffee, bologna sandwiches and dime pies, in a child's version of what meals should be. She was a loving, intelligent, terrorized woman who tried hard to clean our littered house whenever she emerged from her private world, but who could rarely be counted on to finish one task. In many ways, our roles were reversed: I was the mother and she was the child. Yet that didn't help her, for she still worried about me with all the intensity of a frightened mother, plus the special fears of her own world full of threats and hostile voices.

Even then I suppose I must have known that, years before she was thirty-five and I was born, she had been a spirited, adventurous young woman who struggled out of a working-class family and into college, who found work she loved and continued to do, even after she was married and my older sister was there to be cared for. Certainly, our immediate family and nearby relatives, of whom I was by far the youngest, must have remembered her life as a whole and functioning person. She was thirty before she gave up her own career to help my father run the Michigan summer resort that was the most practical of his many dreams, and she worked hard there as everything from bookkeeper to bar manager. The family must have watched this energetic, fun-loving, book-loving woman turn into someone who was afraid to be alone, who could not hang on to reality long enough to hold a job, and who could rarely concentrate enough to read a book.

Yet I don't remember any family speculation about the mystery of my mother's transformation. To the kind ones and those who liked her, this new Ruth was simply a sad event, perhaps a mental case, a family problem to be accepted and cared for until some natural process made her better. To the less kind or those who had resented her earlier independence, she was a willful failure, someone who lived in a filthy house, a woman who simply would not pull herself together.

Unlike the case of my Uncle Ed, exterior events were never suggested as reason enough for her problems. Giving up her own career was never cited as her personal parallel of the Depression. (Nor was there discussion of the Depression itself, though my mother, like millions of others, had made potato soup and cut up blankets to make my sister's winter clothes.) Her fears of dependence and poverty were no match for my uncle's possible political beliefs. The real influence of newspaper editors who had praised her reporting was not taken as seriously as the possible influence of one radical professor.

Even the explanation of mental illness seemed to contain more personal fault when applied to my mother. She had suffered her first "nervous breakdown," as she and everyone else called it, before I was born and when my sister was about five. It followed years of trying to take care of a baby, be the wife of a kind but financially irresponsible man with show-business dreams, and still keep her much-loved job as reporter and newspaper editor. After many months in a sanatorium, she was pronounced recovered. That is, she was able to take care of my sister again, to move away from the city and the job she loved, and to work with my father at the isolated rural lake in Michigan he was trying to transform into a resort worthy of the big dance bands of the 1930s.

But she was never again completely without the spells of depression, anxiety, and visions into some other world that eventually were to turn her into the nonperson I remember. And she was never again without a bottle of dark, acrid-smelling liquid she called "Doc Howard's medicine": a solution of chloral hydrate that I later learned was the main ingredient of "Mickey Finns" or "knockout drops," and that probably made my mother and her doctor the pioneers of modern tranquilizers. Though friends and relatives saw this medicine as one more evidence of weakness and indulgence, to me it always seemed an embarrassing but necessary evil. It slurred her speech and slowed her coordination, making our neighbors and my school friends believe she was a drunk. But without it, she would not sleep for days, even a week at a time, and her feverish eyes began to see only that private world in which wars and hostile voices threatened the people she loved.

Because my parents had divorced and my sister was working in a faraway city, my mother and I were alone together then, living off the meager fixed income that my mother got from leasing her share of the remaining land in Michigan. I remember a long Thanksgiving weekend spent hanging on to her with one hand and holding my eighth-grade assignment of *Tale of Two Cities* in the other, because the war outside our house was so real to my mother that she had plunged her hand through a window, badly cutting her arm in an effort to help us escape. Only when she finally agreed to swallow the medicine could she sleep, and only then could I end the terrible calm that comes with crisis and admit to myself how afraid I had been.

No wonder that no relative in my memory challenged the doctor who prescribed this medicine, asked if some of her suffering and hallucinating might be due to overdose or withdrawal, or even consulted another doctor about its use. It was our relief as well as hers.

But why was she never returned even to that first sanatorium? Or to help that might come from other doctors? It's hard to say. Partly, it was her own fear of returning. Partly, it was too little money, and a family's not-unusual assumption that mental illness is an inevitable part of some-one's personality. Or perhaps other family members had feared something like my experience when, one hot and desperate summer between the sixth and seventh grade, I finally persuaded her to let me take her to the only doctor from those sanatorium days whom she remembered without fear.

Yes, this brusque old man told me after talking to my abstracted, timid mother for twenty minutes: She definitely belongs in a state hospital. I should put her there right away. But even at that age, *Life* magazine and newspaper exposés had told me what horrors went on inside those hospitals. Assuming there to be no other alternative, I took her home and never tried again.

In retrospect, perhaps the biggest reason my mother was cared for but not helped for twenty years was the simplest: her functioning was not that necessary to the world. Like women alcoholics who drink in their kitchens while costly programs are constructed for executives who drink, or like the homemakers subdued with tranquilizers while male patients get therapy and personal attention instead, my mother was not an important worker. She was not even the caretaker of a very young child, as she had been when she was hospitalized the first time. My father had patiently brought home the groceries and kept our odd household going until I was eight or so and my sister went away to college. Two years later when wartime gas rationing closed his summer resort and he had to travel to buy and sell in summer as well as winter, he said: How can I travel and take care of your mother? How can I make a living? He was right. It was impossible to do both. I did not blame him for leaving once I was old enough to be the bringer of meals and answerer of my mother's questions. ("Has your sister been killed in a car crash?" "Are there German soldiers outside?") I replaced my father, my mother was left with one more way of maintaining a sad status quo, and the world went on undisturbed.

That's why our lives, my mother's from forty-six to fifty-three, and my own from ten to seventeen, were spent alone together. There was one sane winter in a house we rented to be near my sister's college in Massachusetts, then one bad summer spent house-sitting in suburbia while my mother hallucinated and my sister struggled to hold down a summer job in New York. But the rest of those years were lived in Toledo where both my mother and father had been born, and on whose city newspapers an earlier Ruth had worked.

First we moved into a basement apartment in a good neighborhood. In those rooms behind a furnace, I made one last stab at being a child. By pretending to be much sicker with a cold than I really was, I hoped my mother would suddenly turn into a sane and cheerful woman bringing me chicken soup à la Hollywood. Of course, she could not. It only made her feel worse that she could not. I stopped pretending.

But for most of those years, we lived in the upstairs of the house my mother had grown up in and that her parents left her—a deteriorating farm house engulfed by the city, with poor but newer houses stacked against it and a major highway a few feet from its sagging front porch. For a while, we could rent the two downstairs apartments to a newlywed factory worker and a local butcher's family. Then the health department condemned our ancient furnace for the final time, sealing it so tight that even my resourceful Uncle Ed couldn't produce illegal heat.

In that house, I remember:

lying in the bed my mother and I shared for warmth, listening on the early morning radio to the royal wedding of Princess Elizabeth and Prince Philip being broadcast live, while we tried to ignore and thus protect each other from the unmistakable sounds of the factory worker downstairs beating up and locking out his pregnant wife.

. . . hanging paper drapes I had bought in the dime store; stacking books and papers in the shape of two armchairs and covering them with blankets; evolving my own dishwashing system (I waited until all the dishes were dirty, then put them in the bathtub); and listening to my mother's high praise for these housekeeping efforts to bring order from chaos, though in retrospect I think they probably depressed her further.

. . . coming back from one of the Eagles' Club shows where I and other veterans of a local tap-dancing school made ten dollars a night for two shows, and finding my mother waiting with a flashlight and no coat in the dark cold of the bus stop, worried about my safety walking home

. . in a good period, when my mother's native adventurousness came through, answering a classified ad together for an amateur acting troupe that performed Biblical dramas in churches, and doing several very corny performances of *Noah's Ark* while my proud mother shook metal sheets backstage to make thunder.

. . . on a hot summer night, being bitten by one of the rats that shared our house and its back alley. It was a terrifying night that turned into a touching one when my mother, summoning courage from some unknown reservoir of love, became a calm, comforting parent who took me to a hospital emergency room despite her terror at leaving home.

. . . coming home from a local library with the three books a week into which I regularly escaped, and discovering that for once there was no need to escape. My mother was calmly planting hollyhocks in the vacant lot next door.

But there were also times when she woke in the early winter dark, too frightened and disoriented to remember that I was at my usual after-school job, and so called the police to find me. Humiliated in front of my friends by sirens and policemen, I would yell at her—and she would bow her head in fear and say "I'm sorry, I'm sorry, I'm sorry," just as she had done so often when my otherwise-kindhearted father had yelled at her in frustration. Perhaps the worst thing about suffering is that it finally hardens the hearts of those around it.

And there were many, many times when I badgered her until her shaking hands had written a small check to cash at the corner grocery and I could leave her alone while I escaped to the comfort of well-heated dime stores that smelled of fresh doughnuts, or to air-conditioned Saturday-afternoon movies that were windows on a very different world.

But my ultimate protection was this: I was just passing through, a guest in the house; perhaps this wasn't my mother at all. Though I knew very well that I was her daughter, I sometimes imagined that I had been adopted and that my real parents would find me, a fantasy I've since discovered is common. (If children wrote more and grown-ups less, being adopted might be seen not only as a fear but also as a hope.) Certainly, I didn't mourn the wasted life of this woman who was scarcely older than I am now. I worried only about the times when she got worse.

Pity takes distance and a certainty of surviving. It was only after our house was bought for demolition by the church next door, and after my sister had performed the miracle of persuading my father to give me a carefree time before college by taking my mother with him to California for a year, that I could afford to think about the sadness of her life. Suddenly, I was far away in Washington, living with my sister and sharing a house with several of her friends. While I finished high school and discovered to my surprise that my classmates felt sorry for me because my mother *wasn't* there, I also realized that my sister, at least in her early childhood, had known a very different person who lived inside our mother, an earlier Ruth.

She was a woman I met for the first time in a mental hospital near Baltimore, a humane place with gardens and trees where I visited her each weekend of the summer after my first year away in college. Fortunately, my sister hadn't been able to work and be our mother's caretaker, too. After my father's year was up, my sister had carefully researched hospitals and found the courage to break the family chain.

At first, this Ruth was the same abstracted, frightened woman I had lived with all those years; though now all the sadder for being approached through long hospital corridors and many locked doors. But gradually she began to talk about her past life, memories that doctors there must have been awakening. I began to meet a Ruth I had never known.

. . . A tall, spirited, auburn-haired high-school girl who loved basketball and reading; who tried to drive her uncle's Stanley Steamer when it was the first car in the neighborhood; who had a gift for gardening and who sometimes, in defiance of convention, wore her father's overalls; a girl with the courage to go to dances even though her church told her that music itself was sinful, and whose sense of adventure almost made up for feeling gawky and unpretty next to her daintier, dark-haired sister.

. . . A very little girl, just learning to walk, discovering the body places where touching was pleasurable, and being punished by her mother who slapped her hard across the kitchen floor.

. . . A daughter of a handsome railroad-engineer and a schoolteacher who felt she had married "beneath her"; the mother who took her two daughters on Christmas trips to faraway New York on an engineer's free railroad pass and showed them the restaurants and theaters they should aspire to—even though they could only stand outside them in the snow.

. . . A good student at Oberlin College, whose freethinking traditions she loved, where friends nicknamed her "Billy"; a student with a talent for both mathematics and poetry, who was not above putting an invisible film of Karo syrup on all the john seats in her dormitory the night of a big prom; a daughter who had to return to Toledo, live with her family, and go to a local university when her ambitious mother—who had scrimped and saved, ghostwritten a minister's sermons, and made her daughters' clothes in order to get them to college at all—ran out of money. At home, this Ruth became a part-time bookkeeper in a lingerie shop for the very rich, commuting to classes and listening to her mother's harsh lectures on the security of becoming a teacher; but also a young woman who was still rebellious enough to fall in love with my father, the editor of her university newspaper, a funny and charming young man who was a terrible student, had no intention of graduating, put on all the campus dances, and was unacceptably Jewish.

I knew from family lore that my mother had married my father twice: once secretly, after he invited her to become the literary editor of his campus newspaper, and once a year later in a public ceremony, which some members of both families refused to attend as the "mixed marriage" of its day.

And I knew that my mother had gone on to earn a teaching certificate. She had used it to scare away truant officers during the winters when, after my father closed the summer resort for the season, we lived in a house trailer and worked our way to Florida or California and back by buying and selling antiques.

But only during those increasingly adventurous weekend outings from the hospital—going shopping, to lunch, to the movies—did I realize that she had taught college calculus for a year in deference to her mother's insistence that she have teaching "to fall back on." And only then did I realize she had fallen in love with newspapers along with my father. After graduating from the university paper, she wrote a gossip column for a local tabloid, under the name "Duncan MacKenzie," since women weren't supposed to do such things, and soon had earned a job as society reporter on one of Toledo's two big dailies. By the time my sister was four or so, she had worked her way up to the coveted position of Sunday editor.

*I*t was a strange experience to look into those brown eyes I had seen so often and realize suddenly how much they were like my own. For the first time, I realized that she might really be my mother.

I began to think about the many pressures that might have led up to that first nervous breakdown: leaving my sister whom she loved very much with a grandmother whose values my mother didn't share; trying to hold on to a job she loved but was being asked to leave by her husband; wanting very much to go with a woman friend to pursue their own dreams in New York; falling in love with a co-worker at the newspaper who frightened her by being more sexually attractive, more supportive of her work than my father, and perhaps the man she should have married; and finally, nearly bleeding to death with a miscarriage because her own mother had little faith in doctors and refused to get help.

Did those months in the sanatorium brainwash her in some Freudian or very traditional way into making what were, for her, probably the wrong choices? I don't know. It almost doesn't matter. Without extraordinary support to the contrary, she was already convinced that divorce was unthinkable. A husband could not be left for another man, and certainly not for a reason as selfish as a career. A daughter could not be deprived of her father and certainly not be uprooted and taken off to an uncertain future in New York. A bride was supposed to be virginal (not "shop-worn," as my euphemistic mother would have said), and if your husband turned out to be kind, but innocent of the possibility of a woman's pleasure, then just be thankful for kindness.

Of course, other women have torn themselves away from work and love and still survived. But a story my mother told me years later has always symbolized for me the formidable forces arrayed against her.

"It was early spring, nothing was open yet. There was nobody for miles around. We had stayed at the lake that winter, so I was alone a lot while your father took the car and traveled around on business. You were a baby. Your sister was in school, and there was no phone. The last straw was that the radio broke. Suddenly it seemed like forever since I'd been able to talk with anyone—or even hear the sound of another voice.

"I bundled you up, took the dog, and walked out to the Brooklyn road. I thought I'd walk the four or five miles to the grocery store, talk to some people, and find somebody to drive me back. I was walking along with Fritzie running up ahead in the empty road—when suddenly a car came out of nowhere and down the hill. It hit Fritzie head on and threw him over to the side of the road. I yelled and screamed at the driver, but he never slowed down. He never looked at us. He never even turned his head.

"Poor Fritzie was all broken and bleeding, but he was still alive. I carried him and sat down in the middle of the road, with his head cradled in my arms. I was going to *make* the next car stop and help.

'But no car ever came. I sat there for hours, I don't know how long, with you in my lap and holding Fritzie, who was whimpering and looking up at me for help. It was dark by the time he finally died. I pulled him over to the side of the road and walked back home with you and washed the blood out of my clothes.

"I don't know what it was about that one day—it was like a breaking point. When your father came home, I said: 'From now on, I'm going with you. I won't bother you. I'll just sit in the car. But I can't bear to be alone again.' "

I think she told me that story to show she had tried to save herself, or perhaps she wanted to exorcise a painful memory by saying it out loud. But hearing it made me understand what could have turned her into the woman I remember: a solitary figure sitting in the car, perspiring through the summer, bundled up in winter, waiting for my father to come out of this or that antique shop, grateful just not to be alone. I was there, too, because I was too young to be left at home, and I loved helping my father wrap and unwrap the newspaper around the china and small objects he had bought at auctions and was selling to dealers. It made me feel necessary and grown-up. But sometimes it was hours before we came back to the car again and to my mother who was always patiently, silently waiting.

At the hospital and later when Ruth told me stories of her past, I used to say, "But why didn't you leave? Why didn't you take the job? Why didn't you marry the other man?" She would always insist it didn't matter, she was lucky to have my sister and me. If I pressed hard enough, she would add, "If I'd left you never would have been born."

I always thought but never had the courage to say: *But you might have been born instead.*

I'd like to tell you that this story has a happy ending. The best I can do is one that is happier than its beginning.

After many months in that Baltimore hospital, my mother lived on her own in a small apartment for two years while I was in college and my sister married and lived nearby. When she felt the old terrors coming back, she returned to the hospital at her own request. She was approaching sixty by the time she emerged from there and from a Quaker

farm that served as a halfway house, but she confounded her psychiatrists' predictions that she would be able to live outside for shorter and
shorter periods. In fact, she never returned. She lived more than another
twenty years, and for six of them, she was well enough to stay in a
rooming house that provided both privacy and company. Even after my
sister and her husband moved to a larger house and generously made two
rooms into an apartment for her, she continued to have some independent
life and many friends. She worked part-time as a "salesgirl" in a china
shop; went away with me on yearly vacations and took one trip to Europe
with relatives; went to women's club meetings; found a multi-racial
church that she loved; took meditation courses; and enjoyed many books.
She still could not bear to see a sad movie, to stay alone with any of her six
grandchildren while they were babies, to live without many tranquilizers,
or to talk about those bad years in Toledo. The old terrors were still in the
back of her mind, and each day was a fight to keep them down.

It was the length of her illness that had made doctors pessimistic. In
fact, they could not identify any serious mental problem and diagnosed
her only as having "an anxiety neurosis": low self-esteem, a fear of being
dependent, a terror of being alone, a constant worry about money. She
also had spells of what now would be called agoraphobia, a problem
almost entirely confined to dependent women: fear of going outside the
house, and incapacitating anxiety attacks in unfamiliar or public places.

Would you say, I asked one of her doctors, that her spirit had been
broken? "I guess that's as good a diagnosis as any," he said. "And it's
hard to mend anything that's been broken for twenty years."

But once out of the hospital for good, she continued to show flashes of
the different woman inside; one with a wry kind of humor, a sense of
adventure, and a love of learning. Books on math, physics, and mysti-
cism occupied a lot of her time. ("Religion," she used to say firmly,
"begins in the laboratory.") When she visited me in New York during her
sixties and seventies, she always told taxi drivers that she was eighty
years old ("so they will tell me how young I look"), and convinced theater
ticket sellers that she was deaf long before she really was ("so they'll give
us seats in the front row"). She made friends easily, with the vulnerability
and charm of a person who feels entirely dependent on the approval of
others. After one of her visits, every shopkeeper within blocks of my
apartment would say, "Oh yes, I know your mother!" At home, she
complained that people her own age were too old and stodgy for her.

Many of her friends were far younger than she. It was as if she were making up for her own lost years.

She was also overly appreciative of any presents given to her—and that made giving them irresistible. I loved to send her clothes, jewelry, exotic soaps, and additions to her collection of tarot cards. She loved receiving them, though we both knew they would end up stored in boxes and drawers. She carried on a correspondence in German with our European relatives, and exchanges with many other friends, all written in her painfully slow, shaky handwriting. She also loved giving gifts. Even as she worried about money and figured out how to save pennies, she would buy or make carefully chosen presents for grandchildren and friends.

Part of the price she paid for this much health was forgetting. A single reminder of those bad years in Toledo was enough to plunge her into days of depression. There were times when this fact created loneliness for me, too. Only two of us had lived most of my childhood. Now, only one of us remembered. But there were also times in later years when, no matter how much I pled with reporters *not* to interview our friends and neighbors in Toledo, *not* to say that my mother had been hospitalized, they published things that hurt her very much and sent her into a downhill slide.

On the other hand, she was also her mother's daughter, a person with a certain amount of social pride and pretension, and some of her objections had less to do with depression than false pride. She complained bitterly about one report that we had lived in a house trailer. She finally asked angrily: "Couldn't they at least say 'vacation mobile home'?" Divorce was still a shame to her. She might cheerfully tell friends, "I don't know *why* Gloria says her father and I were divorced—we never were." I think she justified this to herself with the idea that they had gone through two marriage ceremonies, one in secret and one in public, but been divorced only once. In fact, they were definitely divorced, and my father had briefly married someone else.

She was very proud of my being a published writer, and we generally shared the same values. After her death, I found a mother-daughter morals quiz I once had written for a women's magazine. In her unmistakably shaky writing, she had recorded her own answers, her entirely accurate imagination of what my answers would be, and a score that concluded our differences were less than those "normal for women separated by twenty-odd years." Nonetheless, she was quite capable of putting a made-up name on her name tag when going to a conservative women's club where she feared our shared identity would bring controversy or even just questions. When I finally got up the nerve to tell her I was signing a 1972 petition of women who publicly said we had had abortions and were demanding the repeal of laws that made them illegal and dangerous, her only reply was sharp and aimed to hurt back. "Every starlet says she's had an abortion," she said. "It's just a way of getting publicity." I knew she agreed that abortion should be a legal choice, but I also knew she would never forgive me for embarrassing her in public.

In fact, her anger and a fairly imaginative ability to wound with words increased in her last years when she was most dependent, most focused on herself, and most likely to need the total attention of others. When my sister made a courageous decision to go to law school at the age of fifty, leaving my mother in a house that not only had many loving teenage grandchildren in it but a kindly older woman as a paid companion besides, my mother reduced her to frequent tears by insisting that this was a family with no love in it, no home-cooked food in the refrigerator; not a real family at all. Since arguments about home cooking wouldn't work on me, my punishment was creative and different. She was going to call up *The New York Times*, she said, and tell them that this was what feminism did: it left old sick women all alone.

Some of this bitterness brought on by failing faculties was eventually solved by a nursing home near my sister's house where my mother not only got the twenty-four-hour help her weakening body demanded, but the attention of affectionate nurses besides. She charmed them, they loved her, and she could still get out for an occasional family wedding. If I ever had any doubts about the debt we owe to nurses, those last months laid them to rest.

When my mother died just before her eighty-second birthday in a hospital room where my sister and I were alternating the hours in which her heart wound slowly down to its last sounds, we were alone together for a few hours while my sister slept. My mother seemed bewildered by her surroundings and the tubes that invaded her body, but her consciousness cleared long enough for her to say: "I want to go home. Please take me home." Lying to her one last time, I said I would. "Okay, honey," she said. "I trust you." Those were her last understandable words.

*T*he nurses let my sister and me stay in the room long after there was no more breath. She had asked us to do that. One of her many fears came from a story she had been told as a child about a man whose coma was mistaken for death. She also had made out a living will requesting that no extraordinary measures be used to keep her alive, and that her ashes be sprinkled in the same stream as my father's.

Her memorial service was in the Episcopalian church that she loved because it fed the poor, let the homeless sleep in its pews, had members of almost every race, and had been sued by the Episcopalian hierarchy for having a woman priest. Most of all, she loved the affection with which its members had welcomed her, visited her at home, and driven her to services. I think she would have liked the Quaker-style informality with which people rose to tell their memories of her. I know she would have loved the presence of many friends. It was to this church that she had donated some of her remaining Michigan property in the hope that it could be used as a multiracial camp, thus getting even with those people in the tiny nearby town who had snubbed my father for being Jewish.

I think she also would have been pleased with her obituary. It emphasized her brief career as one of the early women journalists and asked for donations to Oberlin's scholarship fund so others could go to this college she loved so much but had to leave.

I know I will spend the next years figuring out what her life has left in me.

I realize that I've always been more touched by old people than by children. It's the talent and hopes locked up in a failing body that gets to me; a poignant contrast that reminds me of my mother, even when she was strong.

I've always been drawn to any story of a mother and a daughter on their own in the world. I saw *A Taste of Honey* several times as both a play and a film, and never stopped feeling it. Even *Gypsy* I saw over and over again, sneaking in backstage for the musical and going to the movie as well. I told myself that I was learning the tap-dance routines, but actually my eyes were full of tears

I once fell in love with a man only because we both belonged to that large and secret club of children who had "crazy mothers." We traded stories of the shameful houses to which we could never invite our friends. Before he was born, his mother had gone to jail for her pacifist convictions. Then she married the politically ambitious young lawyer who had defended her, stayed home and raised many sons. I fell out of love when he confessed that he wished I wouldn't smoke or swear, and he hoped I wouldn't go on working. His mother's plight had taught him self-pity— nothing else.

I'm no longer obsessed, as I was for many years, with the fear that I would end up in a house like that one in Toledo. Now, I'm obsessed instead with the things I could have done for my mother while she was alive, or the things I should have said.

I still don't understand why so many, many years passed before I saw my mother as a person and before I understood that many of the forces in her life are patterns women share. Like a lot of daughters, I suppose I couldn't afford to admit that what had happened to my mother was not all personal or accidental, and therefore could happen to me.

One mystery has finally cleared. I could never understand why my mother hadn't been helped by Pauline, her mother-in-law; a woman she seemed to love more than her own mother. This paternal grandmother had died when I was five, before my mother's real problems began but long after that "nervous breakdown," and I knew Pauline was once a suffragist who addressed Congress, marched for the vote, and was the first woman member of a school board in Ohio. She must have been a courageous and independent woman, yet I could find no evidence in my mother's reminiscences that Pauline had encouraged or helped my mother toward a life of her own.

I finally realized that my grandmother never changed the politics of her own life, either. She was a feminist who kept a neat house for a husband and four antifeminist sons, a vegetarian among five male meat eaters, and a woman who felt so strongly about the dangers of alcohol that she used only paste vanilla; yet she served both meat and wine to the men of the house and made sure their lives and comforts were continued undisturbed. After the vote was won, Pauline seems to have stopped all feminist activity. My mother greatly admired the fact that her mother-in-law kept a spotless house and prepared a week's meals at a time. Whatever her own internal torments, Pauline was to my mother a woman who seemed able to "do it all." "Whither thou goest, I shall go," my mother used to say to her much-loved mother-in-law, quoting the Ruth of the Bible. In the end, her mother-in-law may have added to my mother's burdens of guilt.

Perhaps like many later suffragists, my grandmother was a public feminist and a private isolationist. That may have been heroic in itself, the most she could be expected to do, but the vote and a legal right to work were not the only kind of help my mother needed.

The world still missed a unique person named Ruth. Though she longed to live in New York and in Europe, she became a woman who was afraid to take a bus across town. Though she drove the first Stanley Steamer, she married a man who never let her drive.

I can only guess what she might have become. The clues are in moments of spirit or humor.

After all the years of fear, she still came to Oberlin with me when I was giving a speech there. She remembered everything about its history as the first college to admit blacks and the first to admit women, and responded to students with the dignity of a professor, the accuracy of a journalist, and a charm that was all her own.

When she could still make trips to Washington's wealth of libraries, she became an expert genealogist, delighting especially in finding the rogues and rebels in our family tree.

Just before I was born, when she had cooked one more enormous meal for all the members of some famous dance band at my father's resort and they failed to clean their plates, she had taken a shotgun down from the kitchen wall and held it over their frightened heads until they had finished the last crumb of strawberry shortcake. Only then did she tell them the gun wasn't loaded. It was a story she told with great satisfaction.

Though sex was a subject she couldn't discuss directly, she had a great appreciation of sensuous men. When a friend I brought home tried to talk to her about cooking, she was furious. ("He came out in the kitchen and talked to me about *stew!*") But she forgave him when we went swimming. She whispered, "He has wonderful legs!"

On her seventy-fifth birthday, she played softball with her grandsons on the beach, and took pride in hitting home runs into the ocean.

Even in the last year of her life, when my sister took her to visit a neighbor's new and luxurious house, she looked at the vertical stripes of a very abstract painting in the hallway and said, tartly, "Is that the price code?"

She worried terribly about being socially accepted herself, but she never withheld her own approval for the wrong reasons. Poverty or style or lack of education couldn't stand between her and a new friend. Though she lived in a mostly white society and worried if I went out with a man of the "wrong" race, just as she had once married a man of the "wrong" religion, she always accepted each person as an individual.

"Is he *very* dark?" she once asked worriedly about a friend. But when she met this very dark person, she only said afterward, "What a kind and nice man!"

My father was the Jewish half of the family, yet it was my mother who taught me to have pride in that tradition. It was she who encouraged me to listen to a radio play about a concentration camp when I was little. "You should know that this can happen," she said. Yet she did it just enough to teach, never enough to frighten.

It was she who introduced me to books and a respect for them, to poetry that she knew by heart, and to the idea that you could never criticize someone unless you "walked miles in their shoes."

It was she who sold that Toledo house, the only home she had, with the determination that the money be used to start me in college. She gave both her daughters the encouragement to leave home for four years of independence that she herself had never had.

After her death, my sister and I found a journal she had kept of her one cherished and belated trip to Europe. It was a trip she had described very little when she came home: she always deplored people who talked boringly about their personal travels and showed slides. Nonetheless, she had written a descriptive essay called "Grandma Goes to Europe." She still must have thought of herself as a writer. Yet she showed this long journal to no one.

I miss her, but perhaps no more in death than I did in life. Dying seems less sad than having lived too little. But at least we're now asking questions about all the Ruths and all our family mysteries.

If her song inspires that, I think she would be the first to say: It was worth the singing.

—1983

OTHER BASIC DISCOVERIES

Words and Change

*T*hink for a minute. Who were you before this wave of feminism began?

Trying to remember our way back into past realities, past rooms, past beliefs is a first step toward measuring the depth of change. Sharing those measures—in the same way we have learned to share current problems and solutions—is probably the most bias-proof way of identifying our own history. After all, if people of diverse experience and age and background begin to see patterns of similarity emerge from changes in the patterns of our lives and even the words we use, then we are probably on the track of an accurate historical pattern. If we write down those changes as we have experienced them, then history may cease to be limited mainly to the documented acts of national leaders, or to the interpretations of scholars proving a particular theory. We can begin to create a women's history, and a people's history, that is accurate and accessible.

New words and phrases are one organic measure of change. They capture transformations of perception, and sometimes of reality itself.

We have terms like *sexual harassment* and *battered women*. A few years ago, they were just called *life*.

Now, we are becoming the men we wanted to marry. Once women were trained to marry a doctor, not be one.

Women's in front of words like *center* or *newspaper, network* or *rock band*, indicates a positive choice. Ten years ago, it was a put-down.

Now, we've made the revolutionary discovery that children have two parents. A decade ago even the kindly Dr. Spock held mothers solely responsible for children.

In 1972, a NASA official's view of women's function in space was "sexual diversion" [on] "long-duration flights such as Mars." Now, women are simply "astronauts."

Until recently, an older woman on campus was an oddity. Now, so many women have returned for a college education once denied them that the median age of the female undergraduate is twenty-seven years old, and colleges are becoming community resources with a new definition of "students."

Until the 1970s most colleges had never heard of Women's Studies. Now, there are over 30,000 such courses.

Ten years ago moving up the economic ladder for a few women meant becoming a doctor not a nurse, a boss not a secretary: a token not a movement. Now, nurses are striking, secretaries are organizing, and there is an uprising in the pink-collar ghetto.

Art used to be definable as what men created. *Crafts* were made by women and natives. Only recently have we discovered they are the same, thus bringing craft techniques into art and art into everyday life.

Now anti-equality politicians in both parties are worried about *the women's vote* or *the gender gap*. Until the 1980s, political experts said there was no such thing.

A decade ago policemen were protesting against the very idea of working with women. Now, females serve in every major city and the *policeman* has become the *police officer*.

In the 1960s Americans talked about white women who *controlled the economy* or black women who were *matriarchs*. Now, more than 70 percent of men and women agree that sex discrimination exists—and that it's wrong.

Until the 1970s women had to choose between *Miss* or *Mrs.*, thus identifying themselves by marital status in a way men did not. Now, more than a third of American women support *Ms.* as an alternative, an exact parallel of *Mr.*, and so do government publications, business, and most of the media.

Ten years ago rape was the only crime in which the victim was put on trial. Today, the laws of evidence have been changed and *sexual assault* in all degrees is understood as a crime of violence

Now some lesbians have kept their jobs, custody of their children, and even been elected to public office, without having to lie or hide. A decade ago *lesbian* was a secret word and *lesbian mother* was thought to be a contradiction in terms.

A few years ago, pregnant women were often forced to leave jobs permanently, and *paternity leave* or *parental leave* wasn't even a phrase. Now the later stages of pregnancy can be considered legally as a routine work disability, and thirty-four national companies plus a few unions offer some form of leave to new fathers as well.

Much of this newness is simple accuracy—for instance, changing *congressmen* to *congresspeople,* or MEN WORKING to PEOPLE WORKING— and even those changes can spell major differences in power. But new coinage is also needed to capture new perceptions.

*B*efore the current wave of feminism, for instance, we were still discussing *population control*: the enlightened answer to *population explosion*. Both were negative phrases, with the first implying the necessity of an outside force, and the second suggesting endless impersonal breeding. Though feminists were expected to come down on the side of *population control*, one of its underlying assumptions was that women themselves could not possibly be given the power to achieve it. Liberal men who were the population experts assumed that women gained security or were fulfilled only through motherhood, and so would bear too many babies if given the power to make the choice. (Unless, of course, they could achieve a higher degree of literacy and education, thus becoming more rational: more like men.) On the other hand, very religious males—a group that often seemed intent on increasing the numbers of the faithful—treated women as potentially sex-obsessed creatures who would use contraception to avoid childbirth totally, behave sinfully, and thus weaken the patriarchal family and civilization itself.

In the seventies, however, feminism transformed the terms of discussion by popularizing *reproductive freedom* as a phrase and as a basic human right. This umbrella term included safe contraception and abortion, as well as freedom from coerced sterilization (of women or of men) and decent health care during pregnancy and birth. In other words, *reproductive freedom* stated the right of the individual to decide to have or not to have a child. Though obviously a right that is more important to women, it also protects men. Furthermore, it allowed the building of new trust and coalitions between white women and women of color, in this country and elsewhere, who had rightly suspected that the power implied by *population control* would be directed at some groups more than others.

To the surprise of the liberal population experts, the choice of *reproductive freedom* has been exercised eagerly by women wherever it was even marginally allowed. Population journals are full of mystified articles about the declining rate of population growth, even in many areas of the world where the rate of illiteracy among women is still tragically high. A 1979 United Nations women's conference of East and West Europe concluded that women were not only limiting their pregnancies for their own health reasons, but were, statistically speaking, on something of a "baby strike" because of double-role problems; that is, the burden of working both outside and inside the home. Some countries recommended the logical remedy of encouraging men to share child rearing and relieve women's burdens, but other more authoritarian governments simply tried to ensure compulsory childbearing by suppressing contraception and abortion. Since some U.S. government experts were speaking of our "unsatisfactorily low birthrate" quite openly by 1979—and some right-wing anti-abortion leaders were openly fearful that cultural differences between white and other birthrates will make the United States "a non-white country"—the question for the future is clear: Will reproductive freedom make childbirth and child rearing a valuable, rewarded function that is supported and aided by both men and women (as feminists advocate)? Or simply functions that are forced on women, especially socially or racially "desirable" women (as the anti-equality right-wing advocates)?

Obviously, *reproductive freedom* is simply a way of stating the basic need that feminism has been advancing for thousands of years. Witches and gypsies were freedom fighters for women because they taught contraception and abortion. It was mainly this knowledge that made them anathema to patriarchs of the past. In the worldwide wave of feminism of the nineteenth and early twentieth century, advocating "birth control" or "fertility control," even for married women, was enough to jail many feminist crusaders.

But the modern contribution is stating *reproductive freedom* as a universal human right, at least as basic as freedom of speech or assembly.

Regardless of marital status, or racist desires to limit or increase certain populations, or nationalistic goals of having more or fewer soldiers and workers, individual women have the right to decide the use of our own bodies. Men who want children must at least find women willing to bear them. That seems little enough to ask. And governments that want increased rates of population growth must resort to such humane measures as lowering infant mortality rates, improving health care during pregnancy, distributing the work of child rearing through child care and equal parenthood, and lengthening the productive lives of older people.

Obviously, this ultimate bargaining power on the part of women is exactly what male supremacists fear most. That's why their authoritarian impulse is so clearly against any sexuality not directed toward family-style procreation (that is, against extramarital sex, homosexuality and lesbianism, as well as contraception and abortion). This understanding helped feminists to understand why the adversaries of such apparently contradictory concerns as contraception and homosexuality are almost always the same. It also helped us to stand up publicly on the side of any consenting, freely chosen sexuality as a rightful form of human expression.

In recent years, words like *lover* (whether referring to someone of the same or different gender), *sexual preference,* or *gay rights* have begun to be commonly used. *Homophobic* was invented to describe the irrational fear of any sexual expression between people of the same gender, a fear so common in the past that it needed no name. There was also a challenge to such rote phrases as *man-hating lesbian.* After all, it's not lesbians but homemakers and other women who depend on men who are more likely to be hurt and thus angry.

*I*n the 1960s, any sex outside marriage was called the *Sexual Revolution,* a nonfeminist phrase that simply meant women's increased availability on men's terms. By the end of the seventies, feminism had brought more understanding that real liberation meant the power to make a choice; that sexuality, for women or men, should be neither forbidden nor forced. With that in mind, words like *virgin, celibacy, autonomy, faithfulness,* and *commitment* took on a positive meaning. Such blameful words as *frigid* and *nymphomaniac* were being replaced by nonjudgmental ones like *preorgasmic* and *sexually active.* Indeed, *nymphomaniac,* a medically nonexistent term, was mainly used to condemn any woman who made more sexual demands than one man could handle.

It still may take some explaining, but many more women are keeping their *birth* names (and not calling them *maiden* names, with all the sexual double standard that implies). A handful of women have even exchanged their *patriarchal* names for *matriarchal* ones ("Mary *Ruthchild*"), or followed the black movement tradition of replacing former owners' names with place names or letters (for instance, "Judy *Chicago*" or "Laura *X*"). Many tried to solve the dilemma of naming with the reformist step of just adding their husband's name ("Mary *Smith Jones*"), but that remained an unequal mark of marriage unless their husbands took both names, too.

Hardly anyone has yet succeeded in interrupting the patriarchal flow of naming children: they are still given their father's name only, or their mother's name as the dispensable one in the middle. It remains for the future to legalize an egalitarian choice, as some European countries have done, by giving children both parents' names, thus indicating their real parentage (and eliminating the need for such constant explanations as, "This is my daughter by my first marriage," "This my son by my second"), and allowing them to choose their own adult name, whether a parental or totally new one, when they are old enough to get a Social Security card or register to vote. After all, the power of naming goes very deep.

Prochoice began to replace the adjective *pro-abortion,* the latter being a media-created term that implied advocacy of abortion, as opposed to support for it as a legal choice. And a decade that had begun with the shocking necessity of proving the Freudian-dictated *vaginal orgasm* to be neurologically nonexistent, plus explaining the *clitoral orgasm* to be literally true, finally ended up more equally with just *orgasm* (no adjectives necessary) being more talked about and experienced.

The feminist spirit has reclaimed some words with defiance and humor. *Witch*, *bitch*, *dyke*, and other formerly pejorative epithets turned up in the brave names of small feminist groups. A few women artists dubbed their new female imagery *cunt art* in celebration of the discovery that not all sexual symbols were phallic. Humor encouraged the invention of *jockocracy* to describe a certain male obsession with athletics and victory; also *loserism* as a rueful recognition of women's cultural discomfort with anything as "unfeminine" as success. *Supermom* and *Superwoman* were words that relieved us all by identifying the Perfect-Wife-and-Mother, plus the Perfect-Career-Woman, as humanly impossible goals.

Women's Lib or *Women's Libber* were trivializing terms that feminists argued against. (Would we say "Algerian Lib"? "Black Libber"?) In the eighties, their use has diminished, but not disappeared.

*T*he nature of *work* has been a major area of new understanding, beginning with the word itself. Before feminism, work was largely defined as what men did or would do. Thus, a *working woman* was someone who labored outside the home for money, masculine-style. Though still alarmingly common, the term is being protested, especially by homemakers who work harder than any other class of worker, and are still called people who "don't work." Feminists have always tried to speak of *work inside the home* or *outside the home*, of *salaried* or *unsalaried workers*. Attributing a financial value to work in the home would go a long way toward making marriage an equal partnership, as the Equal Rights Amendment would also do, and toward ending the semantic slavery inherent in the phrase *women who don't work*

It would also begin to untangle the *double-role problem* identified in the sixties—that is, the double burden of millions of women who work *both* inside and outside the home—by defining human maintenance and home care as a job in itself; a job that men can and should do as well as women.

Equal pay for equal work, the concept with which we entered the sixties, fell short of helping women in the mostly female, nonunionized jobs of the *pink-collar ghetto*—another new term. Blue-collar workers, who are overwhelmingly male, usually earn far more than workers in mostly female jobs. What did *equal pay* do for the nurse, for instance, who was getting the same low salary as the woman working next to her? *Equal pay for comparable work* has become the new goal, and comparability studies are going forward on the many jobs done largely by men that require less education and fewer skills but still get more pay than jobs done largely by women.

*M*any ideas have been transformed by adding one crucial adjective—
women's bank, *women's* music, *women's* studies, *women's* caucus. That
adjective did more than change a phrase. It implied a lot of new content:
child care, flexible work hours, new standards of credit worthiness, new
symbolism, new lyrics. Such groups also experimented with new structures. Whether out of a conscious belief that hierarchy was rooted in
patriarchy or an unconscious discomfort with authority, women's groups
often changed vertical organization into a more lateral one. *Collective,*
communal, supportive, constituency, and *skill sharing* were more likely
to be heard than *organizational chart, credentials,* or *chain of command.*
Though such new forms were often condemned as impractical, their
ability to make individuals more productive—combined with the current
productivity crisis of traditional, hierarchical forms in industry—have
caused some management consultants to look at them as possible models
for the future.

In short, all the truth telling and the creation of alternate institutions
have begun to delineate and give value to a *women's culture,* a set of
perspectives that differs from the more traditional, masculine ones. We
need to learn, but so do men. Together, we can create a shared culture that
includes the most useful and creative features of each.

Power is also being redefined. Women often explain with care that we
mean power to control our lives but not to dominate others.

Language is used to shift some of the burden back where it belongs.
Alimony is sometimes referred to as *back salary* or *reparations.* After all,
if the U.S. Labor Department counts the replacement value of one
homemaker's work at a minimum of eighteen thousand dollars a year, in
this decade, why shouldn't a wife be entitled to some back salary?
Similarly, many feminists stopped pleading with corporations and professional groups for *contributions* and started to ask for *reparations* for past
damages done to women. Women's Studies, Black Studies, Hispanic
Studies, and the like were often referred to as *remedial studies* in order to
put the blame where it belonged (and to show that such courses must one
day be integrated into the basic curriculum for everyone—into human
history). The self-description of the authoritarian, anti-equality backlash
as pro*family* caused many feminists to take great care about using the
plural, *families,* in order to show that there are many different family
forms. The patriarchal nuclear one acceptable to the right wing (father as

breadwinner, woman at home with children) excludes and brands as unacceptable about 85 percent of all American households. Understanding what the right wing means by "family" helps to understand why, in their view, all guarantees of individual rights to women and children *are* antifamily, from the ERA to laws against battered children.

Of course, an importance of words is their power to exclude. *Man, mankind,* and the *family of man* have made women feel left out, usually with good reason. *People, humanity,* and *humankind* are more inclusive. So are rewrites like "Peace on Earth, Good Will to People." Feminists also tried to educate by asking men to imagine receiving a *Spinster of Arts* or *Mistress of Science* degree, and then working hard for a *sistership.* Wouldn't they feel a little left out?

Racial minorities, both women and men, have sometimes been defined in the negative as nonwhite (would we speak of white people as nonblack?), and in any case, those who are counted as minorities in this country are actually the majority in the world. In order to be more accurate and cross-cultural, feminists often adopted the description of *Third World* or *people of color.* For a while, *Fourth World* was also used as a way of describing the commonality of *all* women in the patriarchal world, regardless of race, but that term was taken over in the late seventies as a label for the poorest, nonindustrialized countries. To continue this reference, women are now sometimes self-described as the *Fifth World*—the half of the population that tends to be used as cheap labor and to have the least control over capital or technology, wherever we are.

In order to reach each other across the barrier of race, feminists also tried to be sensitive to other linguistically divisive habits: for instance, using images of darkness or blackness as negative ("the dark side of human nature," "a black heart," "blackmail") and whiteness as positive ("a white lie," "white magic," "fair-haired boy").

Similarly, *qualified* was a word only necessary when describing "out" groups, as if white men were *qualified* by their birth. Furthermore, they remained the adult, the professional (worker, doctor, poet), while the rest of us still needed adjectives (*woman* worker, *black* doctor, *lady* poet).

The difficult efforts to make language more gender free and more accurate often included the invention of such new alternatives as *chair-*

person or *spokesperson*. Clearly, only a single-sex organization can have a position of *chairman* or *chairwoman*. An integrated organization needs to have a position that can be occupied by all its members—thus, *chairperson* or better yet, just *chair*. Given the balance of power, however, these gender-free words were often used to neuterize women and leave men as the status quo. Thus, a woman might be a *spokesperson*, but a man remained a *spokesman*. Females might become people, but men remained men.

This awkward middle stage of change is inevitable, but women sometimes collaborated with our own exclusion by trying to skip to gender-free words too soon. *Humanism* was a special temptation. (As in, "Don't be threatened, feminists are really just talking about humanism.") *Androgyny* also raised the hope that female and male cultures could be perfectly blended in the ideal person; yet because the female side of the equation has yet to be affirmed, *androgyny* usually tilted toward the male. As a concept, it also raised anxiety levels by conjuring up a conformist, unisex vision, the very opposite of the individuality and uniqueness that feminism actually has in mind.

Whether in life or language, integration without equal power means going right back to our usual slots in the hierarchy. Once that is learned, we will be less likely to let our fear of conflict force us into a pretended unity with "mankind." This lesson helps to clarify the need for consciousness-raising through gender-specific language. "Judges will be elected on their merits," for instance, is a perfectly okay sentence. The only problem is that we're all accustomed to visualizing male judges, and a gender-free sentence may do nothing to jog our consciousness. For a while, we may need sentences like "a judge will be elected on her or his merits" to force us to recognize that women judges do exist.

Another symbolic confusion was the invention of *male chauvinist pig*, a hybrid produced by trying to combine feminism with leftist rhetoric, which was often antifeminist in itself: in this case, a willingness to reduce adversaries to something less than human as a first step toward justifying violence against them. (Years of being *chicks*, *dogs*, and *cows* may have led to some understandable desire to turn the tables, but it also taught us what dehumanization feels like.) Police had been *pigs* in the sixties—as in "Off the Pigs!"—so all prejudiced men became the same for a while; a period that has mercifully passed.

In fact, *male chauvinist* itself is a problem. Since *chauvinist* referred to a superpatriot, all we were saying was that this was a man obsessed with loyalty to his country. Instead, many feminist writers began to use *male supremacist* as a more accurate description of the problem at hand, but some male supremacists took advantage of the earlier error by wearing ties and pins proclaiming, "I am a male chauvinist pig." This was an indication, of course, of the lack of seriousness with which sexism is treated. Few of those men would so cheerfully proclaim, "I am an anti-Semite" or "I am a racist."

Battered women is a phrase that uncovered major, long-hidden violence. It helps us to face the fact that, statistically speaking, the most dangerous place for a woman is in her own home, not in the streets. *Sexual harassment* on the job also exposed a form of intimidation that about a third of all women workers suffer. Talking about it openly inspired women to come forward and legal remedies to be created. By identifying *pornography* (literally, "writing about female slavery") as the preaching of woman hatred, and thus quite different from *erotica,* with its connotation of love and mutuality, there was also the beginning of an understanding that pornography is a major way in which violence and dominance are taught and legitimized; that it is as socially harmful as Nazi literature is to Jews or Klan literature is to blacks.

Even *female sexual slavery* (once known by the nineteenth-century racist term *white slavery*, because for the most part it was the only form of slavery to which whites were also subjected) has been redefined and exposed by this wave of feminism. We know now it flourishes in many of our own cities where prostitution and pornography are big business and a fact of international life.

In response to such realizations of injustice, it's no wonder that *radicalism* began to lose some of its equation with excess or unreasonableness. By exposing the injustice of the sexual caste system and its role as a root of other "natural" injustices based on race and class, *radical feminism* laid the groundwork for unity among women. And by challenging this masculine-feminine, dominant-passive structure as a chief cause and justification of violence, it also proved that *radicalism* can not only take nonviolent forms but challenge the origins of violence itself

These new feminist connections among women are very tenuous, but worldwide. Feminism was international—and antinational—during its last massive advance in the nineteenth and early twentieth centuries. (If we call that "the first wave," it's only because we live in such a young country. The feminist revolution has been a contagious and progressive recurrence in history for thousands of years.) The last wave won for many women of the world a *legal identity* as human beings, not the possessions of others. Now we seek to complete that step for all women, and to gain *legal equality*, too. But there will be many more waves of feminism before male-supremacist cultures give way.

In this wave, words and consciousness have forged ahead, so reality can follow. Measuring the distance between the new and the old evokes the unique part of history that lives in each of us.

—1979 AND 1982

In Praise of Women's Bodies

*H*ow long has it been since you spent a few days in the intimate company of women: dressing and undressing, talking, showering, resting—the kind of casual togetherness that seems more common to locker rooms of men?

For me, high-school gym class came the closest. But that was during the repressive fifties, when even the most daring of us hid behind our towels and others were so insecure about our bodies' adolescent changes (or the lack of them) that we went through group showers with our underwear on or endured the damp discomfort of gym suits under our clothes so we never had to undress at all.

By the time we got to college, I suppose we must have been more grown-up and open. Nonetheless, sports for women, still "unfeminine," had become anti-intellectual besides. Those were two good excuses to avoid most situations of casual nudity among women, and thus to go right on concealing the imperfect bodies on which we secretly thought our worldly worth depended.

So I found myself recently, belatedly, having a basic, human, comforting experience that should have been a commonplace in my life. Thanks to a few days at an old-fashioned spa in the company of ninety or so other women, I discovered a simple, visceral consciousness-raising that was just as crucial as the verbal kind. Like many basic experiences women are encouraged to miss, it brought both strength (through self-acceptance) and anger (why didn't I know this before?).

It's a truism, for instance, that a few clothes are more shocking than none. But for women especially, bras, panties, bathing suits, and other stereotypical gear are visual reminders of a commercial, idealized feminine image that our real and diverse female bodies can't possibly fit. Without those visual references, each individual woman's body demands to be accepted on its own terms. We stop being comparatives. We begin to be unique.

Nobody commented on these events, of course. They just happened. The more hours and days we spent together, moving between locker room and exercise classes or pool and sauna, the less we resorted to the silky wisps or formidable elastic of our various underwear styles. Nudity was fine. Exercise leotards were also okay. They coated the body comfortably instead of chopping it up into horizontal strips. But gradually, skinny bikinis, queen-size slips, girdles, and other paraphernalia begin to disappear from our bodies and our lockers, like camouflage in a war we no longer had to fight.

"I've always loved fancy lingerie," said one woman, "but it's beginning to look weird to me."

"That's why my husband likes black garter belts," said a Rubenesque woman in a towel. "They look the *most* weird."

"Did you ever hear the story about Judy Holliday?" asked a woman peeling off a sweaty leotard. "When she went for a movie interview, the head of the studio started chasing her around the desk. So she just reached into her dress, pulled out her falsies, and handed them to him. 'Here,' she said, 'I think this is what you want.' "

"My God," said a big-breasted woman who, by *Playboy*'s standards, should have been very happy. "If only I could do that!"

Gradually there was also less embarrassment about appendectomy scars, stretch marks, Cesarean incisions, and the like. Though I had always resented the anthropological double standard by which scars are supposed to be marks of courage on a male body but marks of ugliness on a female one, I began to realize that I had been assessing such wounds in masculine terms nonetheless. Dueling scars, war wounds, scars-as-violence—those images were part of the reason I had assumed such marks to be shocking on men as well as on women.

But many of women's body scars have a very different context and thus an emotional power all their own. Stretch marks and Cesarean incisions from giving birth are very different from accident, war, and fight scars. They evoke courage without violence, strength without cruelty, and even so, they're far more likely to be worn with diffidence than bragging. That gives them a moving, bittersweet power, like seeing a room where a very emotional event in our lives once took place.

There were other surgical scars that seemed awesome to me, too, but not as evocative as those from childbirth. How do women survive even the routine physical price of skin stretched to its limit? After one Cesarean birth, where do some women find the courage to attempt several more?

True, there are tribal societies that treat women who give birth like honorary male warriors, but that is paying too much honor to war. Childbirth is more admirable than conquest, more amazing than self-defense, and as courageous as either one. Yet one of the strongest, most thoughtful feminists I know still hides in one-piece bathing suits to conceal her two Cesarean scars. And one of the most hypocritical feminists I know (that is, one who loves feminism but dislikes women) had plastic surgery to remove the tiny scar that gave her face character.

Perhaps we'll only be fully at ease with ourselves when we can appreciate scars as symbols of experience, often experiences that other women share, and see our bodies as unique chapters in a shared story.

To do that, we need to be together unself-consciously. We need the regular sight of our diverse reality to wear away the plastic-stereotypical-perfect image against which we've each been encouraged to measure ourselves. The impossible goal of "what we should look like" has worn a groove in our brains. It will take the constant intimacy of many new images to blast us out.

So, from my belated beginnings, I write in praise of diverse women.

- A cheerful, seventyish woman with short white curls held back by an orange ribbon, wearing a satiny green leotard that hugs her gently protruding stomach like a second skin. From her, I learn the beauteous curve of a nonflat stomach. I also learn that a great-grandmother can touch her toes with more flexibility than I, and can leave me panting in aerobic-dance class.

- A small, sturdy young masseuse with strong hands: she dreams of buying a portable massage table so that she can start a business of her own. "My boyfriend's grandmother has arthritis real bad," she explains, "but I massage her hands every day to stop the pain." She also has insomniac clients she massages into drug-free sleep, and clients with painful knots of tension she relaxes through direct pressure. We agree that, if everyone had one good massage a day, there would be fewer wars. From her, I learn there is sisterly satisfaction, not subservience, in serving other women's bodies.

- Two women friends who speak only Spanish and whose arrival causes uncertainty among locker mates who speak no Spanish at all. From them, we soon learn that the language of bodies and gestures is universal.

- A perfectly egg-shaped woman sits upright and serene in the nude sunbathing area every day, proving beyond doubt that only female curves of breasts and stomach make the Buddha image believable.

- A beautiful, tall, slender young woman whose legs dangle from her torso, scarecrowlike, as she leaps in exercise class. Older, stouter women are much more graceful in their movements, and, God knows, more in time with the music. From her, I learn that beauty may be skin-deep, but natural rhythm is deeper.

- A fiftyish locker-room attendant, under five feet tall, jogs five miles every morning. "My husband used to go with me but he had to stop," she says. "The cold air froze his lungs." We are discussing the need for this spa to offer judo or some other self-defense class, and this gray-haired woman agrees. Why? Because she was attacked in the parking lot by a six-foot-tall man with a cement block in his hand; yet she fought him off with self-defense tactics that included a hard blow to the groin. From her, I learn that a small woman can be to a big man what a bullet is to Jell-O.

- A new, no-nonsense athletic director is trying hard to persuade traditional women clients that there's more to fitness than the tape measure and the scale. Since the spa management is still convinced that only men are interested in fitness and health, but women want beauty and pampering, she is relieved at my complaint to management that men in the same spa get cardiovascular and muscle-flexibility tests while women have to request them and pay extra. From each other, we learn the activist value of pressure from both outside and inside any system.

• A tall, calm, dark-haired mother and her tall, calm, dark-haired daughter talk together about their mutual profession of social work, but mostly they seem companionable without needing to talk. A woman's body has given birth to a friend.

• A tough, witty criminal lawyer wants to figure out how to use her legal talents to advance other women. She gifts us with an epigram: "Most men want their wives to have a jobette."

• A no-nonsense young beautician gives a pore-cleaning facial and a discourse on cosmetic surgery at the same time. "I've seen all kinds of scars—breast implants, chin tucks, face lifts, eyelid tucks. There was a woman in here who had such a bad eyelid job that she couldn't close her eyes." I wait to hear some resentment of rich women with little to do but revise their faces, but I am wrong. "Poor things," says the beautician, digging away expertly. "I wouldn't trade places for any amount of money." More silence. "I'm only planning to have a chin tuck myself."

• A few women sit quietly in the steam room, each immersed in a cloud of vapor, her own muscle pains, and her own thoughts. Two newcomers arrive and get help from veterans of a day or two. "Start on the first bench—it gets hotter as you go up."

"Use this ice for your forehead."

"Don't stay more than five minutes the first time." Together, we make a small misty world of diverse sizes, shapes, and colors: a quiet place that cares about the welfare of strangers. The steam that surrounds us seems to communicate our thoughts.

"It's nice that you can come here by yourself or with a group of women," says a voice from the mist.

"And not feel like a nut," finishes another.

"I thought I'd be embarrassed," says a young voice. "I've never been with a bunch of women like . . . like *this* before."

Laughter comes from the steamy Buddha in the corner. "Honey," she says, "what you see is what you get."

• When I return home, caffeine free, sugar free, and relatively healthy, I ask a few much younger women about their experiences of seeing women's bodies. I had assumed this generation would be more at ease than mine, but the spa's younger guests have shaken my faith. From random answers, I learn that though no one is wearing underwear into the shower anymore, this nonverbal consciousness-raising still isn't an accepted part of younger women's lives.

"There's no real place where we can be together like that," says a high-school student thoughtfully. "Sports aren't important, and I don't know anybody who goes to the gym or to a steam bath. It just doesn't happen."

Meanwhile, two editors have reminded me that an evening in a Turkish bath in Jerusalem turned out to be one of the high points of a feminist tour of Israel that *Ms.* magazine organized a few years ago. It was an unexpected bonding among strangers at the beginning of the tour—"instant sisterhood"—and a realization of the beauty of women's bodies on their own terms. The few women who had missed that evening felt they were one step behind the group's intimacy for the rest of the trip.

I had listened to this same story when the tour group came home, but I just hadn't heard. Like other basic experiences, this one is better possessed than described.

But now I know. I know that fat or thin, mature or not, our bodies wouldn't give us such unease if we learned their place in the rainbow spectrum of women. Even great beauties seem less distant, and even mastectomies seem less terrifying, when we stop imagining and try to see them as they really are.

Changing media images would help, but that isn't enough. Like the children who were shown photographs of women and men doing nontraditional jobs—women welding, for instance, and men diapering babies— but reversed those roles in their memories within a few weeks, we only retain a complete image when we have a complete experience. A one-dimensional remedy can't cure a three-dimensional wrong.

Now, like the teenage heroine of *Gypsy,* who is aware of her body only after she becomes a stripper, too many of us experience female bodies, our own and others, in social settings and private bedrooms, only when they are most isolated, artificial, self-conscious, and on display for men.

A little natural togetherness would show us, the Family of Woman, where each of us is beautiful and no one is the same.

—1981

The Importance of Work

*T*oward the end of the 1970s, *The Wall Street Journal* devoted an eight-part, front-page series to "the working woman"—that is, the influx of women into the paid-labor force—as the greatest change in American life since the Industrial Revolution.

Many women readers greeted both the news and the definition with cynicism. After all, women have always worked. If all the productive work of human maintenance that women do in the home were valued at its replacement cost, the gross national product of the United States would go up by 26 percent. It's just that we are now more likely than ever before to leave our poorly rewarded, low-security, high-risk job of homemaking (though we're still trying to explain that it's a perfectly good one and that the problem is male society's refusal both to do it and to give it an economic value) for more secure, independent, and better-paid jobs outside the home.

Obviously, the real work revolution won't come until all productive work is rewarded—including child rearing and other jobs done in the home—and men are integrated into so-called women's work as well as vice versa. But the radical change being touted by the *Journal* and other media is one part of that long integration process: the unprecedented flood of women into salaried jobs, that is, into the labor force as it has been male-defined and previously occupied by men. We are already more than 41 percent of it—the highest proportion in history. Given the fact that women also make up a whopping 69 percent of the "discouraged labor force" (that is, people who need jobs but don't get counted in the unemployment statistics because they've given up looking), plus an official female unemployment rate that is substantially higher than men's, it's clear that we could expand to become fully half of the national work force by 1990.

Faced with this determination of women to find a little independence and to be paid and honored for our work, experts have rushed to ask: "Why?" It's a question rarely directed at male workers. Their basic motivations of survival and personal satisfaction are taken for granted. Indeed, men are regarded as "odd" and therefore subjects for sociological study and journalistic reports only when they *don't* have work, even if they are rich and don't need jobs or are poor and can't find them. Nonetheless, pollsters and sociologists have gone to great expense to prove that women work outside the home because of dire financial need, or if we persist despite the presence of a wage-earning male, out of some desire to buy "little extras" for our families, or even out of good old-fashioned penis envy.

Job interviewers and even our own families may still ask salaried women the big "Why?" If we have small children at home or are in some job regarded as "men's work," the incidence of such questions increases. Condescending or accusatory versions of "What's a nice girl like you doing in a place like this?" have not disappeared from the workplace.

How do we answer these assumptions that we are "working" out of some pressing or peculiar need? Do we feel okay about arguing that it's as natural for us to have salaried jobs as for our husbands—whether or not we have young children at home? Can we enjoy strong career ambitions without worrying about being thought "unfeminine"? When we confront men's growing resentment of women competing in the work force (often in the form of such guilt-producing accusations as "You're taking men's jobs away" or "You're damaging your children"), do we simply state that a decent job is a basic human right for everybody?

I'm afraid the answer is often no. As individuals and as a movement, we tend to retreat into some version of a tactically questionable defense: "Womenworkbecausewehaveto." The phrase has become one word, one key on the typewriter—an economic form of the socially "feminine" stance of passivity and self-sacrifice. Under attack, we still tend to present ourselves as creatures of economic necessity and familial devotion. "Womenworkbecausewehaveto" has become the easiest thing to say.

Like most truisms, this one is easy to prove with statistics. Economic need *is* the most consistent work motive—for women as well as men. In 1976, for instance, 43 percent of all women in the paid-labor force were single, widowed, separated, or divorced, and working to support themselves and their dependents. An additional 21 percent were married to men who had earned less than ten thousand dollars in the previous year, the minimum then required to support a family of four. In fact, if you take men's pensions, stocks, real estate, and various forms of accumulated wealth into account, a good statistical case can be made that there are more women who "have" to work (that is, who have neither the accumulated wealth, nor husbands whose work or wealth can support them for the rest of their lives) than there are men with the same need. If we were going to ask one group "Do you really need this job?", we should ask men.

But the first weakness of the whole "have to work" defense is its deceptiveness. Anyone who has ever experienced dehumanized life on welfare or any other confidence-shaking dependency knows that a paid job may be preferable to the dole, even when the handout is coming from a family member. Yet the will and self-confidence to work on one's own can diminish as dependency and fear increase. That may explain why—contrary to the "have to" rationale—wives of men who earn less than three thousand dollars a year are actually *less* likely to be employed than wives whose husbands make ten thousand dollars a year or more.

Furthermore, the greatest proportion of employed wives is found among families with a total household income of twenty-five to fifty thousand dollars a year. This is the statistical underpinning used by some sociologists to prove that women's work is mainly important for boosting families into the middle or upper middle class. Thus, women's incomes are largely used for buying "luxuries" and "little extras": a neat double-whammy that renders us secondary within our families, and makes our jobs expendable in hard times. We may even go along with this interpretation (at least, up to the point of getting fired so a male can have our job). It preserves a husbandly ego-need to be seen as the primary breadwinner, and still allows us a safe "feminine" excuse for working.

But there are often rewards that we're not confessing. As noted in *The Two-Career Couple,* by Francine and Douglas Hall: "Women who hold jobs by choice, even blue-collar routine jobs, are more satisfied with their lives than are the full-time housewives."

In addition to personal satisfaction, there is also society's need for all its members' talents. Suppose that jobs were given out on only a "have to work" basis to both women and men—one job per household. It would be unthinkable to lose the unique abilities of, for instance, Eleanor Holmes Norton, the distinguished chair of the Equal Employment Opportunity Commission. But would we then be forced to question the important work of her husband, Edward Norton, who is also a distinguished lawyer? Since men earn more than twice as much as women on the average, the wife in most households would be more likely to give up her job. Does that mean the nation could do as well without millions of its nurses, teachers, and secretaries? Or that the rare man who earns less than his wife should give up his job?

It was this kind of waste of human talents on a society-wide scale that traumatized millions of unemployed or underemployed Americans during the Depression. Then, a one-job-per-household rule seemed somewhat justified, yet the concept was used to displace women workers only, create intolerable dependencies, and waste female talent that the country needed. That Depression experience, plus the energy and example of women who were finally allowed to work during the manpower shortage created by World War II, led Congress to reinterpret the meaning of the country's full-employment goal in its Economic Act of 1946. Full employment was officially defined as "the employment of those who want to work, without regard to whether their employment is, by some definition, necessary. This goal applies equally to men and to women." Since bad economic times are again creating a resentment of employed women— as well as creating more need for women to be employed—we need such a goal more than ever. Women are again being caught in a tragic double bind: We are required to be strong and then punished for our strength.

Clearly, anything less than government and popular commitment to this 1946 definition of full employment will leave the less powerful groups, whoever they may be, in danger. Almost as important as the financial penalty paid by the powerless is the suffering that comes from being shut out of paid and recognized work. Without it, we lose much of our self-respect and our ability to prove that we are alive by making some difference in the world. That's just as true for the suburban woman as it is for the unemployed steel worker.

But it won't be easy to give up the passive defense of "wework-becausewehaveto."

When a woman who is struggling to support her children and grandchildren on welfare sees her neighbor working as a waitress, even though that neighbor's husband has a job, she may feel resentful; and the waitress (of course, not the waitress's husband) may feel guilty. Yet unless we establish the obligation to provide a job for everyone who is willing and able to work, that welfare woman may herself be penalized by policies that give out only one public-service job per household. She and her daughter will have to make a painful and divisive decision about which of them gets that precious job, and the whole household will have to survive on only one salary.

A job as a human right is a principle that applies to men as well as women. But women have more cause to fight for it. The phenomenon of the "working woman" has been held responsible for everything from an increase in male impotence (which turned out, incidently, to be attributable to medication for high blood pressure) to the rising cost of steak (which was due to high energy costs and beef import restrictions, not women's refusal to prepare the cheaper, slower-cooking cuts). Unless we see a job as part of every citizen's right to autonomy and personal fulfillment, we will continue to be vulnerable to someone else's idea of what "need" is, and whose "need" counts the most.

In many ways, women who do not have to work for simple survival, but who choose to do so nonetheless, are on the frontier of asserting this right for all women. Those with well-to-do husbands are dangerously easy for us to resent and put down. It's easier still to resent women from families of inherited wealth, even though men generally control and benefit from that wealth. (There is no Rockefeller Sisters Fund, no J. P. Morgan & Daughters, and sons-in-law may be the ones who really sleep their way to power.) But to prevent a woman whose husband or father is wealthy from earning her own living, and from gaining the self-confidence that comes with that ability, is to keep her needful of that unearned power and less willing to disperse it. Moreover, it is to lose forever her unique talents

Perhaps modern feminists have been guilty of a kind of reverse snobbism that keeps us from reaching out to the wives and daughters of wealthy men; yet it was exactly such women who refused the restrictions of class and financed the first wave of feminist revolution.

For most of us, however, "womenworkbecausewehaveto" is just true enough to be seductive as a personal defense.

If we use it without also staking out the larger human right to a job, however, we will never achieve that right. And we will always be subject to the false argument that independence for women is a luxury affordable only in good economic times. Alternatives to layoffs will not be explored, acceptable unemployment will always be used to frighten those with jobs into accepting low wages, and we will never remedy the real cost, both to families and to the country, of dependent women and a massive loss of talent.

Worst of all, we may never learn to find productive, honored work as a natural part of ourselves and as one of life's basic pleasures.

—1979

The Time Factor

*P*lanning ahead is a measure of class. The rich and even the middle class plan for future generations, but the poor can plan ahead only a few weeks or days.

I remember finding this calm insight in some sociological text and feeling instant recognition. Yes, of course, our sense of time was partly a function of power, or the lack of it. It rang true even in the entirely economic sense the writer had in mind. "The guys who own the factories hand them down to their sons and great-grandsons," I remember a boy in my high school saying bitterly. "On this side of town, we just plan for Saturday night."

But it also seemed equally true of most of the women I knew— including myself—regardless of the class we supposedly belonged to. Though I had left my factory-working neighborhood, gone to college, become a journalist, and thus was middle class, I still felt that I couldn't plan ahead. I had to be flexible—first, so that I could be ready to get on a plane for any writing assignment (even though the male writers I knew launched into books and other long-term projects on their own), and then so that I could adapt to the career and priorities of an eventual husband and children (even though I was leading a rewarding life without either). Among the results of this uncertainty were a stunning lack of career planning and such smaller penalties as no savings, no insurance, and an apartment that lacked basic pieces of furniture.

On the other hand, I had friends who were married to men whose long-term career plans were compatible with their own, yet they still lived their lives in day-to-day response to any possible needs of their husbands and children. Moreover, the one male colleague who shared or even understood this sense of powerlessness was a successful black journalist and literary critic who admitted that even after twenty years he planned only one assignment at a time. He couldn't forget his dependence on the approval of white editors.

Clearly there is more to this fear of the future than a conventional definition of class could explain. There is also caste: the unchangeable marks of sex and race that bring a whole constellation of cultural injunctions against power, even the limited power of controlling one's own life.

We haven't yet examined time-sense and future planning as functions of discrimination, but we have begun to struggle with them, consciously or not. As a movement, women have become painfully conscious of too much reaction and living from one emergency to the next, with too little initiative and planned action of our own; hence many of our losses to a much smaller but more entrenched and consistent right wing.

Though the cultural habit of living in the present and glazing over the future goes deep, we've begun to challenge the cultural punishment awaiting the "pushy" and "selfish" women (and the "uppity" minority men) who try to break through it and control their own lives.

Even so, feminist writers and theorists tend to avoid the future by lavishing all our analytical abilities on what's wrong with the present, or on revisions of history and critiques of the influential male thinkers of the past. The big, original, and certainly courageous books of this wave of feminism have been more diagnostic than prescriptive. We need pragmatic planners and visionary futurists, but can we think of even one feminist five-year-plan? Perhaps the closest we have come is visionary architecture or feminist science fiction, but they generally avoid the practical steps of how to get from here to there.

Obviously, many of us need to extend our time-sense—to have the courage to plan for the future, even while most of us are struggling to keep our heads above water in the present. But this does not mean a flat-out imitation of the culturally masculine habit of planning ahead, living in the future, and thus living a deferred life. It doesn't mean the traditional sacrifice of spontaneous action, or a sensitive awareness of the present, that comes from long years of career education with little intrusion of reality, from corporate pressure to work now for the sake of a reward after retirement, or, least logical of all, from patriarchal religions that expect obedience now in return for a reward after death.

In fact, the ability to live in the present, to tolerate uncertainty, and to remain open, spontaneous, and flexible are all culturally female qualities that many men need and have been denied. As usual, both halves of the polarized masculine-feminine division need to learn from each other's experiences. If men spent more time raising small children, for instance, they would be forced to develop more patience and flexibility. If women had more power in the planning of natural resources and other long-term processes—or even in the planning of our own careers and reproductive lives—we would have to develop more sense of the future and of cause and effect.

An obsession with reacting to the present, feminine-style, or on controlling and living in the future, masculine-style, are both wasteful of time.

And time is all there is.

—1980

*O*nce upon a time (that is, just a few years ago), psychologists believed that the way we chose to communicate was largely a function of personality. If certain conversational styles turned out to be more common to one sex than the other (more abstract and aggressive talk for men, for instance, more personal and equivocal talk for women), then this was just another tribute to the influence of biology on personality.

Consciously or otherwise, feminists have challenged this assumption from the beginning. Many of us learned a big lesson in the sixties when our generation spoke out on the injustices of war, as well as of race and class; yet women who used exactly the same words and style as our male counterparts were less likely to be listened to or to be taken seriously. When we tried to talk about this and other frustrations, the lack of listening got worse, with opposition and even ridicule just around every corner. Only women's own meetings and truth telling began to confirm what we had thought each of us was alone in experiencing. It was also those early consciousness-raising groups that began to develop a more cooperative, less combative way of talking, an alternative style that many women have maintained and been strengthened by ever since.

The problem is that this culturally different form has remained an almost totally female event. True, it has helped many, many women arrive at understanding each other and working out strategies for action.

But as an influence on the culturally male style of public talking, it has remained almost as removed as its more domestic versions of the past.

One reason for our decade or so of delay in challenging existing styles of talking makes good tactical sense. Our first task was to change the words themselves. We did not feel included (and usage studies showed that, factually, we were not) in hundreds of such supposedly generic terms as *mankind* and *he, the brotherhood of man* and *statesman.* Nor could we fail to see the racial parallels to being identified as "girls" at advanced ages, or with first names only, or by our personal connection (or lack of one) to a member of the dominant group.

Hard as it was (and still is), this radical act of seizing the power to name ourselves and our experience was easier than taking on the politics of conversation. Documenting society-wide patterns of talking required expensive research and surveys. Documenting the sexism in words, and even conjuring up alternatives, took only one courageous woman scholar and a dictionary (for instance, *Guidelines for Equal Treatment of the Sexes,* the pioneering work of Alma Graham for McGraw-Hill). That was one good economic reason why such works were among the first and best by feminist scholars.

In retrospect, the second cause for delay makes less feminist sense— the long popularity of assertiveness training. Though most women needed to be more assertive (or even more aggressive, though that word was considered too controversial), many of these courses taught women how to play the existing game, not how to change the rules. Unlike the feminist assault on sexist language, which demanded new behavior from men, too, assertiveness training was more reformist than revolutionary. It pushed one-way change for women only, thus seeming to confirm mascu- line-style communication as the only adult model or the most effective one. Certainly, many individual women were helped, and many men were confronted with the educational experience of an assertive woman, but the larger impact was usually to flatter the existing masculine game of talk-politics by imitating it.

Since then, however, a few feminist scholars have had the time and resources to document conversational patterns of mixed- and single-sex groups, both here and in Europe. Traditional scholarship, influenced by feminism, has also begun to look at conversational styles as functions of power and environment. For instance, employees pursue topics raised by their employers more than the reverse, older people feel free to interrupt younger ones, and subordinates are more polite than bosses. Since women share all those conversational habits of the less powerful, even across the many lines of class and status that divide us, how accidental can that be?

Even the new feminist-influenced research has a long way to go in neutralizing the masculine bias of existing studies. For instance, *talking* is assumed to be the important and positive act, while *listening*, certainly a productive function, is the subject of almost no studies at all.

Nonetheless, there is enough new scholarship to document different styles, to point out some deficiencies in the masculine model of communicating, and to give us some ideas on how to create a synthesis of both that could provide a much wider range of alternatives for women *and* for men.

I

Have you assumed that women talk more than men—and thus may dominate in discussion if nowhere else? If so, you're not alone. Researchers of sex differences in language started out with that assumption. So did many feminists, who often explained women's supposedly greater penchant for talking as compensation for a lack of power to act.

In fact, however, when Dale Spender, an English feminist and scholar, surveyed studies of talkativeness for her recent book, *Man Made Language,* she concluded that "perhaps in more than any other research area, findings were in complete contradiction with the stereotype. . . . There has not been one study which provides evidence that women talk more than men, and there have been numerous studies which indicate that men talk more than women."

Her conclusion held true regardless of whether the study in question asked individuals to talk into a tape recorder with no group interaction; or compared men and women talking on television; or measured amounts of talk in mixed groups (even among male and female state legislators); or involved group discussions of a subject on which women might be expected to have more expertise. (At a London workshop on sexism and education, for instance, the five men present managed to talk more than their thirty-two female colleagues combined.)

Some studies of male silence in heterosexual couples might seem to counter these results, but Spender's research supports their conclusion that a major portion of female talk in such one-to-one situations is devoted to drawing the man out, asking questions, introducing multiple subjects until one is accepted by him, or demonstrating interest in the subjects he introduces. Clearly, male silence (or silence from a member of any dominant group) is not necessarily the same as listening. It might mean a rejection of the speaker, a refusal to become vulnerable through self-revelation, or a decision that this conversation is not worthwhile. Similarly, talking by the subordinate group is not necessarily an evidence of power. Its motive may be a Scheherazade-like need to intrigue and thus survive, or simply to explain and justify one's actions.

In addition to a generally greater volume of talk, however, men interrupt women more often than vice versa. This is true both in groups and in couples. Male interruptions of women also bring less social punishment than female interruptions of men. Men also interrupt women more often than women interrupt each other.

Moreover, males are more likely to police the subject matter of conversation in mixed-sex groups. One study of working-class families showed that women might venture into such "masculine" topics as politics or sports, and men might join "feminine" discussions of domestic events, but in both cases, it was the men who ridiculed or otherwise straightened out nonconformers who went too far. Even in that London workshop on sexism, for instance, the concrete experiences of the female participants were suppressed in favor of the abstract, general conclusions on sexism that were preferred by the men. The few males present set the style for all the females.

How did the myth of female talkativeness and conversational dominance get started? Why has this supposed female ability been so accepted that many sociologists, and a few battered women themselves, have even accepted it as a justification for some men's violence against their wives?

The uncomfortable truth seems to be that the amount of talk by women has been measured less against the amount of men's talk than against the expectation of female silence.

Indeed, women who accept and set out to disprove the myth of the talkative woman may pay the highest price of all. In attempting to be the exceptions, we silence ourselves. If that is so, measuring our personal behavior against real situations and real studies should come as a relief, a confirmation of unspoken feelings.

We are not crazy, for instance, if we feel that, when we finally do take the conversational floor in a group, we are out there in exposed verbal flight, like fearful soloists plucked from the chorus. We are not crazy to feel that years of unspoken thoughts are bottled up inside our heads, and come rushing out in a way that may make it hard to speak calmly, even when we finally have the chance.

Once we give up searching for approval by stifling our thoughts, or by imitating the male norm of abstract, assertive communicating, we often find it easier to simply say what needs to be said, and thus to earn respect and approval. Losing self-consciousness and fear allows us to focus on the content of what we are saying instead of on ourselves.

Women's well-developed skill as listeners, perhaps the real source of our much-vaunted "intuition," should not be left behind. We must retain it for ourselves and teach it to men by bringing it with us into our work and daily lives, but that will only happen if we affirm its value. Female culture does have a great deal to contribute to the dominant one. Furthermore, women might feel better about talking equally, selecting subjects, and even interrupting occasionally if we took the reasonable attitude that we are helping men to become attentive and retentive listeners, too. We are paying them the honor of communicating as honestly as we can and treating them as we would want to be treated. After all, if more men gained sensitive listening skills, they would have "intuition," too.

These are practical exercises for achieving a change in the balance of talk. Try tape-recording a dinner-table conversation or meeting (in the guise of recording facts, so participants don't become self-conscious about their talk politics), then play the tape back to the same group, and ask them to add up the number of minutes talked, interruptions, and subject introductions for each gender. Or give a dozen poker chips to each participant in a discussion, and require that one chip be given up each time a person speaks. Or break the silence barrier for those who rarely talk by going around the room once at the beginning of each meeting, consciousness-raising-style, with a question that each participant must answer personally, even if it's only a self-introduction. (It is said that the British Labour party was born only after representatives of its warring factions spent an hour moving their conference table into a larger room. That one communal act broke down individual isolation, just as one round of communal speaking helps break the ice.)

If such methods require more advance planning or influence on the group than you can muster, or if you're trying to sensitize just one person, try some individual acts. Discussing the results of studies on who talks more can produce some very healthy self-consciousness in both women and men. If one group member speaks rarely, try addressing more of your own remarks to her (or him) directly. On the other hand, if one man (or woman) is a domineering interrupter, try objecting directly, interrupting in return, timing the minutes of his or her talk, or just being inattentive. If someone cuts you off, say with humor, "That's one," then promise some conspicuous act when the interruptions get to three. Keep score on "successful" topic introductions, add them up by gender, and announce them at the discussion's end.

If questions and comments following a lecture come mostly from men, stand up and say so. It may be a learning moment for everyone. The prevalence of male speakers in mixed audiences has caused some feminist lecturers to reserve equal time for questions from women only.

To demonstrate the importance of listening as a positive act, try giving a quiz on the content of female and male speakers. Hopefully you *won't* discover the usual: that men often remember what male speakers say better than they remember female speakers' content; that women often remember male content better, too, but that women listen and retain the words of *both* sexes somewhat better than men do.

Check the talk politics concealed in your own behavior. Does your anxiety level go up (and your hostess instincts quiver) when women are talking and men are listening, but not the reverse? For instance, men often seem to feel okay about "talking shop" for hours while women listen, but women seem able to talk in men's presence for only a short time before feeling anxious, apologizing, and encouraging the men to speak. If you start to feel wrongly uncomfortable about making males listen, try this exercise: *keep on talking*, and encourage your sisters to do the same. Honor men by treating them as honestly as you treat women. You will be allowing them to learn.

II

*Here are three popular assumptions: (1) Women talk about them-
selves, personalize, and gossip more than men do. (2) Men would rather
talk to groups of men than to mixed groups, and women prefer mixed
groups to all-female ones. (3) Women speakers and women's issues are
hampered by the feminine style of their presentation.* As you've probably guessed by now, most evidence is to the contrary of all three
beliefs.

After recording the conversational themes of single-sex and mixed-
sex groups, for instance, social psychologist Elizabeth Aries found that
men in all-male groups were more likely to talk about themselves than
were women in all-female ones. Men were also more likely to use
self-mentions to demonstrate superiority or aggressiveness, while women
used them to share an emotional reaction to what was being said by
others.

Phil Donahue, one of the country's most experienced interviewers,
capsulizes the cultural difference between men and women this way: "If
you're in a social situation, and women are talking to each other, and one
woman says, 'I was hit by a car today,' all the other women will say,
'You're kidding! What happened? Where? Are you all right?' In the same
situation with males, one male says, 'I was hit by a car today.' I guarantee
you that there will be another male in the group who will say, 'Wait till I
tell you what happened to *me*.' "

If quantity of talking about oneself is a measure of "personalizing,"
and self-aggrandizement through invoking the weakness of others is one
characteristic of gossip, then men may be far more "gossipy" than
women—especially when one includes sexual bragging.

In addition, subjects introduced by males in mixed groups are far more
likely to "succeed" than subjects introduced by women, and, as Aries
concluded, women in mixed groups are more likely to interact with men
than with other women. Thus, it's not unreasonable to conclude that
mixed groups spend more time discussing the lives and interests of male
participants than of female ones.

On the other hand, research by Aries and others shows that women are
more likely to discuss human relationships. Since "relationships" often
fall under "gossip" in men's view, this may account for the frequent male

observation that women "personalize" everything. Lecturers often comment, for instance, that women in an audience ask practical questions about their own lives, while men ask abstract questions about groups or policies. When the subject is feminism, women tend to ask about practi-cal problems. Men are more likely to say something like, "But how will feminism impact the American family?"

To quote Donahue, who deals with mostly female audiences: "I've always felt a little anxious about the possibility of a program at night with a male audience. The problem as I perceive it—and this is a generalization—is that men tend to give you a speech, whereas women will ask a question and then listen for the answer and make another contribution to the dialogue. In countless situations I have a male in my audience stand up and say in effect, 'I don't know what you're arguing about; here's the answer to this thing.' And then proceed to give a mini-speech."

Aries also documented the more cooperative, rotating style of talk and leadership in women-only groups: the conscious or unconscious habit of "taking turns." As a result, women actually prefer talking in their own single-sex groups for the concrete advantages of both having a conversational turn and being listened to. On the other hand, she confirmed research that shows male-only groups to have more stable hierarchies, with the same one or several talkers dominating most of the time.

As Aries points out, no wonder men prefer the variation and opportunity of mixed-sex audiences. They combine the seriousness of a male presence with more choice of styles—and, as Spender adds caustically, the assurance of at least some noncompetitive listeners.

Women's more gentle delivery, "feminine" choice of adjectives, and greater attention to grammar and politeness have been heavily criticized. Linguist Robin Lakoff pioneered the exposure of "ladylike" speech as a double bind that is both required of little girls, and used as a reason why, as adults, they may not be seen as forceful or serious. (Even Lakoff seems to assume, however, that female speech is to be criticized as the deficient form, while male speech is the norm and thus escapes equal comment.) Sociologist Arlie Hochschild also cites some survival techniques of racial minorities that women of all races seem to share: playing dumb and dissembling, for instance, or expressing frequent approval of others.

But whether this criticism of female speech patterns is justified or not, there is also evidence that a rejection of the way a woman speaks is often a way of blaming or dismissing her without dealing with the content of what she is saying.

For instance, women speakers are more likely to hear some version of "You have a good point, but you're not making it effectively," or "Your style is too aggressive/weak/loud/quiet." It is with such paternalistic criticisms that male politicians often dismiss the serious message of a female colleague, or that husbands turn aside the content of arguments made by their wives.

It is also such criticisms that allow women candidates to be rejected without dealing with the substance of the issues they raise. When Bella Abzug of New York and Gloria Schaeffer of Connecticut both ran for political office in one recent year, each was said to have a personal style that would prevent her from being an effective senator: Abzug because she was "too abrasive and aggressive," and Schaeffer because she was "too ladylike and quiet." Style was made the central issue by the press, and thus became one in the public-opinion polls. Both were defeated.

There are three anomalies that give away this supposedly "helpful" criticism. First, it is rarely used when a woman's message is not challenging to male power. (How often are women criticized for being too fierce in defense of their families? How often was Phyllis Schlafly criticized for being too aggressive in her opposition to the Equal Rights Amendment?) Second, the criticism is rarely accompanied by real support, even when the critic presents himself (or herself) as sympathetic. (Women political candidates say they often get critiques of their fund-raising techniques instead of cash, even from people who agree with them on issues.) Finally, almost everyone, regardless of status, feels a right to criticize. (Women professors report criticism of their teaching style from young students, as do women bosses from their employees.)

Just as there is a conversational topic that men in a group often find more compelling than any introduced by a woman (even when it's exactly the same topic, but reintroduced by a man), or a political issue that is "more important" than any of concern to women, so there is usually a better, more effective style than the one a woman happens to be using.

Men would support us, we are told, if only we learned how to ask for their support in the right way. It's a subtle and effective way of blaming the victim.

What can we do to break through these stereotypes? Keeping notes for one meeting or one week on the male/female ratio of gossip or self-mentions could be educational. Declaring a day's moratorium on all words that end in "—tion" and all generalities might encourage men to state their personal beliefs *without* disguising them as general conclusions.

As a personal exercise, try countering slippery abstractions with tangible examples. When David Susskind and Germaine Greer were guests on the same television talk show, for instance, Susskind used general, pseudoscientific statements about women's monthly emotional changes as a way of excusing the injustices cited by this very intelligent woman. Finally, Greer turned politely to Susskind and said, "Tell me, David. Can you tell if I'm menstruating right now—or not?" She not only eliminated any doubts raised by Susskind's statements, but subdued his pugnacious style for the rest of the show.

Men themselves are working to break down the generalities and competitiveness that a male-dominant culture has imposed on them. Some are meeting in all-male consciousness-raising groups, learning how to communicate more openly and personally among themselves.

Many women are also trying to break down the barriers we ourselves maintain. For instance, women's preference for talking to one another has a great deal to do with the shorthand that shared experience provides. Furthermore, the less powerful group usually knows the powerful one much better than vice versa—blacks have had to understand whites in order to survive, women have had to know men—yet the powerful group can afford to regard the less powerful one as a mystery. Indeed, the idea of differentness and the Mysterious Other may be necessary justifications for the power imbalance and the lack of empathy it requires.

One result is that, even when the powerful group *wants* to listen, the other may despair of talking: it's just too much trouble to explain. Recognizing this unequal knowledge encourages women to talk about themselves to men, at least to match the time they spend talking about themselves. After all, they cannot read our minds.

On issues of style, role reversals are enlightening. For instance, ask a man who is critical of "aggressive" women to try to argue a serious political point while speaking "like a lady." A woman candidate might also ask critics to write a speech in the style they think she should use. Responding in kind can create a quick reversal. There's a certain satisfaction to saying, in the middle of a man's impassioned speech: "I suppose you have a point to make, but you're not expressing it well. Now, if you just used more personal examples. If you changed your language, your timing, and perhaps your suit. . . ."

Finally, if all talk fails, try putting the same message in writing. The point is to get your message across, whether or not the man in question can separate it from the medium.

III

Women's higher-pitched voices and men's lower ones are the result of physiology. Because deep voices are more pleasant and authoritative, women speakers will always have a problem. Besides, female facial expressions and gestures aren't as forceful . . . and so on. It's true that tone of voice is partly created by throat-construction and the resonance of bones. Though there is a big area of male-female overlap in voice tone, as well as in size, strength, and other physical attributes, we assume that all men will have a much deeper pitch than all women.

In fact, however, no one knows exactly how much of our speaking voices are imitative and culturally produced. Studies of young boys before puberty show that their vocal tones may deepen *even before physiological changes can account for it*. They are imitating the way the males around them speak. Dale Spender cites a study of males who were not mute, but who were born deaf and thus unable to imitate sound. Some of them never went through an adolescent voice change at all.

Whatever the mix of physiological and cultural factors, however, the important point is that the *acceptance* of vocal tone is definitely cultural and therefore subject to change.

In Japan, for instance, a woman's traditionally high-pitched, soft speaking voice is considered a very important sexual attribute. (When asked in a public-opinion poll what attribute they found most attractive in women, the majority of Japanese men said "voice.") Though trained to speak in upper registers, Japanese women, like many of their sisters around the world, often speak in lower tones when men are not present.

They may even change their language as well. (A reporter's tapes of Japanese schoolgirls talking among themselves caused a scandal. They were using masculine word endings and verbs in a country where the language is divided into formally masculine and feminine forms.) Thus, Japanese men may find a high voice attractive not for itself but for its tribute to a traditional subservience.

Some American women also cultivate a high, childish, or whispery voice à la Marilyn Monroe. We may sense that a woman is talking to a man on the other end of the phone, or a man to a woman, because she lightens her normal tone and he deepens his.

A childlike or "feminine" vocal style becomes a drawback, however, when women try for any adult or powerful role. Female reporters were kept out of television and radio for years by the argument that their voices were too high, grating, or nonauthoritative to speak the news credibly. Even now, women's voices may be thought more suitable for human interest and "soft news," while men still announce "hard news." In the early days of television, women were allowed to do the weather reports— very sexily. When meteorology and weather maps became the vogue, however, most stations switched to men. Even now, 85 percent of all voice-overs on television ads, including those for women's products, are done by men. Even on floor wax and detergents, men are likely to be the voices of expertise and authority.

In the long run, however, men may suffer more from cultural restrictions on tone of voice than women do. Linguist Ruth Brend's study of male and female intonation patterns in the United States, for instance, disclosed four contrasting levels used by women in normal speech, but only three levels used by men. This isn't a result of physiology: men also have at least four levels available to them, but they rarely use the highest one. Thus, women may speak publicly in both high and low tones with some degree of social acceptability, but men must use their lower tones only. It's okay to flatter the ruling class with imitation, just as it's okay for women to wear pants or for blacks to speak and dress like Establishment whites, but it's less okay for men to wear feminine clothes, for whites to adopt black speech and street style, or for men to imitate or sound like women. (Such upper-class exceptions as the female-impersonating shows put on by the Hasty Pudding Club at Harvard or by the very rich men of the Bohemian Grove in California seem to indicate that even ridicule of women requires security. It's much less likely to happen at the working-class level of bowling clubs and bars.)

As the price of "masculinity," men as a group are losing variety in their speech and an ability to express a full range of emotions. The higher proportion of masculine monotones is also a penalty to the public ear.

In the same way, physical expressiveness may be viewed as "feminine." Women can be vivacious. We are allowed more varieties of facial expression and gestures. Men must be rocklike. Certainly, some emotive and expressive men are being imprisoned by that belief.

The down side is that women's greater range of expression is also used to ridicule females as emotionally unstable. That sad point is made by Nancy Henley in *Body Politics: Power, Sex, and Nonverbal Communication*. "Women's facial expressivity," she explains, "has been allowed a wider range than men's, encompassing within the sex stereotype not only pleasant expressions, but negative ones like crying." Since males are encouraged to leave crying and other emotional expression in their childhoods, females who retain this human ability are often compared to children.

Nonetheless, women's wider range also allows us to recognize more physical expression when we see it. Henley refers to a study showing that women of all races and black men usually do better than white men at identifying nonverbal emotional clues. We're both less imprisoned by the rocklike mask of being in control, and more needful of the survival skill of paying attention.

In short, women need to affirm and expand expressiveness, but men are also missing some major ways of signalling the world and getting signals back.

You can't change vocal cords (theirs or ours), but you can make sure they're being well used. Tape-record women talking together, then record the same people talking to men. It's a good way to find out whether we're sending out geishalike tonal clues. Some women are neglecting our lower range. Others, especially when trying to be taken seriously, are overcompensating for supposed emotionalism by narrowing to a "reasonable" monotone. Men may also change under pressure of taped evidence: for instance, the contrast between their dullness when talking with men and their expressiveness when talking to children. Many actors, female and male, are living testimonials to how much and how quickly—with effort, exercise, and freedom—a vocal range can change.

Most important, remember that there is nothing *wrong* with women's voices, and no subject or emotion they cannot convey. This is especially important for women who are lonely tokens. The first women in law and business schools, the board room, or the assembly line, often report that the sound of their own voices comes as a shock—a major barrier to reciting in class, speaking up on policy, or arguing in union meetings. It may take a while for words said in a female voice to be taken seriously, but a head-turning response to the unusual sound is also a tribute to its owner as a courageous pioneer.

The advent of video recorders is a major breakthrough in understanding and changing our nonverbal expressions. Watching the incontrovertible evidence of how we come across to others can be more useful than years of psychiatry. Many men and boys could also benefit from such expressiveness exercises as a game of charades, or communicating with children. Women and girls can free body movements through sports, a conscious effort to take up more space when sitting or standing, and using body language we may now use only when relaxed with other women. Many of us could benefit from watching female impersonators and learning the many ways in which we have been trained to be female impersonators, too.

*T*he point is not that one gender's cultural style is superior to the other's. The current "feminine" style of communicating may be better suited to, say, the performing arts, medical diagnosis, and conflict resolution. It has perfected emotional expressiveness, careful listening, and a way of leaving an adversary with dignity intact. The current "masculine" style may be better suited to, say, procedural instruction, surgical teams and other situations requiring hierarchical command, and job interviews. It has perfected linear and abstract thinking, quick commands, and a willingness to speak well of oneself or present views with assertiveness. But we will never achieve this full human circle of expression if women imitate the male "adult" style. We have to teach as well as learn.

A feminist assault on the politics of talking, and listening, is a radical act. It's a way of transforming the cultural vessel in which both instant communication and long-term anthropological change are carried. Unlike the written word, or visual imagery, or any form of communication divorced from our presence, talking and listening won't allow us to hide. There is no neutral page, image, sound, or even a genderless name to protect us. We are demanding to be accepted and understood by all the senses and for our whole selves.

That's precisely what makes the change so difficult. And so crucial.

—1981

*F*or much of the female half of the world, food is the first signal of our inferiority. It lets us know that our own families may consider female bodies to be less deserving, less needy, less valuable.

In many poor countries, mothers often breastfeed sons for two years or more, especially when other food is scarce or uncertain. Daughters are usually nursed for less than half that time.

What happens in the mind of a girl child who is denied her own mother's body, or in the mind of her brother who is not?

In India and other countries where the poor must make painful choices, female infanticide is often carried out by the denial of scarce food and health care. Its practice is so common that a ratio of only eighty females to one hundred males is the norm in some parts of the country.

Economists say that scarcity increases value, but that rule doesn't seem to hold when the commodity is female. Mothers of daughters, no matter how poor their health, are expected to bear more and more children until they have sons. Families of bridegrooms go right on demanding dowries from the families of brides. If someone pays the price of scarcity, it seems to be the women themselves. Brides may be kidnapped from neighboring areas. The childbearing burden of a woman may be increased because her husband's brothers have no wives.

The cultural belief in a female's lesser worth goes so deep that many women accept and perpetuate it. "Food distribution within the family arises from the deliberate self-deprivation by women," concludes a 1974 study of nutrition in India, "because they believe that the earning members (and the male members who are potential earning members) are more valuable than those who do domestic work and the child rearing, which they consider devoid of economic value."

What happens to the spirits of women who not only deprive themselves but police the deprivation of their daughters?

Even in this wealthier, luckier country, we may know more than we admit. Black slave women and indentured white women were advertised as breeders or workers, and also as assets who would eat and cost less than males. The hard-working farm women of the frontier served men and boys more plentifully and first, yet the toll of their own hard work and childbearing was so great that the two-mother family was the average: most men married a second time to replace a first wife who died of childbirth, disease, or fatigue. Within our own memories, there are wives and daughters of immigrant families who served meals to fathers and brothers first, sometimes eating only what was left on the men's plates. Right now, tired homemakers save the choice piece of meat for the "man of the house" or "growing boys" more often than for their growing daughters or themselves. Millions of women on welfare eat a poor and starchy diet that can permanently damage the children they bear, yet their heavy bodies are supposed to signify indulgence. Even well-to-do women buy the notion that males need better food, more protein, and more strength. They grow heavy on sugar or weak on diets while preparing good food for their families. Does a woman alone prepare a meal differently for a male guest than for another woman—or for herself? *Perhaps food is still the first sign of respect—or the lack of it—that we pay to each other and to our bodies.*

Of course, women have rebelled. We can guess that from knowing ourselves. We can also guess it from the elaborate, punitive systems that exist to punish female rebellion.

In many areas of Africa and Asia, strict taboos reserve the most valued sources of energy and nourishment for males. Red meat, fish, poultry, eggs, milk, even some fruits and vegetables—each is forbidden to females in some parts of the world. The explanation of these taboos may be a euphemism (for instance, that eating red meat will make women "like men"), or it may play on women's deepest fear (for instance, that drinking milk will destroy a woman's value by making her sterile), but these cultural restrictions go very deep. Some women students from Africa observe them even after years of living in Europe or America. Others report anxiety and nausea when they first force themselves to eat an egg or an orange.

With or without taboos, food itself may be used as punishment or reward. In many cultures, husbands and fathers ration out food from family storerooms to which they alone hold the key. Wives are accountable not only for what they eat but for children, extended family, and servants as well. Even in wealthier societies, wives may be disciplined or rewarded with the treat of "eating out," or given a strict family food budget that holds them accountable for the whole household. In times of inflation, women may be expected to stretch the shrinking food dollar with impossible ingenuity. For instance, when world food prices skyrocketed in the 1970s, a study of families in Great Britain showed that 75 percent of husbands made no increase at all in the housekeeping money they allowed their wives. No wonder food has become a primary source of identity for women.

Some cultures go beyond external controls. In tribal societies of Ethiopia, for instance, a young girl's entry into womanhood and marriageability is marked by the pulling of several crucial teeth, a ritual in the name of beauty that serves to make eating, especially of much-coveted meat, permanently difficult. A gap-toothed smile is regarded as feminine. So are the heavy ankle bracelets a female is bound by at puberty. (Think of the bound feet of the upper-class women of China.) In the same tribes, male decoration is suspiciously confined to body-painting or hair matted with clay and braids—nothing that restricts movement, eating, or freedom.

To deprive females of equal nourishment increases the male food supply and decreases rebellion among wives and daughters. But like all oppression, it is dangerous in the long run.

Poorly nourished women give birth to less healthy children, males as well as females. Even cultures that selectively reward pregnant women with better feeding rarely make up completely for the damage already done in the name of sexual politics. In extreme cases, high infant mortality, poor brain development, and protein-deficiency diseases are the results of poor maternal nutrition, and none of these is any respecter of gender.

We don't have to look far from our own doors to find infant mortality rates and protein deficiency that surpass almost any other industrialized country. The United States is producing ever-growing generations of an impoverished underclass; yet political resistance to food stamps, adequate welfare payments, even feeding programs confined to infants and pregnant or breastfeeding women, continues to increase. So does resistance to the job-training programs, child-care centers, and punishment of sex discrimination in the work place, all of which would allow women to support themselves and their children.

The short-term goal of saving money is cited in all of the above cases; yet that goal is rarely mentioned when discussing the many billions of dollars spent on the military. A dead certain, immediate loss of human talent is simply considered less important than a possible future loss of military superiority.

It makes you wonder: Is the fear of independent women so great, consciously or unconsciously, that our "profamily" leadership will choose short-term female dependency over the country's long-term self-interest? Do they maintain the example of poor women—or any women who can't survive without the goodwill and protection of a man—as a constant reminder to keep us all in line?

Surely women can learn from the politics of food that arguments of enlightened self-interest aren't enough. Sometimes only rebellion will do.

Facts may persuade us of the need to rebel.

The Myth. Males need more and better food because they do more work.

The Fact. According to the United Nations, females do one-third of the paid work in the world, and two-thirds of all work, paid and unpaid. In industrialized societies like the United States, homemakers work harder than any other class of worker: an average of 99.6 hours a week. In Latin America, females make up at least 50 percent of the agricultural labor force, and as much as 90 percent in Africa and Asia. In many societies, most women have two jobs, inside the home and outside it, while most men have only one.

The Myth. Given the famine and malnutrition suffered by much of the world, it is diversionary to focus on how food is distributed. The first and perhaps only question should be how to create more food.

The Fact. The earth already produces enough food to nourish all of its inhabitants. The politics of distribution are the major reason for hunger and starvation. As the Swedish Nutrition Foundation and other international study groups concluded years ago, the use of food and starvation as a political weapon is even more destructive than bacteriological warfare or other weapons that affect all people equally, precisely because withholding nutrition afflicts pregnant women, nursing mothers, and children preferentially.

The Myth. There is no consistent attitude toward females. Some cultures like plump women while others prefer thin ones. It's all a matter of personal preference and style.

The Fact. What is rare and possessed only by the powerful is envied as a symbol of power. Thus, poor societies with little food produce an ideal of feminine beauty that is plump and available only to the rich. Pashas, African chieftains, and American robber barons sometimes force-fed or otherwise fattened up their women as testimonies to their wealth. In more fortunate societies where women become plump on starch and sugar if nothing else, leanness and delicacy in women are rare and envied. Nonetheless, the common denominators are weakness, passivity, and lack of strength. Rich or poor, feminine beauty is equated with subservience to men. Lower-class women, who have to do physical labor and develop some degree of strength, are made to envy this weakness. Middle Eastern peasant women envied and imitated the protection and restriction of the veil that began with women who were the possessions of upperclass men. American farm and factory women may envy the thinness and artifice of the rich.

To many women who are both working for a salary and raising children, life as a childbearer and hostess for a well-to-do man may look desirable by comparison.

Freedom can only be imagined.

*T*hanks to the contagious ideas of feminism, however, imaginations have been working overtime.

Poor women are demanding both the practical means to control the endless births that endanger their health, and improved maternal and infant nutrition to make those fewer children healthier and more likely to survive. This major focus of women in poorer, agricultural countries is also important among the poor inside wealthy, industrialized countries like ours. We may know, for instance, that most poor women in the United States still don't have access to adequate contraception and safe abortion. But do we know that African doctors training here have diagnosed kwashiorkor, the disease that produces the yellow skin and bloated bellies of African famines, in our own inner cities?

Middle-class women are beginning to cultivate fitness and strength. Bodybuilders, everyday joggers, tennis champions, and Olympic athletes have begun to challenge the equation of beauty with weakness. Even upper-class women no longer tolerate the hothouse delicacy that testified to male protection.

All women need strength—health, muscles, endurance—if we are to literally change the world.

Do we think of this as we imagine beauty? Or crave empty calories? Or pass our politics of food on to children and younger sisters?

It will take a lot of nourishment to grow the world's longest revolution.

—1980

*I*f you travel around this country, you can't miss it: networking is becoming to this decade what consciousness-raising was to the last. It's a primary way women discover that we are not crazy, the system is. We also discover that mutual-support groups can create change where the most courageous individual woman could not.

If we've already experienced consciousness-raising (or a feminist book club, mothers' support group—whatever we call the feminist revolutionary cell in our lives), then a women's network built around work or some other shared concern may support the logical next steps in activism and learning. If we missed the sanity-saving revelations of sexual politics that those small C-R groups provided (and still do provide), then truth telling inside networks may produce similar revelations and give us similar support.

But there is a problem. Unlike the old consciousness-raising groups, the new networks are often seen as imitative of Establishment tactics. Some do exclude unsuccessful women instead of breaking down barriers for women as a group, but most suffer only from an image problem that comes from the terms themselves. *Networks* or even *old girls' networks* raise the echo of old boys' clubs in our brains. Though consciousness-raising is also derivative as a concept, its references include the "speaking bitterness" of the Chinese revolution, the "testifying" of the black civil rights movement, the personal support of Alcoholics Anonymous, and other models of profound change. *Networks* may conjure up the status quo.

That is, until you put *women's* in front of it. And until you realize that it's used generically to include everything from specialized national coalitions like the National Women's Health Network or the Feminist Computer Technology Project to such local luncheons and information exchanges as the Women's Forum in New York or the Philadelphia Forum for Executive Women.

In the psychology of naming, I've noticed that networks with *Forum* in the title seem to be the most elitist, while those with words like *Support Group* or *Caucus* tend to be the least so. The city-wide networks that cut across the tops of many professions are also more likely to end up with status as the key ingredient, while those organized around a particular issue or institution tend to include the whole spectrum of women it affects.

More important, the most consistent women's usage of *network* is not as a noun but as a verb. It's a process, not an end in itself. In that sense, *networking* comes across as loosely knit and lateral, a contrast with the more closed, hierarchical style of such male counterparts as professional associations, fraternal orders, interlocking directorates, and old boys' networks themselves.

To be honest, however, there is a problem with content, that is, with what a few women's networks are actually doing. Especially if organized by women dependent on a very male-dominated profession, networks can go through painful, approval-seeking stages of assuming that Establishment opposition will surely melt if only we are "good girls": if only we stick to the narrowest definition of work-related issues, for instance, and don't identify with women as a group by saying a word like "feminist" or by supporting such "unrelated" issues as the Equal Rights Amendment.

Usually, this stage is short-lived. Where money and power are involved, most "good girls" soon find they get the same opposition anyway. Even the sight of a table full of women lunching together in the dining room can get a reaction from male superiors. When Mary Scott Welch wrote a description of successful networking by women at Equitable Life Assurance and the United Storeworkers, she also reported on some less-enlightened employers whose executives ripped down meeting notices and sent female "spies" to report on quite innocent proceedings.

The timidity and conformity of women in some job-related networks are alarming, but that may be one inevitable hazard of organizing around jobs we depend on but don't control.

Such cautious behavior is often condemned by other women as male imitative (by which they mean that women are seeking approval from men and not each other), but, in fact, it is culturally very female indeed. A parallel group of men would be far less likely to count on likability and approval when facing a powerful employer and far more likely to go for collective power.

Even poor, black, Hispanic, and other discriminated-against men seem better able to identify their own self-interest than are most women of any race. It's hard to imagine an organization of Jewish media executives who wouldn't support their own inclusion in the U.S. Constitution, for instance, or a black newscaster who would refuse to join the NAACP because he had to report on racist events. Yet I recently met with one group of sophisticated New York media women, nearly all strong feminists as individuals, who undermined the pro-ERA boycott of unratified states by going without protest to a professional meeting in one of those states. And one of the most prominent women on television, self-identified as a feminist, insists that she cannot contribute to pro-equality groups, or even join the National Organization for Women, because she must report on anti-equality events. In fact, there are still a couple of professional women's networks that are debating whether to use the controversial word *women* in their group names at all.

For sad if obvious reasons, women (especially white women who are seduced by access to the powerful) are the only discriminated-against group whose members seem to think that, if they don't take themselves seriously, someone else will.

As for access, we might take the valuable advice of Carolyn Reed, head of the National Committee on Household Employment. "As a household worker," she said, "I've never confused access with influence."

These problems of networks should serve as a caution, but no discouragement. Carol Kleiman describes hundreds of diverse and successful groups in her book, *Women's Networks: The Complete Guide to Getting a Better Job, Advancing Your Career and Feeling Great as a Woman Through Networking*. Whether they are organized around alco-

holism or architecture, for women's studies or against violence, they tend
to be unconventionally inclusive of women who share that interest across
lines of race, age, class, life-style, or education. They are usually trying
hard to invent open structures and flexible tactics to advance themselves
and their sisters at the same time.

In fact, there are real and functional differences between incumbent
networks who try to guard power, and insurgent networks who try to
disperse it.

We might feel better about our networking sisters, and understand the
survival value of having some female turf in our own lives, if we outlined
these distinctions. For instance:

Women tend to define power differently. Given notions of masculinity, the hierarchical nature of corporations, and the prevalence of inherited wealth, traditional definitions of power have a lot to do with the
ability to dominate other people and benefit unfairly from their work.
This is remarkably distant from the meritocracy that the Establishment
professes, and it doesn't lead to much democratic competition or structure In fact, if you excluded inheritors of wealth and managers of
so much investment money that *not* making a profit might be a challenge, most "old boys' networks" would be decimated. Even at that,
I'm optimistically assuming that male entrepreneurs would survive, but
equal responsibility for raising their own children would cut down their
ranks, too.

We as women, on the other hand, tend to define power as the ability to
use our own talents and to control our own lives. When we are tempted to
act out power's traditional meaning of dominance, the cultural punishments for such "unfeminine" behavior are so great that we tend to pull
back, even at our worst, to the use of guilt and quiet manipulation.

In fact, women's uses of power are so different that management
consultants are now studying women's management style as a source of
more cooperative or collaborative forms, for instance, the habit of saying
"Here's what needs to be done," instead of the usual "You must do this";
or sharing credit by name with everyone who contributes to a project.

Even our much-lamented inability to delegate has an "up" side. We
may end by working as hard or harder than any of our employees, and that
can be leadership by example.

Obviously, we need to learn the useful parts of the more hierarchical, "masculine" style. But no more than most men need to learn the useful parts of ours.

When it comes to content, women's conviction that power has to be earned (especially by women) leads to an emphasis on individual excellence, knowledge, and learning. One network of high-level women already on corporate boards, for instance, meets regularly for the sole purpose of being lectured by the best women economists and management experts. (They had no objection to being lectured by the best men, but found that they tended to condescend.) The percentage of female managers who return for advanced degrees and training far exceeds that of their male counterparts, even though companies are still more likely to subsidize training for men.

When women work in groups instead of being dispersed through existing structures, the differences are easier to see. Hierarchies are usually weaker, more likely to be based on who does the most work, and less likely to be based on status in the outside world. (Even those few professional networks that use salary as a membership criterion usually say "*should* be earning"; a recognition of the fact that few women are getting paid what they are worth.) Meetings are short on formalities or the use of titles and very long on thanking lists of people for working.

Perhaps most distinctive of all, these networks often state a goal that few Establishment groups would consider—"empowerment," that is, giving power to other women.

Like an immigrant group out to pull ourselves up by our bootstraps, women may help each other with public speaking, confidence building, solutions to professional problems, announcements of job openings, or lists of women-owned businesses and services to support. Considering our training to look to men for expertise and authority, it's a victory that we now empower each other as professionals by seeking out women physicians and gynecologists (for whom the demand now exceeds the supply), women rabbis and ministers for group ceremonies, women audio technicians for our meetings and concerts, women stock analysts for our investments, and women piano tuners, company plane pilots, security guards, and carpenters for home or office.

"We're not lowering our standards," said a Houston woman when challenged on her group's choice of a woman architect. "We may even be raising them. Statistically speaking, women professionals had to be better to get where they are."

Even the most traditional skills take on a new meaning. For instance, a retired designer has for years contributed beautifully made clothes to her congresswoman, and a Minnesota homemaker extends the political effectiveness of Koryne Horbal—former United States representative to the United Nations Commission on the Status of Women—by helping to answer her voluminous mail.

More and more, we're seeing the empowerment of another woman as a reciprocal gift. That's a long way from Tom Wolfe's classic definition of power as "making them jump!"

Even when activist networks start out as exclusive, inclusiveness often takes root as good tactics. Suppose you organized a network of all the women corporate vice-presidents in Los Angeles. It would be interesting, and the members could exchange a useful parallel or two. But they wouldn't learn anything additional about their own corporations and, if they got help with a career move, it would mainly be a lateral one.

Suppose instead that each vice-president was part of a network within her own corporation, from women lower down in the hierarchy (including the president's secretary) to those up the line (including the only woman on the board). Clearly, that vice-president could gain information from the president's secretary, as well as unusual access to a board member. If she wanted to move within the company, she would be more likely to know about openings. If she wanted to move elsewhere, she might have a valuable recommendation from a member of her own board. At the same time, the board member would have gained firsthand knowledge of a company for which she is legally liable, and the secretary could have got help with a promotion and unusual access to people at the top.

This boundary-crossing value is especially high where women's numbers are small. According to the United States Bureau of Labor Statistics, about 48 percent of all jobs come through personal contacts. Since we are rarely part of the masculine lines of personal communication, we had better create our own.

At the Women's Media Group in New York, for instance, women rise at expensive monthly lunches, during what is known as the "bulletin board," to announce jobs they need filled or tout the talents of junior colleagues. Since some women executives started out as secretaries themselves, they may have a better understanding of that job's impor- tance and see it as both a step to promotion and a source of valuable advice. "Secretaries know everything," explained one member of a university network that includes faculty and faculty wives as well as clerical and cafeteria workers. "We give them respect, support, and job mobility. They tell us what's really going on."

Here are a few examples of such boundary-crossing networking that I've witnessed.

- One corporate wife forced her husband to raise his secretary's salary.

- One female United States government employee, on her own time and phone, called rape-prevention groups to let them know where federal research money was available.

- One very rich former newspaper publisher and one former Justice Department official—not the sort of women who are supposed to identify downward—both protested *Savvy* magazine's editorial treat- ment of secretaries. ("My dear," sniffed the former publisher, "they only write about how to get good ones, not about how to treat them better.")

- Several black feminists lobbied white male legislators, and several white feminists lobbied black male legislators (all by mutual agree- ment), thus allowing men to get educated on women's issues without feeling threatened by "their" women.

- A network of high-level academic women are supporting, at some professional risk, the discrimination suit of women faculty against Cornell University.

- A small women's caucus of a big California political organization lobbied internally and stopped it from endorsing candidates who opposed reproductive freedom.

One network at an eastern university exemplified the tactical virtues of diversity. First, students protested the lack of gynecological care in student-funded health services and even withheld their money, but nothing happened. Then, women faculty members spent months documenting unequal criteria for tenure, but nothing happened. Finally, telephone operators and other underpaid nonprofessional campus employees petitioned for salary increases, and nothing happened. But when all three groups networked in mutual support *and not one phone call went in or out of that university for a day*, something happened. Each group suddenly got one of its demands. Yet the telephone operators would have been fired if they had struck by themselves, without student and faculty support, and those student and faculty groups might still be trying to get their demands taken seriously, had it not been for the operators.

Finally, women's ability to make bridges out of their shared experience often benefits men, too. The CBS women's group established job ladders and career counseling that men have used as well. Sometimes such bridges built by women are international. The Irish Peace Movement was begun by both Catholic and Protestant women. Arab and Israeli women were meeting long before Camp David. There is even discussion of a joint statement to be made by American, Israeli, and PLO feminists.

Networks are psychic territory. Remember: women of every race are the only discriminated-against group with no territory, no country of our own, not even a neighborhood. Even powerless men can usually point to some part of the globe, past or present, where they were honored in authority—a place to travel, if only in imagination, and gain self-respect. Within their countries, those men also have neighborhoods and bars where they can gather freely. But women rarely do.

In a patriarchy, a poor man's house may be his castle, but even a rich woman's body is not her own.

That's why groups run by and for women are so important to us. They are our psychic turf; our place to discover who we are, or could become, as whole independent human beings. They help us to go beyond our secondary role in the family and in the workplace—to leave the tyranny of society's expectations behind.

They also force us to develop in ourselves those qualities and skills that, in mixed groups, we tend to assign to men.

A few hours a week or a month of making psychic territory can let us know that we are not alone and affirm a new reality. That reality assumes an even bigger importance in an era when national leadership and daily papers are full of top-down assumptions about "what the majority of Americans want," or, for that matter, who the majority is.

But our need may go deeper even than a need for a territory of our own. Since very few of us grew up with mothers who were allowed to be powerful in the world, we often feel motherless. Perhaps in the freedom and support of groups run by and for women, we are becoming each other's mothers.

If so, it's a need that also crosses boundaries.

Devaki Jain, a distinguished economist in India and a friend, has spent twenty years as a feminist working with women in her country. Though family planning, health care, and employment are all important, she has concluded that the most important single element in women's progress is this: one woman-run group outside the family and outside the work force; at least one structure in each woman's life that is a free place for women.

In India, this might be a handicraft cooperative as well as a social network, a group of women who talk by the well every day or a professional association. But without this source of confirmation and mutual support, women may not have the confidence to use the rights they already have, much less the strength to demand more.

Somewhere in our lives, each of us needs a free place, a little psychic territory. Do you have yours?

—1982

*I*n junior high school, I went out for basketball and tried to act like a boy . . . it was a disaster. . . . I've been a woman for three years now, and life is unbelievably satisfying.

—transsexual female

I had this fantasy of being male as far back as I can remember. . . . The surgery was a miracle. . . . My new girl friend depends on me to be the strong one.

—transsexual male

Ever since a tennis-playing ophthalmologist named Richard Raskind had genital surgery, hormone therapy, a change of wardrobe, and became a tennis-playing ophthalmologist named Renee Richards, transsexualism has been a fact in the public consciousness.

Unlike Christine Jorgensen, who made the same transsexual journey and wrote a book about it in the 1950s, Renee Richards arrived in the midst of a big and national wave of feminist activity that is challenging both the justice and the biological basis of sex roles. Unlike Jorgensen, therefore, Richards was and is treated not only as a bizarre exception, an individual choice, but also as an example of sex-role change (and thus a frightening instance of what feminism could lead to) or as a living proof that feminism isn't necessary. After all, if a man wants so badly to be a woman, why can't biological females be happy with what they've got?

Most of all, Richards was greeted with publicity, and an amazing amount of acceptance. Though I'm sure that she herself suffered from ridicule and public attention, the champions of this transsexual woman were surprising in number and identity. Tennis professionals and sports journalists who had fought tooth and nail against equality for women in tennis, and especially against equal prize money, now agitated for Richards's right to play in women's tournaments. They challenged women players who objected as being anti–civil libertarian, poor sports, or cowards who feared they would lose. *The New York Times,* where women who specifically request the use of "Ms." are still denied it, cheerfully changed not only the name of Renee Richards (and other transsexuals) but also the gender of every single pronoun in news stories. Television and other parts of the media produced a commercial boomlet of articles on transsexualism, even though the first young men who challenged the traditional masculine role by refusing to fight in Vietnam had waited months, sometimes years, for equally sympathetic or explanatory coverage. Finally, every active woman on any talk show seemed to be challenged with questions about Renee Richards.

It was this enormous publicity that first made me suspicious. At a minimum, it was a diversion from the widespread problems of sexual inequality. After all, the estimated ten thousand Americans who view themselves as members of the opposite sex, plus the approximately three thousand who have undergone transsexual surgery, hardly balance the millions of women who work at home for no pay, outside the home for unequal pay, subsist on welfare, and struggle to support their own children. When I got the inevitable Renee Richards questions, therefore, I simply defended her right to change her own body if she wished, but pointed out that she was an exception that had little to do with the plight of most women.

The more I listened to the questions, however, the more I realized something else was going on. For one thing, only male-to-female transsexuals were famous. Though biological women had undergone drastic surgery and hormone changes to become men, and had made that change public, their names were not household words. Jorgensen and Richards had been publicized worldwide, as had James Humphrey Morris, a writer and former British Army officer who became Jan Morris, the best-known example of transsexualism in Britain. For another thing, the questions about tennis had a certain glee in them, as if Richards had changed identity only to prove that any man, even an unnatural one, could beat any woman.

When I probed further, I discovered that male-to-female transsexuals were not only used as a handy testimony to the desirability of the traditional female role, but were also the only sort of sex change many interviewers could accept or imagine. For a man to give up his superior role and become a woman was easy—frightening, but no challenge. For a woman to rise out of her inferiority and achieve manhood, however, was unthinkable, impossible—just too big a job. Men were not about to accept even a former female as an equal, but they expected women to accept and even be honored by a former man.

Women tennis players, however, made very different arguments. Was it fair for women to face someone trained physically and culturally for forty years as a man? Like blacks who questioned the fairness of *Black Like Me*, a book by a white man who chemically and briefly darkened his skin, women were pointing out that a lifelong experience can't be duplicated by decree. Why should the hard-won seriousness of women's tennis be turned into a sensational circus by one transsexual? And finally, as one woman tennis professional explained, "If they don't let her play as a woman, they might have to let her play as a man. Then a woman—even a phony one—might beat men."

But the most eye-opening evidence came from the heartrending testimony of transsexuals themselves. As I began to read the medical and journalistic literature, one theme emerged. No matter how different their backgrounds or personalities, and regardless of whether their voyage was male-to-female or vice versa, transsexuals cited a deep conviction that their true personalities had been denied or restricted by the sex role assigned to them at birth. "I thought like a man," said one biological woman. "I felt like a woman," said a biological man. In a landmark doctoral thesis by Jan Raymond, a specialist in medical ethics at Boston College who analyzed in-depth interviews with transsexuals, those themes were repeated over and over again. Their most common expression was the sensation of having a female brain in a male body, or vice versa. But, as Raymond pointed out, "A female mind in a male body only makes sense as a concept in a society that accepts the reality of both."

In other words, transsexuals are paying an extreme tribute to the power of sex roles. In order to set their real human personalities free, they surgically mutilate their own bodies: anything to win from this biased society—where minor differences of hormones and genitals are supposed to dictate total lives and personalities—the right to be who they individually are as human beings.

Raymond understands the crushing societal forces that make transsexuals choose this self-punishment, but she mourns the loss of individuals who might have acted as critics and rebels in this sexually stereotyped society. Instead of accepting the idea of "a female mind in a male body" by mutilating their physical selves, they might have challenged the very idea that there is such a thing as a definitively female or male mind, and demonstrated that gender is only one of many elements that makes up each unique individual.

For that reason, she is also critical of the medical establishment that has grown up around the new possibility and the demand (and the big payments) for transsexual surgery plus long-term hormonal treatments. Instead of serving more lifesaving but often less lucrative needs for their surgical and hormone-therapy skills, some physicians are aiding individuals who are desperately trying to conform to an unjust society. It's a small group of successful physicians she names "the transsexual empire."

Of course, not all sexual surgery or hormone therapy is put to such use. Babies born with ambiguous genitalia are rescued by the same techniques, so their external selves conform to their internal chromosomal structure or reproductive capacities. So are some adults who could not otherwise perform the only physical functions restricted by gender—impregnation for males, gestation for females.

In a way, transsexuals themselves are also making a positive contribution by proving that chromosomes aren't everything. By ignoring this internal structure they cannot change, and focusing on external body appearances and socialization, they are demonstrating that both women and men have within them the full range of human possibilities. Unfortunately, this isn't a point made in the popular press. On the contrary, transsexualism is used mostly as a testimony to the importance of sex roles as dictated by a society obsessed with body image, genitals, and "masculine" or "feminine" behavior.

But the main question is whether some individuals are being forced into self-mutilation by the biases around them, and whether their self-mutilation is then used and publicized to prove that those biases are true.

Feminists are right to feel uncomfortable about the need for and the uses of transsexualism. Even while we protect the right of an informed individual to make that decision, and to be identified as he or she wishes, we have to make clear that this is not the goal we have in mind. The point is to transform society so that a female *can* "go out for basketball" and a male doesn't *have* to be "the strong one." Better to turn anger outward toward changing the world than inward toward transforming and mutilating bodies.

In the meantime, we shouldn't be surprised at the amount of publicity and commercial exploitation conferred on a handful of transsexuals. Sex-role traditionalists know a political tribute when they see one.

But the question remains: If the shoe doesn't fit, must we change the foot?

—1977

Why Young Women Are
More Conservative

*I*f you had asked me a decade or more ago, I certainly would have said the campus was the first place to look for the feminist or any other revolution. I also would have assumed that student-age women, like student-age men, were much more likely to be activist and open to change than their parents. After all, campus revolts have a long and well-publicized tradition, from the students of medieval France, whose "heresy" was suggesting that the university be separate from the church, through the anticolonial student riots of British India; from students who led the cultural revolution of the People's Republic of China, to campus demonstrations against the Shah of Iran. Even in this country, with far less tradition of student activism, the populist movement to end the war in Vietnam was symbolized by campus protests and mistrust of anyone over thirty.

It has taken me many years of traveling as a feminist speaker and organizer to understand that I was wrong about women; at least, about women acting on their own behalf. In activism, as in so many other things, I had been educated to assume that men's cultural pattern was the natural or the only one. If student years were the peak time of rebellion and openness to change for men, then the same must be true for women. In fact, a decade of listening to every kind of women's group—from brown-bag lunchtime lectures organized by office workers to all-night rap sessions at campus women's centers; from housewives' self-help groups to campus rallies—has convinced me that the reverse is more often true.

Women may be the one group that grows more radical with age. Though some students are big exceptions to this rule, women in general don't begin to challenge the politics of our own lives until later.

Looking back, I realize that this pattern has been true for my life, too. My college years were full of uncertainties and the personal conservatism that comes from trying to win approval and fit into the proper grown-up and womanly role, whether that means finding a well-to-do man to be supported by or a male radical to support. Nonetheless, I went right on assuming that brave exploring youth and cowardly conservative old age were the norms for everybody, and that I must be just an isolated and guilty accident. Though every generalization based on female culture has many exceptions, and should never be used as a crutch or excuse, I think we might be less hard on ourselves and each other as students, feel better about our potential for change as we grow older—and educate reporters who announce feminism's demise because its red-hot center is not on campus—if we figured out that for most of us as women, the traditional college period is an unrealistic and cautious time. Consider a few of the reasons.

As students, women are probably treated with more equality than we ever will be again. For one thing, we're consumers. The school is only too glad to get the tuitions we pay, or that our familes or government grants pay on our behalf. With population rates declining because of women's increased power over childbearing, that money is even more vital to a school's existence. Yet more than most consumers, we're too transient to have much power as a group. If our families are paying our tuition, we may have even less power.

As young women, whether students or not, we're still in the stage most valued by male-dominant cultures: we have our full potential as workers, wives, sex partners, and childbearers.

That means we haven't yet experienced the life events that are most radicalizing for women: entering the paid-labor force and discovering how women are treated there; marrying and finding out that it is not yet an equal partnership; having children and discovering who is responsible for them and who is not; and aging, still a greater penalty for women than for men.

Furthermore, new ambitions nourished by the rebirth of feminism may make young women feel and behave a little like a classical immigrant group. We are determined to prove ourselves, to achieve academic excellence, and to prepare for interesting and successful careers. More noses are kept to more grindstones in an effort to demonstrate newfound abilities, and perhaps to allay suspicions that women still have to have more and better credentials than men. This doesn't leave much time for activism. Indeed, we may not yet know that it is necessary.

In addition, the very progress into previously all-male careers that may be revolutionary for women is seen as conservative and conformist by outside critics. Assuming male radicalism to be the measure of change, they interpret any concern with careers as evidence of "campus conservatism." In fact, "dropping out" may be a departure for men, but "dropping in" is a new thing for women. Progress lies in the direction we have not been.

Like most groups of the newly arrived or awakened, our faith in education and paper degrees also has yet to be shaken. For instance, the percentage of women enrolled in colleges and universities has been increasing at the same time that the percentage of men has been decreasing. Among students entering college in 1978, women *outnumbered* men for the first time. This hope of excelling at the existing game is probably reinforced by the greater cultural pressure on females to be "good girls" and observe somebody else's rules.

Though we may know intellectually that we need to have new games with new rules, we probably haven't quite absorbed such facts as the high unemployment rate among female Ph.D.s; the lower average salary among women college graduates of all races than among counterpart males who graduated from high school or less; the middle-management ceiling against which even those eagerly hired new business-school graduates seem to bump their heads after five or ten years; and the barrier-breaking women in nontraditional fields who become the first fired when recession hits. Sadly enough, we may have to personally experience some of these reality checks before we accept the idea that lawsuits, activism, and group pressure will have to accompany our individual excellence and crisp new degrees.

Then there is the female guilt trip, student edition. If we're not sailing along as planned, it must be *our* fault. If our mothers didn't "do anything" with their educations, it must have been *their* fault. If we can't study as hard as we think we must (because women still have to be better prepared than men), and have a substantial personal and sexual life at the same time (because women are supposed to care more about relationships than men do), then we feel inadequate, as if each of us were individually at fault for a problem that is actually culture-wide.

I've yet to be on a campus where most women weren't worrying about some aspect of combining marriage, children, and a career. I've yet to find one where many men were worrying about the same thing. Yet women will go right on suffering from the double-role problem and terminal guilt until men are encouraged, pressured, or otherwise forced, individually and collectively, to integrate themselves into the "women's work" of raising children and homemaking. Until then, and until there are changed job patterns to allow equal parenthood, children will go right on growing up with the belief that only women can be loving and nurturing, and only men can be intellectual or active outside the home. Each half of the world will go on limiting the full range of its human talent.

Finally, there is the intimate political training that hits women in the teens and early twenties: the countless ways we are still brainwashed into assuming that women are dependent on men for our basic identities, both in our work and our personal lives, much more than vice versa. After all, if we're going to enter a marriage system that's still legally designed for a person and a half, submit to an economy in which women still average about fifty-nine cents on the dollar earned by men, and work mainly as support staff and assistants, or *co*-directors and *vice*-presidents at best, then we have to be convinced that we are not whole people on our own.

In order to make sure that we will see ourselves as half-people, and thus be addicted to getting our identity from serving others, society tries hard to convert us as young women into "man junkies"; that is, into people who are addicted to regular shots of male-approval and presence, both professionally and personally. We need a man standing next to us, actually and figuratively, whether it's at work, on Saturday night, or throughout life. (If only men realized how little it matters *which* man is standing there, they would understand that this addiction depersonalizes them, too.) Given the danger to a male-dominant system if young women stop internalizing this political message of derived identity, it's no wonder that those who try to kick the addiction—and, worse yet, to help other women do the same—are likely to be regarded as odd or dangerous by everyone from parents to peers.

With all that pressure combined with little experience, it's no wonder that younger women are often less able to support each other. Even young women who espouse feminist goals as individuals may refrain from identifying themselves as "feminist": it's okay to want equal pay for yourself (just one small reform) but it's not okay to want equal pay for women as a group (an economic revolution). Some retreat into individualized career obsessions as a way of avoiding this dangerous discovery of shared experience with women as a group. Others retreat into the safe middle ground of "I'm not a feminist but. . . . " Still others become politically active, but only on issues that are taken seriously by their male counterparts.

The same lesson about the personal conservatism of younger women is taught by the history of feminism. If I hadn't been conned into believing the masculine stereotype of youth as the "natural" time for freedom and rebellion, a time of "sowing wild oats" that actually is made possible by the assurance of power and security later on, I could have figured out the female pattern of activism by looking at women's movements of the past.

In this country, for instance, the nineteenth-century wave of feminism was started by older women who had been through the radicalizing experience of getting married and becoming the legal chattel of their husbands (or the equally radicalizing experience of *not* getting married and being treated as spinsters). Most of them had also worked in the antislavery movement and learned from the political parallels between race and sex. In other countries, that wave was also led by women who were past the point of maximum pressure toward marriageability and conservatism.

Looking at the first decade of this second wave, it's clear that the early feminist activist and consciousness-raising groups of the 1960s were organized by women who had experienced the civil rights movement, or homemakers who had discovered that raising kids and cooking didn't occupy all their talents. While most campuses of the late sixties were still circulating the names of illegal abortionists privately (after all, abortion could damage our marriage value), slightly older women were holding press conferences and speak-outs about the reality of abortions (including their own, even though that often meant confessing to an illegal act) and demanding reform or repeal of antichoice laws. Though rape had been a quiet epidemic on campus for generations, younger women victims were still understandably fearful of speaking up, and campuses encouraged silence in order to retain their reputation for safety with tuition-paying parents. It took many off-campus speak-outs, demonstrations against laws of evidence and police procedures, and testimonies in state legislatures before most student groups began to make demands on campus and local cops for greater rape protection. In fact, "date rape"—the common campus phenomenon of a young woman being raped by someone she knows, perhaps even by several students in a fraternity house—is just now being exposed. Marital rape, a more difficult legal issue, was taken up several years ago. As for battered women and the attendant exposé of husbands and lovers as more statistically dangerous than unknown muggers in the street, that issue still seems to be thought of as a largely noncampus concern, yet at many of the colleges and universities where I've spoken, there has been at least one case within current student memory of a young woman beaten or murdered by a jealous lover.

This cultural pattern of youthful conservatism makes the growing number of older women going back to school very important. They are life examples and pragmatic activists who radicalize women young enough to be their daughters. Now that the median female undergraduate age in this country is twenty-seven because so many older women have returned, the campus is becoming a major place for cross-generational connections.

None of this should denigrate the courageous efforts of young women, especially women on campus, and the many changes they've pioneered. On the contrary, they should be seen as even more remarkable for surviving the conservative pressures, recognizing societal problems they haven't yet fully experienced, and organizing successfully in the midst of a transient student population. Every women's history course, rape hot line, or campus newspaper that is finally covering *all* the news; every feminist professor whose job has been created or tenure saved by student pressure, or male administrator whose consciousness has been permanently changed; every counselor who's stopped guiding women one way and men another; every lawsuit that's been fueled by student energies against unequal athletic funds or graduate school requirements: all those accomplishments are even more impressive when seen against the backdrop of the female pattern of activism.

Finally, it would help to remember that a feminist revolution rarely resembles a masculine-style one—just as a young woman's most radical act toward her mother (that is, connecting as women in order to help each other get some power) doesn't look much like a young man's most radical act toward his father (that is, breaking the father-son connection in order to separate identities or take over existing power).

It's those father-son conflicts at a generational, national level that have often provided the conventional definition of revolution; yet they've gone on for centuries without basically changing the role of the female half of the world. They have also failed to reduce the level of violence in society, since both fathers and sons have included some degree of aggressiveness and superiority to women in their definition of masculinity, thus preserving the anthropological model of dominance.

Furthermore, what current leaders and theoreticians define as revolution is usually little more than taking over the army and the radio stations. Women have much more in mind than that. We have to uproot the sexual caste system that is the most pervasive power structure in society, and that means transforming the patriarchal values of those who run the institutions, whether they are politically the "right" or the "left," the fathers or the sons. This cultural part of the change goes very deep, and is often seen as too intimate, and perhaps too threatening, to be considered as either serious or possible. Only conflicts among men are "serious." Only a takeover of existing institutions is "possible."

That's why the definition of "political," on campus as elsewhere, tends to be limited to who's running for president, who's demonstrating against corporate investments in South Africa, or which is the "moral" side of some conventional revolution, preferably one that is thousands of miles away.

As important as such activities are, they are also the most comfortable ones when we're young. They provide a sense of virtue without much disruption in the power structure of our daily lives. Even when the most consistent energies on campus are actually concentrated around feminist issues, they may be treated as apolitical and invisible. Asked "What's happening on campus?" a student may reply, "The antinuke movement," even though that resulted in one demonstration of two hours, while student antirape squads have been patrolling the campus every night for two years and women's studies have begun to transform the very textbooks we read.

No wonder reporters and sociologists looking for revolution on campus often miss the depth of feminist change and activity that is really there. Women students themselves may dismiss it as not political and not serious. Certainly, it rarely comes in the masculine sixties style of bombing buildings or burning draft cards. In fact, it goes much deeper than protesting a temporary symptom—say, the draft—and challenges the right of one group to dominate another, which is the disease itself.

Young women have a big task of resisting pressures and challenging definitions. Their increasing success is a miracle of foresight and courage that should make us all proud. But they should know that they, too, may grow more radical with age.

One day, an army of gray-haired women may quietly take over the earth

—1979

Erotica vs. Pornography

*L*ook at or imagine images of people making love; really making love. Those images may be very diverse, but there is likely to be a mutual pleasure and touch and warmth, an empathy for each other's bodies and nerve endings, a shared sensuality and a spontaneous sense of two people who are there because they *want* to be.

Now look at or imagine images of sex in which there is force, violence, or symbols of unequal power. They may be very blatant: whips and chains of bondage, even torture and murder presented as sexually titillating, the clear evidence of wounds and bruises, or an adult's power being used sexually over a child. They may be more subtle: the use of class, race, authority, or just body poses to convey conqueror and victim; unequal nudity, with one person's body exposed and vulnerable while the other is armored with clothes; or even a woman by herself, exposed for an unseen but powerful viewer whom she clearly is trying to please. (It's interesting that, even when only the woman is seen, we often know whether she is there for her own pleasure or being displayed for someone else's.) But blatant or subtle, there is no equal power or mutuality. In fact, much of the tension and drama comes from the clear idea that one person is dominating another.

These two sorts of images are as different as love is from rape, as dignity is from humiliation, as partnership is from slavery, as pleasure is from pain. Yet they are confused and lumped together as "pornography" or "obscenity," "erotica" or "explicit sex," because sex and violence are so dangerously intertwined and confused. After all, it takes violence or the threat of it to maintain the unearned dominance of any group of human beings over another. Moreover, the threat must be the most persuasive wherever men and women come together intimately and are most in danger of recognizing each other's humanity.

The confusion of sex with violence is most obvious in any form of sadomasochism. The gender-based barrier to empathy has become so great that a torturer or even murderer may actually believe pain or loss of life to be the natural fate of the victim; and the victim may have been so deprived of self-respect or of empathetic human contact that she expects pain or loss of freedom as the price of any intimacy or attention at all. It's unlikely that even a masochist expects death. Nonetheless, "snuff" movies and much current pornographic literature insist that a slow death from sexual torture is the final orgasm and ultimate pleasure. It's a form of "suicide" reserved for women. Though men in fact are far more likely to kill themselves, male suicide is almost never presented as sexually pleasurable. But sex is also confused with violence and aggression in all forms of popular culture, and in respectable theories of psychology and sexual behavior as well. The idea that aggression is a "normal" part of male sexuality, and that passivity or even the need for male aggression is a "normal" part of female sexuality, are part of the male-dominant culture we live in, the books we learn from, and the air we breathe.

Even the words we are given to express our feelings are suffused with the same assumptions. Sexual phrases are the most common synonyms for conquering and humiliation (*being had*, *being screwed*, *getting fucked*); the sexually aggressive woman is a *slut* or a *nymphomaniac*, but the sexually aggressive man is just *normal*; and real or scientific descriptions of sex may perpetuate the same roles, for instance, a woman is always *penetrated* by a man though she might also be said to have *enveloped* him.

Obviously, untangling sex from aggression and violence or the threat of it is going to take a very long time. And the process is going to be greatly resisted as a challenge to the very heart of male dominance and male centrality.

But we do have the common sense of our bodies to guide us. Pain is a warning of damage and danger. If that sensation is not mixed with all the intimacy we know as children, we are unlikely to confuse pain with pleasure and love. As we discover our free will and strength, we are also more likely to discover our own initiative and pleasure in sex. As men no longer can dominate and have to find an identity that doesn't depend on superiority, they also discover that cooperation is more interesting than submission, that empathy with their sex partner increases their own pleasure, and that anxieties about their own ability to "perform" tend to disappear along with stereotyped ideas about masculinity.

But women will be the main fighters of this new sexual revolution. It is our freedom, our safety, our lives, and our pleasure that are mostly at stake.

We began by trying to separate sex and violence in those areas where the physical danger was and is the most immediate: challenging rape as the one crime that was considered biologically irresistible for the criminal and perhaps invited by the victim; refusing to allow male-female beatings to be classified as "domestic violence" and ignored by the law; exposing forced prostitution and sexual slavery as national and international crimes. With the exception of wife beating, those challenges were made somewhat easier by men who wanted to punish other men for taking their female property. Women still rarely have the power to protect each other.

Such instances of real antiwoman warfare led us directly to the propaganda that teaches and legitimizes them—pornography. Just as we had begun to separate rape from sex, we realized that we must find some way of separating pornographic depictions of sex as an antiwoman weapon from those images of freely chosen, mutual sexuality.

Fortunately, there is truth in the origin of words. *Pornography* comes from the Greek root *porné* (harlot, prostitute, or female captive) and *graphos* (writing about or description of). Thus, it means a description of either the purchase of sex, which implies an imbalance of power in itself, or sexual slavery.

This definition includes, and should include, all such degradation, regardless of whether it is females who are the slaves and males who are the captors or vice versa. There is certainly homosexual pornography, for instance, with a man in the "feminine" role of victim. There is also role-reversal pornography, with a woman whipping or punishing a man, though it's significant that this genre is created by men for their own pleasure, not by or for women, and allows men to *pretend* to be victims— but without real danger. There could also be lesbian pornography, with a woman assuming the "masculine" role of victimizing another woman.

That women rarely choose this role of victimizer is due to no biological superiority, but a culture that doesn't addict women to violence. But whatever the gender of the participants, all pornography is an imitation of the male-female, conqueror-victim paradigm, and almost all of it actually portrays or implies enslaved woman and master.

Even the 1970 Presidential Commission on Obscenity and Pornography, whose report is often accused of suppressing or ignoring evidence of the causal link between pornography and violence against women, defined the subject of their study as pictorial or verbal descriptions of sexual behavior characterized by "the degrading and demeaning portrayal of the role and status of the human female."

In short, pornography is not about sex. It's about an imbalance of male-female power that allows and even requires sex to be used as a form of aggression.

Erotica may be the word that can differentiate sex from violence and rescue sexual pleasure. It comes from the Greek root *eros* (sexual desire or passionate love, named for Eros, the son of Aphrodite), and so contains the idea of love, positive choice, and the yearning for a particular person. Unlike pornography's reference to a harlot or prostitute, *erotica* leaves entirely open the question of gender. (In fact, we may owe its sense of shared power to the Greek idea that a man's love for another man was more worthy than love for a woman, but at least that bias isn't present in the word.) Though both erotica and pornography refer to verbal or pictorial representations of sexual behavior, they are as different as a room with doors open and one with doors locked. The first might be a home, but the second could only be a prison.

The problem is that there is so little erotica. Women have rarely been free enough to pursue erotic pleasure in our own lives, much less to create it in the worlds of film, magazines, art, books, television, and popular culture—all the areas of communication we rarely control. Very few male authors and filmmakers have been able to escape society's message of what a man should do, much less to imagine their way into the identity of a woman. Some women and men are trying to portray equal and erotic sex, but it is still not a part of popular culture.

And the problem is there is so much pornography. This underground stream of antiwoman propaganda that exists in all male-dominant societies has now become a flood in our streets and theaters and even our homes. Perhaps that's better in the long run. Women can no longer pretend pornography does not exist. We must either face our own humiliation and torture every day on magazine covers and television screens or fight back. There is hardly a newsstand without women's bodies in chains and bondage, in full labial display for the conquering male viewer, bruised or on our knees, screaming in real or pretended pain, pretending to enjoy what we don't enjoy. The same images are in mainstream movie theaters and respectable hotel rooms via closed-circuit TV for the traveling businessman. They are brought into our own homes not only in magazines, but in the new form of video cassettes. Even video games offer such features as a smiling, rope-bound woman and a male figure with an erection, the game's object being to rape the woman as many times as possible. (Like much of pornography, that game is fascist on racial grounds as well as sexual ones. The smiling woman is an Indian maiden, the rapist is General Custer, and the game is called "Custer's Revenge.") Though "snuff" movies in which real women were eviscerated and finally killed have been driven underground (in part because the graves of many murdered women were discovered around the shack of just one filmmaker in California), movies that simulate the torture murders of women are still going strong. (*Snuff* is the porn term for killing a woman for sexual pleasure. There is not even the seriousness of a word like *murder*.) So are the "kiddie porn" or "chicken porn" movies and magazines that show adult men undressing, fondling, and sexually using children; often with the titillating theme that "fathers" are raping "daughters." Some "chicken porn" magazines offer explicit tips on how to use a child sexually without leaving physical evidence of rape, the premise being that children's testimony is even less likely to be believed than that of adult women.

Add this pornography industry up, from magazines like *Playboy* and *Hustler*, to movies like *Love Gestapo Style*, *Deep Throat*, or *Angels in Pain,* and the total sales come to a staggering eight billion dollars a year—more than all the sales of the conventional film and record industry combined. And that doesn't count the fact that many "conventional" film and music images are also pornographic, from gynocidal record jackets like the famous *I'm "Black and Blue" from the Rolling Stones—and I Love It!* (which showed a seminude black woman bound to a chair) to the hundreds of teenage sex-and-horror movies in which young women die sadistic deaths and rape is presented not as a crime but as sexual excitement. Nor do those industries include the sales of the supposedly "literary" forms of pornography, from *The Story of O* to the works of the Marquis de Sade.

If Nazi propaganda that justified the torture and killing of Jews were the theme of half of our most popular movies and magazines, would we not be outraged? If Ku Klux Klan propaganda that preached and even glamorized the enslavement of blacks were the subject of much-praised "classic" novels, would we not protest? We know that such racist propaganda precedes and justifies the racist acts of pogroms and lynchings. We know that watching a violent film causes test subjects to both condone more violence afterward and to be willing to perpetuate it themselves. Why is the propaganda of sexual aggression against women of all races the one form in which the "conventional wisdom" sees no danger? Why is pornography the only media violence that is supposed to be a "safety valve" to satisfy men's "natural" aggressiveness somewhere short of acting it out?

*T*he first reason is the confusion of *all* nonprocreative sex with pornography. Any description of sexual behavior, or even nudity, may be called pornographic or obscene (a word whose Latin derivative means *dirty* or *containing filth*) by those who insist that the only moral purpose of sex is procreative, or even that any portrayal of sexuality or nudity is against the will of God.

In fact, human beings seem to be the only animals that experience the same sex drive and pleasure at times when we can and cannot conceive. Other animals experience periods of heat or estrus. Humans do not.

Just as we developed uniquely human capacities for language, planning, memory, and invention along our evolutionary path, we also developed sexuality as a form of expression, a way of communicating that is separable from our reproductive need. For human beings, sexuality can be and often is a way of bonding, of giving and receiving pleasure, bridging differentness, discovering sameness, and communicating emotion.

We developed this and other human gifts through our ability to change our environment, adapt to it physically, and so in the very long run to affect our own evolution. But as an emotional result of this spiraling path away from other animals, we seem to alternate between periods of exploring our unique abilities and feelings of loneliness in the unknown that we ourselves have created, a fear that sometimes sends us back to the comfort of the animal world by encouraging us to look for a sameness that is not there.

For instance, the separation of "play" from "work" is a feature of the human world. So is the difference between art and nature, or an intellectual accomplishment and a physical one. As a result, we celebrate play, art, and invention as pleasurable and important leaps into the unknown; yet any temporary trouble can send us back to a nostalgia for our primate past and a conviction that the basics of survival, nature, and physical labor are somehow more worthwhile or even more moral.

In the same way, we have explored our sexuality as separable from conception: a pleasurable, empathetic, important bridge to others of our species. We have even invented contraception, a skill that has probably existed in some form since our ancestors figured out the process of conception and birth, in order to extend and protect this uniquely human gift. Yet we also have times of atavistic suspicion that sex is not complete, or even legal or intended by God, if it does not or could not end in conception.

No wonder the very different concepts of "erotica" and "pornography" can be so confused. Both assume that sex can be separated from conception; that human sexuality has additional uses and goals. This is the major reason why, even in our current culture, both may still be condemned as equally obscene and immoral. Such gross condemnation of all sexuality that isn't harnessed to childbirth (and to patriarchal marriage so that children are properly "owned" by men) has been increased by the current backlash against women's independence. Out of fear that the whole patriarchal structure will be eventually upset if we as women really have the autonomous power to decide our sexual and reproductive futures (that is, if we can control our own bodies, and thus the means of reproduction), anti-equality groups are not only denouncing sex education and family planning as "pornographic," but are trying to use obscenity laws to stop the sending of all contraceptive information through the mails. Any sex or nudity outside the context of patriarchal marriage and forced childbirth is their target. In fact, Phyllis Schlafly has denounced the entire women's movement as "obscene."

Not surprisingly, this religious, visceral backlash has a secular, intellectual counterpart that relies heavily on applying the "natural" behavior of some selected part of the animal world to humans. This is questionable in itself, but such Lionel Tiger-ish studies make their political purpose even more clear by the animals they choose and the habits they emphasize. For example, some male primates carry and generally "mother" their infants, male lions care for their young, female elephants often lead the clan, and male penguins literally do everything except give birth, from hatching the eggs to sacrificing their own membranes to feed the new arrivals. Perhaps that's why many male supremacists prefer to discuss chimps and baboons (many of whom are studied in atypical conditions of captivity) whose behavior is suitably male-dominant. The message is that human females should accept their animal "destiny" of being sexually dependent and devote themselves to bearing and rearing their young.

Defending against such repression and reaction leads to the temptation to merely reverse the terms and declare that *all* nonprocreative sex is good. In fact, however, this human activity can be as constructive or destructive, moral or immoral, as any other. Sex as communication can send messages as different as mutual pleasure and dominance, life and death, "erotica" and "pornography."

The second kind of problem comes not from those who oppose women's equality in nonsexual areas, whether on grounds of God or nature, but from men (and some women, too) who present themselves as friends of civil liberties and progress. Their opposition may take the form of a concern about privacy, on the grounds that a challenge to pornography invades private sexual behavior and the philosophy of "whatever turns you on." It may be a concern about class bias, on the premise that pornography is just "workingmen's erotica." Sometimes, it's the simple argument that they themselves like pornography and therefore it must be okay. Most often, however, this resistance attaches itself to or hides behind an expressed concern about censorship, freedom of the press, and the First Amendment.

In each case, such liberal objections are more easily countered than the anti-equality ones because they are less based on fact. It's true, for instance, that women's independence and autonomy would upset the whole patriarchal apple cart: the conservatives are right to be worried. It's not true, however, that pornography is a private concern. If it were just a matter of men making male-supremacist literature in their own basements to assuage their own sexual hang-ups, there would be sorrow and avoidance among women, but not the anger, outrage, and fear produced by being confronted with the preaching of sexual fascism on our newsstands, movie screens, television sets, and public streets. It is a multi-billion-dollar industry, which involves the making of public policy, if only to decide whether, as is now the case, crimes committed in the manufacture and sale of pornography will continue to go largely unprosecuted. Zoning regulations on the public display of pornography are not enforced, the sexual slavery and exploitation of children goes unpunished, the forcible use of teenage runaways is ignored by police, and even the torture and murder of prostitutes for men's sexual titillation is obscured by some mitigating notion that the women asked for it.

In all other areas of privacy, the limitation is infringement on the rights and lives and safety of others. That must become true for pornography. Right now, it is exempt: almost "below the law."

As for class bias, it's simply not accurate to say that pornography is erotica with less education. From the origins of the words, as well as the careful way that feminists working against pornography are trying to use them, it's clear there is a substantive difference, not an artistic or economic one. Pornography is about dominance. Erotica is about mutuality. (Any man able to empathize with women can easily tell the difference by looking at a photograph or film and putting himself in the woman's skin. There is some evidence that poor or discriminated-against men are better able to do this than rich ones.) Perhaps the most revealing thing is that this argument is generally made *on behalf* of the working class by pro-pornography liberals, but not *by* working-class spokespeople themselves.

Of course, the idea that enjoying pornography makes it okay is an overwhelmingly male one. From Kinsey forward, research has confirmed that men are the purchasers of pornography, and that the majority of men are turned on by it, while the majority of women find it angering, humiliating, and not a turn-on at all. This was true even though women were shown sexually explicit material that may have included erotica, since Kinsey and others did not make that distinction. If such rare examples of equal sex were entirely deleted, pornography itself could probably serve as sex aversion-therapy for most women; yet many men and some psychologists continue to call women prudish, frigid, or generally unhealthy if they are not turned on by their own domination. The same men might be less likely to argue that anti-Semitic and racist literature was equally okay because it gave them pleasure, or that they wanted their children to grow up with the same feelings about people of other races, other classes, that had been inflicted on them. The problem is that the degradation of women of all races is still thought to be normal.

Nonetheless, there are a few well-meaning women who are both turned on by pornography and angered that other women are not. Some of their anger is misunderstanding: objections to pornography are not condemnations of women who have been raised to believe sex and domination are synonymous, but objections to the idea that such domination is the only form that normal sexuality can take. Sometimes, this anger results from an underestimation of themselves: being turned on by a rape fantasy is not the same thing as wanting to be raped. As Robin Morgan has pointed out, the distinguishing feature of a fantasy is that the fantasizer herself is in control. Both men and women have "ravishment" fantasies in which we are passive while others act out our unspoken wishes—but they are still *our* wishes. And some anger, especially when it comes from women who consider themselves feminists, is a refusal to differentiate between what may be true for them now and what might be improved for all women in the future. To use a small but related example, a woman may now be attracted only to men who are taller, heavier, and older than she, but still understand that such superficial restrictions on the men she loves and enjoys going to bed with won't exist in a more free and less-stereotyped future. Similarly, some lesbians may find themselves following the masculine-feminine patterns that were our only model for intimate relationships, heterosexual or not, but still see these old patterns clearly and try to equalize them. It isn't that women attracted to pornography cannot also be feminists, but that pornography itself must be recognized as an adversary of women's safety and equality, and therefore, in the long run, of feminism.

Finally, there is the First Amendment argument against feminist anti-pornography campaigns: the most respectable and public opposition, but also the one with the least basis in fact.

Feminist groups are not arguing for censorship of pornography, or for censorship of Nazi literature or racist propaganda of the Ku Klux Klan.

For one thing, any societal definition of pornography in a male-dominant society (or of racist literature in a racist society) probably would punish the wrong people. Freely chosen homosexual expression might be considered more "pornographic" than snuff movies, or contraceptive courses for teenagers more "obscene" than bondage. Furthermore, censorship in itself, even with the proper definitions, would only drive pornography into more underground activity and, were it to follow the pattern of drug traffic, into even more profitability. Most important, the First Amendment is part of a statement of individual rights against government intervention that feminism seeks to expand, not contract: for instance, a woman's right to decide whether and when to have children. When we protest against pornography and educate others about it, as I am doing now, we are strengthening the First Amendment by exercising it.

The only legal steps suggested by feminists thus far have been the prosecution of those pornography makers who are accused of murder or assault and battery, prosecution of those who use children under the age of consent, enforcement of existing zoning and other codes that are breached because of payoffs to law-enforcement officials and enormous rents paid to pornography's landlords, and use of public-nuisance statutes to require that pornography not be displayed in public places where its sight cannot reasonably be avoided. All of those measures involve enforcement of existing law, and none has been interpreted as a danger to the First Amendment.

Perhaps the reason for this controversy is less substance than smokescreen. Just as earlier feminist campaigns to combat rape were condemned by some civil libertarians as efforts that would end by putting only men of color or poor men in jail, or in perpetuating the death penalty, anti-pornography campaigns are now similarly opposed. In fact, the greater publicity given to rape exposed the fact that white psychiatrists, educators, and other professionals were just as likely to be rapists, and changes in the law reduced penalties to ones that were more appropriate and thus more likely to be administered. Feminist efforts also changed the definition to sexual assault so that men were protected, too.

Though there are no statistics on the purchasers of pornography, clerks, movie-house owners, video-cassette dealers, mail-order houses, and others who serve this clientele usually remark on their respectability, their professional standing, suits, briefcases, white skins, and middle-class zip codes. For instance, the last screening of a snuff movie showing a real murder was traced to the monthly pornographic film showings of a senior partner in a respected law firm; an event regularly held by him for a group of friends including other lawyers and judges. One who was present reported that many were "embarrassed" and "didn't know what to say." But not one man was willing to object, much less offer this evidence of murder to the police. Though some concern about censorship is sincere—the result of false reports that feminist anti-pornography campaigns were really calling for censorship, or of confusion with right-wing groups who both misdefine pornography and want to censor it—much of it seems to be a cover for the preservation of the pornographic status quo.

*I*n fact, the obstacles to taking on pornography seem suspiciously like the virgin-whore divisions that have been women's only choices in the past. The right wing says all that is not virginal or motherly is pornographic, and thus they campaign against sexuality and nudity in general. The left wing says all sex is good as long as it's male-defined, and thus pornography must be protected. Women who feel endangered by being the victim, and men who feel demeaned by being the victimizer, have a long struggle ahead. In fact, pornography will continue as long as boys are raised to believe they must control or conquer women as a measure of manhood, as long as society rewards men who believe that success or even functioning—in sex as in other areas of life—depends on women's subservience.

But we now have words to describe our outrage and separate sex from violence. We now have the courage to demonstrate publicly against pornography, to keep its magazines and films out of our houses, to boycott its purveyors, to treat even friends and family members who support it as seriously as we would treat someone who supported and enjoyed Nazi literature or the teachings of the Klan.

But until we finally untangle sexuality and aggression, there will be more pornography and less erotica. There will be little murders in our beds—and very little love.

—1977 AND 1978

FIVE WOMEN

Marilyn Monroe: The Woman Who Died Too Soon

Saturday afternoon movies—no matter how poorly made or incredible the plot, they were a refuge from my neighborhood and all my teenage miseries. Serials that never ended, Doris Day, who never capitulated, cheap travelogues, sci-fi features with zippers in the monster suits: I loved them all, believed them all, and never dreamed of leaving until the screen went sickeningly blank.

But I walked out on Marilyn Monroe. I remember her on the screen, huge as a colossus doll, mincing and whispering and simply hoping her way into total vulnerability. Watching her, I felt angry, even humiliated, but I didn't understand why.

After all, Jane Russell was in the movie, too (a very bad-taste version of *Gentlemen Prefer Blondes*), so it wasn't just the vulnerability that all big-breasted women seem to share. (If women viewers prefer actresses who are smaller, neater—the Audrey Hepburns of the world—it isn't because we're jealous of the *zoftig* ones as men suppose. It's just that we would rather identify with a woman we don't have to worry about, someone who doesn't seem in constant danger.) Compared to Marilyn, Jane Russell seemed in control of her body and even of the absurd situations in this movie.

Perhaps it was the uncertainty in the eyes of this big, blond child-woman; the terrible desire for approval that made her different from Jane Russell. How dare she expose the neediness that so many women feel, but try so hard to hide? How dare she, a movie star, be just as unconfident as I was?

233

So I disliked her and avoided her movies, as we avoid that which reflects our fears about ourselves. If there were jokes made on her name and image when I was around, I joined in. I contributed to the laughing, the ridicule, the put-downs, thus proving that I was nothing like her. Nothing at all.

I, too, got out of my neighborhood in later years, just as she had escaped from a much worse life of lovelessness, child abuse, and foster homes. I didn't do it, as she did, through nude calendar photographs and starlet bits. (Even had there been such opportunities for mildly pretty girls in Toledo, Ohio, I would never have had the courage to make myself so vulnerable.) Yes, I was American enough to have show-business dreams. The boys in my neighborhood hoped to get out of a lifetime in the factories through sports; the girls, if we imagined anything other than marrying a few steps up in the world, always dreamed of show-business careers. But after high-school years as a dancer on the Toledo show-business circuit, or what passed for show business there, it seemed hopeless even to me. In the end, it was luck and an encouraging mother and a facility with words that got me out; a facility that helped me fake my way through the college entrance exams for which I was totally unprepared.

But there's not much more confidence in girls who scrape past college boards than there is in those who, like Marilyn, parade past beauty-contest judges. By the time I saw her again, I was a respectful student watching the celebrated members of the Actors Studio do scenes from what seemed to me very impressive and highbrow plays (Arthur Miller and Eugene O'Neill were to be served up that day). She was a student, too, a pupil of Lee Strasberg, leader of the Actors Studio and American guru of the Stanislavski method, but her status as a movie star and sex symbol seemed to keep her from being taken seriously even there. She was allowed to observe, but not to do scenes with her colleagues.

So the two of us sat there, mutually awed, I think, in the presence of such theater people as Ben Gazzara and Rip Torn, mutually insecure in the masculine world of High Culture, mutually trying to fade into the woodwork.

I remember thinking that Strasberg and his actors seemed to take positive pleasure in their power to ignore this great and powerful movie star who had come to learn. Their greetings to her were a little too studiously casual, their whispers to each other about her being there a little too self-conscious and condescending. Though she stayed in the back of the room, her blond head swathed in a black scarf and her body hidden in a shapeless black sweater and slacks, she gradually became a presence, if only because the group was trying so hard *not* to look, to remain oblivious and cool.

As we filed slowly out of the shabby room after the session was over, Marilyn listened eagerly to the professional postmortem being carried on by Ben Gazzara and others who walked ahead of us, her fingers nervously tracing a face that was luminous and without makeup, as if she were trying to hide herself, to apologize for being there. I was suddenly glad she hadn't participated and hadn't been subjected to the criticisms of this rather vulturous group. (Perhaps it was an unschooled reaction, but I hadn't enjoyed watching Strasberg encourage an intimate love scene between an actor and actress, and then pick them apart with humiliating authority.) Summoning my nerve, I did ask the shy, blond woman in front of me if she could imagine playing a scene for this group.

"Oh, no," Marilyn said, her voice childish, but much less whispery than on the screen, "I admire all these people so much. I'm just not good enough." Then, after a few beats of silence: "Lee Strasberg is a genius, you know. I plan to do what he says."

Her marriage to Arthur Miller seemed quite understandable to me and to other women, even those who were threatened by Miller's casting off of a middle-aged wife to take a younger, far more glamorous one. If you can't be taken seriously in your work, if you have an emotional and intellectual insecurity complex, then marry a man who has the seriousness you've been denied. It's a traditional female option—far more acceptable than trying to achieve that identity on one's own.

Of course, Marilyn's image didn't really gain seriousness and intellectuality. Women don't gain serious status by sexual association any more easily than they do by hard work. (At least, not unless the serious man dies and we confine ourselves to being keepers of the flame. As Margaret Mead has pointed out, widows are almost the only women this country honors in authority.) Even Marilyn's brave refusal to be intimidated by threats that she would never work in films again if she married Miller, who was then a "subversive" called to testify before the House Un-American Activities Committee, was considered less brave than Miller's refusal to testify. Indeed, it was barely reported at all.

Perhaps she didn't take her own bravery seriously either. She might be giving up her livelihood, the work that meant so much to her, but she was about to give that up for marriage anyway. As Mrs. Arthur Miller, she retired to a Connecticut farm and tried to limit her life to his solitary work habits, his friends, and his two children. Only when they badly needed money did she come out of retirement again, and that was to act in *The Misfits*, a film written by her husband.

On the other hand, the public interpretation was very different. She was an egocentric actress forcing one of America's most important playwrights to tailor a screenplay to her inferior talents: that was the gossip-column story here and in Europe. But her own pattern argues the case for her. In two previous marriages, to an aircraft factory worker at the age of sixteen and later to Joe Di Maggio, she had cut herself off from the world and put all her energies into being a housewife. When it didn't work out, she blamed herself, not the role, and added one more failure to her list of insecurities. "I have too many fantasies to be a housewife," she told a woman friend sadly. And finally, to an interviewer: "I guess I *am* a fantasy."

The Misfits seemed to convey some facets of the real Marilyn: honesty, an innocence and belief that survived all experience to the contrary, kindness toward other women, a respect for the life of plants and animals. Because for the first time she wasn't only a sex object and victim, I also was unembarrassed enough to notice her acting ability. I began to see her earlier movies—those few in which, unlike *Gentlemen Prefer Blondes*, she wasn't called upon to act the female impersonator.

For me as for so many people, she was a presence in the world, a life force.

Over the years, I heard other clues to her character. When Ella Fitzgerald, a black artist and perhaps the greatest singer of popular songs, hadn't been able to get a booking at an important Los Angeles nightclub in the fifties, it was Marilyn who called the owner and promised to sit at a front table every night while she sang. The owner hired Ella, Marilyn was faithful to her promise each night, the press went wild, and, as Ella remembers with gratitude, "After that, I never had to play a small jazz club again."

Even more movingly, there was her last interview. She pled with the reporter to end with, "What I really want to say: That what the world really needs is a real feeling of kinship. Everybody: stars, laborers,

Negroes, Jews, Arabs. We are all brothers. . . . Please don't make me a joke. End the interview with what I believe."

And then she was gone. I remember being told, in the middle of a chaotic student meeting in Europe, that she was dead. I remember that precise moment on August 5, 1962—the people around me, what the room looked like—and I've discovered that many other people remember that moment of hearing the news, too. It's a phenomenon usually reserved for the death of family and presidents.

She was an actress, a person on whom no one's fate depended, and yet her energy and terrible openness to life had made a connection to strangers. Within days after her body was discovered, eight young and beautiful women took their lives in individual incidents clearly patterned after Marilyn Monroe's death. Some of them left notes to make that connection clear.

Two years later, Arthur Miller's autobiographical play, *After the Fall*, brought Marilyn back to life in the character of Maggie. But somehow that Maggie didn't seem the same. She had Marilyn's pathetic insecurity, the same need to use her sexual self as her only way of getting recognition and feeling alive. But, perhaps naturally, the play was about Miller's suffering, not Marilyn's. He seemed honestly to include some of his own destructive acts. (He had kept a writer's diary of his movie-star wife, for instance, and Marilyn's discovery of it was an emotional blow, the beginning of the end for that marriage. It made her wonder: Was her husband exploiting her, as most men had done, but in a more intellectual way?) Nonetheless, the message of the play was mostly Miller's view of his attempts to shore up a creature of almost endless insecurities; someone doomed beyond his helping by a mysterious lack of confidence.

To women, that lack was less mysterious. Writer Diana Trilling, who had never met Marilyn, wrote an essay just after her death that some of Marilyn's friends praised as a more accurate portrayal than Miller's. She described the public's "mockery of [Marilyn's] wish to be educated"; the sexual awareness that came only from outside, from men's reactions, "leaving a great emptiness where a true sexuality would have supplied her with a sense of herself as a person with connection and content." She questioned whether Marilyn had really wanted to die, or only to be asleep, not to be conscious through the loneliness of that particular Saturday night.

Trilling also recorded that feeling of connection to Marilyn's loneliness felt by so many strangers ("especially women to whose protectiveness her extreme vulnerability spoke so directly"), so much so that we fantasized our ability to save her, if only we had been there. "But we were the friends," as Trilling wrote sadly, "of whom she knew nothing."

"She was an unusual woman—a little ahead of her times," said Ella Fitzgerald. "And she didn't know it."

Now that women's self-vision is changing, we are thinking again about the life of Marilyn Monroe. Might our new confidence in women's existence with or without the approval of men have helped a thirty-six-year-old woman of talent to stand on her own? To resist the insecurity and ridicule? To stop depending on sexual attractiveness as the only proof that she was alive—and therefore to face aging with confidence? Because the ability to bear a child was denied to her, could these new ideas have helped her to know that being a woman included much more? Could she have challenged the Freudian analysts to whom she turned in her suffering?

Most of all, we wonder if the support and friendship of other women could have helped. Her early experiences of men were not good. She was the illegitimate daughter of a man who would not even contribute for her baby clothes; her mother's earliest memory of her own father, Marilyn's grandfather, was his smashing a pet kitten against the fireplace in a fit of anger; Marilyn herself said she was sexually attacked by a foster father while still a child; and she was married off at sixteen because another foster family could not take care of her. Yet she was forced always to depend for her security on the goodwill and recognition of men; even to be interpreted by them in writing because she feared that sexual competition made women dislike her. Even if they had wanted to, the women in her life did not have the power to protect her. In films, photographs, and books, even after her death as well as before, she has been mainly seen through men's eyes.

We are too late. We cannot know whether we could have helped Norma Jean Baker or the Marilyn Monroe she became. But we are not too late to do as she asked. At last, we can take her seriously.

—1972

I would like to thank Ms. cofounder and editor, Harriet Lyons, whose idea this was.

Patricia Nixon Flying

*I*n 1968, during ten days spent on the Nixon campaign plane as a
political reporter for New York magazine (see the essay entitled "Campaigning"), I requested an interview with Richard Nixon and was given
Pat Nixon instead. Though the total article was a long one on Nixon and
his staff, this brief section aroused more interest. My regret is that the
impersonal style of that article didn't allow me to say that I liked her much
better after this interview than before: I thought I understood her resentment. My deeper regret is that my attempts to make some personal and
friendly connection just didn't work.

*F*rom Denver, back into our three jets for a teenage rally (mostly
private and parochial students) in St. Louis; then another flight to Louis-
ville, Kentucky, for a ride on the last Mississippi riverboat in existence.
The first leg of this flight yielded an interview with Pat Nixon.

She had worked her way through college, tried to be an actress, and
had become a teacher of shorthand and typing in a small California high
school; married her husband with apparent reluctance after a two-year
courtship at the age of twenty-eight (he had proposed on the first date) and
been introduced by him during his famous Checkers speech as "a wonderful stenographer." She had shared all the vilification and praise without
ever emerging in public as an individual. I was eager to meet her, but all
her other interviewers said Mrs. Nixon had put them straight to sleep.

She was sitting in the front of the plane, freckled hands neatly folded,

239

ankles neatly crossed, and smiling a public smile as a sleek young staff man sat me next to her. I didn't want to ask the questions she had answered so blandly and often about her husband ("I just think he'd make a wonderful president") or politics ("You'll have to ask Dick about that"), but to ask about herself.

Explaining my doubts about writing from clips, I asked if there were any persistent mistakes in the press that I should take care not to repeat. "No, no," she said, smoothing her skirt. "You ladies of the press do a fine job. I think the stories have been very fine." Did that mean she liked everything that had been written? "Well, actually, I haven't had time to read a lot of them lately." (Other "ladies of the press" had told me she read everything and had been annoyed by a Seattle story that made her seem a catatonic smiler.) But she liked all the stories from past campaigns? "Yes, of course; I don't object to what's been written. I know you do your best, and most of you have been very kind." We went round with that a few more times. Then she was, I told her, the only person I'd ever met, including myself, who liked everything written about them. There was a flicker of annoyance behind the hazel eyes—the first sign of life.

But after painfully slow questioning, I learned only the following: No, she was never bored with campaigning, brought no books along, needed no distraction. ("I'm always interested in the rallies, they're so different. Some are outside; some are inside. Some have old people; some have young people like the one today.") There was nothing special she wanted to do with her influence as First Lady. ("I think a person has to just be herself.") But she was glad she'd had so much "on-the-job training" for the entertaining she would have to do. Her only other interest was education. ("As a teacher, I agree with Dick's education program one hundred percent. I'd like to work on job and educational opportunities for all. I don't like this dropout system we have now.") She was keeping a journal on her life as Mrs. Nixon for her daughters, but never used anecdotes, of course, because she might have to write down the names of real people. She liked the theater, especially *My Fair Lady*, and had seen *Hello, Dolly!* three times: twice with visitors, and once because their "family friend," Ginger Rogers, was doing it. ("I feel there's enough seriousness in the world without seeing it in the theater.") She liked historical novels, especially the lives of Queen Victoria and Mary Todd Lincoln, also Thomas Wolfe's novels, but seldom had time to read "just for entertainment," or to go to fashion shows. ("I'm pretty selfless about things like that. I just keep busy with all our friends. Instead of a long lunch, I like to take them to a museum or the park. I find we all like that much better than just making social conversation.") There is no Generation Gap at all in her family. ("Why only the other day, Tricia and Julie didn't go to one of their parties. I said, 'Aren't you going out?' And they said, 'Oh, no, we'd much rather have dinner with you and Daddy.' ") The woman in history she most admires and would want to be like is Mrs. Eisenhower. Why? "Because she meant so much to young people."

Each of these answers had required several questions. She wasn't pleased at having to dredge around for such subjective information as what she identified with, other than daughters and husband. (She didn't answer that one at all.) And I wasn't overjoyed with so many bland answers. Mrs. Eisenhower was the last straw.

I was in college during the Eisenhower years, I told her, and I didn't think Mrs. Eisenhower had any special influence on youth. "You didn't?" Long pause. "Well, I do," she said finally. "Young people looked up to her because she was so brave all the time her husband was away at war." Longer pause. We eyed each other warily as I searched around for some fresh subject.

Then the dam broke. Not out of control but low-voiced and resentful, like a long accusation, the words flowed out.

"I never had time to think about things like that—who I wanted to be, or who I admired, or to have ideas. I never had time to dream about being anyone else. I had to work. My parents died when I was a teenager, and I had to work my way through college. I drove people all the way cross-country so I could get to New York and take training as an X-ray technician so I could work my way through college. I worked in a bank while Dick was in the service. Oh, I could have sat for those months doing nothing like everybody else, but I worked in the bank and talked with people and learned about all their funny little customs. Now, I have friends in all the countries of the world. I haven't just sat back and thought of myself or my ideas or what I wanted to do. Oh, no, I've stayed interested in people. I've kept working. Right here in the plane I keep this case with me, and the minute I sit down, I write my thank-you notes. Nobody gets by without a personal note. I don't have time to worry about who I admire or who I identify with. I've never had it easy. I'm not like all you . . all those people who had it easy."

The staff man had been signaling vainly to me for some time. We had landed, stopped at the ramp, and I was interfering with routine. Mrs. Nixon fingered her old-fashioned diamond ring for a moment, then, public smile refixed firmly, she patted my arm. "Now I hope we see you again soon; I really do; bye now; take care," she said, standard phrase upon standard phrase. "I've really enjoyed our talk. Take care!"

For the first time, I could see Mrs. Nixon's connection with her husband: two people with great drive, and a deep suspicion that "other people had it easy"—in her phrase, "glamour boys," or "buddy-buddy boys" in his—would somehow pull gracefully ahead of them in spite of all their work. Like gate crashers at a party, they supported each other in a critical world. It must have been a very special hell for them, running against the Kennedys; as if all their deepest suspicions had been proved true.

—1968

The Real Linda Lovelace

Remember *Deep Throat*? It was the porn movie that made porn movies chic; the first stag film to reach beyond the bounds of X-rated theaters and into much bigger audiences. Though it was created in 1972 as a cheap feature that took only forty thousand dollars and a few days to make, it ended the decade with an estimated gross income of six hundred million dollars from paying customers for the film itself plus its subindustry of sequels, cassettes, T-shirts, bumper stickers, and sexual aids. In fact, so much of the media rewarded it with amusement or approval that *Deep Throat* entered our language and our consciousness, whether we ever saw the film or not. From the serious Watergate journalists of the Washington *Post* who immortalized "Deep Throat" by bestowing that title on their top-secret news source, to the sleazy pornocrats of *Screw* magazine—a range that may be, on a scale of male supremacy, the distance from *A* to *B*—strange media bedfellows turned this cheap feature into a universal dirty joke and an international profit center.

At the heart of this dirty joke was Linda Lovelace (née Linda Boreman) whose innocent face and unjaded manner was credited with much of the film's success. She offered moviegoers the titillating thought that even the girl next door might love to be the object of porn-style sex.

Using Linda had been the idea of Gerry Damiano, the director-writer of *Deep Throat*. "The most amazing thing about Linda, the truly amazing thing," she remembers him saying enthusiastically to Lou Peraino, who

243

bankrolled the movie, "is that she still looks sweet and innocent." Nonetheless, Peraino (who was later arrested by the FBI as a figure in alleged organized-crime activities in the illicit-film industry) complained that Linda wasn't the "blond with big boobs" that he had in mind for his first porn flick. He continued to complain, even after she had been ordered to service him sexually.

In fact, watching Linda perform in public as a prostitute had given Damiano the idea for *Deep Throat* in the first place. He had been at a party where men lined up to be the beneficiaries of the sexual sword-swallower trick Linda had been taught by her husband and keeper, Chuck Traynor. By relaxing her throat muscles, she learned to receive the full-length plunge of a penis without choking; a desperate survival technique for her, but a constant source of amusement and novelty for clients. Thus creatively inspired, Damiano had thought up a movie gimmick, one that was second only to Freud's complete elimination of the clitoris as a proper source of female pleasure and invention of the vaginal orgasm. Damiano decided to tell the story of a woman whose clitoris was in her throat and who was constantly eager for oral sex with men.

Though his physiological fiction about *one* woman was far less ambitious than Freud's fiction about *all* women, his porn movie had a whammo audiovisual impact; a teaching device that Freudian theory had lacked.

Literally millions of women seem to have been taken to *Deep Throat* by their boyfriends or husbands (not to mention prostitutes who were taken by their pimps) so that each one might learn what a woman could do to please a man *if she really wanted to*. This instructive value seems to have been a major reason for the movie's popularity and its reach beyond the usual male-only viewers.

Of course, if the female viewer were really a spoilsport, she might identify with the woman on screen and sense her humiliation, danger, and pain—but the smiling, happy face of Linda Lovelace could serve to cut off empathy, too. *She's there because she wants to be. Who's forcing her? See how she's smiling? See how a real woman enjoys this?*

Eight years later, Linda told us the humiliating and painful answer in *Ordeal*, her autobiography. She described years as a sexual prisoner during which she was tortured and restricted from all normal human contact.

Nonetheless, it's important to understand how difficult it would have been at the time (and probably still is, in the case of other victims) to know the truth.

At the height of *Deep Throat*'s popularity, for instance, Nora Ephron wrote an essay about going to see it. She was determined not to react like those "crazy feminists carrying on, criticizing nonpolitical films in political terms." Nonetheless, she sat terrified through a scene in which a hollow glass dildo is inserted in Linda Lovelace's vagina and then filled with Coca-Cola, which is drunk through a surgical straw. ("All I could think about," she confessed, "was what would happen if the glass broke.") Feeling humiliated and angry, but told by her male friends that she was "overreacting," that the Coca-Cola scene was "hilarious," she used her license as a writer to get a telephone interview with Linda Lovelace. "I totally enjoyed myself making the movie," she was told by Linda. "I don't have any inhibitions about sex. I just hope that everybody who goes to see the film . . . loses some of their inhibitions."

So Nora wrote an article that assumed Linda to be a happy and willing porn queen who was enjoying " . . . $250 a week . . . and a piece of the profits." And she wrote off her own reaction as that of a "puritanical feminist who lost her sense of humor at a skin flick."

What she did not know (how could any interviewer know?) was that Linda would later list these and other answers as being dictated by Chuck Traynor for just such journalistic occasions; that he punished her for showing any unacceptable emotion (when, for instance, she cried while being gang-banged by five men in a motel room, thus causing one customer to refuse to pay); in fact, that she had been beaten and raped so severely and regularly that she suffered rectal damage plus permanent injury to the blood vessels in her legs.

What Nora did not know was that Linda would also write of her three escape attempts and three forcible returns to this life of sexual servitude: first by the betrayal of another prostitute; then by her own mother who was charmed by Chuck Traynor's protestations of remorse and innocence into telling him where her daughter was hiding; and finally by Linda's fear for the lives of two friends who had sheltered her after hearing that she had been made to do a sex film with a dog, and outside whose home Traynor had parked a van that contained, Linda believed, his collection of hand grenades and a machine gun.

Even now, these and other facts about Traynor must be read with the word "alleged" in front of them. Because of Linda's long period of fear and hiding after she escaped, the time limitations of the law, and the fact that Traynor forced her to marry him, legal charges are difficult to bring. Linda's book documents her account of more than two years of fear, sadism, and forced prostitution. Traynor has been quoted as calling these charges "so ridiculous I can't take them seriously." He has also been quoted as saying: "when I first dated her she was so shy, it shocked her to be seen nude by a man. . . . *I created Linda Lovelace.*"

Linda's account of being "created" includes guns put to her head, turning tricks while being watched through a peephole to make sure she couldn't escape, and having water forced up her rectum with a garden hose if she refused to offer such amusements as exposing herself in restaurants or to passing drivers on the highway.

Ordeal is a very difficult book to read. It must have been far more difficult to write. But Linda says she wanted to purge forever the idea that she had become "Linda Lovelace" of her own free will.

Was profit a motive for this book? Certainly she badly needs money for herself, her three-year-old son, her imminently expected second baby, and her husband, a childhood friend named Larry Marchiano, whose work as a TV cable installer has been jeopardized by his co-workers' discovery of Linda's past. For a while, they were living partially on welfare. But Linda points out that she has refused offers of more than three million dollars to do another porn movie like *Deep Throat.* (For that filming, Linda was paid twelve hundred dollars; a sum that, like her fees for turning tricks as a prostitute, she says she never saw.)* "I wouldn't do any of that again," she says, "even if I could get fifty million dollars."

A different motive for writing *Ordeal* is clear from Linda's response to a postcard written by a young woman who had been coerced into prostitution, a woman who said she got the courage to escape after seeing Linda on television. "Women have to be given the courage to try to escape, and to know that you *can* get your self-respect back," she says. "It meant the whole world to me to get that postcard."

Ironically, her own hope of escape came with the surprising success of *Deep Throat.* She had become a valuable property. She had to be brought

---

*Since this writing, a judgment has been brought against Linda for "contract failure" during what she says was her period of imprisonment, and her payments for *Ordeal* have been attached. The book may end by financially benefiting Traynor's former lawyer. The punishment goes on.

into contact with outsiders occasionally, with a world that she says had been denied to her, even in the form of radio or newspapers. Now, she says soberly, "I thank God today that they weren't making snuff movies back then. . . ."

She says she escaped by feigning trustworthiness for ten minutes, then a little longer each time, until, six months later, she was left unguarded during rehearsals for a stage version of *Linda Lovelace*. Even then, she spent weeks hiding out in hotels alone, convinced she might be beaten or killed for this fourth try at escape, but feeling stronger this time for having only her own life to worry about. It took a long period of hiding, with help and disguises supplied by a sympathetic secretary from Traynor's newly successful Linda Lovelace Enterprises (but no help from police, who said they could do nothing to protect her "until the man with the gun is in the room with you"), before the terror finally dwindled into a nagging fear. Traynor continued to issue calls and entreaties for her return. He filed a lawsuit against her for breach of contract. But he had also found another woman to star in his porn films—Marilyn Chambers, the model who appeared in a comparatively nonviolent porn movie called *Behind the Green Door*.

And then suddenly, she got word through a lawyer that Traynor was willing to sign divorce papers. The threats and entreaties to return just stopped.

Free of hiding and disguises at last, she tried to turn her created identity into real acting by filming *Linda Lovelace for President*, a comedy that was supposed to have no explicit sex, but she discovered that producers who offered her roles always expected nudity in return. She went to a Cannes Film Festival but was depressed by her very acceptance among celebrities she respected. "I had been in a disgusting film with disgusting people. . . . What were they doing watching a movie like that in the first place?"

Once she started giving her own answers to questions and trying to explain her years of coercion, she discovered that reporters were reluctant to rush into print. Her story was depressing, not glamorous or titillating at all. Because she had been passed around like a sexual trading coin, sometimes to men who were famous, there was also fear of lawsuits.

Only in 1978, when she was interviewed by Mike McGrady, a respected newspaper reporter on Long Island where she had moved with her new husband, did her story begin the long process of reaching the public. McGrady believed her. In order to convince publishers, he also put her through an eleven-hour lie-detector test with the former chief polygraphist of the New York district attorney's office, a test that included great detail and brutal cross-questioning. But even with those results and with McGrady himself as a collaborator, several major book publishers turned down the manuscript. It was finally believed and accepted by Lyle Stuart, a maverick in the world of publishing who often takes on sensational or controversial subjects.

One wonders: Would a male political prisoner or hostage telling a similar story have been so disbelieved? *Ordeal* attacks the myth of female masochism that insists women enjoy sexual domination and even pain, but prostitution and pornography are big businesses built on that myth. When challenged about her inability to escape earlier, Linda wrote: "I can understand why some people have such trouble accepting the truth. When I was younger, when I heard about a woman being raped, my secret feeling was *that could never happen to me*. I would never *permit* it to happen. Now I realize that can be about as meaningful as saying I won't permit an avalanche."

There are other, nameless victims of sexual servitude: the young blonds from the Minnesota Pipeline, runaways from the Scandinavian farming towns of Minnesota, who are given drugs and "seasoned" by pimps and set up in Times Square; the welfare mothers who are pressured to get off welfare and into prostitution; the "exotic" dancers imported from poorer countries for porn films and topless bars; the torture victims whose murders were filmed in Latin America for snuff movies popular here, or others whose bodies were found buried around a California filmmaker's shack; the body of a prostitute found headless and handless in a Times Square hotel, a lesson to her sisters. Perhaps some of their number will be the next voiceless, much-blamed women to speak out and begin placing the blame where it belongs. Perhaps Linda's example will give them hope that, if they return, some of society will accept them. Right now, however, they are just as disbelieved as rape victims and battered women were a few years ago.

*T*o publicize her book, Linda is sitting quiet and soft-spoken on TV's "Phil Donahue Show." Under her slacks she wears surgical stockings to shield the veins that were damaged by the beatings in which she curled up, fetuslike, to protect her stomach and breasts from kicks and blows: this she explains under Donahue's questioning. Probably, she will need surgery after her baby is born. The silicone injected in her breasts by a doctor (who, like many other professionals to whom she was taken, was paid by Linda's sexual services) has shifted painfully, and surgery may be necessary there, too.

Yet Donahue, usually a sensitive interviewer, is asking her psychological questions about her background: How did she get along with her parents? What did they tell her about sex? Didn't her fate have something to do with the fact that she had been pregnant when she was nineteen and had given birth to a baby that Linda's mother put up for adoption?

Some of the women in the audience take up this line of questioning, too. *They* had been poor. *They* had strict and authoritarian parents; yet *they* didn't end up as part of the pornographic underground. The air is thick with self-congratulation. Donahue talks on about the tragedy of teenage pregnancy, and what parents can do to keep their children from a Linda-like fate.

Because Traynor did have a marriage ceremony performed somewhere along the way (Linda says this was to make sure she couldn't testify against him on drug charges), she has to nod when he is referred to as "your husband." On her own, however, she refers to him as "Mr. Traynor."

Linda listens patiently to doubts and objections, but she never gives up trying to make the audience understand. If another woman had met a man of violence and sadism who "got off on pain," as Linda has described in her book, *she might have ended up exactly the same way*. No, she never loved him: he was the object of her hatred and terror. Yes, he was very nice, very gentlemanly when they first met. They had no sexual relationship at all. He had just offered an apartment as a refuge from her strict childlike regime at home. *And then he did a 180-degree turn*. She became, she says quietly, a prisoner. A prisoner of immediate violence and the fear of much more.

She describes being so isolated and controlled that she was not allowed to speak in public or to go to the bathroom without Traynor's permission. *There was no choice. It could happen to anyone*. She says this simply, over and over again, and to many women in the audience the point finally comes through. But to some, it never does. Donahue continues to ask questions about her childhood, her background. What attracted her to this fate? How can we raise our daughters to avoid it? If you accept the truth of Linda's story, the questions are enraging, like saying, "What in your background led you to a concentration camp?"

No one asks how we can stop raising men who fit Linda's terrified description of Chuck Traynor. Or what attracted the millions of people who went to *Deep Throat*. Or what to do about the millions of "normal" men who assume that some violence and aggression in sex are quite okay.

A woman in the audience asks if this isn't an issue for feminism. Linda says that yes, she has heard there are anti-pornography groups, she is getting in touch with Susan Brownmiller who wrote *Against Our Will*. That definitive book on rape has led Brownmiller to attack other pornographic violence against women.

But it's clear that, for Linda, this is a new hope and new connection.

For women who want to support Linda now and to save others being used sexually against their will, this may be the greatest sadness. At no time during those months of suffering and dreams of escape, not even during the years of silence that followed, was Linda aware of any signal from the world around her that strong women as a group or feminists or something called the women's movement might be there to help her.

Surely, a victim of anti-Semitism would know the Jewish community was there to help, or a victim of racism would look to the civil rights movement. But feminist groups are not yet strong enough to be a public presence in the world of pornography, prostitution, and gynocide; or in the world of welfare and the working poor that Linda then joined. Even now, most of her help and support come from sympathetic men: from McGrady who believed her life story, from her husband who loses jobs in defense of her honor, from the male God of her obedient Catholic girlhood to whom she prayed as a sexual prisoner and prays now in her daily life as homemaker and mother.

Even her feelings of betrayal are attached to her father, not her mother. During her long lie-detector test, the only time she cried and completely broke down was over an innocuous mention of his name. "I was watching that movie *Hardcore*," she explained, "where George C. Scott searches and searches for his daughter. Why didn't my father come looking for me? He saw *Deep Throat*. He should've known. . . . He should've done something. Anything!"

After all, who among us had mothers with the power to rescue us, to *do something*? We don't even expect it. In mythology, Demeter rescued her daughter who had been abducted and raped by the King of the Underworld. She was a strong and raging mother who turned the earth to winter in anger at her daughter's fate. Could a powerful mother now rescue her daughter from the underworld of pornography? Not even Hollywood can fantasize that plot.

But Linda has begun to uncover her own rage, if only when talking about her fears for other women as pornography becomes more violent. "Next," she says quietly, as if to herself, "they're going to be selling women's skins by the side of the road."

And women have at least begun to bond together to rescue each other as sisters. There are centers for battered women, with publicized phone numbers for the victims but private shelters where they cannot be followed. It's a system that might work for victims of prostitution and pornography as well, if it existed, and if women knew it was there.

In the meantime, Linda takes time out from cleaning her tiny house on Long Island ("I clean it twice a day," she says proudly) to do interviews, to send out her message of hope and strength to other women who may be living in sexual servitude right now, and to lecture against pornography with other women, who are now her friends. She keeps answering questions, most of them from interviewers who are far less sympathetic than Donahue.

How could she write such a book when her son will someday read it? "I've already explained to him," she says firmly, "that some people hurt Mommy—a long time ago." How can her husband stand to have a wife with such a sexual past? ("It wasn't sexual. I never experienced any sexual pleasure, not one orgasm, nothing. I learned how to fake pleasure so I wouldn't get punished for doing a bad job.") And the most popular doubt of all: *If she really wanted to, couldn't she have escaped sooner?*

Linda explains as best she can. As I watch her, I come to believe the question should be different: *Where did she find the courage to escape at all?*

Inside the patience with which she answers these questions—the result of childhood training to be a "good girl" that may make victims of us all—there is some core of strength and stubbornness that is itself the answer. She *will* make people understand. She will *not* give up.

In the microcosm of this one woman, there is a familiar miracle: the way in which women survive—and fight back.

And a fight there must be.

Deep Throat plays continuously in a New York theater and probably in many other cities of the world. Bruises are visible on Linda's legs in the film itself, supporting her testimony that she was a prisoner while she made it. Do viewers see the bruises or only her smile?

So far, no invasion of privacy or legal means has been found to stop this film. Money continues to be made.

Deep Throat has popularized a whole new genre of pornography. Added to all the familiar varieties of rape, there is now an ambition to rape the throat. Porn novels treat this theme endlessly. Some emergency-room doctors believe that victims of suffocation are on the increase.

As for Chuck Traynor himself, he is still the husband and manager of Marilyn Chambers.

Larry Fields, a columnist for the Philadelphia *Daily News,* remembers interviewing them both for his column a few years ago when Marilyn was performing a song-and-dance act in a local nightclub. Traynor bragged that he had taught Linda Lovelace everything she knew, but that "Marilyn's got what Linda never had—talent."

While Traynor was answering questions on Marilyn's behalf, she asked him for permission to go to the bathroom. Permission was refused. "Not right now," Fields remembers him saying to her. And when she objected that she was about to appear onstage: "Just sit there and shut up."

When Fields also objected, Traynor was adamant. "I don't tell you how to write your column," he said angrily. "Don't tell me how to treat my broads."

—1980

Jackie Reconsidered

*I*n 1964, while Jacqueline Bouvier Kennedy was still secluded in her year of mourning, I wrote a long article about this woman I barely knew. As a journalistic assignment, it consisted of reporting the views of friends, relatives, adversaries, politicians, and various public figures on a question that much of the world's media seemed to be asking at the time. What would this thirty-five-year-old widow do with her life?

Most people said she should play an international, public role. Serving as ambassador to France, becoming a kind of glamorous Eleanor Roosevelt, or marrying Adlai Stevenson (in order to turn him into a viable presidential candidate again) were all on the list.

A few others, especially friends and relatives, thought she had done enough for the world already. A White House correspondent said that, in her role as widow, she had saved the country's sanity by behaving with a sense of history, dignity, and courage throughout the complicated events surrounding the death and funeral. Robert Kennedy reacted with a kind of laissez-faire admiration. "Jackie has always kept her own identity," he explained, "and been different."

As for the subject herself—she wasn't saying. While still in the White House, she had reacted with humor to similar questions about her future. "I'll just retire to Boston," she had said, "and try to convince John, Jr., that his father was once the president." Since her year of mourning excluded all interviews (and indeed, she has made almost no public statements ever since), the first clue to her future plans was her interest in the continuation of her husband's work. "He changed our world," she said firmly, "and I hope people will remember him and miss him all their lives." The second was her future as what we would think of, were she any less famous woman, as a single parent. "I was reading Carlyle," she told a reporter, "and he said you should do the duty that lies nearest you. And the thing that lies nearest me is the children."

In retrospect, the most interesting thing about the barrage of directives and suggestions for her future was what they left out. With the possible exception of Robert Kennedy, no one even mentioned the idea that she might lead a life of her own. With feminist hindsight, I realize that neither I nor anyone I interviewed was paying her the honor of considering her as a separate human being; as the person she was and would have been, whether or not she had married a future president. True, she must have been changed by those Kennedy years and all the personal and historical events they contained, but she was still more than the sum of them. Yet we behaved as if she could not (or should not) create any future independent of the powerful Kennedy image.

It was this refusal to see her as a separate woman that increased the public shock when she married Aristotle Onassis. Without an understanding of her own problems and daily life, not to mention the penalties of just existing as the most famous living symbol of the Kennedy era, her second marriage just didn't make sense. It's a problem understood by any woman who's had the experience of being treated like a totally different person because the identity of the man standing next to her has changed.

Even when she was alone again after Onassis's death, the speculation about her future plans only seemed to split in two. Would she become a Kennedy again (that is, more political, American, and serious) or remain an Onassis (that is, more social, international, and simply rich)?

What no one predicted was her return to the publishing world she had entered briefly after college—to the kind of job she could have had years ago, completely on her own. And that's exactly what she did.

On my way to work every day, I pass a lunch counter, a tiny restaurant that specializes in giant hamburgers. In its window is a blown-up newspaper photo of Jackie sitting alone at the counter. She is just holding her coffee cup, obviously unaware of any camera, yet this photograph was taken and published without her permission, and is now being displayed to promote hamburgers.

This small symbol of a life in which private moments are in constant danger of becoming public makes me think again about the appeal of a private Greek island and a strong protective friend—especially in those postassassination years when crowds waited outside her apartment each day. It also makes me seriously consider the strength and resolve she must need to enter the ordinary world of work. She has been doing this regularly now for more than four years, something that her many fervent critics either don't know or ignore.

First, she must survive the professional Jackie-watchers and photographers who still lurk around corners, and the spurts of newspaper speculation on the Kennedy assassination or Jack Kennedy's personal life, the stream of books about both of her husbands, and the occasional movie in which some young actress achieves fame by dramatizing a part of her past. On top of that, she must make herself vulnerable to a whole group of skeptical New York publishing professionals with a "show me" attitude about her skills and an inclination to gossip. I suppose there are also many occasional friends and colleagues who respect and like her, as I always have, but who tend to keep quiet about it, as I'm afraid I used to. It's a peculiarity of knowing her and having an occasional work lunch that you feel like a name-dropper if you tell someone what you did that day.

Despite all of us, however, she gradually has found her own life.

In 1975, shortly after Onassis's death, Dorothy Schiff, then the successful publisher of the New York *Post*, invited Jackie to lunch to suggest that she consider running for the U.S. Senate against Daniel Patrick Moynihan. Jackie quickly refused that suggestion, but spent the afternoon enthusiastically touring the *Post*'s editorial offices and pressrooms instead. As she explained to Dorothy Schiff, the day brought back good memories of her early career as a young newspaper reporter in Washington. About the same time, she contributed a nicely written but unsigned piece to *The New Yorker* on the opening of the International Center of Photography, a project of her friend Cornell Capa. But neither of these events prepared many of her friends, much less the public, for the decision she soon announced: she would join the Viking Press as a consulting editor. Media commentators seemed both shocked and skeptical. Neither of her husbands had been in publishing. What made her think she could go off on a career of her own? There was much media speculation about her salary and how long she would pursue this new whim. Like parents who couldn't believe their child was old enough for a first day at school, camera crews and reporters lined up on the sidewalk to record her first day at work.

Despite this public skepticism, she continued to work there four days a week for two years, phoning in conscientiously for messages on her one day off. She went to editorial meetings, suggested ideas and authors, got her own coffee, made her own phone calls, waited at the Xerox machine to do her own copying, worked on a variety of book projects, and made ten thousand dollars a year.

None of that daily routine would need to be explained, of course, about an ordinary person who "had to work." As it was, however, such down-to-earth behavior ran contrary to her public image. So did her colleagues' accounts of Jackie as the editor of a book of eighteenth-century American women's history called *Remember the Ladies*. She supported the author's inclusion of working-class, black, and Native American women in its pages; pored over an eighteenth-century sex manual with information about a root that women chewed to induce abortion; and, according to Muffie Brandon, an originator of the book, "crawled around the floor, arranging picture layouts."

By the time she moved to Doubleday (partly as a result of her objections to a Viking novel about the assassination of a thinly disguised version of Ted Kennedy), she had become a full-time associate editor. She could work at home or in the office, or be out doing research and having author's lunches, with less danger of being accused of dilettantism. Her own apartment floor became the space covered by Atget, the French photographer whose collection she edited, or other book layouts. But many people at all levels in publishing are still surprised to pick up the phone and hear her unmistakable voice on the line, without benefit of secretarial announcement. And many more in the world at large are surprised to learn that she's traveling in order to research ideas, seeking out authors, arranging book promotion events—or still working at all.

I don't mean to suggest that the Most Famous Woman in the World is just like everyone else. On the contrary, she is like no one else. Part of her uniqueness is an ability to distance herself from her public image, to ignore the obsessive interest of strangers, and to refuse to read most of what is written about her.

Certainly, this ability has helped her to survive with her sanity and humor pretty much intact. Probably, it is the habit that most frustrates those who wish she would use her public power for various political ends. (I, for instance, wish with all my heart that she would use some of her derived influence to work publicly for the issues of powerless groups in general and women in particular.) But wanting her to use that power from her other lives may be unfairly close to wanting to use her, however worthwhile the cause.

She personally contributes money to many projects, including ones that help women toward some power of their own, but will not be publicly active for the Equal Rights Amendment she privately supports or for any other political issue. She has remained steadfast over the years in working for such Kennedy-initiated projects as Bedford-Stuyvesant Restoration, a successful community development project in New York's largest black ghetto. But she is still more publicly associated with the art and cultural events that have long been her own personal interests. Saving New York buildings for the Municipal Art Society or rescuing Forty-second Street from its current decline into pornography and crime—these are also projects on which she quietly lavishes time.

That's the individual she is: neither Kennedy nor Onassis nor even her own glamorous public image, but a woman who remains serious, hard-working, sensitive, funny, and even slightly outrageous. (In conversation, she's the sort of person to whom you find yourself saying things you had previously only thought, indiscreet things that her own gentle rebelliousness encourages you to say.) She is a kind of quiet, one-woman consciousness-raising group among her friends, encouraging a rich wife to stand on her own two feet, helping a newly divorced friend to get her first job. She is creative, intelligent, consistent in her interests over the years, loyal to her friends, very demanding of loyalty, and the very private center of a very public storm.

Her example poses interesting questions for each of us to ask ourselves: given the options of using Kennedy power or living the international life-style of an Onassis, how many of us would have chosen to return to our own talents and less spectacular careers? How many of us would have the strength to choose work over derived influence?

In the long run, her insistence on work that is her own may be more helpful to other women than any use of the conventional power she has declined

—1979

Alice Walker: Do You Know This Woman? She Knows You

*T*here must be thousands of people scattered around this country, each one of whom thinks only she or he knows how major and unique a writer Alice Walker is.

Even "writer" may be too distant a word. Traveling and listening over the years, I've noticed that the readers of Alice Walker's work tend to speak about her as a friend: someone who has rescued them from passivity or anger, someone who has taught them sensuality or self-respect, humor or redemption.

"I've been a much better person," explained an angry young novelist to a roomful of his peers, "since I've been under the care and feeding of Alice Walker's writing." That was the only introduction he gave before Alice rose to read her work before that formidable audience—and he was right. By the time she had finished a moving short story about the death of an obscure, heroic, much-loved old man, the room had lost its lethal edge of competition and anger.

"While I'm reading her novels, I'm completely unaware of her style," said a literary critic who is a writer herself. "It's like a glass that contains whatever she wants you to see. Yet I can read a few paragraphs of hers and know immediately: That's Alice."

"She's certainly not the only writer who sees personal cruelty and social injustice," explained a woman who has grown old in the struggle for civil rights in general and black women's dignity in particular. "But she's the only writer I know who sees it all: what happens to black people here, to women everywhere; the outrages against history and the earth; everything. Yet she has also taught me that cruelty turns back on itself, which gives me faith to keep on fighting. She takes people who seem completely irredeemable, and then writes about their redemption. That gives me faith in change, and allows me to change, too. When I read something by Alice, I'm never quite the same person when I finish as I was when I began."

I've heard many such comments over the past decade or so Because people know that I work for *Ms.* magazine where Alice Walker has published and being a contributing editor over the years, I'm the accidental recipient of personal testimonies wherever I go. When readers suspect that I might know Alice herself, the comments turn to questions: When is a new story coming out? Why aren't her books in more book-stores? Interestingly, I don't hear the usual celebrity question: What is Alice Walker really like? Readers feel they already know her personally from her writing. But lives touched by her work form a small, secret, far-flung network that touches almost every campus and town.

Of course, the existence of such readers, even unknown to each other, means that Alice Walker is not really a secret writer. Her three novels, three books of poetry, and two collections of short stories have sold and been reviewed respectably. She has also edited a reader of the work of Zora Neale Hurston, the black writer and folklorist of the 1930s, and written an introduction to Hurston's biography. For young readers, she has published a biography of Langston Hughes. Her first collection of short stories, *In Love and Trouble*, won the Rosenthal Award of the National Institute of Arts and Letters. Her second novel, *Meridian*, is often cited as the best novel of the civil rights movement and taught as part of American history as well as literature courses. *Revolutionary Petunias*, her second book of poetry, won the Lillian Smith Award and was nominated for a National Book Award.

But her visibility as a major American talent has been obscured by a familiar bias: white male writers and the literature they create are the norm, so black women (and all women of color) must be doubly removed and "special." Only lately has the work of novelists like Toni Morrison or Maya Angelou begun to be read beyond the restrictions implied by the adjectives *black woman* modifying *writer*. (Only white men require no adjectives. Perhaps we should begin to speak of Norman Mailer *et al* as *white male writers*.) In fact, Toni Cade Bambara, June Jordan, Paule

Marshall, Ntozake Shange, and other valuable current American writers are still missing from the mainstream (and the mainstream is missing them) because of this bias against the universality of what they have to say. So are all those Zora Neale Hurstons and Nella Larsens of the past whose works have been allowed to go out of print and out of mind.

Even with Black Studies, Women's Studies, and other new courses now trying hard, it's going to take a while to change the academic and cultural assumptions that American readers will cross boundaries of country, time, and language to identify with Dostoevsky or Tolstoy, but can't be expected to walk next door to meet Baldwin or Ellison; that women can and should identify with male leading characters, but there's something perverse about expecting male readers to see life through a woman's eyes. Of course, Alice Walker creates male protagonists too, as she did in her first novel, *The Third Life of Grange Copeland*, but there she ran into a parallel bias: Yes, male artists can create women but how can a woman writer have the authority to create a believable man?

As usual, however, people are ahead of their leaders, and readers are ahead of academics and critics. It's true and important that a disproportionate number of people who seek out Alice Walker's hard-to-find books are black women. After all, she comes at universality through the path of that experience and is even brave enough to write about such delicate themes as interracial sex in America or women's oppression in Africa. ("Do you have *any idea* what she means to us?" a Spelman College student once asked me with tears in her eyes.) But women of many different backgrounds also feel personally connected to Alice Walker. The struggle to have work and minds of our own, our physical vulnerability, our debt to our mothers, the realities of childbirth, friendships among women, the destructiveness of loving men who treat us as less than themselves, sensuality, violence—all these are major themes of her fiction and poetry. In *The Third Life of Grange Copeland*, she exposed violence against women, years before we had begun to tell the truth in public about beatings by husbands and lovers. Her novel paid a critical price for being ahead of its time. In fact, she speaks the female experience more powerfully for being able to pursue and describe it across boundaries of race and class.

And she never gives in. No female character is ever allowed to disappear behind a sex role, any more than she would allow a black character to sink into a stereotype of race.

As the young novelist said, "I've become a much better person . . .," and that seems to be a frequent reaction of her readers who are black men. They comment on her loving use of black folk English, her understanding of what goes right and wrong between men and women, and her clear-eyed rendering of the rural black South in which many of them grew up.

It's true that a disproportionate number of her negative reviews have been by black men. But those few seemed to be reviewing their own conviction that black men should have everything white men have had, including dominance over women, or reflecting their fear that black women's truth telling would be misused by a racist society, or their alarm at her "life-style," a euphemism for the fact that Alice was married for ten years to a white civil rights worker. And those were usually critics, as Alice has written, "who were themselves frequently interracially married and who, moreover, hung on every word from Richard Wright, Jean Toomer, Langston Hughes, James Baldwin, John A. Williams, and LeRoi Jones, to name a few, all of whom were at some time in their lives interracially connected. . . . I, a black woman, had dared to exercise the same prerogative as they."

On the other hand, as Alice also points out, "At least those black reviewers take me seriously enough to get mad at. Most of the white ones just seem perplexed."

As for white male readers, their first stumbling-block seems to be a conviction that her books "aren't written for us." Once they read Alice's work, they often cite an increased understanding of black rage or a new conviction that they themselves have been deprived of seeing the world whole; an irony considering the fears expressed by those black male critics. Susan Kirschner, an English professor who made a study of all the reviews of *Meridian*, concluded that the only critic to examine seriously the moral themes of the novel, not just respectfully describe its plot, was Greil Marcus, a white male reviewer writing in *The New Yorker*.

After all, who could fail to share the rage of the poet who wrote these lines:

i sit for hours staring at my own right hand
wondering if it would help me shoot the judge
who called us chimpanzees from behind his bench
and would it help pour sweet arsenic

into the governor's coffeepot
or drop cyanide into yours.
you don't have to tell me;
i understand these are the clichéd fantasies
of twenty-five million longings
that spring spontaneously to life
every generation.
it is hard for me to write
what everybody already knows;
still, it appears to me
i have pardoned the dead
*enough.**

And who could resist this rebellious spirit:

In me there is a rage to defy
the order of the stars
despite their pretty patterns.
To see if Gods who hold forth now
on human thrones
can will away my lust
to dare
and press to order the anarchy
I would serve.†

And who would not want to say these freely given words:

I have learned not to worry about love;
but to honor its coming
with all my heart.
To examine the dark mysteries
of the blood
with headless heed and
swirl,
to know the rush of feelings

*"January 10, 1973," *Goodnight, Willie Leer, I'll See You in the Morning* (New York: Dial, 1979).
†"Rage," *Revolutionary Petunias & Other Poems* (New York: Harcourt, Brace, Jovanovich, 1973)

swift and flowing
as water.
The source appears to be
some inexhaustible
spring
within our twin and triple
selves;
the new face I turn up
to you
no one else on earth
has ever
*seen.**

I've suspected for a long time that a convention of all the scattered Alice Walker readers might look surprisingly big and diverse. It might look something like the country.

II

Her readers may be about to find their numbers greatly increased. *The Color Purple*, Alice Walker's third and latest novel, may be the kind of literary event that transforms a small and intense reputation into a popular one.

For one thing, the storytelling style of *The Color Purple* is irresistible.

The speaker is Celie, the downest and outest of women. Because she must survive against impossible odds and has no one to talk to, she writes about her life with great honesty and down-home realism in the guise of letters to God. When she discovers that Nettie, her much-loved sister, is not dead after all but is living in Africa, she begins to write letters to Nettie instead. (Clearly, the author is telling us something about the origin of God—about when we need to invent an unseen powerful friend and when we don't.) The point is that, whether anyone ever reads her words or not, she must confirm her own existence by writing the truth. Like a Scheherazade whose enemy is everywhere but inside her own head, Celie is writing this story to save her life.

*"New Face," *Revolutionary Petunias & Other Poems* (New York; Harcourt, Brace, Jovanovich, 1973).

The result is a dead-honest, surprising novel that is the success-ful culmination of Alice Walker's longer and longer trips outside the safety of standard English and into the speech of her characters. Here, she takes the leap completely. There is no third-person narrator to dis-tance the reader from feelings and events. We are inside Celie's head, seeing through her eyes, experiencing her suffering and humor, and observing the world with a clarity that may only be possible from the bottom up.

Moreover, Celie turns out to be a no-nonsense storyteller with a gift for cramming a complicated turn of events and the essence of a person's character into very few words. Like E. L. Doctorow in *Ragtime*, the rhythm of the telling adds to the momentum of suspense, but what that book did with the pace of episodes and chapters, Celie does with the choice of a line, a phrase, a verb. It's the fast, compressed kind of novel that could be written only by a poet. If God were getting these letters, God would definitely be hooked.

With this novel, reviewers should understand why Alice Walker has always preferred to describe her characters' speech as "black folk En-glish" and not "dialect," a word she feels has been used in a condescend-ing, often racist way. When Celie talks or records the talk of her friends, there are no self-conscious apostrophes and contractions to assure us that the writer really knows what the proper spelling or grammar should be, and no quotation marks to keep us at our distance. Celie just puts words down the way they sound and feel. She literally writes her heart out. Pretty soon, the reader can't imagine why anyone would bother to write any other way.

As always with Alice Walker's work, a pleasure of *The Color Purple* is watching people redeem themselves and grow, or wither and turn inward. It depends on the ways they do or don't work out the moral themes in their lives. As always, however, this morality is not a set of external dictates. It doesn't matter if you love the people society says you shouldn't love, or do or don't have children with more than one of them. It doesn't matter if you have money, go to church, or obey the law. What matters is that you are not cruel or wasteful; that you don't keep the truth from those who need it, suppress someone's will or talent, take more than you need from nature, or fail to use your own talent and will. It's an organic morality of dignity, autonomy, nurturing, and balance.

What also matters is the acknowledgment that everybody, no matter how poor or passive on the outside, has these possibilities inside.

Perhaps that's why Alice puts us in Celie's unlikely hands. As the teenage daughter in a dirt-poor southern family, she is hardworking, spiritless, silent, and not pretty. In the first few pages, she is raped more than once by her mother's husband, forced to leave the school she loves because she is pregnant, deprived even of the two children who are born of those rapes, and married off to a widower who uses her as a worker to take care of his many children. Her life seems hopeless and over.

In fact, the main danger to this book is that its first few pages will cause readers to put it down in despair.

But her violent stepfather's warning after the rape to "tell no one but God" starts her secret letters. She writes down everything, survives her husband's routine beatings by becoming "like a tree," and breaks the chain of cruelty by refusing to inflict her own suffering on another woman.

Celie saves herself through small feats of empathy and courage. She resists her husband, the widower Mr. ———, a man so stony and cruel that she refuses to write his name. (By the end of the novel, Mr. ——— has become a rather nice man named Albert. Such are the powers of change and redemption.) She also is forced by him to nurse back to health Shug Avery, the woman her husband really loves; a local singer with the talent of Bessie Smith and the independent spirit of Zora Neale Hurston. The love that Celie also comes to feel for Shug is returned in ways both sisterly and sensuous. When Celie discovers that Mr. ——— has intercepted all the letters from her sister Nettie in Africa, allowing her to think that Nettie is dead, Celie's rage finally breaks through her passivity. She wants to kill him, and is only kept from doing so by Shug, who punishes him in more effective ways. Eventually Celie discovers that standing up to him, laughing at him, and just leaving him alone with his own sins for a while cause him to change, too.

That's only a sample of the plot. No Russian novel could outdo it for complicated family relationships, wide scope, and human coincidence. To these novelistic pleasures, add a sense of humor and an expectation of justice that are very American, plus succinct discussions about the existence of God, the politics of religion, and what's going on in the daily news, all of which are pure Alice. (There are also many surprises that, as in life, seem inevitable in retrospect.) But, whatever else is going on, the plot and its ideas keep unfolding with an economy of words that follows Picasso's rule of art. Every line is necessary. Nothing could be deleted without changing everything.

Once Nettie's letters have been recovered, for instance, they expand the story beyond the rural South to England and to Africa. Her personal, blow-by-blow account of what happens when a British rubber plantation buys the village where she lives as a missionary explains more about the intimate workings of colonialism than do many academic tomes. It should be included in international economics courses for that reason. The author's sense of moral balance and retribution is so contagious that we find ourselves wondering if England might not now be paying for its past colonial sins in an only slightly larger version of Celie's husband paying for his cruelty to Celie.

By the end of the novel, we understand that this poor, nameless patch of land in the American South is really the world, and vice versa. Conversations between Celie and Shug have brought us theories of philosophy, ethics, and metaphysics. The color purple, a rare miracle in nature, has come to symbolize the miracle of human possibilities.

In the tradition of Gorky, Steinbeck, Dickens, Ernest Gaines, Hurston, Baldwin, Ousmane Sembene, Bessie Head, and many others, Alice Walker has written an empathetic novel about the poorest of the poor. Unlike most novels that expose the injustice of race and class, however, *The Color Purple* doesn't treat male-female injustice as secondary or natural. And unlike many would-be feminist novels, it doesn't exclude some women because of race or class. Equally unusual among books about the poor and powerless, it is not written *about* one group but *for* another, *about* the poor but *for* the middle class. It is populist, in the best sense. The people in it could read and enjoy it, too.

In fact, it's hard to imagine anyone in the country this novel couldn't reach.

III

Alice and I are sitting in her quiet apartment in San Francisco, drinking tea and tiptoeing around the edges of an interview. We have shared work, parties, and marches for a decade, but the truth is that this is only the second or third time we have talked by ourselves. Like so many others, I think I know her from her work—but do I?

For instance, this is the first time I have been in a totally Alice-created environment. There is one small room with a large wooden work shelf where she writes; one bedroom that her twelve-year-old daughter Rebecca has painted with a motif of rainbows; Alice's own bedroom filled almost wall-to-wall with an ornately carved, old-fashioned wooden bed; a kitchen stocked with fresh herbs and pottery made from Mississippi clay; and a living room with a big couch, plants, quilts, an old rocker, and many, many books.

In spite of the big city outside, Celie, Nettie, and Shug would all feel at home here. It's warm, peaceful, and solid, with rural southern photographs and women's art on the walls for Celie, many books and African prints for Nettie, and enough bright colors and sophistication to please the blues singer in Shug.

"The people in the book were willing to visit me," explained Alice, "but only after I stopped interrupting with poetry readings and lectures and getting on some plane." Even more than most novelists, she feels that her characters have a separate life, that they come alive in her head and walk around on their own. "They took a lot of quiet and attention. For a while when Rebecca first came back from staying with her father, I thought even she might be too much. Then she came home from school one day looking all beat up and said, 'Don't worry, Mom. You should see the other guy!' Right away, Celie liked her.

"If you're silent for a long time, people just arrive in your mind. It makes you believe the world was created in silence."

It's a surprise to hear Alice sounding uniquely like herself. In the three years since she moved away from New York where I live, her characters' voices have become more familiar to me than her own. I realize that they are the parts—but Alice is the whole.

"Writing *The Color Purple* was writing in my first language," explained Alice. She is the youngest of eight children from a sharecropping family in Georgia. "I had to do a lot of living to get the knowledge, but the writing itself was easy. There was a moment when I remember feeling real rage that black people or other people of color who have different patterns of speech can't just routinely write in this natural, flowing way."

She seems all of a piece with her past, yet no one else in her small town or big family had ever become a poet or a writer. It made me wonder if she, like many creative people, had ever felt so different that she believed she had been "found" or adopted.

"Sometimes I thought I'd gotten into the family by mistake," she admits. "I always seemed to need more peace and quiet than anybody else. That's very difficult when you're living with ten people in three or four rooms. So I found what privacy I had by walking in the fields. We had to get our water from a spring, so that was a time to be alone, too. I spent so much time out of doors that when I started writing—and I found myself writing my first book of poems, *Once*, under a tree in Kenya—it seemed quite normal.

"I also had terrific teachers. When I was four and my mother had to go to work in the fields, my first-grade teacher let me start in her class. Right on through grammar school and high school and college there was one, sometimes even two, teachers who saved me from feeling alone; from worrying that the world I was stretching to find might not even exist.

"Of course, the schools were all black, and that gave us a feeling that they really belonged to us. If they needed desks or a stage, the men in the community built them. My parents gave what they called get-togethers to raise money for the grammar school when I was there. There was a lot of self-help and community.

"My teachers lent me books—*Jane Eyre* was my friend for a long time. Books became my world because the world I was in was very hard. My mother was working as a maid, so she was away from six-thirty in the morning until after dark. Because one sister was living up North and the other one had become a beautician, I was supposed to take care of the house and do the cooking. I was twelve, coming home to an empty house and cleaning and fixing dinner—for people who didn't really appreciate the struggle it was to fix it. I missed my mother very much."

Echoes of Alice's stories and characters are all there. Like Celie, she began to write as a way of surviving.

"From the time I was eight, I kept a notebook. I found it lately and I was surprised—they were horrible poems, but they were poems. There's even a preface that thanks all the people who were forced to hear this material—my mother, my teacher, my blind Uncle Frank."

Like the first-person voice in many of her poems and stories, she had a mother whose courage and wisdom she counted on. She still does. Nearly seventy and still living in the same small town in Georgia, her mother only recently became too weak to keep working. Alice visits her often. She counts the two gifts her mother once scrimped and saved to give her, a suitcase and a typewriter, as clear permission to adventure and to work. Her father, who died nine years ago, was a troubled and complicated man to whom she was very close as a child but who didn't understand the woman she became.

In her essay, "My Father's Country Is the Poor," she writes about this separation that neither of them wanted: a distance between parent and child that extreme poverty and sacrifices for the progress of the next generation often create.

Like Meridian, the central character of her second novel, she won a scholarship and went away to Spelman, a black women's college in Atlanta. For Alice, however, that opportunity was partly an ironic result of a childhood accident that had shadowed her life and left her "handicapped."

At the age of eight, while playing with her older brothers, she was wounded by a shot from one of their BB guns. It blinded her right eye. A local doctor predicted that she would eventually lose the sight in her other eye as well, and though he was proved wrong, she lived with that fear for many years.

She also lived with scar tissue that had grown over the injured eye like a giant cataract. "I used to pray every night that I would wake up and somehow it would be gone," she remembers. "I couldn't look at people directly because I thought I was ugly. Flannery O'Connor says that a writer has to be able to stare, to see everything that's going on. I never looked up.

"Then when I was fourteen, I visited my brother Bill to take care of his children in the summer. He took me to a hospital where they removed most of the scar tissue—and I was a *changed person*.

"I promptly went home, scooped up the best-looking guy, and by the time I graduated from high school, I was valedictorian, voted 'Most Popular,' and crowned queen!"

She is laughing at herself, but much of the fear of those earlier years is still there. Alice has just explained one of the few mysteries about herself that her writing does not: why she never seems to know that she is beautiful.

Perhaps those childhood years also explain why she can write from inside the head of someone like Celie, someone society has discarded as poor, black, and ugly besides.

"I used to have a dream in which there was a bus coming down the road," Alice said thoughtfully, "and the bus driver would get out where I was waiting with my bag. He would hold his hand out for the fare—and I would put an eye in it.

"Of course, that's really true. If I had not lost the sight of one eye permanently, I wouldn't have qualified for the half scholarship and free textbooks that the Georgia Department of Rehabilitation gives people who are 'handicapped.' The other half of my tuition came from Spelman because of my excellent high-school grades, emphatic recommendations from my principal and teachers, and the fact that I was high-school valedictorian—and not too black. (A high school teacher of mine swears she got into Spelman because her folks were too poor to attach a photograph to her application.) But in a literal sense, it cost an eye to get out."

And so she went off to Spelman as the beginning of a long journey, then transferred to Sarah Lawrence College in New York on another scholarship, then traveled to Africa and back like Nettie, and worked in the civil rights movement in Mississippi like Meridian. She was writing all the while.

There is another mystery of the visible Alice that only her writing explains. Sitting across from me now, she is soft-spoken, gentle, reticent. I have seen her sit for hours without speaking in a meeting about whose subject I know she cares—"an unlikely warrior," as one writer called her. Yet the rage, retribution and the imaginings of righteous murders that are in her writing are also in her. You just have to know her long enough to see the anger flash.

I remember listening to Alice after she had met with editors from *The New York Times Magazine* to discuss an article she had written on their assignment about the New South. They asked for a rewrite because she had not included "enough white people" in her essay. Having made this mistake, they compounded it by noting that, after all, she had been "married to a white man."

"He's not a group," she told them fiercely. "He's Mel—a person."

She later fired off a letter to the unfortunate editors. It referred to her seven years in Mississippi facing southern sheriffs with hoses and dogs, and made clear that on the whole and compared to their lunch meeting, she preferred the dogs.

"It's true that I fantasize revenge for injustices," she said, smiling at my memory of her letter's fierceness, and not regretting it one bit. "I imagine how wonderful it must feel to kill the white man who oppresses you. My dream used to be sitting in some racist politician's lap with a hand grenade and blowing us both up."

It's significant that, even in her most murderous rages, she can't imagine killing another human being without killing herself. Like the title figures in both *Meridian* and *The Third Life of Grange Copeland*, she can support murder of an enemy for righteous reasons, but only at the price of one righteous life. That sense of moral balance is the restraint on her desire for revenge.

"Lately," she added, "I've come to believe that you have some help when you fight. If a country or person oppresses folks, it or he will pay for it. That happens more often than not. Years after the Indians died on the Trail of Tears, Andrew Jackson, who had been president at the time, had to be wrapped like a mummy to keep the flesh on his bones.

"I think black people's absence from the antinuclear movement has to do with that belief in justice, too. Since white men lived by raping the earth and then by threatening us all with the bomb—why not let them die by it? On the other hand, we don't want to die with them. That's why we're now beginning to work against nuclear war, too."

This lust for justice comes from a woman whose childhood was filled with stories of past lynchings and who later felt even those stories had been incomplete. ("When young black girls were raped and killed and dumped in the river," she explains, "no one said they were lynched. But they were.") At twelve, the same little white girls who had been her daily playmates were suddenly supposed to be called "Miss"—a change she refused to make. That strength and self-respect were created in a small community where almost everyone—ministers, teachers, neighbors—was black. White adults were seen not as individuals, but as a group of distant adversaries.

Yet when she was a college student, she refused the honor and badly needed money of a major prize from Spelman because she felt its black president had fired Howard Zinn, a white professor, for being too left wing, too involved in the civil rights movement, too willing to make his students laugh, too "incorrect."

After Sarah Lawrence, where she found support for her writing but the alienation of being in an almost totally white society for the first time, she spent a summer traveling in Africa on a fellowship, looking for a spiritual home. But she was often seen more as a peculiar kind of American than as a returning daughter. She also felt the suffering of women and the condescension of many men.

An unpublished short story from that period, "The Suicide of an American Girl," describes the meeting of a young black American and an African student. Because he is attracted and angered by her independence, he rapes her. As a kind of chosen sacrifice to his need for power, the girl doesn't resist. But after he is gone, she turns on the gas and quietly waits for death. It's a conflict of wills that Alice would no longer resolve by giving up. In her most recent book of poetry, *Goodnight Willie Lee, I'll See You in the Morning*, as well as in *The Color Purple*, she writes about the fate of specific African women with irony and anger. "We're going to have to debunk the myth that Africa is a heaven for black people—especially black women," she now says firmly. "We've been the mule of the world there and the mule of the world here."

In Mississippi in the late 1960s, Alice began to write about the life stories of ordinary black women in the South; women like her own mother. While registering voters and working for welfare rights, she collected the folklore stories they told and recorded the details of their days. It was during this research that she discovered the work of Zora Neale Hurston, a relief from white writers who often recorded black folklore with condescension. Hurston's work became an important influence in Alice's life. So did the effort to bring that work back into print and public attention. She also sought out the obscure, segregated cemetery where Hurston had been buried after dying in poverty in a welfare home, and bought a tombstone to honor her unmarked grave.

It was during those Mississippi years that she met Mel Leventhal, the civil rights lawyer who was her husband for ten years, and who is the father with whom Rebecca now spends half her time. They remain friends in spite of divorce.

"Mel and I had been living together perfectly happily for almost a year," she explains, "but we could see that, given the history, we couldn't go off into the world and do political work unless we were married. We could challenge the laws against intermarriage at the same time, in addition to which, we really loved each other. Love, politics, work—it was a mighty coming together.

"He was also the first person who consistently supported me in my struggle to write. Whenever we moved, the first thing he did was to fix a place for me to work. He might be astonished and sometimes horrified at what came out, but he was always right there."

Though she says she can't imagine marrying again, she has been living companionably for several years with Robert Allen, a writer and the editor of *The Black Scholar*. They keep separate apartments but share their weekends in the country.

Once *The Color Purple* was sent into the world, Alice began traveling occasionally for poetry readings and lectures. As a Distinguished Writer in the Department of Afro-American Studies at Berkeley, she taught a course, The Inner Life—Visions of the Spirit, and she also taught creative writing for a semester at Brandeis University. As a teacher, critic, and editor, she introduces American students and readers to such important African authors as Bessie Head, Ama Ata Aidoo, and insists that black writers be included in Women's Studies courses and that Black Studies not neglect women.

But teaching and poetry readings are mainly ways of financing another long period of silence. ("Everything," she says, "comes out of silence.") She is looking forward to another novel.

In the meantime, she has collected her own essays for the book, *In Search of Our Mothers' Gardens: A Collection of Womanist Prose*. (She prefers "womanist" to "feminist" on the grounds that it sounds stronger and more inclusive.) She is also as politically active as a solitary person who dislikes meetings can be. With friend and novelist Tillie Olsen, Alice co-sponsored a San Francisco meeting of the Women's Party for Survival, a protest against nuclear weapons, and this concern for the fragility of our future is a theme of her new poems.

"Books are by-products of our lives," she explains. "Deliver me from writers who say the way they live doesn't matter. I'm not sure a bad person can write a good book. If art doesn't make us better, then what on earth is it for?"

All this talk about activism suddenly reminds me of a trip with Alice to Atlanta in the early 1970s for a march to celebrate Martin Luther King's birthday. I lost Alice in the crowded streets but found a group of Spelman students who had been searching for her. They knew every word of her work and had come to Atlanta in the hope of meeting her. They had even gone to see her childhood home in Georgia, just as Alice had sought out the life of Zora Neale Hurston.

The parallel had given me a chill then, when Alice's work was less plentiful and less well known. Even now, the thought wouldn't disappear: Could Alice Walker and her work ever be lost? Like Hurston, she had been introduced to us when her productive years happened to coincide with a movement for social justice, but what would happen when that coincidence was gone? Was Ralph Ellison right in saying that Americans reject serious novels until their time has passed and they have lost their moral cutting edge?

Perhaps we need to campaign just as energetically to get and keep good books in print as to get and keep good leaders in power. If critics and academics have too much invested in safer and more distant literary pantheons, we will have to create our own networks and publishing houses, as many feminists and others are now doing, as well as pressuring to change those that already exist.

If so, I suggest one populist criterion: Could we trust a particular writer to understand the complexities and realities of our own lives? Can she or he see us clearly, without bias for or against us, and with a compassionate heart?

I think we can trust Alice Walker to know us. And we can change for the better if we know her.

—1982

POSTSCRIPT

In the spring of 1983, Alice Walker received the American Book Award and the Pulitzer Prize for *The Color Purple*.

—1983

TRANSFORMING POLITICS

Houston and History

W*ere our State a pure democracy there would still be excluded from our deliberations women who, to prevent deprivation of morals and ambiguity of issues, should not mix promiscuously in gatherings of men.*

—Thomas Jefferson

In 1972 the United Nations declared 1975 to be the official International Year of the Woman. Among the world's women themselves, reaction was not all good. Was this like the International Year of the Handicapped? Or was it an admission that everything else was the Year of the Man?

Nonetheless, most governments began to collect statistics to present at the International Women's Year Conference in Mexico City, and that was a worthwhile result in itself. In some countries, this was the first time that research had been focused on the status of females. Many individual women and their organizations decided to use this world spotlight as an opportunity to meet each other and to further the cause of equality in any way they could. In this country, President Ford appointed an International Women's Year Commission of thirty-nine members to round up statistics and recommendations, and to travel to Mexico City as delegates. Thousands of individual American women also went there to take part in the unofficial events that often outnumbered and overshadowed the official ones. By the end of those few days, at least one other world

conference had been called for, and Women's Year had become
Women's Decade.

For most official and unofficial Americans, this was the first, mind-
expanding experience of a massive multicultural women's meeting. It
was also a source of learning. The range of women's concerns was both
culturally diverse and amazingly similar on the basic problems of women
in male-dominant societies. The nationalist divisions among women who
otherwise agreed on those basics were destructive and embittering. And,
like the women of most countries, the female half of the United States was
represented by a delegation and an official national agenda that might or
might not be what we had in mind. Despite many presidential commissions and other goodwill efforts to "study" American women, no one had
ever asked us.

It was this desire to work out women's own agenda of issues, goals,
and timetables that had motivated Congresswomen Bella Abzug and
Patsy Mink earlier in 1975 when they drafted and got support from other
congresswomen for Public Law 94-167—a proposal for a public, govern-
ment-funded conference in every state and territory that would identify
issues and elect delegates to a U.S. National Women's Conference. As a
kind of Constitutional Convention for women and a remedy for the
founding fathers who had excluded all women from the first one, this
national elected body would then recommend to Congress and the president those changes in laws, government procedures, and the Constitution
itself that would remove barriers to women's equality.

After Mexico City, there was enough enthusiasm and international
publicity to lobby this bill through. Of course, Congress didn't pass and
fund it until too late for the 1976 Bicentennial year in which the conference was supposed to happen, and its modest requested appropriation of
ten million dollars was cut to five million dollars: less than the cost of
sending one postcard to every adult woman. Nonetheless, a new International Women's Year Commission was appointed by President Carter,
this time for the purpose of carrying out the complex process of convening
a representative conference in every state and territory and electing
delegates proportionate to populations.

Thanks to the enthusiasm, energy, and sacrifice of women who
responded and spent months of outreach and organizing within their own
states, some of those fifty-six, two-day conferences were attended by as

many as twenty thousand women and interested men. They were the biggest and most economically and racially representative statewide political meetings ever held. The result was not only the identification of barriers to equality in twenty-six areas, from arts and humanities to welfare, but the election of two thousand delegates who were the first (and still the only) national political representatives in which family incomes of less than twenty thousand dollars a year, racial minorities, and all ages over eighteen were represented in proportion to their real presence in the population.

Once in Houston where the First National Women's Conference was held in November 1977, fifteen thousand participants, including observers from other countries, joined the two thousand voting delegates. A careful debate and balloting procedure allowed four days of discussion and voting on each of the twenty-six areas recommended by state conferences.* Though anti-equality women and men also rallied in protest in another part of Houston, led by right-wing Congressman Robert Dornan and anti-ERA activist Phyllis Schlafly, their views were fairly, perhaps disproportionately, represented among the voting delegates themselves. In some states, calculated and disproportionate flooding of the conferences by such groups as Mormons, fundamentalist Baptists, and, in Mississippi, the Ku Klux Klan had produced elected delegates whose positions did not match their states' majority opinions in elections and public opinion polls. Nonetheless, resolutions were passed that were pro-equality and, according to post-Houston national opinion polls, did have the majority support of Americans, women and men.

As journalist Lindsy Van Gelder reported from Houston, "It was like a supermarket check-out line from Anywhere, U.S.A. transposed to the political arena: homemakers and nuns, teenagers and senior citizens, secretaries and farmers and lawyers, mahogany skins and white and café au lait. We were an all-woman Carl Sandburg poem come to life."

Certainly the Houston conference itself was more representative by race, class, and age than either the U.S. House of Representatives or the Senate, and more democratic in its procedures—from allowing floor debate, amendments, and substitute motions to encouraging voting by

---

*For a full text of this National Plan of Action, see Caroline Bird, *What Women Want: The National Women's Conference* (New York: Simon and Schuster, 1979).

individual conscience rather than by geographical blocks or for political reward—than the national presidential conventions that were its closest models. The long and complex process leading up to Houston was often frustrating and never perfect, but its impressive results surprised many Americans, including some of the women who had worked hardest to make it happen.

This mammoth project begins to sound unprecedented, and there are many factual ways in which that is true. But comparable events *have* happened in the past. Women have taken action against the political systems of male dominance for as many centuries as they have existed, and some of those actions have been at least as impressive and, in their own contexts, more courageous. If we are to be successful in preserving the spirit of Houston, we should be aware that similar changeful, challenging, women-run events have been unrecorded, suppressed, ridiculed, or met with violence in the past.

As a student learning American history from the textbooks of the 1950s, I read that white and black women had been "given" the vote in 1920, an unexplained fifty years after black men had been "given" the vote as a result of a civil war fought on their behalf. I learned little about the many black people who had risen up in revolt and fought for their own freedom, and nothing about the more than one hundred years of struggle by nationwide networks of white and black women who organized and lectured around the country for both Negro and women's suffrage at a time when they were not even supposed to speak in public. They lobbied their all-male legislatures, demonstrated in the streets, went on hunger strikes and went to jail, and opposed this country's right to "fight for democracy" in World War I when half of American citizens had no political rights at all. In short, I did not learn that several generations of our foremothers had nearly brought the country to a halt in order to win a legal identity as human beings for women of all races.

At least the right to vote was cited in history books, however, as one that American women had not always enjoyed. Other parts of that legal identity—the goal of this country's long, first wave of feminism—were not mentioned. How many of us learned what it meant, for instance, for females to be the human property of husbands and fathers, and to die a "civil death" under the marriage laws? It was a condition of chattel so clear that the first seventeenth-century American slaveholders simply adopted it, as Gunnar Myrdal has pointed out, as the "nearest and most natural analogy" for the legal status of slaves.* As young students, how many of us understood that the right of an adult American female to own property, to sue in court, or to sign a will; to keep a salary she earned instead of turning it over to a husband or father who "owned" her; to go to school, to have legal custody of her own children, to leave her husband's home without danger of being forcibly and legally returned; to escape a husband's right to physically discipline her; to challenge the social prison of being a lifelong minor if she remained unmarried or a legal nonperson if she did marry—how many of us were instructed that all of these rights had been won through generations of effort by an independent women's movement?

When we studied American progress toward religious freedom, did we read about the many nineteenth-century feminists who challenged the patriarchal structure of the church, who dared question such scriptural rhetoric as the injunction of the Apostle Paul to "Wives, submit yourselves unto your husbands as unto the Lord"? Were we given a book called *The Woman's Bible*, a scholarly and very courageous revision of the scriptures undertaken by Elizabeth Cady Stanton?

If we read about religious and political persecution in America, did we learn that the frenzy of the New England witch trials, tortures, and burnings were usually the persecutions of independent or knowledgeable women, of midwives who performed abortions and taught contraception, of women who challenged the masculine power structure in many ways?

When we heard about courageous people who harbored runaway slaves, did they include women like Susan B. Anthony, who scandalized and alienated abolitionist allies by helping not only black slaves, but runaway wives and children who were escaping the brutality of white husbands and fathers who "owned" them?

Of course, to record the fact that both blacks and women were legal chattel, or that their parallel myths of "natural" inferiority were (and sometimes still are) used to turn both into a source of cheap labor, is not to be confused with equating these two groups. Black women and men

*Gunnar Myrdal, *An American Dilemma* (New York: Harper and Brothers, 1944), 1073.

often suffered more awful restrictions on their freedom, a more overt cruelty and violence, and their lives were put at greater risk. To teach a white girl child to read might be condemned as dangerous and even sinful, but it was not against the law, as it was for blacks in many slave states of the South. White women were far less likely than black slaves to risk their lives or be separated from their children, and particularly less so than black women who were forced to be breeders of more slaves as well as slaves themselves. Angelina Grimke, one of the courageous white southern feminists who worked against both race and sex slavery, always pointed out that "We have not felt the slaveholder's lash . . . we have not had our hands manacled."*

Nonetheless, white women were sometimes tortured or killed in "justified" domestic beatings or sold as indentured workers as a punishment for poverty, or for a liaison with a black man, or for breaking a law of obedience. Hard work combined with the years of coerced childbearing designed to populate this new land may have made white women's life expectancy as low as half that of white men. Early American graveyards full of young women who died in childbirth testify to the desperation with which many women must have sought out midwives for contraception or abortion. The most typical white female punishment was humiliation, the loss of freedom and identity, or to have her health and spirit broken. As Angelina Grimke explained, "I rejoice exceedingly that our resolution should combine us with the Negro. I feel that we have been with him; that the iron has entered into our souls . . . our *hearts* have been crushed."†

But why did so many of my history books assume that white women and blacks could have no issues in common, so much so that they failed to report on the real coalitions of the past? Historians seem to pay little attention to movements among the powerless. Perhaps the intimate, majority challenge presented by women of all races and men of color was (and still is) too threatening to the power of a white male minority.

Certainly, the lessons of history were not ignored because they were invisible at the time. Much of the long struggle for black and female personhood had been spent as a functioning, conscious coalition. ("*Resolved*. There never can be a true peace in this Republic until the civil and

---

*Angelina Grimke, in Elizabeth Cady Stanton et al., *The History of Woman Suffrage*, Vol. II. (Rochester: Charles Mann, 1899).
†Ibid.

political rights of all citizens of African descent and all women are practically established."* That statement was made by Elizabeth Cady Stanton and passed at a New York convention in 1863.) Like most early feminists, Stanton believed that sex and race prejudice had to be fought together; that both were "produced by the same cause, and manifested very much in the same way. The Negro's skin and the woman's sex are both [used as] *prima facie* evidence that they were intended to be in subjection to the white Saxon man."† Frederick Douglass, the fugitive slave who became an important national leader of the movement to abolish slavery and to establish the personhood of all females, vowed in his autobiography that, "When the true history of the antislavery cause shall be written, women will occupy a large space in its pages, for the cause of the slave has been peculiarly women's cause."‡ When Douglass died, newspapers reported a national mourning for him as a "friend of women" as well as an abolitionist pioneer. And there were many more such conscious statements and obvious lessons.

If more of us had learned the parallels and origins of the abolitionist and suffragist movements, there might have been less surprise when a new movement called "women's liberation" grew from the politicization of white and black women in the civil rights movement of the 1960s. Certainly a familiarity with the words of Frederick Douglass might have prevented some of the white and black men in both the civil rights and peace movements from feeling that their dignity depended on women's second-classness, or from seeing that they themselves were sometimes waging a sexual war against women, in Vietnam villages and at home. If women had been taught that feelings of emotional connection to other powerless groups were logical—that women also lacked power as a caste, and that we might feel understandably supportive when peace or civil rights sit-ins rejected violence as proofs of manhood—certainly I and many other women of my generation would have wasted less time being mystified by our odd and frequent sense of identification with all the "wrong" groups: the black movement, migrant workers, or with male contemporaries who were defying the "masculine" role by refusing to fight in Vietnam.

*Ibid.
†Ibid.
‡*The Life and Times of Frederick Douglass* (New York: Collier, 1962), p. 469.

As it was, however, suffragists were often portrayed as boring, ludicrous bluestockings when they were in history books at all: certainly no heroines you would need in modern America where we were, as male authorities kept telling us resentfully, "the most privileged women in the world." Some of us were further discouraged from exploring our real human strengths by accusations of Freudian penis envy, the dominating-mother syndrome, careerism, a black matriarchy that was (according to some white sociologists) more dangerous to black men than white racism, plus other punishable offenses. Men often emerged from World War II, Freudian analysis, and locker rooms with vague threats that they would replace any uppity women with more subservient ones—an Asian or European war bride instead of a "spoiled" American, a "feminine" white woman to replace a black "matriarch," or just some worshipful young "other woman."

There were many painful years of reinventing the wheel before we relearned the lessons that our foremothers could have taught us: that a false mythology of inferiority based on sex and race was being used to turn both groups into a support system. Limited intellectual ability, childlike natures, special job skills (always the poorly paid ones), greater emotionalism and closeness to nature, an inability to get along with our own group, chronic lateness and irresponsibility, happiness with our "natural" place—all these similar arguments were used against women of every race and men of color.

"The parallel between women and Negroes is the deepest truth of American life, for together they form the unpaid or underpaid labor on which America runs."* That was Gunnar Myrdal writing in 1944 in a rather obscure appendix to his landmark study on racism, *An American Dilemma*. Even in the sixties when I discovered those words (and wished devoutly that I had read them years before), I still did not know that Susan B. Anthony had put the issue even more succinctly almost a century before Myrdal. "Woman," she said, "has been the great unpaid laborer of the world."†

The current movements toward racial and sexual justice have had some success in pressuring for courses in women's history, black history, the study of Hispanic Americans, Native Americans, and many others,

*Myrdal, 1077.
†Susan B. Anthony, in Stanton, Vol. I.

but these subjects still tend to be special studies taken only by those with the most interest and the least need. They are rarely an integrated, inescapable part of the American history texts read by all students.

And if the recent past of our own country is still incomplete for many of us, how much less do we learn about other countries and more distant times?

What do we know about the African warrior queens of Dahomey, for instance, who led their armies against colonial invaders? Or the market women of modern West Africa who run the daily businesses of their countries? If we know little about the relationship of the witch hunts of New England to patriarchal politics, how much less do we know about the more than eight million women who were burned at the stake in medieval Europe, clearly as an effort to wipe out remains of a pre-Christian religion that honored the power of women and nature? If we know not even Stanton's *Woman's Bible* of the nineteenth century, what about the first-century texts of the Bible itself that show a much less patriarchal version of Christ's teachings? If the exceptional American women who were explorers, outlaws, ranchers, pirates, publishers, soldiers, and inventors are only just being rediscovered, what about those Native American nations and tribes that honored women in authority far more than the "advanced" European cultures that invaded their shores?

How are we to interpret the discovery that many of the "pagan idols," "false gods," and "pagan temples" so despised by Judeo-Christian tradition and the current Bible were representations of a female power: a god with a womb and breasts? How will our vision of prehistory change now that archaeologists have discovered that some skeletons long assumed to be male—because of their large-boned strength or because they were buried with weapons and scholarly scrolls—are really female? (In America, the famous archaeological find described as the Minnesota Man has recently been redesignated the Minnesota Woman. In Europe, the graves of young warriors killed by battle wounds have turned out to contain the skeletons of females.) Now that we are beginning to rediscover the interdependency of sexual and racial caste systems in our own nation's history, and the parallels in modern forms of job discrimination, will political-science courses begin to explain that a power structure dependent on race or class "purity"—whether it is whites in the American South and South Africa or Aryans in Nazi Germany—must place greater restrictions on the freedom of women in order to perpetuate that "purity"? Will we finally be allowed to confront these caste systems together, and therefore successfully in the long run, instead of facing constant divide-and-conquer tactics in the short run?

Such revolts against birth-based caste systems have always been international, and contagious. Anticolonial movements against external dominations of one race by another have deepened into movements against internal dominations based on racial or sexual caste. Together, they are the most profound and vital movements of this century and the last. They are changing both our hopes for the future and our assumptions about the past.

But some revelations about the past can be both rewarding and angering. It seems that our ancestors knew so much that we should not have had to relearn.

Among the resolutions in the National Plan of Action adopted at Houston, for instance, there are many echoes of the first wave of American feminism. The high incidence of battered women, the inadequacy of laws to protect them, and the reluctance of police to interfere—all those facts struck many Americans as shocking new discoveries. If we had known more about the history of a husband's legal right to "own" his wife, and therefore to "discipline" her physically with the explicit permission of the law, we could have uncovered this major form of violence much sooner. A wife's loss of her own name, legal residence, credit rating, and many other civil rights might have seemed less "natural" and inevitable if we had known that our marriage laws were still rooted in the same common-law precedent ("husband and wife are one person in law . . . that of the husband")* that nineteenth-century English and American women had struggled so hard to reform. We would have been better prepared for arguments that the Equal Rights Amendment would "destroy the family" or force women to become "like men" if we had known that the same accusations, almost word for word, were leveled against the suffrage movement. (The possibility of two political opinions in one family was said to be a sure way to destroy it. Our own foremothers were called "unsexed women," "entirely devoid of personal attraction," who had only been "disappointed in their endeavors to appropriate

*Blackstone, *Commentaries*

breeches," all because they wanted to vote and own property.) Even the charge that the ERA would be contrary to states' rights and constitute a "federal power grab" is a repeat of the argument that a citizen's right to vote should be left entirely up to the states; a stumbling block that caused suffragists to proceed state by state, and to delay focusing on a Nineteenth Amendment to the Constitution for many years.

In a way, the unity represented by the minority women's resolution—perhaps the single greatest accomplishment of the Houston Conference, because it brought together all Americans of color for the first time, from Asian to Puerto Rican—was also the greatest example of the high price of lost history. After all, black women had been the flesh-and-blood links between abolition and suffrage; yet they had suffered from double discrimination and invisibility even then. ("There is a great stir about colored men getting their rights," warned Sojourner Truth, the great black feminist and antislavery leader, "but not a word about colored women.")* When American male political leaders destroyed the coalition for universal adult suffrage by offering the vote to its smallest segment—that is, to black males—but refused the half of the country that was female, black women were forced to painfully and artificially slice up their identities They could either support their brothers in, as the slogan of the era put it, "the Negroes' hour," even though no black woman was included; or, like Sojourner Truth, they could advocate "keeping the thing going . . . because if we wait till it is still, it will take a great while to get things going again."† Once it was clear that black men were going to get the vote first, no matter what any woman said, black women were further isolated by some white suffragists who, embittered by the desertion of both white and black male allies, began to use the racist argument that the white female "educated" vote was necessary to outweigh the black male "uneducated" vote. Divisions deepened. Sojourner Truth's prediction that it would "take a great while to get things going again" if the two great parallel causes were divided turned out to be true. It was a half century later, and many years after Sojourner Truth's death, before women of all races won the vote.

Even so, many scars of the rift between white and black women remain. So does the cruel and false argument that black women must

*Sojourner Truth, in Stanton, Vol. II, 193.
†Ibid.

suppress their own talents on behalf of black men, thus weakening the black community by half. White male "liberals" had tried a divide-and-conquer tactic by separating out black men, and, in many sad ways, they won.

When the first reformist prelude to feminism started up again in the early and mid sixties, it was largely a protest of middle-class white housewives against the "feminine mystique" that kept them trapped in the suburbs. For black women who often had no choice but to be in the labor force, that was a life-style that some envied and few could afford. Only after the civil rights movement and feminism's emergence again in the later sixties—after the analysis of all women as a caste, not just as a privileged and integrationist few—did the organic ties between the movements against racial and sexual caste begin to grow again. In spite of enduring racism in society, in spite of an economic and social structure that exploits racial divisions among women and also manufactures social and economic tensions between black women and men, the women's movement has become the most racially and economically integrated movement in the country—and even so, it is not integrated enough. Despite the enduring argument that male supremacy is a social norm to which all should aspire, the black movement and its political leaders now include a few more women than do their white counterparts—but even so, there is far from a balance.

For this wave of feminism, Houston was the first public landmark in a long, suspicion-filled journey across racial barriers. At last there were enough women of color (more than a third of all delegates and thus a greater proportion than the population) to have a strong voice. There were not only black women, but Hispanic women (from Chicana to Puerto Rican, Latina to Cuban) as the second largest American minority, Asian Pacific women, Alaskan Native, and American Indian women from many different nations, who themselves were often meeting for the first time. But how much less perilous this journey would have been if we had maintained the bridges of the past; if we had not had to build new roads to coalitions through what seemed to us an uncharted wilderness.

*F*or myself, Houston and all the events surrounding it have become a landmark in personal history, the sort of milestone that divides our sense of time. Figuring out the date of any other event now means remember-ing: Was it before or after Houston?

The reason has a lot to do with learning. In retrospect, I realize that I had been skeptical about the time and effort spent on this First National Women's Conference. Could a government-sponsored conference really be populist and inclusive? Even after the state conferences made clear that the combination of public and private outreach was working, I still feared the culmination in Houston as if it were an approaching trial. Would this enormous meeting attract national and international attention, only to highlight disorder? Would the anti-equality counterconference be taken as proof that "women can't get along"? As a member of the new International Women's Year Commission appointed by President Carter, I had worked throughout that year of state conferences and preparation, but as their culmination in Houston came closer, I still would have given anything to stop worrying, avoid conflict, stay home, or just indefinitely delay this event about which I cared too much.

I thought my fears were rational and objective. They were not.

Yes, I had learned, finally, that *individual women* could be compe-tent, courageous, and loyal to each other. Despite growing up with no experience of women in positions of worldly authority, I had learned that much. But I still did not believe that *women as a group* could be competent, courageous, and loyal to each other. I didn't believe that we could conduct large, complex events that celebrated our own diversity. I wasn't sure that we could make a history that was our own.

But we can. Houston taught us that. The question is: Will this lesson be lost again?

—1979

The International Crime of Genital Mutilation

ROBIN MORGAN
AND GLORIA STEINEM*

arning: These words are painful to read. They describe facts of life as far away as our most fearful imagination and as close as any denial of women's sexual freedom.

As you read this, an estimated thirty million women in the world are suffering the results of genital mutilation. The main varieties of this extensive custom are:

1. Sunna "circumcision," or removal of the prepuce and/or tip of the clitoris.

2. Clitoridectomy, or the excision of the entire clitoris (both prepuce and glans), plus the adjacent parts of the labia minora.

3. Infibulation (from the Latin *fibula,* or "clasp"), that is, the removal of the entire clitoris, the labia minora, and labia majora—plus the joining of the scraped sides of the vulva across the vagina, where they are secured with thorns or sewn with catgut or thread. A small opening is preserved by inserting a sliver of wood (commonly a matchstick) into the wound during the healing process, thus allowing passage of urine and menstrual blood. An infibulated woman must be cut open to permit intercourse, and cut further to permit childbirth. Often, she is

*Though this article is co-authored, we have chosen to publish it as part of our respective work because of the subject's importance.

closed up again after delivery, and thus may be subject to such procedures repeatedly during her reproductive life.

The age at which these ritual sexual mutilations are performed varies with the type of procedure and local tradition. A female may undergo some such rite as early as the eighth day after birth, or at puberty, or after she herself has borne children. In most areas, however, the ritual is carried out when the child is between the ages of three and eight, and she may be considered unclean, improper, or unmarriagable if it is not done.

To readers for whom such customs come as horrifying news, it is vital that we immediately recognize the connection between these patriarchal practices and our own. They are different in scope and degree, but not in kind. Not only have American and European women experienced the psychic clitoridectomy that was legitimized by Freud,* but Western nineteenth-century medical texts also proclaim genital mutilation as an accepted treatment for "nymphomania," "hysteria," masturbation, and other nonconforming behavior. Indeed, there are women living in the United States and Europe today who have suffered this form (as well as other, more familiar forms) of gynophobic, medically unnecessary, mutilating surgery.

As a general practice and precondition of marriage, however, some researchers cite recent evidence for genital mutilation in areas as diverse as Australia, Brazil, Malaya, Pakistan, and among the Skoptsi Christian sect in the Soviet Union. In El Salvador, it is still not uncommon for a mother to carve the sign of the cross with a razor blade on the clitoris of her little girl for reasons such as to "make her a better worker and keep her from getting ideas." But international health authorities find the most extensive evidence of such customs on the African continent and the Arabian peninsula. The majority of mutilations take place without anesthetic at home (in the city or village), but many are now performed in hospitals as approved procedures. Nor are these rites limited to one religion; they are practiced by some Islamic peoples, some Coptic Christians, members of various indigenous tribal religions, some Catholics and Protestants, and some Fellasha, an ancient Jewish sect living in the Ethiopian highlands.

*"The elimination of clitoral sexuality is a necessary precondition for the development of femininity." *Sexuality and the Psychology of Love* (New York: Macmillan, 1963).

The form most common on the African continent is clitoridectomy, which is practiced in more than twenty-six countries from the Horn of Africa and the Red Sea across to the Atlantic coast, and from Egypt in the north to Mozambique in the south, also including Botswana and Lesotho. According to Awa Thiam, the Senegalese writer, clitoridectomy—in the form of either complete excision or the more "moderate" Sunna variant— also can be found in the two Yemens, Saudi Arabia, Iraq, Jordan, Syria, and southern Algeria. Infibulation appears to be fairly standard in the whole of the Horn—Somalia, most of Ethiopia, the Sudan (despite legislation prohibiting it in 1946), Kenya, Nigeria, Mali, Upper Volta, and parts of Ivory Coast. Many ethnic groups have local versions: some cauterize the clitoris with fire or rub a special kind of nettle across the organs in order to destroy nerve endings; some stanch the flow of blood with compounds made of herbs, milk, honey, and sometimes ashes or animal droppings.

The health consequences of such practices include primary fatalities due to shock, hemorrhage, or septicemia, and such later complications as genital malformation, delayed menarche, dyspareunia (pain suffered during intercourse), chronic pelvic complications, incontinence, calcification deposits in the vaginal walls, recto-vaginal fistulas, vulval cysts and abscesses, recurrent urinary retention and infection, scarring and keloid formation, infertility, and an entire array of obstetric complications. There is also increased probability of injury to the fetus (by infection) during pregnancy and to the infant during birth. Psychological responses among women range from temporary trauma and permanent frigidity to psychoses. A high rate of mortality is suspected by health officials, although there are few fatality records available, because of the informality or secrecy surrounding the custom in many areas.

Although such practices are frequently described as "female circumcision," the degree of damage is not comparable to the far more minor circumcision of males. Certainly, the two procedures are related: both are widely practiced without medical necessity and are extreme proofs of subservience to patriarchal authority—whether tribal, religious, or cultural—over all sexual and reproductive functions. But there the parallel stops. Clitoridectomy is more analogous to penisectomy than to circumcision: the clitoris has as many nerve endings as the penis. On the other hand, male circumcision involves cutting the tip of the protective "hood" of skin that covers the penis, an area whose number of nerve endings are analogous to those in the earlobe, but not damaging the penis. This procedure does not destroy its victim's capacity for sexual pleasure; indeed, some justify the practice as increasing it by exposing more of the sensitive area. The misnomer "female circumcision" seems to stem from conscious or unconscious political motives: to make it appear that women are merely experiencing something men also undergo—no more, no less

Politics are also evident in the attribution of this custom. The Sudanese name for infibulation credits it to Egypt ("Pharaonic circumcision"), while the Egyptians call the same operation "Sudanese circumcision." The more moderate "Sunna circumcision" was supposedly recommended by the Prophet Muhammed, who is said to have counseled, "Reduce, but don't destroy," thus reforming, and legitimizing, the ritual. That version was termed "Sunna," or traditional, perhaps in an attempt to placate strict traditionalists, although such rituals are mentioned nowhere in the Koran, a fact Islamic women who oppose this mutilation cite in their arguments.

The overt justifications for genital mutilation are as contradictory as are theories about its origins. Explanations include custom, religion, family honor, cleanliness, protection against spells, initiation, insurance of virginity at marriage, and prevention of female promiscuity by physically reducing, or terrorizing women out of, sexual desire, this last especially in polygamous cultures. On the other hand, the fact that some women in the Middle East who are prostitutes also have been clitoridectomized is cited as proof that it *doesn't* reduce pleasure, as if women become prostitutes out of desire.

A superstition is a practice or belief justified by simultaneous and utterly opposing sets of arguments. (For instance, male circumcision is not only said to increase desire but to decrease it through toughening of the exposed skin or removing the friction-causing "hood.") Thus, a frequently given reason for sexual mutilation is that it makes a woman more fertile, yet in 1978 Dr. R. T. Ravenholt, then director of the United States Agency for International Development's Population Bureau, failed to oppose it on the ground that it was a *contraceptive* method, claiming that "because it aimed at reducing female sex desire, [clitoridectomy/infibulation] undoubtedly has fertility control as part of its motivation." In fact, some women's behavior indicates the reverse. The pain of intercourse often leads mutilated women to seek pregnancy as a temporary relief from sexual demands.

In some cultures, the justification is even less obscure. Myths of the Mossi of Upper Volta, and the Dogon and Bambaras of Mali, clearly express the fear of an initially hermaphroditic human nature and of women's sexuality: the clitoris is considered a dangerous organ, fatal to a man if brought into contact with his penis.

Similarly, in nineteenth-century London, Dr. Isaac Baker Brown justified scissoring off the clitoris of some of his own English patients as a cure for such various ills as insomnia, sterility, and "unhappy marriages." In 1859, Dr. Charles Meigs recommended application of a nitrate of silver solution to the clitoris of female children who masturbated. Until 1925 in the United States, a medical association called the Orificial Surgery Society offered surgical training in clitoridectomy and infibula-tion "because of the vast amount of sickness and suffering which could be saved the gentler sex. . . ." Such operations (and justifications) occurred as recently as the 1940s and 1950s in the United States. For instance, in New York alone, the daughter of a well-to-do family was clitoridecto-mized as a "treatment" for masturbation recommended by a family physician. Some prostitutes were encouraged by well-meaning church social workers to have this procedure as a form of "rehabilitation."

During the 1970s, clitoral "relocation"—termed "Love Surgery"—entered some medical practice. As late as 1979, the feminist news service Hersay carried the story of Dr. James Burt, an Ohio gynecologist who offered a fifteen-hundred-dollar "Mark Two" operation, which involved vaginal reconstruction in order to "make the clitoris more accessible to direct penile stimulation."

Whatever the supposed justifications for these efforts to make women's bodies conform to societal expectations, we can explore the real reasons for them only within the context of patriarchy. It must control women's bodies as the means of reproduction, and thus repress the independent power of women's sexuality. Both motives are enforced by socioeconomic rewards and punishments.

If marriage is the primary means of economic survival for a woman, then whatever will make her more marriageable becomes desirable. If a bride who lacks virginity literally risks death or renunciation on her wedding night, then a chastity belt forged of her own flesh is a gesture of parental concern. If the tribal role of clitoridectomist or midwife who performs such mutilations is the sole position of honor, power, or even independent livelihood available to women, then the "token women" who perform such rites will fight to preserve them. If those who organize the ceremonies of excision (sometimes whole families by inherited prerogative) have the right, as they do in some cultures, to "adopt" the excised children to work in their fields for two or three years, then such families have a considerable economic motive for perpetuating the custom. If Western male gynecologists also believed women's independent sexuality to be dangerous and unnatural, then surgery was justified to remove its cause. If a modern gynecologist still presumes that men may not be willing to learn how to find or stimulate the clitoris for female pleasure, then he will think it natural to move the clitoris closer to the customary site of penile pleasure.

Illogical responses can be carried to new depths by bureaucrats. The White House and its concern for "human rights," the various desks of the United States State Department, and such agencies as the United Nations International Children's Fund and the World Health Organization all have expressed reluctance to interfere with "social and cultural attitudes" regarding female genital mutilation. This sensitivity has been markedly absent on other issues, for example, campaigns to disseminate vaccines or vitamins despite resistance from local traditionalists.

Clearly, "culture" is that which affects women while "politics" affects men. Even human-rights and other admirable political statements do not include those of special importance to the female majority of humanity. (This is true not only for genital mutilation and other areas of reproductive freedom. Most women of the Middle East cannot leave their countries without a male family member's written permission, yet this is not classed with, for instance, Jews who are forbidden to leave the Soviet Union, or other travel restrictions that affect men as well.) Some international agencies take a reformist position—that clitoridectomy and/or infibulation should be done in hospitals under hygienic conditions and proper medical supervision. Feminist groups and such respected organizations as Terre des Hommes, the (ironically named) Swiss-based international agency dedicated to the protection of children, repeatedly have urged a strengthening of this position to one condemning the practice outright.

The situation is further complicated by the understandable suspicion on the part of many African and Arab governments and individuals that Western interest in the matter is motivated not by humanitarian concerns but by a racist or neocolonialist desire to eradicate indigenous cultures. In fact, as Jomo Kenyatta, Kenya's first president, noted in his book, *Facing Mount Kenya*, the key mobilization of many forces for Kenyan independence from the British was in direct response to attempts by Church of Scotland missionaries in 1929 to suppress clitoridectomy. Patriarchal authorities, whether tribal *or* imperial, have always considered as central to their freedom and power the right to define what is done with "their" women. But past campaigns against female mutilation, conducted for whatever ambiguous or even deplorable reasons, need not preclude new approaches that might be more effective because they would be sensitive to the cultures involved and, most important, supportive of the *women* affected, and in response to *their* leadership.

Precisely such an initiative began in February 1979, at a historic meeting in Khartoum, Sudan, attended by delegates (including physicians, midwives, and health officials) from ten African and Arab nations and supported by many who could not attend. Initiated by the WHO Regional Office for the Eastern Mediterranean with the assistance of the Sudanese government, this meeting was cautiously called a seminar on "Traditional Practices Affecting the Health of Women and Children"— such practices as child marriage, and nutritional taboos during pregnancy and lactation, but also including genital mutilation. Four recommendations resulted:

1. Adoption of clear national policies for the abolition of "female circumcision."

2. Establishment of national commissions to coordinate activities, including the enactment of abolition legislation.

3. Intensification of general education on the dangers and undesirability of the practice.

4. Intensification of education programs for birth attendants, midwives, healers, and other practitioners of traditional medicine, with a view to enlisting their support.

Later in 1979, a United Nations conference held in Lusaka, Zambia— one of the series of regional preparatory meetings for the United Nations' 1980 World Conference for the Decade for Women—also dealt with the subject. Adopting a resolution sponsored by Edna Adan Ismail of Somalia, the meeting condemned female mutilations and called on all women's organizations *in the countries concerned* "to mobilize information and health-education campaigns on the harmful medical and social consequences of the practices."

It is also true, however, that genital mutilation is not always cited as a priority by women in developing countries: the elimination of famine, general health, agricultural and industrial development may take precedence. Yet the Khartoum and Lusaka meetings showed clearly that many women, and men of conscience, throughout the African and Arab countries have for a long time been actively opposing clitoridectomy and infibulation. Such groups as the Voltaic Women's Federation and the Somali Women's Democratic Organization, and such individuals as Dr. Fatima Abdul Mahmoud, minister of social affairs of the Sudan, Mehani Saleh of the Aden Ministry of Health, Awa Thiam of Senegal, and Esther Ogunmodede, the crusading journalist of Nigeria, have been campaigning in different ways against genital mutilation, with little international support. In fact, according to Fran P. Hosken, a feminist who for years has been trying to mobilize American and international consciousness on this issue, "International and UN agencies, as well as charitable and church groups and family-planning organizations working in Africa, have engaged in a 'conspiracy of silence.' . . . As a result, those Africans who are working for a change in their own countries have been completely isolated or ignored."

Now, victims and witnesses are beginning to be heard as they speak personally about the suffering inflicted, whether in a village hut, a modern apartment, or a sterile operating room, by genital mutilation—suffering that may continue for a lifetime. Their voices are unforgettable. It's long past time that we heard them and understood what is being done—to them, and to all of us. It's time that we began to act—*with* them, the most immediate victims, and in the shared interest of women as a people.

—1979

POSTSCRIPT

When this article was written, we used the most conservative estimate of 30 million women who were suffering the results of genital mutilation.

Since then, official estimates made by the World Health Organization have increased the number to 75 million.

UNICEF was the only UN agency that had made the elimination of these practices a goal of its program, and then only as a part of its larger concern with children's health. For the first time, UNICEF's executive board meeting in May 1980, raised "female circumcision" among the issues in a special report on women and the overall development and economic well-being of their countries. WHO has also taken up this concern as a formal part of its program. Furthermore, the four recommendations listed earlier, the results of the first WHO conference on the subject in 1979, were approved by the World Conference for the UN Decade for Women which met in July 1980, in Copenhagen.

In 1982, President Daniel Arap Moi of Kenya banned the practice of genital mutilation after fourteen excised girls had died.

Norway, Denmark, and Sweden have banned excision procedures by law. African and Middle Eastern families residing there had made this traditional practice an issue by requesting that it be done in hospitals. It is not banned in France or England, however, and there are many reports of local surgeons who perform it for a substantial fee. In 1982, the father of a family from Mali that was residing in France was arrested for removing his three-month-old daughter's clitoris with a pocketknife. There have been some unconfirmed reports that a few American women who have converted to Islam have had, or been pressured to have, this operation as a tribute to cultural nationalism.

The most hopeful sign is that women themselves in the most affected countries are now being heard and taking the leadership on the elimination of genital mutilation. It's hopeful, too, that such patriarchal practices are beginning to be understood as a universal problem in varying degrees, not the fault of only one culture or religion.

This article itself is being distributed by UNICEF.

—1983

R_X Fantasies: For Temporary Relief of Pain Due to Injustice

I write this on the eighth birthday of *Ms*. magazine, just before the United Nations Women's Conference in Copenhagen.

These two events fill me with a combination of hope and anger. I look back at early issues of *Ms*. and am alarmed to find that many articles are still entirely current: the objective conditions of life haven't changed very much for the majority of women. I study the documents for yet another UN conference, and realize that our official representatives and points of conflict are still dictated by governments, not by the women they govern.

On the other hand, I know there is a new American majority support for equality issues that weren't even recognized as issues a few years ago, and *Ms*. is a flourishing forum that started with barely enough money to last eight months, much less eight years. I also hope that cross-cultural gatherings like Copenhagen might just yield enough woman-to-woman contacts to create some future International Revolutionary Feminist Government-in-Exile.

Suddenly, I begin to feel better. Most of this rush of hope is based on reality, but some of it is a fantasy of empowerment for the female half of the world that grows from inventing phrases like the International Revolutionary Feminist Government-in-Exile.

Fantasies bolster our psychic strength, and sometimes advance our vision. They may also combine laughter and revenge in a very medicinal way. I offer here a Fantasy Starter Set, so each of us can create fantasies to suit the crimes.

*F*eminists get together a small international army and take over Saudi Arabia. We are able to do this with a minimum of violence because the men of the royal family are so freaked out at the idea of being attacked by women—and so unable to take the attack seriously—that they barely fight back. They are victims of their own prejudice.

We then free Saudi women from the palace women's quarters, harems, veils, and a status as chattel so complete that they are not allowed to drive cars and legally can be executed for infidelity. (Actually, we've had subversive agents there for some time: the fed-up wives of American oil executives, and reliable reports of *Ms.* magazine being read in the harem. More important, Saudi women have been coming in disguise to international women's conferences.) Together, we turn to the world, and say: "Now *deal*. You want this oil? Here's what you have to do for women and all your powerless groups. Here's how you redistribute the wealth, and overthrow systems based on sex, race, and class. Otherwise—no oil."

Nurtured and elaborated, this fantasy can make you happy for at least ten minutes. (For instance, the army of my imagination is sometimes led by lawyer, black activist, and feminist Florynce Kennedy. This gives us our own "Florynce of Arabia.")

*S*ome feminist (pick one of your choice, preferably yourself) has just defeated (select one) the pope, the president of the Mormon Church, the Lubevitche Rebbe, Ronald Reagan, William Buckley, Jimmy Carter, William Shockley, Lionel Tiger, George Gilder, Gay Talese, the Ayatollah Khomeini, or ———— in public debate. He is being laughed off the stage. The whole thing is telecast by satellite in every language of the world.

*T*he New York Times is inherited by women who break with family tradition and do *not* pass its control to husbands, brothers, sons, or sons-in-law. (Like hemophilia, *The Times* is passed through women but received by men.) Instead, they assume publishing power themselves and fire every editor and manager who was responsible for the bias cited by the staff members in their landmark sex- and race-discrimination suits. Then they say to the litigants: "There, my dears—now *you* decide who will run *The New York Times*."

*A*t night in the office buildings of Wall Street, a group of cleaning women plot, organize, read up on computer technology, and carry out an elaborate heist in which they rig the computers of the six biggest multinationals to transfer 41 percent of all assets into the cleaning women's Swiss bank account. Though they leave a printout explaining what they did and why ("Gentlemen: Since women workers receive only fifty-nine cents for each dollar paid to men . . . "), the boards of directors are too humiliated to admit that they have been handily outsmarted by their own *cleaning women*. Instead of prosecuting, they announce bankruptcy due to "technical difficulties." Their multinationals are broken up and turned over to the workers.

Meanwhile, the mysterious Cleaning Women Gang distributes its loot to Americans below the poverty line (men, too; they're building coalitions), saving just enough to finance training missions to Europe, Asia, Africa, et cetera. There, they pass their knowledge on to other Cleaning Women Gangs in London . . . Rome . . . Moscow . . . Tokyo . . . Pretoria. . . .

*F*or the second time this year, Pope John Paul announces one more time that the church should stay out of politics—only this time, *he really means it*. All church attempts to influence legislation on contraception, sexuality, abortion, the family, and other private matters come to an immediate halt. Taxes begin to flow in from parking lots, hotels, shopping centers, and all other church property not being used for religious purposes. We actually achieve separation of church and state.

*C*lerical workers, researchers, analysts, office cleaners, and all other women working in the Pentagon and the Defense Department go on strike—*for just one day*. They also serve notice. Unless 25 percent of the military budget is transferred into social programs *immediately,* they will go on a similar strike approximately once a month, and then *twice* a month . . . and so on. They bring the Pentagon to its knees.

*W*ives and secretaries begin to tell each other everything they know, and hold press conferences besides. Women who work for big corporations also tell each other their salaries. They tell the world the corporate executives' salaries—and many other secrets. Every woman who has been impregnated and encouraged to have an abortion by an anti-abortion politician goes on television and . . . well, you get the idea. Knowledge is power.

*P*lease don't think that all my fantasies are cheerful. Many are very paranoid indeed. Given the increasing ability to predetermine a baby's sex, for instance, plus the bias toward having sons, and the development of extrauterine birth, the worst of my fantasies stretches through decades of a decreasing female population. It ends in some international zoo of the future with a dozen of us in cages and a sign: "Please don't feed the women."

Nonetheless, a strong fantasy life is our own personal science fiction. It's a source of relief, escape, and even a few far-out ideas.

Take the women's self-help health movement, for instance. Its pioneers have helped us learn about the amazing resilience, strength, and sensitivity of the cervix. Suppose that knowledge were combined with biofeedback techniques that taught us how to control those muscles. Women who have been unable to carry babies to term might be able to do so. Women who didn't wish to be pregnant might be able to self-abort. By the year 2000, if women used every publication and every national and international conference to teach each other this subversive technique in geometrically increasing numbers, we might be able to declare a selective "baby strike." Not only would we have seized control of the means of reproduction, but nobody would be able to do one damn thing about it.

It certainly would be a great use of women's conferences—and these pages.

—1980

If Hitler Were Alive, Whose Side Would He Be On?

*S*ix million is the number generally assigned not only to Jews who died under Hitler but to babies who have died under the Supreme Court.

—Patrick Riley
National Catholic Register,
May 13, 1979

AUSCHWITZ, DACHAU, AND MARGARET SANGER: THREE OF A KIND
—sign at the 1979
Right-to-Life Convention

Just as the Jews were depicted as untermenschen, *so the unborn are depicted as nonhuman.*

—Raymond J. Adamek
Human Life Review,
Fall 1977

Using the same analogy to Nazi Germany made by many of the speakers, [Congressman Robert K.] Dornan said, "We know in this country what is going on. Some of the Germans had the excuse they weren't sure."

—*The Washington Post,*
January 23, 1977

This is not the time to "cool the rhetoric." . . . *We are not "sliding toward Auschwitz." We are not "headed for a Holocaust." We are living in the very midst of one.* . . . *The American Abolitionist League calls on the conscience of the pro-life community to* . . . *padlock the slaughter-houses. Stage sit-ins. Let this nation know that the laws of the Supreme Being take precedence over the laws of the Supreme Court.*

> —*The Abolitionist,*
> (an anti-abortion
> newsletter published
> in Pittsburgh)

[At the National Right-to-Life Convention] Professor William C. Brennan . . . *said [the company] which manufactures devices and medicines used in abortion [is] in the same position as I. G. Farben, the German firm that made chemicals used in the mass execution of Jews.*

> —*The Catholic News,*
> July 5, 1979

I

If you haven't been at an anti-abortion rally lately, or stumbled on the right-wing efforts to achieve a constitutional ban against abortion, then the quotations you've just read may seem bizarre and exceptional.

Certainly, the groups that use these and other inflammatory arguments don't trust the major media. (The same Professor Brennan quoted above, for instance, went on to compare the American press with that in Nazi Germany and to condemn it for "concealing the facts.") That's why they have created their own media world of right-wing newsletters, pamphlets, and books distributed through churches and local organizations or through computerized mailing lists for which they claim ten million names, plus television shows that reach fourteen million homes weekly.

But feminists who have been working especially on the issues of reproductive freedom, and those few reporters who research the ultraright wing, have been sending back warnings of this increasingly vicious campaign ever since the 1973 Supreme Court decisions on abortion. By

1974, for instance, Marion K. Sanders, a distinguished reporter for *Harper's* magazine, reported that "the analogy with Hitler's extermination program . . . has proved potent propaganda. The implication is that legal abortion is only a first step toward compulsory abortion for 'undesirables,' raising the specter of genocide for black people."

As it turned out, most of the black community rejected this genocide argument based on its source if nothing else: overwhelmingly white, right-wing groups that also opposed most integration and civil rights efforts. If some black women were having a disproportionate number of abortions, as the anti-abortion groups often cited as proof of "genocide," it was because they had less access to good health care and contraception. In fact, the white birthrate declined proportionately as much as the black birthrate after contraception and abortion became legal, and it remains lower than that for black Americans. More important, a very disproportionate number of the women whose health and lives are saved by safe, legal abortion are black. (For instance, in New York City's Harlem Hospital alone, in the first year following the 1971 liberalization of New York State's abortion law, there were about 750 fewer admissions of women suffering from self-induced or illegal abortions.) Finally, legally available or Medicaid-funded abortions as a matter of right have meant that black and other minority women are less vulnerable to racist "bargaining": a safe abortion, in return for agreeing to be sterilized.

Altogether, many of the anti-abortion groups seemed more motivated by concern with the decline of the white birthrate to a low unprecedented in American history—even producing too few "adoptable" white infants to meet the demand—than with the need to protect the reproductive rights of poor or minority Americans. (In some states, anti-abortion leaders and legislators had advocated withholding welfare from women with three or more children unless those women agreed to be sterilized.) The self-description of "abolitionist" by groups working to abolish legal abortion tries for an emotional connection between the antichoice movement and the movement against slavery. So does their odd equating of the Dred Scott and the 1973 Supreme Court decisions, as if denying legal personhood to a slave and to a fetus were exactly the same thing. But right-wing literature now focuses less on blacks and other minorities and more on those who fear change most: the white middle class, the elderly, religious fundamentalists; and others who may feel that their power and their life-styles are endangered.

To them, abortion is constantly presented as the symbolic beginning of some horrifying future. It will destroy marriage and morality by removing childbearing as the only goal of sex and as God's will; it will limit the number of future people like them, thus jeopardizing the future of a white majority; it will endanger old or handicapped people by paving the way for euthanasia; it will masculinize women by allowing them to choose an identity other than being vessels for other people's lives; and finally it will be the same as legalizing murder.

The nature of the fear may vary, but the metaphor for terror is often the same: Hitler's philosophy and concentration camps—the closest modern memory can come to an earthly version of hell.

"Is there much difference between the concept of a 'Master Race' (quality race)," Dr. and Mrs. J. C. Willke ask rhetorically in their *Handbook on Abortion*, "and the 'quality of life' of our modern pro-abortionist social planners?" According to this obscurely published, widely distributed paperback (with a photograph of a white teenage girl listening attentively to a white male doctor on the cover), the answer is no. "Although never legalized, abortion had become in fact the accepted answer for the mother's social problem in the 1920s and 1930s in Germany," the Willkes allege. "The above physicians, accustomed to accepting the killing of one group of humans who were socially burdensome (the unborn), were apparently able to move logically to killing other classes of humans."

By focusing only on the doctor and ignoring the rights and requests of the patients, these authors equate two opposite acts: an abortion performed at the request of a woman who has freely chosen it (and who has a logical right to decide whether or not a pregnancy will go forward with the use of her body and all its life-support systems), and the death of an autonomous person who has requested no such thing (not even, presumably, the right to suicide or a planned and peaceful death). The crucial questions of *who decides* and *where the authority lies* are never discussed in these emotional comparisons between abortion and death camps; between a belief in reproductive choice as an individual right *against* the dictates of government, and a Nazi authoritarianism that opposed the very idea of individual rights.

"True idealism," as Hitler wrote in *Mein Kampf*, "is nothing but the subordination of the interests and life of the individual to the community. . . . The sacrifice of personal existence is necessary to secure the preservation of the species."

Does this begin to sound familiar? It should, because the second flaw in the libelous equation of prochoice advocates with Nazis is that Hitler himself, and the Nazi doctrine he created, were unequivocally opposed to any individual right to abortion. In fact, Hitler's National Socialist Movement preached against and punished contraception, homosexuality, any women whose main purpose was not motherhood, men who did not prove their manhood by fathering many children, and anything else that failed to preserve and expand the Germanic people and the German state.

In *Mein Kampf*, Hitler wrote that "We must also do away with the conception that the treatment of the body is the affair of every individual."

Those words were a direct slap at the feminist movement of Germany in the late-nineteenth and early-twentieth centuries, an influential force for, among other things, divorce, contraception, and abortion; in short, for a woman's right to own and control her own body.

Not only did German feminists share these goals of their sisters in other countries, but they had won some earlier and greater successes. They achieved the vote in 1918, for instance, as part of the Weimar Constitution that followed World War I. By 1926, moderate feminists had elected thirty-two women deputies to the Reichstag, the national parliamentary body that politically symbolized this brief burst of democracy, just as it was culturally symbolized by the great German novelists, the Bauhaus, and the between-the-wars flowering of literature and art. (In the same era, there were only fifteen women members of the British Parliament, and women in the United States Congress had reached a total of three.) Radical German feminists had also begun to organize against the protective legislation that kept women out of many jobs, and to work toward such international goals as alliances with their counterparts in other countries, demilitarization, and pacifism. German families had become much smaller, married women had gained the legal right to keep their own salaries, and both married and single women were joining the paid-labor force in record numbers.

Precisely because such changes were both obvious in daily life-styles and profound in their potential effect, they were often resented by those who longed for the old male supremacist, hierarchical, "undefeated" days before the war. As unemployment and inflation grew worse, feminists in particular and women in the work force in general were scape-goated along with Marxists and Jews, and any group that challenged the Aryan idea of power based on race, sex, and class. Because of right-wing pressure, the Weimar Republic began to ban married women from competing with men for government jobs. Because of that political pressure plus alarm at the declining birthrate, it also re-stricted access to contraception. But the Nazi party promised much more. And much worse.

"The right of personal freedom," Hitler explained in *Mein Kampf*, "recedes before the duty to preserve the race." The Nazi leaders said they would not deprive women of the vote, but they ridiculed feminists, liberals, and socialists who were "masculinizing" women by treating them *the same as men*. Their own answer to women was "*gleichwertig aber nicht gleichartig*": "*equivalent but not the same.*"

A return to a strong family life; women's primary identity as mothers; tax penalties for remaining single; loans for young married couples and subsidies for childbearing; prohibition of prostitution, homosexuality, contraception, and abortion: all these were issues that the Roman Catholic church, the Catholic Center party, and the Nazi party could and did agree on. True, they disagreed bitterly on which patriarchy should prevail, the church or the state, but the place of women and the need for an authoritar-ian family life was a shared platform, and bond, and a reason for coalition.

As British historian Tim Mason wrote: "This type of partial or appar-ent consensus on a basic issue among different sectional interests and elite groups was one of the most important foundations of Nazi rule. . . . Antifeminism was not a minor or opportunistic component of National Socialism, but a central part of it."

And once Hitler came to power, popularly elected in part by a patriarchal backlash against feminist successes, he delivered immediately on his promise to restore male supremacy.

Whether moderate or radical, feminist organizations were disbanded. Feminist publications were closed down or censored. At the same time, traditional women's organizations, like the Evangelical Women's Asso-ciation or the National Association of German Housewives, were strengthened by being welcomed into *Frauenfront*, the Nazi women's association. In 1933, feminists were removed by law from teaching and other public posts: the same law that removed all "non-Aryans" from such jobs. All women, feminist or not, were banned from the Reichstag, from judgeships, and from other decision-making posts.

To the extent that labor needs allowed, married women were persuaded or forced to stay at home and leave paid jobs to men. Propaganda portrayed the ideal woman as healthy, blond, no makeup; a chaste and energetic worker while single, a devoted wife and mother as soon as possible. The magazine advertisements for contraception that had been commonplace were outlawed as pornographic (as many right-wing groups suggest today). Birth-control and abortion clinics were padlocked (much as some anti-abortion groups are demanding today).

Under Hitler, choosing abortion became sabotage—a crime punishable by imprisonment and hard labor for the woman and a possible death penalty for the abortionist. It was an act of the individual against the state; an exaggeration in degree, but not kind, of current fundamentalist arguments that women must have children "for Jesus and the church"; or, as the Supreme Court ruled in denying poor women the choice of Medicaid-funded abortion, for "legitimate government interest."

As Hitler wrote, "It must be considered as reprehensible conduct to refrain from giving healthy children to the nation."

The key word was, of course, *healthy*. Since non-Aryans were "racially impure" and thus unhealthy, Jews, gypsies, Poles, and victims of serious handicaps and diseases (Hitler was, for instance, obsessed with syphilis) were all discouraged or prevented from reproducing by methods that varied from segregation of the sexes, threats, labor camps, and forced abortion or sterilization, to imprisonment or death in a concentration camp. The choice of method depended largely on whether and for how long the "unhealthy" were needed as workers. It also depended on convenience. A pregnant worker was easier to gas than to coerce into an abortion.

Nonetheless, the horrors of concentration camps appear over and over again in current right-wing literature as the analogue of abortion clinics. These extremist arguments may well incite, consciously or not, such violent and increasingly frequent acts as the fire-bombing of abortion clinics, harassment and death threats of patients and doctors, the picketing and actual invasion of clinics, the sabotage of telephones and other private communications, and the taunts of "baby killer" for prochoice elected leaders.

There are anti-abortion activists who also fear such results. Dr. Bernard Nathanson, a physician who once performed abortions and who now has co-written a militantly anti-abortion book called *Aborting America*, explains: "As a Jew, I cannot remain silent at this facile use of the Nazi analogy, though I realize that some anti-abortion Jews use it. If this argument is so compelling, why do Jews remain generally favorable toward abortion?"

Liberal Catholic publications, like most individual Catholics, are alarmed by these false comparisons, especially coming from a Right-to-Life movement that is publicly identified with the Catholic hierarchy. "There is something wrong in a movement," the *National Catholic Reporter* editorialized, "which in spite of its current clever adaptation of abolitionist sloganeering, can value life in just one stage of human development."

But even such objectors may use words like *exaggeration*, as if abortion were lesser in degree, similar in kind.

*W*e still need to draw the clear line of difference based on *where the power lies* if we're to identify authoritarianism in all its forms. Though Hitler stated the crucial difference between the individual's right to choose and the state's right to impose—whether it was abortion or anything else—today's religious ultrarightists may obscure that difference with rhetoric.

"If you are prolife and then support capital punishment or the arms race," a student was reported as arguing at a Right-to-Life Convention in St. Louis, "you're inconsistent."

"But," the report continued, "a common rebuke to that argument among Right-to-Life members was that unborn life is 'perfect' life, born life 'imperfect.' " In fact, there is a high correlation between those who are anti-abortion and those in favor of both capital punishment and military spending. It's okay to kill life that is not "innocent," and it's the state that decides.

The same reservation is repeated in secular form in *The Phyllis Schlafly Report*, the publication of the Eagle Forum, which carefully advocates only "the right to life of all *innocent* persons from conception to natural death." That proviso accompanies support for the killing of the "guilty" through both capital punishment and the military.

Interestingly, Hitler also supported capital punishment "because of its deterrent effect."

The argument among authoritarians is what level and kind of patriarchal power will be supreme—national or international, secular or religious. What all seem to agree on, however, is the patriarchal family as the basis and training ground for any further authoritarianism. It was the basic cell (*Keimzelle*) of the state for Germany's national socialism. In the more mixed philosophy of the Eagle Forum, it is just "the basic unit of society." For more religious groups like the American Life Lobby, it's a three-step progression of authoritarian units—"the family, the nation, the very laws of God."

But at that first level of the family, and the resistance to any self-determination for women within it—authoritarian preachings sound alike. For that matter, even some civil libertarians who cherish individual rights against the state will not guarantee individual and equal rights to women within either state or family. Individuals are men, the family is their basic unit of security in which the state has no right to interfere, and women are nowhere. It's as if a basic right of men *is* to dominate women and the family.

A current and popular anti-abortion argument includes a description of a family with poor health, many members, and great hardship. When the audience agrees that the mother should have the right to an abortion under those circumstances, the lecturer says, "Congratulations. You have just killed Bach."

In fact, the rationale sounds like this: "Supposing Bach's mother, after her fifth or sixth or even twelfth child, had said 'That'll do, enough is enough'—the works of Bach would never have been written."

That last quote comes from Heinrich Himmler, founder of the SS, head of all concentration camps, and originator of the Lebensborn homes where Aryan pregnant women who were unwed, deserted, or having children by lovers other than their husbands were encouraged to have the children Himmler feared might otherwise be illegally aborted. They could choose to keep the child and be supported by the state, or give it up for adoption to a good Aryan family of carefully matched social background. What they couldn't do was to choose *not* to have the child, and thus seize control of the means of reproduction, their own bodies, in defiance of the patriarchal state.

*T*here are echoes and parallels here between Germany between-the-wars and the United States after the 1970s: a hopeful burst of individual rights, both racial and sexual, followed by an ultraright-wing backlash; economic troubles and unemployment; a loss of international prestige through the loss of a war. Perhaps anti-abortion groups that accuse feminists and the prochoice majority of being Nazis have done us an inadvertent favor by sending us back to read history in self-defense.

II

In Germany before World War I, when Adolf Hitler himself was still a child, nineteenth-century feminism was already accomplishing a great deal. Politicians and the press were gradually becoming more sympathetic to its goals. Women in industry, offices, and the professions weren't oddities anymore. Unlike feminist movements in most other Western countries, this one was giving organizational support to radical feminist demands for sexual and economic equality, the same rights for "illegitimate" children as for those of married parents, an end to the idea that childbearing was the only purpose of women or of marriage, and a "new morality" that required equal rights and consideration for women and men in or outside marriage.

In addition, most activist women were focused on issues that seemed more immediate than achieving the right to vote. Top-down change always seems remote at best, and in Germany before World War I, parliamentary democracy was a very new and limited possibility. But German feminists had won public support for their unprecedented campaign to decriminalize prostitution (its illegality created the familiar result of brothels protected or run by the police), and they almost succeeded in their careful lobbying effort to delete abortion from the criminal code completely by arguing that "the competence of the modern State . . . is limited by the necessity of preserving the freedom of the individual over his [or her] own body."

This challenge to the sexual caste system met great resistance from the more agricultural, religious, and military parts of German society, plus reservations from some reformist or religious women who worked to replace radical feminist leaders of national organizations with those who cited motherhood and "superior morality" as reasons that women should be given more (but not equal) rights. The national obsession with a declining birthrate, combined with new Darwinian theories on who should or should not be encouraged to reproduce, encouraged these nonfeminist reformers to cite healthy German motherhood as their justification for educational and other rights.

Nonetheless, feminists in the early 1900s were changing minds and eroding public hostility by the end of a half century or so of activism. They were, that is, until 1912 when a small group of military officers, conservative politicians, racist geneticists, and academics resentful of female competition (all of whom, as the press noted, shared the distinction of being unknown or so out-of-date as to be "among the living dead") formed the League for the Prevention of the Emancipation of Women.

For the first time, there was an organized antifeminist group turning out anti-equality propaganda. As a tribute to both German conservatism and feminist successes, the "Anti-League" felt compelled to issue an antifeminist manifesto. In a press report of its first congress, an ultraright-wing aristocrat explained: "The German Empire was created with blood and iron. That was man's work! If women helped, [they] stood behind their men in battle and fired them on to kill as many enemies as possible. (Fervent applause.)"

By 1913, the Anti-League had gained support from a white-collar union of male clerks convinced that Jews, the lower classes, and "the invasion of female elements into the profession" were taking their jobs away. Union leaders condemned feminists as "men-women," "degenerate," and "perverse."

In 1914 the Anti-League imported Lady Griselda Cheape, an English antisuffrage leader—perhaps the Phyllis Schlafly of her day—to give lectures in Berlin and to tour the country.

Though feminists were divided on whether to take this challenge seriously or to ignore it (some thought it ridiculous enough to be inadvertently helpful), its theme of woman-hating struck a deep chord in patriarchal society. Groups such as the Anti-League never had many members (just as the Eagle Forum or the Moral Majority and other anti-equality groups spawned here in the 1970s do not), but they did publicly scapegoat feminists in particular and active women in general for all that was changing or difficult in modern life. This was something that the military, the church, and other traditionalists could agree on, even when they could agree on nothing else.

As Richard Evans, one of the few male scholars to take women's history seriously, explained in *The Feminist Movement in Germany: 1894-1933*, antifeminist arguments

> were based on the belief that Germany was subject to growing hostility and danger from forces inside the country and without. . . . The women's movement was creating fresh divisions by . . . destroying the family . . . by encouraging married women to take jobs, by supporting unmarried mothers, and by urging women in general to be more independent. It was endangering Germany's military potential by discouraging marriage [plus encouraging family planning and thus lowering the birthrate]. It was outraging nature by campaigning for the systematic equalization of the sexes and by inciting women to do things they were unsuited for. It was international in spirit and unpatriotic.

In other words, the later Nazi post-World War I campaign against feminism as anti-German, subversive—and therefore an obvious product of a Communist-Jewish conspiracy—was not invented by Hitler or by the philosophy of national socialism. His promise to return women to "Children, Cooking, Church" (*"Kinder, Küche, Kirche"*), and thus to restore the male-dominant family as the model of an authoritarian society, was an appeal to religious and other ultraright-wing discontent that had been around since the early twentieth century. True, that discontent was deepened into bitterness by Germany's humiliation during and after World War I, but the atavistic elements of this obsession with male supremacy and restoration of "the Fatherland" were already there. It just took a national leader willing to pander to such desires, to add the force and respectability of a party platform in which they were key emotional planks.

In 1972 a group of American historians became concerned enough about apparent parallels between modern political tensions in the United

States and in the Germany of the Weimar Republic, the period that preceded Hitler's popular election, to hold a special conference on the subject.* Given such similar developments as race- and sex-based challenges to traditional power, reduced influence in the world, division over Vietnam, pressures of inflation and unemployment at home, and an increasing impatience with elected leadership, could Americans go down the same authoritarian path?

Their conclusion was no. After all, the United States had a much longer tradition of democratic government and acceptance of diversity than did the Germans after World War I. Even developments that seemed alarmingly similar in kind were still very different in degree.

In the years since then, America has suffered its first humiliating defeat in war. The loss of fifty-seven thousand soldiers in faraway Vietnam is hardly comparable to Germany's homeland devastation and loss of two million in World War I. Furthermore, many fewer Americans perceived our government's defeat as unjust or due to weakness: years before it happened, polls showed 70 percent support for United States withdrawal. Nonetheless, justifications of our military presence in Vietnam continue to get big emotional responses from some powerful constituencies. The Veterans of Foreign Wars, for instance, gave Ronald Reagan an ovation for describing Vietnam as "in truth, a noble cause" during his 1980 presidential campaign. They broke an eighty-year tradition of nonendorsement to support him. A spate of revisionist theorists, from Norman Podhoretz to members of Congress, now maintain that the only tragedy in Vietnam was our unwillingness to use our full military strength, and our ultimate departure.

In addition, the international pressure of an energy crisis has made us intimately dependent on and vulnerable to "foreigners" for the first time—and on non-Westerners and non-Christians at that. United States industrial and trade supremacy has also leveled off, the Iranian hostage crisis dramatized U.S. impotence, inflation and unemployment are populist concerns, the challenge from racial minorities and women of every description continues, confidence in our elected leadership is low, and visible right-wing leadership now legitimizes an especially militaristic, religious, and "back-to-basics" kind of patriotism.

---

*Proceedings published in *Social Research*, Summer, 1972.

In a 1976 Gallup poll, Americans were asked if they thought the country needed "really strong leadership that would try to solve problems directly without worrying about how Congress or the Supreme Court might feel." Forty-nine percent agreed. By 1979, 66 percent of those questioned in a *New York Times*–CBS poll said they would vote for "someone who would step on some toes and bend some rules to get things done."

This impatience with our national situation does not mean, as right-wing wishful thinkers often insist, that "the whole country has moved to the right." On almost every issue of social justice—from more equitable distribution of income to a new equality based on race and sex, even a willingness to cut back on material living standards if it makes environmental sense to do so—there is majority support. In national polls, these majorities continue to grow. When right-wing candidates who don't represent these majority views get elected, it is mainly because too many Americans are either too complaisant or too turned off to vote.

But a tolerance of or desire for strong "top-down" leadership was also a hallmark of the Weimar Republic in which national socialism grew, and not all such longing came from the traditional right wing.

Hitler presented himself as a champion of the lower classes against inherited wealth and power (hence his "socialism"), as well as against the "international conspiracy" of powerful Jews. From a working-class family himself, he replaced upper-class superiority with race superiority, thus justifying his own right to rise to the top. Basic texts like *The Nazi Primer* emphasized hard work and talent as the ways any real German—that is, any Aryan-German—could succeed (hence, "*national* socialism").

A repressed would-be architecture student shocked by the sinfulness of Munich; a vegetarian who didn't smoke or drink and who was obsessed by imagined sexual attacks on nice German girls (though only if the attacks came from "the black-haired Jewish youth [who] lurks in wait," as Hitler wrote in *Mein Kampf*); an obscure and angry worker who felt exploited by the rich and powerful—Adolf Hitler entered the city's beer halls and workingmen's clubs. His gift for emotional speechmaking unlocked dreams of revenge.

Evil is obvious only in retrospect. It's important to remember that Hitler, champion of everyman against the rich and aristocratic, often seemed both selfless and charming. "The Führer comes to greet me with outstretched hand," a woman journalist for *Paris-Soir* wrote in 1936. "I am surprised and astonished by the blue of his eyes, which look brown in photographs, and I prefer the reality—the face that brims with intelligence and energy and lights up when he speaks. At this moment, I comprehend the magical influence . . . and his power over the masses."

The message of the interviewer's own second-class status as a female was sugarcoated; a parallel to the national socialist description of non-Aryans: "No real differences in quality, but rather differences in kind."

"I grant women the same right as men, but I don't think they're identical," Hitler explained jovially. "Woman is man's companion in life. She shouldn't be burdened with the tasks for which man was created. I don't envisage any women's battalions . . . women are better suited to social work."

However sugarcoated and ambiguous, every form of authoritarianism must start with a belief in some group's greater right to power, whether that right is justified by sex, race, class, religion, or all four. However far it may expand, the progression inevitably rests on unequal power and airtight roles within the family.

ITEMS

• "If the man's world is said to be the State . . . [the woman's] world is her husband, her family, her children, and her home. . . . Every child that a woman brings into the world is a battle, a battle waged for the existence of her people. . . . It is not true . . . that respect depends on the overlapping of the spheres of activity of the sexes; this respect demands that neither sex should try to do that which belongs to the sphere of the other."

> —Hitler's speech to the National
> Socialist Women's Organization,
> September 1934.

• " . . . the attack on the family is an attack on civilization itself. . . . Men are by nature mobile and aggressive, whereas women are by nature committed to stability, permanence, and futurity. . . . Welfare, day-care centers, and affirmative action or preferential hiring of women diminish the role of the male as a provider. . . . They thus promote the dissolution of society. . . ."

> —From a pamphlet entitled
> "Communism, the Family, and the
> Equal Rights Amendment,"
> Christian Anti-Communist Crusade,
> California, March 1975.

• "Perhaps the three points most stressed in family theory," U.S. sociologist Clifford Kirkpatrick wrote in 1937 about Nazi Germany, "are reproduction, sex differences, and strengthened homelife."

• "Ninety percent of our problems with children," explained a booklet distributed by members of the Pro-Family Caucus at the 1981 White House Conference on Families, "are probably the result of a mother who has 1) failed to learn how to really love her man and submit to him, 2) tried to escape staying at home, or 3) hindered her husband in the discipline of the children."

• "A Child's Declaration of Rights," published by Phyllis Schlafly's Eagle Forum, includes the right: "To be taught from textbooks that honor the traditional family as a basic unit of society, women's role as wife and mother, and man's role as provider and protector. . . ."

• "No funds [will be] authorized . . . under federal law [for] purchase or preparation of any educational materials or studies relating to the preparation of educational materials, if such materials would tend to denigrate, diminish, or deny the role differences between the sexes. . . ."

> —The Family Protection Act, an omnibus
> federal bill introduced in 1979 by
> Senator Paul Laxalt (R.-Nev.). (It would
> also forbid federal laws against child
> abuse and federal funding of battered
> women's shelters, abortion rights, school
> desegregation, gay rights, etc.)

Once we grow callous in our earliest, most intimate world to a power difference among our own family members, how much easier is it to accept all other hierarchies? If one sex is born to greater power, then why not one race? If women were allowed to marry and have children with men of their own choosing, how could race and class be kept "pure"? If a man is not allowed to dictate to a wife and children beneath him, how is he to tolerate the dictation he must accept from above?

ITEMS

- "The slogan 'Emancipation of Women' was invented by Jewish intellectuals. . . . Our National Socialist women's movement has in reality but one single point," Hitler told women in his 1934 speech, "and that point is the child. . . ." In *Mein Kampf*, a copy of which was presented to every newly married Aryan couple in Germany, he wrote, "Just as [the Jew] himself systematically ruins women and girls . . . it was and is Jews who bring Negroes into the Rhineland . . . ruining the hated white race by the necessarily resulting bastardization . . . rising [himself] to be its master."

- "Russia has an ERA and their birthrate has fallen below population zero," reported *The Thunderbolt*, a publication of the avowedly white-supremacist National States Rights party. "The time is *now* to act to protect the family and *motherhood* itself. . . . Laws requiring men and women to be separated in prison would be invalidated [by the ERA]. A negro judge has already used these equality laws in Chattanooga to lock a White woman in the same cell with a black man. She was then raped. . . ."

- Father Paul Marx, director of the Human Life Center, an anti-abortion "think tank" in Minnesota, has traveled to more than thirty countries as part of his campaign against abortion and contraception. As characterized and quoted by the Minneapolis *Star*, he fears that "the white Western world is committing suicide through abortion and contraception," and explains: "I guess we have 250,000 Vietnamese here already, and they are going to have large families—the Orientals always do. There are Koreans, and Filipinos . . . God knows how many Mexicans come across the border every night. . . . And if we ever have to fight the Russians, I wonder if these people will be willing to stake their lives."

Extreme ideas? Maybe. But the belief that men must control women if men are to maintain race and class divisions, the supply of workers and soldiers for the state, and ownership of their own children is the root injustice from which all these flowers of evil grow.

In pleading for women's freedom seventy years ago, one German feminist said, "Woman has often been reduced—callously, if unconsciously—to the level of a childbearing machine, her children regarded as the property of the State while still in the womb." Another said angrily, "If we women do not take a stand for our own responsibility for ourselves here, in the most female of all tasks in life, that of 'giving life,' if we do not take a stand against our being regarded merely as the involuntary producers of cannon fodder, then in my opinion, we do not deserve to be regarded as anything else!"

Many women in Hitler's Germany did take a public stand against his sexual caste system, as well as against the anti-Semitism that, as a punishment from which many men also suffered, was better understood as an injustice. "National Socialism has grown big in its fight against Jews and women," said a leader of Germany's largest feminist organization. "Today, I am for struggle."

Many demonstrated in the streets against Hitler's closing of family planning clinics, an act that one German feminist, now a resident of this country, remembers as "the first thing Hitler did." The individual right to abortion was so suppressed that even women who miscarried had to prove they had not tried to abort or else risk criminal prosecution.

Other activist women tried unsuccessfully to save their organizations by becoming less "political," by fighting the Nazi diatribe against them with dry "factual corrections," or even by using Hitler's own racist arguments to get Aryan women into positions of influence where they might reform from within.

Jewish women in Germany were not only purged from any important jobs, but often abandoned by their own non-Jewish husbands or friends. First discouraged from marriage or having children, then forced out of both, they were eventually used as forced labor or sent to concentration camps. (Ravensbrück, the one camp exclusively for women, was also the site of most Nazi "medical experiments." Though Jewish men underwent similar atrocities elsewhere, Aryan male doctors seemed better able to disassociate from bodies so different from their own.)

Meanwhile, Hitler assumed that women were or should be attracted to his military image. He stayed single partly to inspire the devotion and romantic fantasies of women followers. (Privately, he was reported as saying that he would not have children because no son of his, being partly the product of a woman, could be as great as he.) Though some national socialists claimed "it was the women's vote that brought Hitler to triumph," that was no more true than the current argument that women voters defeated the ERA. Hindenberg, president of Germany from 1925 to 1934, got more women's votes in 1932 than did Hitler, both in absolute numbers and percentage.

But some women did vote for national socialism. Most were the very young who knew little or nothing of past feminist struggles. Some were excited by the romance of Hitler's heroine-goddess images of German womanhood. Others wanted to stay at home as housewives instead of being poorly paid workers and housewives besides. Still others were attracted by Hitler's promise of a bridegroom for every young woman, a seductive if unlikely campaign promise in a country where World War I had decimated the male population.

Ironically, women's traditional workload and their skepticism about getting help from any men, including national socialists, saved many from Nazi involvement. "The mass of German women did not want to be organized," wrote historian Jill Stephenson, "and their passive resistance to attempts to involve the housebound housewife, above all in the 'women's work of the nation,' ensured that the Nazi women's organization remained a minority concern."

*T*here can be no doubt that feminists would have been more effective in opposing Hitler if they had possessed local centers as did the churches, or work communities as did the unions, or an international network as did both.

As it was, their major organizations were dependent on public meeting places and communications. They were easily outlawed or taken over. And their diverse, multi-issue approach was no match for the simple, driving emotionalism of the opposition. "Whereas the cause of women's emancipation," explained historian Tim Mason, "[was] promoted by a very wide range of small and normally uncoordinated groups with different partial goals and political outlooks, the cause of the restoration of men's preeminence could be made to appear a relatively simple single issue and could be preempted by a single political movement of incomparably greater power."

The result was tragic for men as well as women, not only in Germany but in every area decimated by German expansion. Feminists had been virtually alone in challenging the patriarchal family as the basic unit of an authoritarian society, and in trying to replace its primacy with the primacy of the individual rights and thus the possibility of democratic families. Many of the powerful religious groups supported Hitler's view of the family and of women and supported the early growth of national socialism because of it. True, they disagreed with state supremacy over the church—a development that came after "Kinder, Küche, Kirche"—but by then it was too late. Even liberal, radical, and union groups that had supported women's rights in the marketplace and the voting booth had abandoned that support at the family door.

*A*ccording to our own current right-wing and anti-equality backlash, a major goal is to protect and restore a family clearly defined by them as male-led and hierarchical. Thus, they condemn as "antifamily" any direct federal guarantee of rights to women or to children by the law. Thus, the Equal Rights Amendment is antifamily. So are laws against child abuse and funding for battered women's shelters. So is any individual right to sexual expression outside the family, whether homosexual or heterosexual. So are abortion, contraception, and any other means of separating sexual expression from childbirth.

This authoritarian thrust is further reflected in right-wing tax policy, media censorship, and interference in public schools to establish family ownership of children and control of what they may read or study. The nightmare of abortion as a crime against the state, punishable as murder, is also promised by the right-wing-sponsored Human Life Amendment that would confer legal personhood on the fertilized egg. In all ways, the family is to be the basic unit, not the individual. Women are to be subordinate within it.

Many Americans are surprised that our right-wing groups focus on issues of the family and reproduction. Some of our most able and democratic political leaders are unwilling or unable to deal with issues that seem to them unfamiliar, embarrassing, or small.

But many Europeans are surprised that we're surprised. They say: Where have you been? Where do you think authoritarianism starts?

They've been through this before.

*T*here are other disquieting parallels between past and present. The current spate of right-wing efforts to censor school libraries, for instance, starts with books that are "antifamily," often those written by family-planning experts, feminist authors, and black authors. Is this a less dramatic version of Nazi-style book burnings that also started with antifamily, "anti-German" books by family planners, Jews, and feminists? Could the effort of some current politicians to appease the right wing by giving in on "social issues" be as disastrous a mistake as the concessions made by the Wiemar Republic on women in the work force and other domestic concerns?

Certainly there are enormous, and let us hope lifesaving, differences in degree as well as in content. Our nationalism doesn't use anti-Semitism as an internal and external danger. Yet our own anticommunism sometimes borders on paranoia and is used to condemn critics as "bad Americans." Hostility to human rights for women and minorities hasn't forced us out of responsible jobs. Yet there is an increase in subtle scapegoating for everything from divorce and juvenile delinquency to crime and unemployment. A white male who does well economically is a public-spirited creator of jobs, but women and minorities who do well may be seen as selfish, a part of the "Me Generation."

Furthermore, feminists still seem to be the only cohesive force taking on the right wing at the level of family issues and fighting for individual rights—from the bottom up. Anti-equality forces may see this more clearly than our liberal allies do. "Orthodox feminism is an especially militant manifestation," warned *The Human Life Review*, an anti-abortion quarterly, "of a larger, increasingly prevalent social philosophy which holds that the 'needs' of the individual are self-validating and that no person or institution may restrict those needs." This is heresy for those who worship family, church, or state.

As in Germany, there is also a disquieting sameness between those

who wish to enforce the traditional family and those who want increased
military spending and a more confrontational attitude toward the world.
Most disquieting of all, this sameness is found in high places. A much-
quoted political cartoon of Ronald Reagan shows him in a Western hat
and saying: "A gun in every holster, a pregnant woman in every home.
Make America a man again."

It all sounds a little too familiar. But at least we know now that
feminism has a history—and that it is the keystone of any organic or
lasting democracy.

—1980

Night Thoughts of a
Media Watcher

After a childhood of listening to radio soap operas and a decade of staying in motel rooms where the same sagas are on TV, I've finally figured out why soap operas are, and logically should be, so popular with generations of housebound women. *They are the only place in our culture where grown-up men take seriously all the things that grown-up women have to deal with all day long.* Family illnesses, problems with kids, getting along with neighbors, sexual jealousy, worry about losing our own jobs through divorce, worry about a husband losing his job and our income; what goes on in the bedroom, at the dinner table, in hospital rooms—all these are the stuff of women's lives. For at least a few hours each day, a fictional world takes them seriously, too.

Like "race movies" made for black audiences in the 1920s and 1930s, with glamorous and suspenseful stories populated by black actors and a few overwhelmed white ones, soap operas validate and glorify a segregated world. Since the less powerful are stuck with it anyway, we are grateful and intrigued.

This same formula is supposed to be on prime-time TV in the form of all the melodramatic series like "Dallas," but it's not the same. In order to attract male interest (or at least to be thought worthy of it), nighttime conflicts center on such grown-up concerns as big business deals, crime, violence, or masculine rivalry for the legacy of a powerful father. The daytime staples of errant children, infidelity, alcoholism, and illness are relegated to subplots.

327

Sexual politics may change from day to evening, but class and race remain the same. Though a really poor person or family is rarely a major part of a TV series at any time (it's too depressing), a Ph.D. thesis could be done on why comedies focus on working-class families (occasionally black), while melodramas focus on the rich and powerful (always white). Personally, I think it's a semiconscious plot to preserve the social order. The idea is to convince us that it's *fun* to be poor, or even to live in the ghetto, but being rich is a terrible burden we shouldn't want to try

Television also proves Margaret Mead's conclusion that in a patriarchy, widows are the only women honored in authority. If you're born female, what you have to do is marry the newspaper publisher, senator, corporate stockholder, or whatever man has the position you want, and live out your time as wife-mother-hostess. When he dies, you may be allowed to carry on in his place. Until recently, widowhood was the major way that women got into Congress.

A powerful woman on television is allowed to be an older woman and a widow like Mrs. Pynchon on the "Lou Grant" show. Though she still isn't important enough to have a show of her own, and she is portrayed as a little silly and out of touch in a way that male inheritors of great power rarely are, Mrs. Pynchon is one of the few female characters who are allowed to be both powerful and admirable.

In television and in reality, perhaps men should think twice before making widowhood our only path to power

II

The Equal Rights Amendment began its long ratification process in 1972, yet to my knowledge, not one major newspaper or radio station, not one network news department or national television show, has ever done an independent investigative report on what the ERA will and will not do.

Instead, the major media have been content to present occasional interviews, debates, and contradictory reports from those who are for or against. One expert is quoted as saying that the ERA will strengthen the legal rights of women in general and homemakers in particular by causing the courts to view marriage as a partnership, and the next one says the ERA will force wives to work outside the home and eliminate alimony.

One political leader explains on camera that the ERA protects women and men from discriminatory federal laws; then another politician calls the ERA a federal power grab that will reduce individual rights. One activist says that the ERA is a simple guarantee of democracy that should have been part of the Bill of Rights, had the Constitution not been written by and for property-owning white males, and the next one insists it will destroy the family, eliminate heterosexuality, and integrate bathrooms.

Understandably, the audience is confused. We thought the sky was blue to begin with, but equal time and prestige given to an insistence that it's really green may finally cause us to doubt our perceptions. It's true that the majority of women and men have continued to support the ERA (by a margin that has increased since the Reagan administration demonstrated that existing progress could be reversed without it), but I'm not sure the media can take much credit for that fact. There is some evidence that 50–50, so-called objective reporting has actually *impeded* the building of a larger majority.

For instance, reading or hearing the actual twenty-four words of the ERA* is the most reliable path to its support. Many people are still surprised to learn that there's no mention of *unisex* or *abortion* or *combat* in its text; such is the confusion created by anti-ERA arguments. Yet most ERA news coverage never quotes its text at all.

Among reporters and news executives, however, there is great self-righteousness. They have followed the so-called fairness doctrine. They have presented "both sides of the issue" by devoting the same number of minutes or amount of space to the "pro" and the "con." This has remained true, even though majority support for the ERA means a "con" is often tough to find. I've frequently been called by an interviewer and asked, "Would you bring an 'anti' with you?"

One result of this prizefight school of journalism is that Phyllis Schlafly, who was not a nationally famous person pre-ERA, has become the only name that most Americans can think of when asked what women oppose it. In a real sense, she is an artificial creation of the fairness doctrine. Another result is the idea that *women* voted against the ERA; not

Equality of rights under the law shall not be denied or abridged by the United States or by any state on account of sex.

the two dozen or so aging white male state legislators, plus economic and religious interests, who are the actual culprits. A third result is the notion that black Americans don't support the ERA, though black state legislators have voted overwhelmingly for it. If black women and men had been represented in legislatures in proportion to their present numbers in the population, especially in southern states, the ERA would have passed long ago.

In the early days of the civil rights movement, most journalists followed the same "equal time" formula. When they reported on black voter registration in the South, for instance, they quoted civil rights workers saying they had been beaten up in jail. Then they quoted the sheriff saying that these young people had attacked the police or had beaten up each other. Readers were left with either their confusion or their original biases intact.

Eventually, however, most serious media assumed responsibility for doing their own investigations. They reported, to the best of their ability, what the facts really were.

Unfortunately, that has yet to be done for the ERA. It isn't that such independent reporting would be difficult. More than fifty years of legislative history is available to explain the impact intended by Congress. An issue of *The Yale Law Journal* and many authoritative books have been devoted to projecting its impact in scholarly detail. Finally, there are a few states that have already begun to enforce statewide ERAs with the same or similar wording proposed federally. Pennsylvania, for instance, adopted its ERA more than a decade ago. Bathrooms have not been integrated, abortion and homosexual rights have not been affected, for better or worse, but women's economic rights have been strengthened; equality in education, employment, and insurance benefits has advanced; and sex-based discriminatory laws against men also have been struck down.

So why haven't independent, in-depth reports been done? Why don't the media of your town (and mine) take this historic issue seriously? Why do they allow legislators to vote against the majority opinion in their own districts, as reflected in independent polls, without fearing a journalistic exposé of the special interests they are responding to?

We must ask them. A future with or without the ERA is at stake. And so is good or lousy journalism.

III

I've noticed that, from Dostoevsky's novels to Las Vegas's TV shows, big-time gambling is portrayed as a male-only obsession. Someone once asked me why women don't gamble as much as men do, and I gave the common-sensical reply that we don't have as much money. That was a true but incomplete answer. In fact, women's total instinct for gambling is satisfied by marriage.

If men doubt the magnitude of the gamble, consider just how tough it is to know that the person you are about to marry, who is, by tradition and by lack of economic alternative, your lifetime identity and meal ticket, really is going to have the law career or foreman's job or political office that you want for yourself and for your security. Not so easy, right?

In the fifties, I remember college friends taking their fiancé's poems, architectural drawings, or senior thesis to the appropriate professor and asking, "Is this guy any good?"

Of course, this gamble has been diminished by our increased ability to support ourselves and to find our own work lives. But until pay and power are equal, and women no longer have to take on men's names and social identities, it's not going to end. Novels and other media still allow this marriage motive only to "bad women."

They're missing a lot of good plots.

IV

It's high time that someone publicly thanked Gay Talese for titling his exhaustive catalog of impersonal sex, *Thy Neighbor's Wife*. Since women don't have wives, we are warned by the author (however inadvertently) that we need not buy this book. So are male readers who no longer think of women as other men's possessions. That leaves a narrow but fervent readership for Mr. Talese: men who are, sexually speaking, on automatic pilot.

Sophie's Choice, however, another best-seller (and the basis of a motion picture besides) is much more deceptive. By putting a woman in the title of his novel, William Styron (author-narrator-protagonist) encourages us to believe that he can write about a woman with empathy. In his last novel, *The Confessions of Nat Turner*, Styron, who is white, promised the same about a black man. He was greatly criticized for turning that leader of a courageous slave revolt into a white male fantasy; even portraying him as sexually obsessed with, and the murderer of, a young white woman, although there is no historical evidence that he was either. Unfortunately, Sophie (supposing, as Styron asks us to, that she really existed) left not even the slender historical record of a slave, but she seems to be just as much a prisoner of Styron's infuriating and stereotypical bias. Like Turner, she is assumed to be motivated by sex and to have a mainly sexual-psychological value, not an activist-historical one. Like other female protagonists in Styron's work, from *Lie Down in Darkness* forward, she is masochistic and suicidal.

Even accepting the factual outlines of her life as supplied by Styron's novel, I have a hard time believing she was either. For instance, though Sophie survived the loss of her two children and years of starvation and atrocities in a Nazi concentration camp, though she had vowed to (and does) live longer than its hated commandant so that he will not triumph, we are asked to believe that she freely chooses to stay with and love a sexual fascist in New York, a drug-addicted and clinically crazy lover who saves her from malnutrition only to beat her and subject her to jealous rages because she might have used sex to survive the concentration camp. (What if she did? The author-narrator seems to accept the crazed lover's premise that nothing is more important about a woman than her sexual behavior. Indeed, he presents much of her lover's sadistic and controlling behavior as a normal male mating style.) Though Sophie is a refugee with almost zero alternatives, she has enough strength and self-respect to express relief when her violent lover temporarily takes off—but for that disloyalty, the author-narrator rebukes her.* He also accepts as okay, and collaborates with, the refusal on the part of the lover's brother to let Sophie know that this man she is living with has totally fabricated his background as a Nobel-quality biologist and has actually been violent and in and out of mental hospitals all his life.

Though the narrator is (God knows) sexually obsessed with Sophie

*Readers who have seen the film, which was released after this essay was published, will note that this episode in the book was left out. Indeed, Meryl Streep's virtuoso performance as Sophie almost rescues her on screen, and both the sadistic lover and the narrator are softened and sanitized. Nonetheless, the basic questions of their morality and Sophie's "masochism" remain.

and professes to love her, that "love" takes the form of wanting to have her for himself, not to warn her of real danger or to help her live on her own. In fact, the narrator only gets alarmed when the lover finally threatens to kill not just Sophie, but the narrator, too.

Even when the narrator "saves" Sophie by taking her out of reach of her crazy lover, it is on the clear condition that she marry the narrator. Given the choice between these two men, Sophie's decision to commit suicide becomes almost believable. (Of course, the narrator presents her suicide as inevitable: a result of her self-punishing guilt at having survived a concentration camp. Though he examines every other motive at incredible length, he never questions a possible connection between going to bed with him for the first time and deciding to kill herself hours later.) Nonetheless, this choice of suicide is not the only reference for *Sophie's Choice*.

In flashbacks to the concentration camp, we learn that a Nazi officer had forced Sophie to choose which of her two children would live. If she did not send one to the gas ovens, both would die.

Sophie chooses to save her son. This choice is given scarcely more space than I have given it here. Her motive is not examined at all.

This is especially odd since Styron examines everything else in exhaustive detail. (It is part of his pretentious style to write two long sentences where one short phrase would do.) For instance, he speculates at great length about the possible motive of the Nazi officer who forced this unthinkable choice, and comes to the odd conclusion that it was a religious desire to force a sinful decision.

Nonetheless, he spends *not one single word* on the sexual politics that might have been embodied in Sophie's decision *not* to save her daughter. In the author's mind, son-preference needs no comment. It's as natural as female masochism, male sadism, and suicidal women.

It's hard to get angry at an author who seems so oblivious of his own biases. Reading *Sophie's Choice* is like reading a case history by Freud in which he stoutly maintains a woman patient was not really raped by her father as a child, but just made up this story because she had hoped it would happen. Of course, we're now discovering from Freud's letters that he knew such women patients were telling the truth, but went right on blaming the victim in order to make his case histories acceptable to society It's possible that Styron also knew what he was doing. (If so, they are equally guilty.) In the end, the reader is left with the sad suspicion that, if Sophie hadn't been beautiful and the author hadn't spent a long summer trying to go to bed with her, he wouldn't have bothered to record her existence at all. On an enormous canvas of concentration camps, human suffering, child murder, and insanity, the author has painted the portrait of a white southern sex-obsessed young writer who finally succeeds in losing his virginity.

My first hope is that there was no real Sophie, that Styron just made her up completely. Like Freud's women patients, however, she is just real and believable enough to break your heart; all the more so because she is recorded by someone who describes but never understands.

Perhaps we should print stickers for the jackets of both *The Confessions of Nat Turner* and *Sophie's Choice*: "Please help me. I am a prisoner in a book by William Styron."

V

To the extent that women can dictate terms of any national debate, I think we made a media mistake in allowing the enemies of the Equal Rights Amendment to trap us into tacit approval of the draft by supporting women's eligibility for it.

The draft is *their* ground, not ours. Though most American women (and men) are opposed to a peacetime draft, and so greeted draft-based anti-ERA arguments with a ritual disclaimer, "I'm opposed to the draft for men or women," we often ended up arguing defensively that if there *were* a national emergency, women should serve under the same exemptions for parenthood, age, and health that men do. Then we were right back in hot water again, with many parents feeling they could lose their daughters as well as their sons, and many women fearing that they would be forced to go against our majority conviction that violence is rarely an effective way of solving any conflict.

From a media and long-term feminist point of view, our ground should have been—and should be in the future—freedom of choice. The idea is not to dictate what a choice shall be, but to give each person the power to make it. That means our most effective argument is the right of women to *volunteer* for the military, including combat positions, on the same basis as men.

A big media advantage of this argument is putting our anti-equality adversaries on the defensive. They are almost uniformly against women in combat and frequently against women in any part of the armed services, yet they also profess patriotism and the right of each citizen to bear arms.

Furthermore, if we allow ourselves to go along with the argument that the draft is a precondition to equal citizenship, we ignore reality. Most men's rights weren't tied to military service. The draft has only existed for thirty of this country's more than two hundred years, and only about 5 percent of those who do go into the military ever see combat. Putting obligations before opportunities, or making more people vulnerable to what is already an unpopular institution is no way to build a movement.

On the other hand, to support women's right to volunteer on the same basis as men, without quota or combat restriction, remains true to the principle of freedom of choice, for women and for men. It also supports the equal promotional opportunities being sought by women already in the military, and confronts the male-dominant argument that women shouldn't learn to fight back.

Many military men with combat experience (as opposed to congressmen with armchair experience) believe that no war can be won if most of its combat troops are being forced to fight. A system that rests on the willingness of both men and women to volunteer is likely to offer better pay and conditions within the military and to have a cause that volunteers believe is worth fighting for—an interesting check on such military adventurism as Vietnam was, and countries like El Salvador could become.

Finally, the current ban on allowing willing-and-able women into combat positions is the pretext for limiting the number of women volunteers and for keeping women clustered in the lower ranks. This preserves for men the military's best job-training spots and all of its decision making. Despite the military's much-publicized lack of adequately educated soldiers and its need to save money, lower educational and test scores are still okay for men. Male recruits are still more sought after. The military must spend thirty-five hundred dollars more to recruit each man than to recruit one woman.

In fact, if women could volunteer for service in the numbers we are already willing and able to, current personnel needs of the military could be met without any need to draft men. Clifford Alexander, former secretary of the army, reports that even in the worst recruiting year of the volunteer era, the army was only sixteen thousand soldiers short of its goal. Without restrictive quotas, women would easily surpass that number. Saving men from the draft is not a bad offer. Women may be pardoned for our suspicions about why it is refused.

Why do the same right-wing forces that campaign for an equal-opportunity death penalty and oppose shelters for battered women, still insist on "protecting" women from military service in general and voluntary combat duty in particular? Margaret Mead and other anthropologists have conducted cross-cultural studies that show women to be just as fierce as men in self-defense. Women have fought in most wars that involved civilian populations and a few that sent us to the front lines. Even in World War II, Korea, and Vietnam, some women have served in combat zones as nurses and communications officers. Apparently, we can be shot at—and occasionally killed. We're just not supposed to shoot back.

No wonder there is a deep conviction among many women that this society just doesn't want us to learn how to use force. What would happen if all the underpaid waitresses and rape victims and battered wives had a little military training? What if welfare mothers had learned the same skills that many poor men did in Vietnam? How would just your ordinary dependent wife change if she had been through a year or two of universal national service?

Perhaps what we need most is some organizing and a good lawsuit by women who want to volunteer for the military and for combat. After all, a point of feminism is the power to choose.

—1980, 1981

If Men Could Menstruate

*L*iving in India made me understand that a white minority of the world has spent centuries conning us into thinking a white skin makes people superior, even though the only thing it really does is make them more subject to ultraviolet rays and wrinkles.

Reading Freud made me just as skeptical about penis envy. The power of giving birth makes "womb envy" more logical, and an organ as external and unprotected as the penis makes men very vulnerable indeed

But listening recently to a woman describe the unexpected arrival of her menstrual period (a red stain had spread on her dress as she argued heatedly on the public stage) still made me cringe with embarrassment. That is, until she explained that, when finally informed in whispers of the obvious event, she had said to the all-male audience, "and you should be *proud* to have a menstruating woman on your stage. It's probably the first real thing that's happened to this group in years!"

Laughter. Relief. She had turned a negative into a positive. Somehow her story merged with India and Freud to make me finally understand the power of positive thinking. Whatever a "superior" group has will be used to justify its superiority, and whatever an "inferior" group has will be used to justify its plight. Black men were given poorly paid jobs because they were said to be "stronger" than white men, while all women were relegated to poorly paid jobs because they were said to be "weaker." As the little boy said when asked if he wanted to be a lawyer like his mother, "Oh no, that's women's work." Logic has nothing to do with oppression.

So what would happen if suddenly, magically, men could menstruate and women could not?

Clearly, menstruation would become an enviable, boast-worthy, masculine event:

Men would brag about how long and how much.

Young boys would talk about it as the envied beginning of manhood. Gifts, religious ceremonies, family dinners, and stag parties would mark the day.

To prevent monthly work loss among the powerful, Congress would fund a National Institute of Dysmenorrhea. Doctors would research little about heart attacks, from which men were hormonally protected, but everything about cramps.

Sanitary supplies would be federally funded and free. Of course, some men would still pay for the prestige of such commercial brands as Paul Newman Tampons, Muhammad Ali's Rope-a-Dope Pads, John Wayne Maxi Pads, and Joe Namath Jock Shields—"For Those Light Bachelor Days."

Statistical surveys would show that men did better in sports and won more Olympic medals during their periods.

Generals, right-wing politicians, and religious fundamentalists would cite menstruation ("*men*-struation") as proof that only men could serve God and country in combat ("You have to give blood to take blood"), occupy high political office ("Can women be properly fierce without a monthly cycle governed by the planet Mars?"), be priests, ministers, God Himself ("He gave this blood for our sins"), or rabbis ("Without a monthly purge of impurities, women are unclean").

Male liberals or radicals, however, would insist that women are equal, just different; and that any woman could join their ranks if only she were willing to recognize the primacy of menstrual rights ("Everything else is a single issue") or self-inflict a major wound every month ("You *must* give blood for the revolution").

Street guys would invent slang ("He's a three-pad man") and "give fives" on the corner with some exchange like, "Man, you lookin' *good!*"

"Yeah, man, I'm on the rag!"

TV shows would treat the subject openly. (*Happy Days*: Richie and Potsie try to convince Fonzie that he is still "The Fonz," though he has missed two periods in a row. *Hill Street Blues*: The whole precinct hits the same cycle.) So would newspapers. (SUMMER SHARK SCARE THREATENS MENSTRUATING MEN. JUDGE CITES MONTHLIES IN PARDONING RAPIST.) And so would movies. (Newman and Redford in *Blood Brothers!*)

Men would convince women that sex was *more* pleasurable at "that time of the month." Lesbians would be said to fear blood and therefore life itself, though all they needed was a good menstruating man.

Medical schools would limit women's entry ("they might faint at the sight of blood").

Of course, intellectuals would offer the most moral and logical arguments. Without that biological gift for measuring the cycles of the moon and planets, how could a woman master any discipline that demanded a sense of time, space, mathematics—or the ability to measure anything at all? In philosophy and religion, how could women compensate for being disconnected from the rhythm of the universe? Or for their lack of symbolic death and resurrection every month?

Menopause would be celebrated as a positive event, the symbol that men had accumulated enough years of cyclical wisdom to need no more.

Liberal males in every field would try to be kind. The fact that "these people" have no gift for measuring life, the liberals would explain, should be punishment enough.

And how would women be trained to react? One can imagine right-wing women agreeing to all these arguments with a staunch and smiling masochism. ("The ERA would force housewives to wound themselves every month": Phyllis Schlafly. "Your husband's blood is as sacred as that of Jesus—and so sexy, too!": Marabel Morgan.) Reformers and Queen Bees would adjust their lives to the cycles of the men around them. Feminists would explain endlessly that men, too, needed to be liberated from the false idea of Martian aggressiveness, just as women needed to escape the bonds of "menses-envy." Radical feminists would add that the oppression of the nonmenstrual was the pattern for all other oppressions. ("Vampires were our first freedom fighters!") Cultural feminists would exalt a female bloodless imagery in art and literature. Socialist feminists would insist that, once capitalism and imperialism were overthrown, women would menstruate, too. ("If women aren't yet menstruating in Russia," they would explain, "it's only because true socialism can't exist within capitalist encirclement.")

In short, we would discover, as we should already guess, that logic is in the eye of the logician. (For instance, here's an idea for theorists and logicians: If women are supposed to be less rational and more emotional at the beginning of our menstrual cycle when the female hormone is at its lowest level, then why isn't it logical to say that, in those few days, women behave the most like the way men behave all month long? I leave further improvisations up to you.)*

The truth is that, if men could menstruate, the power justifications would go on and on.

If we let them.

—1978

*With thanks to Stan Pottinger for many of the improvisations already here

I

DEPTH-SOUNDING I

n the peace movement and feminist surge of the early 1970s, Bella Abzug is elected to Congress. She advances the issues of women and other powerless groups, is the first member of Congress to call for the impeachment of President Nixon, becomes respected for her lawyerly skill in writing legislation and researching little-used shortcuts in congressional procedure, and is elected by her peers, after only two terms in the House of Representatives, as one of its three "most influential" members. In 1976, she dares to become the first woman to run for the Senate from New York, loses by a very small margin, and the following year, becomes the first woman to run on a major party ticket for mayor of New York City.

Is she commended for the courage it takes to leave a safe seat in Congress and be a "first" in tough races? Is she praised for having raised more political money—largely through small donations at that—than any other woman (and many men) in American history? Does she at least get sympathy for expending all that life energy, and losing? Definitely not. She is condemned by supposedly profeminist liberals as being "too aggressive" or "abrasive," and by a right-wing media campaign that labels her "antifamily," "pro-Communist," and "Queen of the Perverts." As a result, even her effort to regain a House seat is destroyed: a white, male, Republican millionaire is elected in her stead. In the press, and even in a few parts of the women's movement, her defeat is humiliatingly diagnosed as being "her own fault."

DEPTH-SOUNDING II

The Equal Rights Amendment earns majority support from Americans, both women and men, in nationwide public-opinion polls, and is ratified by the thirty-five states in which most Americans live. Nonetheless, a handful of firmly entrenched, white male legislators control enough votes in the remaining few states to keep its victory just three states away. Are those local legislators blamed for not responding to a national consensus? Do reporters, or Americans in general, demand to know what special interests are controlling state legislatures? No, the most popular question seems to be, "Why are women against the ERA?" The second most popular query not only blames the victims, but introduces some wishful thinking besides. You know, the one that goes, "Why is the women's movement dying?"

DEPTH-SOUNDING III

In 1973, after a long feminist campaign to galvanize America's prochoice majority, the Supreme Court rules that the constitutionally guaranteed right to privacy protects a woman's right to choose abortion. Though the health and lives of many women are saved by the increased availability of legal abortion, both candidates in the 1976 presidential campaign personally oppose abortion, thus legitimizing the view of the antichoice minority. By 1977, most welfare recipients, the least politically powerful among women, have been deprived of public funding for abortion. Compulsory motherhood and butchery or death from self-induced and illegal operations are the inevitable results. Meanwhile, the vociferous, antichoice lobby accelerates its campaign to further restrict and finally outlaw abortion, and begins to harass patients as well. Clinics are picketed, blockaded by demonstrators, and even set on fire. Several are invaded by antichoice gangs while women are on the operating table. Most of this is done in the name of a religious belief that, even when phrased in the most rational way by public-opinion polls, isn't supported by a majority of anybody, including members of the major religions supposed to hold that belief. Indeed, antichoice activists in the Catholic hierarchy may be endangering their own women especially, since Catholic women's more limited use of contraception means that they tend to have more abortions, proportionate to their numbers in the population, than do their sisters in other religions.

Are these antichoice forces seen as a tyrannical minority; one whose power jeopardizes individual rights, as well as the separation of church and state? Does a casual newspaper reader get the impression that some 60 to 70 percent of Americans support the right to choose? On the contrary, anti-abortion groups are often credited with being part of a "turn to the right" on the part of the "majority of Americans." And they are seriously, constantly referred to as "prolife."

DEPTH-SOUNDING IV

For five million dollars, less than a quarter of the gift offered by the government to one presidential candidate, women work nationwide for two years, hold fifty-six state and territorial conferences, and a meeting of twenty thousand observers and delegates known as the National Conference in Houston. It is probably the most representative, democratic, biggest, and cheapest meeting of elected national representatives in history.

Is everybody congratulated for hard work, frugality, and a democratic process? Does Congress give some commendation to one of the few federally funded projects ever to fulfill its mandate without coming back for more cash? Not at all. On the contrary, right-wing groups charge that five million tax dollars were "wasted," and their allegations are printed with little investigation by many reporters and believed with little justification by many congressmen. So are some accusations that the 1977 National Women's Conference tax dollars were used to pay for "pornography" and "a national scandal." Material that has nothing to do with the conference is displayed to congressmen and state legislators and tours many state capitals.

So much mud is flung that some of it sticks. Though a post-Houston opinion poll conducted by Louis Harris shows that a majority or plurality of Americans actually supports each of the main resolutions passed by conference delegates, the conference itself isn't viewed with the same approval: 29 percent disapprove of it altogether; 52 percent aren't sure how they feel; and only 19 percent approve. It is a partial but disturbing victory of easy media image over hard-won realities.

*T*hose few stories only symbolize the emotional, complex events that keep us swimming through a river of change marked by hope, revelation, tiredness, and rage. And of course, besides those public soundings, there are private ones. How many of us have had our dreams set free but still can't budge everyday realities? How many of us went courageously back to school, for instance, only to find ourselves among the female unemployed who grow larger in number and better educated every year? Or with one full-time job outside the home and one in it? How many of us are trying to help children become free, individual people, but face a whole culture devoted to mass-producing them as roles? How many of us try to keep love and mutual support flowing between equals, only to find it dammed up by some imbalance of self-confidence or power?

This seems to be where we are, after the first full decade of the second wave of feminism. Raised hopes, a hunger for change, and years of hard work are running head-on into a frustrating realization that each battle must be fought over and over again at different depths. One inevitable result of winning a majority change in consciousness is a backlash from those forces whose power depended on the old one.

Perhaps that's the first Survival Lesson we need to remember if we are to keep going: *serious opposition is a measure of success*. Women have been trained to measure our effectiveness in love and approval, not conflict or resistance. That makes it tough to be personally independent or to advocate change. But the truth is that there was no major organized backlash against us when we were still paying for women's conferences out of our own pockets and living-room benefits. That happened only after we were strong enough to get a few of our own tax dollars back. Traditional churches and fundamentalist leaders didn't organize against feminists politically until the contagion of justice caused nuns to question the authority of priests, Mormon women to chafe at the sex-race restrictions by which that well-to-do establishment is run, Jewish and Protestant women to become rabbis and ministers, and the very personification of God the Father to be questioned.

As for the principle of equal pay for comparable work, you will remember that this demand was once known as "the-part-I-agree-with." Sometimes, it still is. But that easy agreement usually precedes the realization of how many women *are* doing comparable work without equal pay, or how many more women would like to join their sisters who already make up more than 40 percent of the salaried-labor force, or what massive redistribution of wealth could result if women as a group were no longer available as a cheap, unorganized, surplus labor force.

In other words, if even the work we are now doing were paid according to its logical, comparable value in "men's work," we would cause a major redistribution of wealth. Which is exactly why we should keep forcing this demand. A system that rests on cheap labor and allows unearned wealth to accumulate deserves to be transformed by pressures of the many on the few.

The realization of the populist, radical potential of "equal pay" is now beginning to dawn on everybody—those with profits to lose as well as those with equality to gain. The logical results are both deeper resistance and broader support. It depends, of course, on whether someone benefits from women's cheap labor (as an employer, investor, stockholder, or even a husband may do); or whether someone is a salaried woman herself, is dependent on a woman's wage-earning power, or is just a person who happens to believe that society would be improved for everyone in the long run by rewarding merit and restricting unearned wealth.

If we weren't culturally prepared as women for meeting such resistance, we were rarely prepared as students or citizens either. Wasn't equal opportunity one of the rocks on which America was built? Why should we fight for, or expect resistance to, something we thought we already had?

In fact, our own experience has been the best school and textbook. We might have started by discovering, for instance, that women who answered phones in city hall got $170 a week, while policemen who answered phones in police precincts earned $306. Or that "maintenance men" got $185 a week for the upkeep of office buildings in the daytime, while "scrubwomen" got $170 for doing comparable work at night. Or that a registered nurse got paid no more than the garbagemen who served the same hospital and much less than a pharmacist who had equal training but belonged to a mostly male profession. Sometimes we complained and got some financial relief from employers. More often, we realized the necessity of much longer and more massive pressure. Always, we learned lessons in how to organize. But we frequently got some version of the same reply: "This could break every city government and hospital in the country." Or from very frank private employers: "We only hire women here because they're cheaper than men."

Those are evocative examples. Each of us could supply many more. But it's important to remember the real economic consequences of equality, as we ourselves can see and assess them, if we are to understand both the logic and the tribute of the stiff opposition we continue to get.

Ironically, even those of us who had studied other economic revolutions weren't necessarily better prepared for this resistance than those of us who were acting on a general faith in fair play. Political theorists usually presented women's inequality as an incidental by-product of other "larger" economic questions. Their supposition was that change must start at the top, and the top doesn't include women.

Those nonfeminist theorists might or might not be right about a particular revolution, but there had to be more than one way to create change. So we started where it was possible for us to start—at the bottom. Since we weren't undertaking armed rebellion, nationalization, or worker takeover of the factories, we had few models of what tactics to use or what resistance to expect.

In fact, many of us in the 1960s and early 1970s had spurned such legislative measures as the Equal Rights Amendment precisely because it didn't sound radical enough. We had all the doubts of the sixties about making any change through the electoral system or any effort that appeared to depend on infiltrating the Establishment, one feminist at a time. Both politics and temperament put me in that skeptical camp. I didn't love structure of any kind (no doubt a trait of free-lance writers), and besides, the ERA seemed like a leftover from a time when our once-radical foremothers had been persuaded to put too much faith in the vote.

In the past few years, however, the slowly revealed cumulative potential of mass-movement pressure has made a lot of us change our minds. So has the right-wing backlash and its implicit testimony to the importance of a constitutional principle of equality.

But, as some smart person once said, one evidence of intelligence is the absence of surprise. If we ourselves had figured out the possible economic impact of the ERA more thoroughly and sooner, we might have worked harder to get the necessary ratifications early, while the right wing was still dozing at its legislative command posts. We even might have educated the media better on the where and why of the opposition, so that fewer reporters would now be accepting the legislators' false arguments that *"my* women constituents are against it" or that the problem is the mythical specter of coed bathrooms.

In the absence of real economic analysis, however, we tended to present the ERA as sweet reason; without adding that equity, when introduced to systems that depend on inequity (in the workplace and at home) can turn out to be very radical indeed.

Of course, no degree of preparedness might have increased the present pace of change. As women, we have to be careful not to succumb to our social disease of terminal guilt. *States' rights* and *local legislative control* have always been code words for racial bias and economic conservatism; it's just that the ERA experience has engraved that fact on our skins. In some parts of the country we were faced with having to transform legislatures that have been a Catch-22 of democracy since the Civil War: North Carolina, for example, only ratified the amendment giving women the vote in 1976 and Mississippi is still holding out.* Kentucky didn't ratify the antislavery amendment until 1976.

In Nevada, eleven legislators who had pledged to support the ERA, and who had been supported by pro-equality groups because of that public promise, voted against it once they were in office. Why? Because the right-wing leadership of the legislature made it clear that they had little chance of chairing committees or otherwise having a political future unless they voted no. In Virginia, women even performed the impossible feat of electing a pro-ERA Republican in the Democratic district of an anti-ERA Democratic leader of the legislature. But, as one feminist put it, "That only made them mad. Now, the other legislators want to punish us even more."

It may be good for the country in the long run that the ERA has exposed the lack of democracy in many state legislatures, but it some-

*Mississippi finally ratified the amendment giving women the vote in 1982.

times feels as if we're being asked to reconstruct the entire nationwide phone system just to get one message through.

For the future, however, we should understand that this process of democratizing a state legislative system takes time. Changing a few faces is not enough, just as earning majority support of a legislator's constituents doesn't help if he has been put there by special interests. You have to be around long enough to out-organize the special interests and change the legislature's leadership.

When the ERA is finally part of the Constitution (as it eventually will be) and historians look back at our journey, they may count acceptance of the initial seven-year ratification deadline as the greatest single error. Most constitutional amendments have had no deadlines at all. The first suggested one for the ERA was thirty-five years. When Alice Paul, the suffragist who wrote and introduced the ERA, heard that its congressional sponsors had accepted seven years, she despaired of success. After all, if it took a Civil War plus nearly a century to get racial equality into the Constitution, why should we be surprised that legal equality for half the population would take a long and sustained effort?*

*I*t also takes a while for a critical mass of any movement as enormous as this wave of feminism to learn that the paths to change prescribed in our civics texts are just not enough. Working inside political parties, explaining problems to leaders, electing or dis-electing, gaining the support of the majority—all these make sense. Occasionally they even work. But our textbooks didn't prepare us for the fact that some power considerations have nothing to do with majorities (for instance, which special interests make the biggest political contributions, who appoints committee chairs, who can quash some legislator's ethics rap, and which legislators just are not going to vote for equality because "God didn't intend women to be equal"); or that majority support can exist for years on some issue (like gun control, full employment, or getting out of Vietnam) without giving it the power to win.

---

*The Equal Rights Amendment was reintroduced in Congress immediately after its failure to be ratified by the July 1982 deadline. By the November elections of the same year, pro-equality voters had changed enough legislators in Florida and Illinois—two of the key states in stopping the ERA—so that those legislatures could now pass it. Nonetheless, if the same ratification process is to be followed, most estimates say that another ten years is a probable minimum.

*T*hose of us who came of political age in the masculine-style left, however, also had textbooks. They said you couldn't win by the ballot, lobbying, or getting majority support for anything less than revolt. You had to adopt such "outside-the-system" methods as street demonstrations, passive (or maybe violent) resistance to the system, and a desertion of allegiances to people who didn't agree with all of the above.

In practice and under the right conditions, both "inside" and "outside" strategies worked—but both also tended to fizzle out. The reformers or "inside" people often got absorbed or immobilized. The revolutionaries or "outside" people often got so fixed on immediate drastic impact that they became isolated or demoralized when major change wasn't evident right away (or at least, before they reached the age of thirty).

Consciously and otherwise, we carried versions of these polarized, prefeminist styles with us into the women's movement. In the 1960s and early 1970s, we divided into "reformist" or "liberal" feminists (sometimes including the more hesitant category of "I'm not a feminist but . . .") and "socialist" or "radical" feminists (often used synonymously, though the first tend to think that class is more important than caste, while the second group believes the reverse). Even after most of us had identified with the women's movement as a first priority, some mutations of these divisions still turned up. For instance, there was (and still is) a distinction between "political feminists" (who have an impulse toward economic actions or analyses and coalitions with the nonfeminist Left) and "cultural feminists" (who are more into anthropology, self-transformation, and building a woman's culture).

In real life, however, the same individual or group might feel attracted to *both* of these worthwhile goals and want to combine them in imaginative ways. The tragedy was that an artificial choice was often imposed anyway. We weren't supposed to be working both "inside" and "outside" the system. We risked being accused of hypocrisy if we tried both to earn academic credentials and to challenge the system that required them.

It was as if feminism had pointed out the injustice of dividing human nature into the false polarities of "feminine" or "masculine," but hadn't yet become strong or organic enough to get us past other bipartite either/or divisions that imitated them.

The worst penalty was the deadening of our perceptions. In reality, for instance, most situations turn out to contain varieties of actions and ideas that number a dozen, fourteen, a hundred, or just one. To polarize everything into opposing pairs was to deprive ourselves of accuracy, subtlety, invention, and growth. It kept us from seeing the total spectrum of actions from which we could choose.

In a male-supremacist culture, a vital function of polarization is to set up a win-lose situation. Women, of course, are supposed to be on the giving or losing side: that's the way we achieve virtue, sympathy, and society's support. Even among feminists, moral purity and rightness often retains this association with failure, a notion that can cause us to reward weakness in each other and to punish strength.

One recent example of this is the division of feminists into the "moderate" or even "conservative" majority versus the "radical" or "pure" few. In this version of polarization, any group or person who has succeeded, or even survived, is supposed to be in the sellout category, and anyone who is isolated and embittered is probably in the camp of the pure. Thus, one may read in some parts of the press (though not those controlled by the right wing, which knows better) that the "conservatives" or "moderates" have taken over the women's movement from the "true feminist" few.*

One giveaway of this division's purpose is the extreme imbalance of its two groups. You can be sure that the majority of feminists will be on the condemned side, since only the tiny minority can be allowed to be "pure." Sometimes, this is a paternalistic way that political observers outside the movement try to define it out of existence. Often, it's the self-defeating way that a very few women choose to declare their moral superiority and ownership of feminism

In either case, it's important to ignore labels and look at the record of issues and actions, and they often disclose something quite different. The majority group may well have survived and grown precisely because it *was* feminist and therefore radical enough to attack fundamental, shared problems and to make women of different experiences and backgrounds

*Relative to other movements and interest groups, the women's movement is also measurably more radical; that is, much more interested in fundamental change. A 1976 Harvard University Center for International Affairs/*Washington Post* survey of leadership groups in the United States (youth groups, the black movement, and many more) found that feminists were consistently more willing to address questions of basic change (for instance, public ownership of utilities and oil firms, redistribution of income) than any other group. The majority questioned were members of NOW and the National Women's Political Caucus, the very groups often cited as "conservative" feminists.

feel welcome. The "pure" and now embittered few, on the other hand, may have become isolated precisely because they were feminist in rhetoric but exclusive or authoritarian in behavior and style. Whether they came from the Right or the Left, they tend to carve out some territory, claim ownership or other unique authority, and demand perpetual homage to that claim.

In fact, however, the most recognizable characteristic of feminists and feminist acts is their effort to be inclusive. The radical vision of feminism depends on its possibility of transforming the status of all women, not just a correct few.

*T*his is not to say that internal distinctions and criticisms can't be constructive. They can, providing that they describe authentic differences and don't push us unnecessarily far apart.* In the label department, for instance, I would prefer to be called simply "a feminist." After all, the belief in the full humanity of women leads to the necessity of transforming male-supremacist structures and, thus, removing the model and continuing support for other systems of birth-determined privilege. That should be radical enough. However, because there are feminists who believe that women can integrate or imitate existing structures (or conversely, that we must wait until class structures are eliminated, whereupon women's subordinate position will change automatically), I feel I should identify myself as a "radical feminist." "Radical" means "going to the root," and I think that the sexual caste system *is* the root. Whether or not it developed as the chronologically first dominance model in prehistory, it is clear right now that women's freedom is the most restricted in societies that are also devoted to keeping some race or class groups "pure" by birth in order to perpetuate their power.

Because I do believe that the sexual caste system is this kind of crucial, anthropological root cause, I also think that all effective actions taken against it will contribute to society's radical transformation in the end. And this will happen whether the acts are taken by radical feminists or by someone who says uncertainly, "I'm not a feminist, but. . . ." Therefore, I feel fine about supporting and working with women who

*For a description of groups and trends inside the feminist movement, in both the first and second waves, see Shulamith Firestone, *Dialectic of Sex* (New York: Bantam Books, 1971), 15-40.

don't share my chosen label Yes, we may disagree on analyses in the long run: I don't think feminism *can* just be imitative or integrationist. By definition, it must transform. But in the short run, there are goals we agree on. And it's in the short run that we must act.

*M*ost feminists have begun to see varied, orchestrated tactics and styles as an asset. We've learned something from the experience of working together across race, age, class, and sexuality differences. We've learned from examples like the women's health movement or changing rape laws or starting battered women's shelters, all of which benefited from diverse approaches: not just "inside" or "outside" tactics, but creating alternative feminist structures *and* translating as many of their lessons as possible into the dominant system itself.

Each issue goes through a similar ontogeny: naming the problem; speaking out, consciousness-raising, and researching; creating alternate structures to deal with it; and beginning to create or change society's laws and structures to solve the problem for the majority. Perhaps that is the second Survival Lesson: *we have to push ourselves far beyond prefeminist, either/or, polarized thinking, and use a whole spectrum of talents and tactics. We must surround our goals.*

We have often said that diversity would be a hallmark of a hoped-for, feminist future. But we're just beginning to understand it as a tactical advantage right now. We're also gaining enough confidence to dispense with the idea that everyone who doesn't choose our particular style is rejecting or criticizing us. This frees us to use diverse means, and to see that, in the organic integrity that feminism demands, the means *are* the ends. We won't have diversity at the end unless we nurture it along the way.

*I*n the history of this wave of feminism, for instance, the campaign for the ERA may appear as the first massive, shared experience that blasted a critical mass of the women's movement out of its inside-the-system/outside-the-system rut. The next struggle is much less likely to find radicals ignoring the power of elected officials, or reformers insisting that all will be well if we just act ladylike, wear skirts, and avoid controversy.

This is no attempt to be Pollyannaish. An ERA victory would save us years of struggle. Defeat is seen as a failure of the women's movement, no matter how clear it may be that state legislatures are at fault.

But we are only a decade or so into this current wave of the longest revolution. The last wave endured for more than a century, and there will be others pushed forward by our sisters to come. It's important to extract lessons for future action.

*T*ake the loss of Bella Abzug at the polls. If we had not left her out there on the cutting edge, with no visible movement in the streets, no sit-ins, or door-to-door organizing to make clear that she had a fearsome constituency, she might not have been so easily cut down as the farthest-out voice within earshot of the politicians or the press. As it was, a lot of us succumbed to the polarized argument that we were (or she was) inside the system and that the street days of the early 1970s were therefore over. Some of us even agreed that her aggressive wave-making had invited defeat. But wasn't Bella's style a lot like that of Fiorello La Guardia, New York's most beloved mayor?

Perhaps we would have been more willing to press from outside the political structure, and to honor Bella's style, if we had read more statements like this:

Cautious, careful people always casting about to preserve their reputation or social standards never can bring about reform. Those who are really in earnest are willing to be anything or nothing in the world's estimation, and publicly and privately, in season and out, avow their sympathies with despised ideas and their advocates, and bear the consequences.

That was Susan B. Anthony in 1873. Without the knowledge of quotes like these, we sometimes think of the first-wave activists as tame. But how many of their tactics can we match for variety or force?

Even the later suffragists, the ones who are most often labeled reformist because of their concentration on the vote, used radical tactics. Yes, they lobbied politely, sometimes, and took tea with their friends in Congress, but they also picketed the White House and engaged in the civil disobedience that those same congressmen abhorred. Wives of well-known men, preferably personal friends of President Wilson, were arrested (very dramatic for the press), and labor-union women riding in bunting-trimmed cars down main streets were a decorous surprise—not the stereotype of "immoral" working girls and immigrants at all. Suffragists wore cloth banners folded under their clothes so they could smuggle them into dignified meetings or well-guarded picket lines. When one set of banners had been unfurled and seized by police, a dozen others could take its place. Our foremothers had a great gift for pageantry: everybody marching in the same capes, carrying the same color flowers, presenting a three-mile-long petition, or (when they thought more toughness was in order) burning the president's speeches, even when he was abroad, in the streets of Washington, D.C., to embarrass him internationally. They also had a disciplined precomputer lobbying system in which letters, cables, and phone calls could be sent out by national signal, plus a fine sense of timing. Suffragist meetings were often scheduled on the eve of some Establishment event—say, a national political convention—to take advantage of the gathering of bored, news-hungry reporters.

Chaining themselves to the White House fence, going to jail, declaring a hunger strike, being cruelly force-fed: those events are now famous. But the range of tactics included humor, theatrics, passive resistance, persuasion, and, whenever possible, the subversion of Establishment contacts and wives.

The antiwoman backlash of their day also accused them of being free-love advocates, antifamily, anti-God, masculine, and unnatural women. Sound familiar?

Ideas for actions, conflict resolution, and a reminder of similar hostility in the past—all these are practical reasons for Survival Lesson number three: *we need to know the history of our sisters, both for inspiration and for accumulating a full arsenal of ideas, and adopt what translates into the present.* Very few tactics are either completely new, or completely out-of-date. Even after we as individuals have exhausted our ability to make them fresh, other feminists can repeat, enlarge, and change them.

We are all organizers, and no organizer should ever end a meeting or a book or an article without ideas for practical action. After all, a

movement depends on people moving. What *are* we going to do differently when we get up tomorrow?

In fact, the great strength of feminism—like that of the black movement here, the Gandhian movement in India, and all the organic struggles
for self-rule and simple justice—has always been encouragement for each
of us to act, without waiting and theorizing about some future takeover at
the top. It's no accident that, when some small group does accomplish a
momentous top-down revolution, the change seems to benefit only those
who made it. Even with the best intentions of giving "power to the
people," the revolution is betrayed.

Power can be taken, but not given. The process of the taking is
empowerment in itself.

So we ask ourselves: What might a spectrum of diverse, mutually
supportive tactics really look like for us as individuals, for family and
community groups, for men who care about equality, for children, and for
political movements as a whole? Some actions will always be unique to
particular situations and thus unforeseeable. Others will be suited to times
of great energy in our lives, and still others will make sense for those who
are burnt out and need to know that a time of contemplation and assess-
ment is okay. But here are some that may inspire action, if only to say,
"No, that's not right. But this is what I choose to do instead."

AS INDIVIDUALS

In the early 1970s when I was traveling and lecturing with feminist
lawyer and black activist Florynce Kennedy, one of her many epigrams
went like this: "Unity in a movement situation is overrated. If you were
the Establishment, which would you rather see coming in the door, five
hundred mice or one lion?"

Mindful of her teaching, I now often end lectures with an organizer's
deal. If each person in the room promises that in the twenty-four hours
beginning the very next day she or he will do at least *one outrageous thing*
in the cause of simple justice, then I promise I will, too. It doesn't matter
whether the act is as small as saying, "Pick it up yourself" (a major step
for those of us who have been our family's servants) or as large as calling
a strike. The point is that, if each of us does as promised, we can be pretty
sure of two results. First, the world one day later won't be quite the same.

Second, we will have such a good time that we will never again get up in the morning saying, *"Will* I do anything outrageous?" but only *"What* outrageous act will I do today?"

Here are some samples I've recorded from the outrageous acts of real life.

- Announced a permanent refusal to contribute more money to a church or synagogue until women too can become priests, ministers, and rabbis.

- Asked for a long-deserved raise, or, in the case of men and/or white folks, refused an undeserved one that is being given over the heads of others because of their race or sex.

- Written a well-reasoned critique of a sexist or racist textbook and passed it out on campus.

- Challenged some bit of woman-hating humor or imagery with the seriousness more often reserved for slurs based on religion or race.

- Shared with colleagues the knowledge of each other's salaries so that unfairnesses can be calculated. (It's interesting that employers try to keep us from telling the one fact we know.)

- Cared for a child or children so that an overworked mother could have a day that is her own. (This is especially revolutionary when done by a man.)

- Returned to a birth name or, in the case of a man, gave his children both parents' names.

- Left home for a week so that the father of your young child could learn to be a parent. (As one woman later reported calmly, "When I came home, my husband and the baby had bonded, just the way women and babies do.")

- Petitioned for a Women's Studies section in a local library or bookstore.

- Checked a corporate employer's giving programs, see if they are really inclusive by benefiting women with at least half of their dollars, and made suggestions if not.

- Personally talked to a politician who needed persuasion to support, or reward for helping, issues of equality.

- Redivided a conventional house so that each person has a space for which he or she is solely responsible, with turns taken caring for kitchen, bathroom, and other shared rooms.

- Got married to an equal, or divorced from an unequal.

- Left a violent lover or husband.

- Led a walkout from a movie that presents rape scenes or other violence as titillating and just fine.

- Made a formal complaint about working (or living) in a white ghetto. White people are also being culturally deprived

- Told the truth to a child, or a parent.

- Said proudly, "I am a feminist." (Because this word means a believer in equality, it's especially helpful when said by a man.)

- Organized a block, apartment house, or dormitory to register and vote.

- Personally picketed and/or sued a bigoted employer/teacher/athletic coach/foreman/union boss

In addition to one-time outrageous acts, these are also the regular ones that should be the bottom line for each of us: writing five letters a week to lobby, criticize, or praise anything from TV shows to a senator; giving 10 percent of our incomes to social justice; going to one demonstration a month or one consciousness-raising group a week just to keep support and energy up; and figuring out how to lead our daily lives in a way that reflects what we believe. People who actually incorporate such day-by-day changes into their lives report that it isn't difficult: five lobbying letters can be written while watching "The Late Show"; giving 10 percent of their incomes often turns out to be the best investment they ever made; meetings create a free space, friends, and an antidote to isolation; and trying to transform a job or a family or a life-style in order to reflect beliefs, instead of the other way around, gives a satisfying sense of affecting the world.

If each of us only reached out and changed *five other people in our lifetimes*, the spiral of revolution would widen enormously—and we can do much more than that.

IN GROUPS

Some of the most effective group actions are the simplest:

- Dividing membership lists according to political district, from precinct level up, so we can inform and get out the pro-equality vote.

- Asking each organization we belong to, whether community or professional, union or religious, to support issues of equality in their formal agendas.

- Making sure that the nonfeminist groups we're supporting don't have mostly women doing the work and mostly men on their boards.

- Making feminist groups *feminist;* that is, relevant to women of the widest diversity of age, race, economics, life-styles, and political labels practical for the work at hand. (An inclusiveness that's best begun among the founders. It's much tougher to start any group and only later reach out to "others.")

- Offering support where it's needed without being asked—for instance, to the school librarian who's fighting right-wing censorship of feminist and other books; or to the new family feeling racially isolated in the neighborhood. (Would you want to have to ask people to help you?)

- Identifying groups for coalitions and allies for issues.

- Streamlining communications. If there were an emergency next week—a victim of discrimination who needed defending, a piece of sinister legislation gliding through city council—could your membership be alerted?

- Putting the group's money where its heart is, and not where it isn't. That may mean contributing to the local battered women's shelter and protesting a community fund that gives far more to Boy Scouts than to Girl Scouts; or publishing a directory of women-owned businesses; or withholding student-activity fees from a campus program that invites mostly white male speakers. (Be sure and let the other side know how much money they're missing. To be more forceful, put your contributions in an escrow account, with payment contingent on a specific improvement.)

- Organizing speak-outs and press conferences. There's nothing like personal testimonies from the people who have experienced the problem firsthand.

- Giving public awards and dinners to women (and men) who've made a positive difference.

- Bringing in speakers or Women's Studies courses to inform your members; running speakers' bureaus so your group's message gets out to the community.

- Making sure new members feel invited and welcome once they arrive, with old members assigned to brief them and transfer group knowledge.

- Connecting with other groups like yours regionally or nationally for shared experience, actions, and some insurance against reinventing the wheel.

Obviously, we must be able to choose the appropriate action from a full vocabulary of tactics, from voting to civil disobedience, from supporting women in the trades to economic boycotts and tax revolts, from congressional hearings to zap actions with humor and an eye to the evening news.

Given the feminization of poverty, however, groups are also assuming another importance. Since women are an underdeveloped, undercapitalized labor force with an unequal knowledge of technology—in other words, a Third World country wherever we are—we re beginning to realize that the Horatio Alger model of individualistic economic progress doesn't work very well for us. Probably we have more to learn about economic development from our sisters in countries recognized as the Third World. Cooperative ownership forms and communal capital formation may be as important to our future as concepts of equal pay.

So far, these experiments have started small: three single mothers who combine children and resources to buy a house not one of them could afford alone; two women who buy a truck for long-distance hauling jobs; a dozen women who pool their savings to start a bakery or a housecleaning service, or single mothers and feminist architects who transform old buildings into new homes.

But we're beginning to look at Third World examples of bigger efforts. If the poorest women in rural Kenya can pool their savings for years, buy a bus, make money from passengers, and build a cooperative store, why can't we with our greater resources help each other to do the same? If illiterate women in India can found and run their own credit cooperative, thus giving them low-interest loans for the goods they sell in the streets, how dare American women be immobilized by a poor economy? It's also a healthy reversal of the usual flow of expertise from developed to underdeveloped country that may help feminists build bridges across national chasms of condescension and mistrust. Groups and organizations have been the base of our issue-oriented, electoral, consciousness-raising, and direct-action progress. In the future, they may be our economic base as well.

AS STRATEGISTS

We've spent the first decade or so of the second wave of feminism on the riverbank, rescuing each other from drowning. In the survival areas of rape, battery, and other terrorist violence against women, for instance, we've begun to organize help through shelters, hot lines, pressure on police to provide protection, reforms in social services and legislation. and an insistence that society stop blaming the victim.

Now, some of us must go to the head of the river and keep the victims from falling in.

For instance, we can pursue new strategies that have proved effective in treating wife batterers and other violent men. Such strategies have been successful precisely because they came from experiences and feminist insight: violence is an addiction that a male-dominant society creates by teaching us that "real men" must dominate and control the world in general and women in particular. When some men inevitably become addicted to violence to prove their masculinity, conventional Freudian-style treatment has only said: "Yes, men are natural aggressors, but you must learn to control the degree." That's like telling a drug addict that he can have just a little heroin.

Treatment based on experience, on the other hand, says: "No, men are not natural aggressors; you must unhook your sense of identity and masculinity from violence, and kick the habit completely."

The few such programs that exist have been helpful to batterers, rapists, and other violent men, criminals and dangerous citizens who have been judged untreatable precisely because they saw themselves as normal men. This fundamental challenge to cultural ideas of masculinity might also hold hope for less violent ways of solving conflicts on this fragile Spaceship Earth.

That's one of hundreds of futurist examples. There are many other strategies centered around four great goals: *reproductive freedom*; *work redefined*; *democratic families; and depoliticized culture*.

Clearly, these goals can only be reached a long distance in the future. We are very far from the opposite shore.

But the image of crossing a river may be too linear to describe the reality we experience. In fact, we repeat similar struggles that seem cyclical and discouraging in the short run, yet each one is on slightly changed territory. One full revolution is not complete until it has passed through the superficiality of novelty and even law to become an accepted part of the culture. Only when we look back over a long passage of time do we see that each of these cycles has been moving in a direction. We see the spiral of history.

*I*n my first days of activism, I thought I would do this ("this" being feminism) for a few years and then return to my real life (what my "real life" might be, I did not know). Partly, that was a naïve belief that injustice only had to be pointed out in order to be cured. Partly, it was a simple lack of courage.

But like so many others now and in movements past, I've learned that this is not just something we care about for a year or two or three. We are in it for life—and for our lives. Not even the spiral of history is needed to show the distance traveled. We have only to look back at the less complete people we ourselves used to be.

And that is the last Survival Lesson: *we look at how far we've come, and then we know—there can be no turning back.*

—1978, 1982

*I*f the struggle of the last decades was against the colonialism that allowed one nation to rule another, the current and future struggle will be about the internal colonialism that allows one race or one sex to dominate another.

One day our descendents will think it incredible that we paid so much attention to things like the amount of melanin in our skin or the shape of our eyes or our gender instead of the unique identities of each of us as complex human beings.

—Franklin Thomas
The Liberty of the Citizen